SEX IN THE ANCIENT WORLD
FROM A TO Z

THE ANCIENT WORLD FROM A TO Z

What were the ancient fashions in men's shoes? How did you cook a tunny or spice a dormouse? What was the daily wage of a Syracusan builder? What did Romans use for contraception?

This new Routledge series will provide the answers to such questions, which are often overlooked by standard reference works. Volumes will cover key topics in ancient culture and society – from food, sex and sport to money, dress and domestic life.

Each author will be an acknowledged expert in their field, offering readers vivid, immediate and academically sound insights into the fascinating details of daily life in antiquity. The main focus will be on Greece and Rome, though some volumes will also encompass Egypt and the Near East.

The series will be suitable both as background for those studying classical subjects and as enjoyable reading for anyone with an interest in the ancient world.

Already published:

Food in the Ancient World from A to Z
Andrew Dalby

Sport in the Ancient World from A to Z
Mark Golden

Sex in the Ancient World from A to Z
John G. Younger

Forthcoming titles:

Birds in the Ancient World from A to Z
Geoffrey Arnott

Money in the Ancient World from A to Z
Andrew Meadows

Domestic Life in the Ancient World from A to Z
Ruth Westgate and Kate Gilliver

Dress in the Ancient World from A to Z
Lloyd Llewellyn-Jones *et al.*

SEX IN THE ANCIENT WORLD FROM A TO Z

John G. Younger

Routledge
Taylor & Francis Group

LONDON AND NEW YORK

First published 2005
by Routledge
2 Park Square, Milton Park, Abingdon, Oxfordshire, OX14 4RN

Simultaneously published in the USA and Canada
by Routledge
270 Madison Ave., New York, NY 10016

Routledge is an imprint of the Taylor & Francis Group

Typeset in Sabon by Taylor & Francis Books Ltd
Printed and bound in Great Britain by
TJ International Ltd, Padstow, Cornwall

British Library Cataloguing in Publication Data
A catalogue record for this book is available from the British Library

Library of Congress Cataloging in Publication Data
A catalog record for this title has been requested

ISBN 0–415–24252–5

TO PAUL

Contents

Illustrations

Plates

Preface

The contents of this book

This encyclopedia concentrates on the sexual practices, expressions, and attitudes of the Greeks and Romans in the lands around the Mediterranean in the period between 1000 BCE and 300 CE; occasionally it will stray into peripheral cultures, into times earlier and later, and into subjects that may not seem like sex at all.

Sex and sexuality are difficult to define. In English, "sex" denotes primarily the biological sex of a person (male, female, other; in Greek and Latin, one's *genus*); gender is the way a person is expected to act in society because they are male or female. Sex secondarily means activities that involve the genitals and related body areas. Sexuality is more personal and seems to allude to the individual's promise of or availability for sexual activity. Behind this personal quality lies, however, the social construction of sexuality, how society views sex and the individual.

For some ancient cultures, sexual practices are virtually invisible (Celtic and Minoan-Mycenaean). Greeks and Romans, however, depicted and wrote about sex candidly and constantly. In general, sex was for procreation, recreation, and political advancement. Within this broad spectrum, details of ancient sex sometimes seem peculiar. For instance, their favorite position for intercourse was rear entry ("a tergo"); they thought ravens conceived their young through fellatio; they put phalluses everywhere (indoors and outdoors) for good luck; Greeks and Romans (men and women) used their slaves sexually; and both Greeks and Romans made their politicians out to be sex-crazed profligates. In other words, Greeks and Romans were not sexually repressed.

I have tried to keep this encyclopedia focused on specific ancient subjects: people, behavior, and attitudes, words, works of literature, depictions, artifacts. I have tried to focus more on sex and less on gender. I have tried to keep the entries factual, without too much over-interpretation; sometimes, however, the evidence warrants a more interpretive statement. I have also avoided illustrating those objects that are commonly found in handbooks (see Works of art cited).

Our sources for classical sex and sexuality are limited in several ways. Most ancient writings have been lost due to neglect, to the practice of anthologizing texts for teaching, to the male bias against the writings of women, and to the prudish Bowdlerism of late and post-antique scholarship. Much of our artifactual evidence was deliberately lost or locked away in "secret cabinets" and "curiosity collections," which only recently have been opened for a more appreciative and tolerant public. For instance, the Naples Museum had a "Gabinetto degli Oggetti Osceni" (Cabinet of Obscene Objects) which it has now opened to the public as the "Raccoltà Pornografica" (Pornographic Collection). It is still, however, a separate collection, reflecting our tendency to see sex apart from the rest of culture.

Because almost all of our sources are male-authored, it is difficult to obtain a balanced view of men's and women's sexuality, sex practices, and desires. Nonetheless, it is well worth the effort. For instance, though representations of vaginas are rare, one woman dedicated a sculptural representation of hers "to Aphrodite, for her favors: rejoice all you passers-by!"

Terminology

I have tried to keep the terminology unoffensive; I have occasionally used an English obscene expression, but only to translate the force of the ancient one. If my vocabulary seems dry, perhaps it will help the reader concentrate on the differences between ancient and modern practices and behaviors.

Similarly, I have tried not to use a vocabulary that is inappropriate for describing what the ancients did and thought. Most men were, and were assumed to be, attracted to both young women and boys and almost all got married. Within these parameters, the term "bisexual" is inappropriate. The term "heterosexual" applies only to those few men (like Ovid and Claudius) who liked women (almost) exclusively. In some instances, it is possible to show women's "heterosexual" desires for men, but for others a "lesbian" desire is more appropriate. Similarly, men who were attracted to boys and youths will be discussed under Greek "paiderastia," which is an anthropologically attested, eroticized male socialization ritual, and under Roman "boy-love," which citizen men felt almost exclusively for youthful non-citizen males. For those few men who maintained same-sex relationships into adulthood, I use the term "male homosexual."

The following are terms found throughout this book:

agora	market place (Greek)
archon	a high city magistrate
"a tergo"	sexual penetration from the rear
erastes	the older "lover" in a paiderastic relationship
eromenos	the younger "beloved" in a paiderastic relationship
ephebe	military cadet (18–20 years old, in Athens)
hetaira	expensive prostitute
forum	market place (Roman)

metic   a foreign resident
pallakê/ós concubine (female, male)
pornê   inexpensive prostitute
tyrant   a dictator, usually favorably disposed toward the merchant class, of
            the early Greek period

Notes to readers

The names of Greek authors are given in conventional Latinate spelling; words and other names follow Greek spelling unless well known.

Internal references will appear in small capitals, both the proper title of the entry and variations (thus, both PROSTITUTED and PROSTITUTION refer to the entry PROSTITUTES).

Dates are specified as BCE or CE; dates of authors are given in the "Ancient sources cited" section at the end of the book.

Bold numbers in the entries refer to the items in the "Works of art cited" section at the end of the book.

Quotations are abbreviated; the intention here is not to mislead the reader but to make them more readable. All translations are the author's, unless otherwise stated.

Much information has been drawn from basic, unreferenced sources like *LIMC*, *OCD*, *RE*, Hubbard 2003 (see Bibliography); and the "Perseus" online website (http://perseus.tufts.edu).

Acknowledgments

I wish to thank the students in my courses on Perspectives in Lesbian, Gay, Bisexual, and Transgender Studies at Duke University, on Gender and Sexuality in the Ancient World at both Duke University and the University of Kansas, and on Classical Women Writers at the University of Kansas – and special thanks to Brian Walters, Susanne Fletcher, Christina Ponig, and Cara Snyder. As always, I am grateful to Paul Rehak who read this manuscript, heard my thoughts, and gave me many suggestions, criticisms, and some difficult questions. Paul passed away while this book was in press; I dedicate it to him in loving memory and in memory of our love.

Theory and modern scholarship

Theories

Essentialism and constructionism

Essentialism holds that human beings have in-grained behaviors and attitudes. Constructionism holds that some behaviors are dependent on the particular society, time, and place. What about sex? Is it "natural"? Is it socially constructed? For instance, western civilization prefers the "missionary" position (woman supine, man on top, for facing vaginal intercourse; Marks 1978); but classical society preferred intercourse "a tergo" (SEXUAL POSITIONS).

If the preference for a sexual position has changed, what about other preferences? For instance, there was greater tolerance for homoerotic behavior in antiquity. Was there therefore "homosexuality" in antiquity? Some scholars say "no" (the term was only coined in 1869; see Padgug 1989: 60; Halperin 1990, 1994; Halperin *et al.* 1990). A few scholars (like Boswell 1980 and 1994), however, have identified what look like modern homosexuals and modern homosexual behavior in antiquity (cf. ARISTOPHANES's myth in PLATO's SYMPOSIUM 191d–193a). I am convinced by this evidence, that the modern concept of homosexuality was more or less known in antiquity but rarely practiced (MALE HOMOSEXUALITY; LESBIANISM). If so, then it is the practice that is constructed, not the basic desire (Stein 1999).

Penetration = domination

In the late twentieth century it became fashionable to assume that penile penetration expressed the power of the penetrator and the subordination of the penetrated (Foucault 1976/80–1984/6; Keuls 1985; Parker 1992). Many studies then concluded, rightly I feel, that men had sexual access to all those beneath them in society (unmarried females, non-citizen males, slaves; Richlin 1992: xviii; Sutton 1992: 5); only proper women and citizen males were off limits.

The assumption turns on the subordination of the penetrated. My own experience as a gay man tells me, however, that who has power during sexual activity can be negotiated. For instance, the penetrated could exercise control. We hear how LAIS 2 so perfected the "a tergo" technique that she called the posture her own, the *léaina* (the lioness). The second most popular sexual position, the equestrian, had the woman on top where she could control sexual stimulation (cf. Johns 1982: 136–7; Myerowitz 1992: 153). And in Roman practice there were two kinds of oral-penis stimulation, fellatio (performed by the mouth of the penetrated) and irrumation (performed by the penis of the penetrator [i.e. rape of the mouth]). The Romans therefore distinguished between who had control of the sexual stimulation, the penetrator (irrumatio) or the penetrated (fellatio).

The origin of homosexuality

Many scholars have written much about early paiderastia – since Homer does not mention it, some scholars argue that it must be an innovation of the later Iron Age. Scholars then look for causes (population control [Percy 1996], or a byproduct of athletic nudity [Scanlon 2002]). Paiderastia, however, is not homosexuality; it is a coming-of-age rite, and as such it has anthropological parallels that situate it in a stage of state-formation, at the tribal level. In that case, paiderastia should originate in the Bronze Age (Cantarella 1992: 5), and I myself would put its development no later than the Middle Bronze Age (ca. 1900–1600 BCE).

Men and women

In antiquity men and women saw each other as different; accordingly, they developed complex taxonomies (philosophical explanations) for understanding anatomical, physiological, emotional, and rational differences. Some of these differences seem profoundly odd to us moderns. For instance, women had many pockets in their body that needed to be broken through to (hence the necessity for penetrative intercourse) and women's bodies were moist (hence the need to menstruate); conversely, men's bodies were dense (hence the need for physical exercise) and hot and dry (hence the need to stay active and outdoors).

In modern society, masculinity is primarily performed as a set of repeated and routinized behaviors (men are taught to be "tall, dark, handsome, restrained, strong, unemotional"). Femininity is also performed, but with seemingly greater variety (women are taught to be "flighty, indecisive, emotional, and conscious of appearance"). In antiquity we find similar performances: women's thoughts and emotions are fluid, men's controlled.

With women constructed as closer to unmanageable nature (Aristotle, *Problems* 29; Ortner 1972), men may have felt constantly in danger: surely spending too much time with women emasculates a man. Not coincidentally, therefore, we occasionally hear men lamenting that women are necessary for procreation (SEXUAL ATTITUDES).

Erotic art and pornography

Modern discussions about erotic art have often concerned the place of women: to what extent are they objects of social manipulation, to what extent can they be subjects? Since men probably made most art and most literature, many scholars have concluded that ancient women are basically unknowable (Rabinowitz 1992: 38–50; Kappeler and MacKinnon 1992: 252).

As an archaeologist, however, I feel that too much emphasis has been placed on literature and not enough on the artifactual evidence. Women viewed erotic art; they undoubtedly saw the Greek sympotic drinking cups and contemplated the wall paintings in their Roman homes. And in doing so, they must have speculated on their own sexuality.

Much of the debate over pornography concerns two issues: its objectification of all participants and the effects of that objectification. Will erotic objectification cause people (men) to objectify their actual partners during sex, or will pornography cause a catharsis of such (negative) feelings? Since homosexual pornography is rampant today but homosexual rape is rare, homosexual pornography (at least) may have little negative effect on behavior (Shapiro 1992: 55).

Moral decay

A common attitude in antiquity was that toleration of immoderation (luxury, food, drink, sex) would induce cultural decline. That culture has declined is an assumption in Hesiod, and that present laxity overturns accepted morality is a theme in Aristophanes's *Clouds*. Writers constantly accused politicians and other notables for sexual perversity (INVECTIVE). "A well-known theme of Latin literature locates the initiation of the state's supposed moral ruin in the second century BC, and attributes that decline to the influx of wealth from the East" (Wyke 1994: 140). LAWS were enacted to stem the erosion of public decency (BACCHANALIA). In the Justinianic codes, sexual immorality was an offence to God, and since God could exact revenge on the state, the state's punishment was capital.

For sexual morality, the topic turned, and still turns, on the participants (what biological sex, what class, what age), activities (what positions, penetrations of what), and reasons (procreation, pleasure, political ambition). All these factors are subject to scrutiny, especially along lines of what is considered "natural" (SEXUAL ATTITUDES), as if human behavior had any "natural" analog. As Winkler (1990: 17–44) clearly saw, what is "natural" in human behavior is usually cultural. For antiquity, I take no moral stance; they practiced sex because they could.

Modern scholarship

By the late eighteenth century Greek culture was being castigated for inspiring "pederasty" ("Greek," "Socratic" love). In the early nineteenth century Friedrich

Welcker (1816 [1845]) made a strong case for Sappho as a heterosexual, ideal mother, which brought Sappho's poetry back into the classical canon. William Mure (1857) demolished Welcker's view, opening the dialogue on ancient sexual behaviors. John Addington Symonds published privately two essays (1883, 1891) that discussed Greek paiderastia and the characterization of modern homosexuality. Early twentieth-century scholars thus tried to approach Greek and Roman sexuality with some objectivity (Licht 1925–8, 1932; Vorberg 1932).

In the late twentieth century lavishly illustrated books (e.g. Marcadé 1962 and 1965; Grant and Mulas 1965; Boardman and LaRocca 1975; Johns 1982) allowed an interested public to examine ancient erotic art leisurely; and Brendel 1970 discussed it in comfortable art historical terms. Michel Foucault (1976/80–1984/6) systematized ancient sexuality as a (male) cultural construct (with a history), at the same time feminist scholars began recovering ancient women and their sexuality (Pomeroy 1975; Keuls 1985). Wilhelm Krenkel's remarkable series of articles (1979–89) on ancient sexual practices went unduly neglected, but they deserve careful reading. Ancient homoeroticism was a major theme in the 1980s (e.g. Boswell 1980; Lilja 1983; Koch-Harnack 1983; Reinsberg 1989; Dover 1989).

From 1990 to the present day ancient sexuality has gone mainstream, being offered in university classrooms and quoted in America's lawcourts (Nussbaum 1994; Skinner 1996; and the 2003 Supreme Court decision that overturned sodomy laws). Especially influential studies include Lefkowitz and Fant 1992; Richlin 1992; Dean-Jones 1994; Kampen 1996; Clarke 1998; and Davidson 1998.

A

Abortion Since conception was considered a continuous process (seven days for Aristotle or longer for SORANUS), and since it was also unclear when life began (at conception [Pythagoreans], at birth [Diogenes, Stoics], or gradually through PREGNANCY [Soranus]), CONTRACEPTION and abortion are conflated in antiquity.

Methods of abortion (*ekbólia*) include drugs to stimulate blood flow (oral pessaries or external poultices; PLANTS), strenuous activity (DANCE), physical interventions, and MAGIC. Elephantis (first century BCE) was a well known woman author on abortifacients (Pliny, *HN* 28.51).

Abortions for female slaves and PROSTITUTES were common (Hippocrates, *Nat. puer.*); the BROTHEL at Ashkalon produced many fetus skeletons in its drains (Faerman 1998). Abortions for citizen women, however, were avoided since they gave women a power over their own bodies (OVID, *Amores* 2.13–14) and bypassed the father's right to accept the child into the household (AMPHIDROMIA). After Augustus's LAWS promoting MARRIAGE and multiple children, people began to consider the fetus the primary victim of abortion.

The statement in the Hippocratic oath, "I will not give to a woman a pessary to procure an abortion," does not forbid other means and does not specify when this prohibition should apply; consequently, doctors made their own decisions based on individual cases.

Abortion was apparently not illegal in antiquity, nor was it hateful to the GODS. Under Septimius Severus and Caracalla a few cases criminalized abortion because the husband did not consent. The *Digest* mentions abortion only because of dangerous drugs (48.19.38.5).

See also: CONTRACEPTION; MEDICINE.

Richlin 1997: 237–9; Kapparis 2002.

Abstinence was a man's concern in antiquity (except in ARISTOPHANES, *Lysistrata*). In general, it was thought to preserve potency. Continence contributed to good health, allowing a man "to store up his seed" (Plutarch, *Mor.* 129d ff.). Prolonged abstinence, however, could do harm. "Athletes or singers who lead totally sexless lives have thin and wrinkled genitals like OLD men's" (Galen 8:451–2 Kühn). In contrast, Aristotle (*Gen. An.* 7.1) notes that the male voice deepens during puberty and with SEXUAL ACTIVITY.

Abstinence from intercourse was practiced by singers (Horace, *Ars P.* 414; cf. Suetonius, *Domitian* 10), although they could perform FELLATIO and CUNNILINGUS (Aristophanes, *Knights* 1278 f., and scholiast; Juvenal 6.73; Martial 7.82, 11.75, 14.215).

ATHLETES especially abstained from sex, since any loss of SEMEN sapped strength. "If any man retains his semen, he is strong, and the proof is athletes who are abstinent" (Aretaeus, *De causis morb.* 2.5.4; cf. Plato, *Laws* 839e–840c). Athletes were advised even to avoid MASTUR-BATION and NOCTURNAL EMISSIONS by wearing lead plates under their thighs (Galen 9:12, 12:232 Kühn; cf. NERO). Modern admonitions against masturbation often address adolescents: it depletes "the sex fluid formed by the testicles. Keep control in sex matters. It's manly to do so. It's important for one's life, happiness, efficiency and the whole human race as well" (Boy Scouts of America 1910: 448–9). And modern coaches discourage sex especially on nights before competition.

Both Plutarch (*Anecd. Par.* 2.154.20–25) and Aelian (*NA* 6.1) mention the Olympic pankratiast Kleitomachos who "turned away when he saw dogs mating" (Aelian) and "did not tolerate the mere mention of sex" (Plutarch). Aelian also characterizes the Olympic pentathlete Ikkos (444 BCE) as "inexperienced in sexual intercourse for the whole period of his training, for Ikkos was in love with the Olympic and Pythian Games" (cf. Plato, *Laws* 839e–840a).

To help them avoid DESIRE, athletes rubbed their bodies with an ointment that stained the skin yellow; Philostratus's description ("oil thickened with dust," *Gym.* 31–40) implies that this is KONISA-LOS (cf. Martial 7.32.9, 11.47.1–8). Other means for reducing desire included ana-phrodisiacs (APHRODISIACS), CHASTITY BELTS, and the DOGKNOT.

See also: BODY MODIFICATION.

Sweet 1985; Scanlon 2002: 227–36.

Achilles, son of Peleus and Thetis, hero of the TROJAN WAR. Since Achilles was willing to choose a short but famous life, Thetis hid him, when Agamemnon was assembling his Trojan expedition, at the court of Lykomedes on the island of Scyros, dressed as a girl (AGE GRADES, TRANSVESTISM). There he has a son, Neoptolemos by Deidameia, one of the king's daughters. Odysseus and Palamedes arrive to look for him, and Odysseus drops armor on the floor to attract Achilles's attention. Thus found out, he joins the expedition. At Aulis, to assuage ARTEMIS, Agamemnon sacrifices his daughter Iphigeneia on the pretext of MARRYING her to Achilles (cf. VERGINIA). At Troy, Achilles ambushes and kills Troilos by either cutting off his head or raping him to death. At the start of the *Iliad*, Achilles is forced to give up his prize, Briseis, to king Agamemnon. He sulks in his tent, but his best friend Patroklos dons Achilles' armor and is killed by Hector. In poems that deal with later events, Achilles kills Penthesileia queen of the AMAZONS, but only seconds after they had fallen in love at first sight (NECROPHILIA). After Paris kills Achilles, Polyxena is sacrificed to him.

Achilles may also have been the erome-nos of Antilochos (Homer, *Odyssey* 24.78–9; cf. **40**). In Homer, Patroklos is older than Achilles, and the two are just friends. Aeschylus (*Myrmidons* fr. 228 Mette) and Plato (*Symp.* 180a.4), however, make Achilles the elder erastes and Patroklos the younger eromenos (**89**, **166**).

Adonis, the son of Cinyras, king of Cyprus, and of Cinyras's daughter Myr-rha who had seduced him (INCEST). Myr-rha then became the myrtle tree (fruiting in mid-June) out of which was born Adonis (*myrton*, clitoris; cf. ATTIS). APH-RODITE seduces him. A boar kills him and she keeps the body fresh with nectar (cf. Nossis, *Greek Anth.* 6.275) or changes him into a flower, the *adonium*.

Women mourn his death annually in Athens and Argos at the Adonia (mid-June?; Ammianus 22.9.15). They force PLANTS to sprout (the Gardens of Adonis) and carry them to rooftops where they wither. The festivities on the rooftops were raucous (Oakley and Sinos 1993: 40). Finally, the women carry an image of Adonis around the city and cast it in the sea. The "Mutilation of the HERMS" and the departure of the Syracusan expedition of 415 BCE took place during the festival (Plutarch, *Alc.* 18).

Ovid, *Met.* 10.519–36; Apollodorus 1.3.2; 1.9.9, 11 and 12; 3.14.3 and 4; Pausanias 2.20.6; 6.24.7; 9.16.4; 9.29.8; 9.41.2; Keuls 1985: 391, 395; Reed 1995; Simms 1997; 1998.

Adultery assumes that one spouse is the property of the other, used without approval by another person; additionally, an adulteress betrays her lawful guardian (Wells 1979). Most adultery in antiquity is committed by the wife, although ALCIBIADES's wife tries to divorce him for letting PROSTITUTES stay in the house.

In Athens, if the husband catches his wife in the act of adultery, he may kill the other man with impunity (cf. Lysias, *Eratosthenes*), although the usual penalty was to pay money to the husband (Callias 1 K–A). There were other punishments against the male adulterer: stuffing a radish or mullet into his anus, or irrumating him (FELLATIO; Aristophanes, *Clouds* 1079–85; Catullus 15, 74; Martial 2.47.4). Seducers of unmarried women, however, could be forced to MARRY them. Adulterous wives in Athens were denied access to public festivals, displayed in the agora, or led through the city bound.

In Rome, a husband, in consultation with his wife's relatives, could kill his wife for adultery, drinking, counterfeiting his keys, or poison (Dio. Hal. 2.25; Plutarch, *Rom.* 25). In 36 BCE a man caught his wife in bed with another woman, and he killed them both (Plutarch, *Ant.* 24.5; Strabo 660; LESBIANISM). The *lex Julia de adulteriis coercendis* (18 BCE; LAWS) defined criminal adultery as involving a married woman.

Husbands could allow their wives to be seduced by someone important for political gain. Phaüllos of Argos sneaked his wife to king Philip V. Gabba gave a dinner for Maecenas and pretended to go to sleep so he could dally with his wife; when a slave attempted to steal some wine, Gabba blurted, "it's only for Maecenas that I'm asleep!" paraphrasing Lucilius 251 (Plutarch, *Erotikos* 760a–b cites both stories).

See also: DIVORCE

Aeschines (ca. 397–22 BCE), Athenian politician. In 346/5, Demosthenes, supported by Timarchus, prosecuted Aeschines for bribery, and Aeschines successfully counter-prosecuted Timarchus for PROSTITUTING himself (Aeschines, *In Timarchum*) and then having taken part in politics (CITIZENSHIP). Timarchus's behavior was common knowledge (*In Timarchum* 44, 73–6): he had been wealthy (97), but had wasted his inheritance on flutegirls and hetairai (75, 95–105); he even sold his property for ready cash; he had moved in with five different men, the last one also a prostitute. Can such a man be trusted with state business? (95–6). "The man who has sold the right to his own body would be ready to sell the state as well" (29).

Agaristê (fl. 575 BCE), daughter of Cleisthenes, tyrant of Sikyon. At the Olympic games ca. 576 BCE Cleisthenes invited suitors to woo his daughter Agaristê. The successful suitor seemed to be Hippokleides son of Tisander of Athens. But the night when Cleisthenes was to announce his choice, the suitors stayed up late drinking and Hippocleides DANCED on a table Laconian-style, then Attic-style, and then upside-down, his legs dancing in the air. When Cleisthenes remonstrated that he had just danced away his MARRIAGE, he replies, "Not a care to Hippokleides!" Agaristê was therefore married to Megacles son of Alcmaeon of Athens, and became the mother of Cleisthenes the lawgiver, Agaristê II (wife of PEISISTRATOS), and Hippokrates the father of Agaristê III, the mother of Perikles.

Herodotus 6.126–131.

Age Grades, socially marked, important stages in life. Such stages include: infancy, childhood, adolescence (puberty), adulthood (further subdivided by MARRIAGE, parenthood, and CITIZENSHIP), and OLD AGE.

Greek males went from CHILDHOOD (age 7 or 8) or adolescence (twelve, PAIDERASTIA) to warriors (eighteen, ephebes), husbands (late twenties), and full citizens (thirty-five); their adolescence further included ATHLETIC and military training and socialization into male society. Females underwent a shorter period of transition to adult, from 7 or 8 (footraces) to 15 or 20 years old, during which they experienced puberty (MENSTRUATION), got married, and gave BIRTH.

Terminology for the age grades differed; for the earliest stages, there were, for both boys and girls, "infant" perhaps up to age three, and then "child" up to age seven or so. At SPARTA, boys became *paídes* at age seven, *paidískoi* (14–20; as eromenoi), youths or *hébontes* 20–30 (as erasteis, full members of a messhall), *ándres* ("men," 30, and full citizens). The Chigi jug (**32**) presents a simpler tripartite division: boys in the lowest zone, youths in the middle zone, and adult warriors in the top zone (Hurwitt 2002).

Infancy can be subdivided: the announcement of a child's birth (at the house entrance: wool for a girl, olive wreaths for a boy) and the father's acceptance and naming of the child a week later (AMPHIDROMIA/LUSTRATIO). At Athens, when a child was at least 3 years old, it first participated in "Choes" (ANTHESTERIA).

Childhood seems to have lasted until about seven years. In Athens, girls could be selected by the state to be "Arrhe-

phoroi," to live on the Acropolis, serve ATHENA, and help weave her *péplos* (robe). In Sparta and Crete, boys (aged 12–14) begin to frequent the *andreía* (clubhouse) of their fathers; a *paidonómos* supervised them and taught them grammar and music and organized them into "herds" (*agélai*) that ate and slept together. The father of the herd's leader led them in hunting, exercise, mock battles, and running.

Running was an important component in the adolescence of both boys and girls (ATHLETICS). Young females ran footraces in the Heraia games, in honor of DIONYSUS Kolonatas at Sparta, and at the ARKTEIA for ARTEMIS in Attica. Plato recommends that unmarried girls to age 18 or 20 should compete in footraces, while girls under thirteen should compete NUDE (*Laws* 833c–834d). Women's footraces may have celebrated the transition from a "wild" unmarried state to a "tamed" wife (Scanlon 2002; Spiro 1900; ATALANTA).

Footraces and other contests were also common for young men. They constituted the earliest events at the men's Olympics (seventeen or older); boys' footraces were added in 632. At Sparta, boys ran the *staphylodrómos* (running with grapes; OSCHOPHORIA) during the festival of APOLLO Karneus: a youth filleted with wool prays for benefits to the state, and the staphylodromoi, a group of unmarried men, chase him (Pausanias 3.14.6). At the *gymnopaídia*, nude males of various ages competed in choral DANCES that imitated, very slowly, athletic events. In Crete, the word for racecourse, *drómos*, is used to designate a pre-citizen (*apodrómos*) and citizen (*dromeús*).

Other general marks of the transition from adolescence to adulthood include changes in hairstyle (dedicating HAIR to a divinity: women to APHRODITE or ARTEMIS, men to APOLLO or HERAKLES), and changes in dress (EKDYSIA; LEUKIPPOS 2; TRANSVESTISM). At Athens, graduation from the ephebeia at age twenty may have involved a change of dress since Philok-leon could see their genitals (ARISTO-PHANES, *Wasps* 578). For women about to be married, it was also a time to dedicate dolls, toys, musical instruments, and their belt (Van Straten 1981: 90–1).

In Rome, males passed through adolescence over a shorter period of time and with fewer ceremonies: exchanging the *toga praetextus* for the *toga virilis* at age fifteen, and shaving one's first beard (NERO).

Von Gennep's tripartite division for these transitions (1909/60: removal from society, marginalization, and reintegration) predicts that, especially in adolescence, males and females will be taken aside, educated in their new roles, and brought back into mainstream society through important ceremonies. Exiting and re-entering society during the transition to adulthood could both be marked by pain. In Sparta, the boys raced to an altar in the sanctuary of Artemis Orthia between two lines of men who beat them. Women too were beaten at the feast of Dionysus (Pausanias 8.23.1). In Attica at Halai Araphenides, boys participated in a blood-letting ceremony (Euripides, *Iph. Taur.* 1439 ff.). Circumcision (BODY MOD-IFICATION) for both boys and girls was practiced in the east.

Alcibiades (451/0–404/3 BCE), Athenian aristocrat, general, and politician. On the eve of the expedition's departure for Sicily (415) HERMS were mutilated (ADONIS), but the fleet departed anyway under the command of Alcibiades, Nicias, and Lamachus. After it had reached Sicily, the Athenians recalled Alcibiades, charging him with sacrilege both for the mutilation of the herms and for mocking the Mysteries. He escaped to SPARTA where he was accused of impregnating the Spartan queen (412); he fled to Persia. He was made general by the Athenian democrats in Samos, won several battles against the Spartans, and was acquitted of sacrilege (407). He withdrew to the Thracian Chersonese (406), attempted to advise the Athenians at Aegispotamoi (405), and after their defeat he sought asylum in Persia; he was murdered in Phrygia the next year.

In Plato's *Symposium*, Alcibiades makes a tipsy entrance, and tells of his infatuation with Socrates, and of his attempts to seduce him in the GYMNASIUM and to bed him under their military CLOAK. Socrates may have been in love with him (Plato, *Alc.* 103a; cf. Athenaeus 5.187e–f). Athenaeus continues the story, weaving bits from Plato, that ASPASIA chided Socrates for being in love with Alcibiades, now thirty, and she advises him to search for love elsewhere (5.219b–220a). Anytos, the eventual prosecutor of Socrates, did, however, successfully woo Alcibiades as his eromenos. He gave a symposium which Alcibiades crashed taking half the cups; when his guests complained, Anytus replied that "it was most kind of him to leave me as many as he did" (Plutarch, *Alc.* 4).

In Abydos, Alcibiades and his friend Axiochus reportedly MARRIED the same woman, who gave birth to a daughter. When the girl matured both men had sex with her, saying she was the daughter of the other (Athenaeus 12.534f, 12.535a, 13.574e). The Socratic philosopher Antisthenes charged Alcibiades with INCEST "with his mother, his sister, and his daughter" (Athenaeus 5.220c). And the historian Callisthenes characterized him as being "a woman's man without actually being a man" (FGrH 124 F34; cf. JULIUS CAESAR).

Two "portraits" of Alcibiades exist, a marble relief depicting "Alcibiades" and his hetairai (252) and a Roman mosaic from Sparta.

Ellis 1989.

Alexander III of Macedon, "The Great" (356–22 BCE), son of Philip II of Macedon and Olympias of Epirus. At the battle of Chaironeia, Philip ordered him to eradicate the SACRED BAND. After the assassination of Philip (336), Alexander was elected to lead the Greeks across the Hellespont (spring 334) against king Darius II. By October 331 he had taken over the Persian empire; in 327 he marched into India. He returned to Persia (325) and died at Babylon in the early summer of 323, age thirty-two, having gotten sick from drinking too much wine at a SYMPOSIUM. His general Ptolemy interred him in a fabled coffin in Alexandria.

Alexander is said to have set fire to the palace of Darius at Persepolis at the urging of the Athenian hetaira THAÏS. In Bactria, he MARRIED Roxanê the daughter of the chief of Sogdiana, Oxyartes (327); shortly after Alexander's death she bore Alexander IV Aigos. After his Indian campaign, he ordered eighty of his officers to take Asian wives in a mass ceremony, at which he also MARRIED his second wife Barsanê, daughter of Darius (POLYGAMY); she bore him Herakles. Eventually, Cassander had Roxanê, Barsanê, Alexander IV, and Herakles assassinated, 311. When his closest friend Hephaistion died in Ecbatana, Alexander grieved by cutting the manes and tails of his horses, crucifying the attending physician, and slaughtering tribes of barbarians.

Plutarch, *Alex.*

Amazons, legendary warrior daughters of Ares and the naiad Harmonia. Originally, they lived in Scythia near lake Maeotis. Queen Lysippê eventually moved them to Themiskyra on the south coast of the Black Sea where they prospered. Other Amazons lived in Hespera, the island in the middle of Lake Tritonis in southern Numidia. When Gorgons massacred them, queen Myrinê and her followers fled east to Egypt and Arabia. It is these Amazons that Athenian vase painters depicted on white ground "Negro" alabastra (von Bothmer 1957: pl. 73.3–5); it is perhaps not coincidental that an Athe-

nian vase found at Meroë in Ethiopia (137) also depicts Amazons.

While their men performed domestic duties (their arms and legs broken in childhood), Amazon women governed and fought with bronze bows and shields shaped like half-moons; they were the first to use horses in war. Amazons are first shown wearing skins, but from ca. 440 BCE their COSTUME consists of a patterned suit (shirt and pants) and Phrygian caps. On horse, Amazons wear a short tunic. They were said to have removed their right breast in order to gain greater freedom in archery (although no Amazon is so depicted), and Libyan Amazons had no breasts at all (Diodorus Siculus 3.53–54). The popular etymology for "Amazon" (from a+*mázos*, without a breast) probably contributed to this idea.

Most stories concern the Amazons at Themiskyra. THESEUS and Pirithoös had joined Herakles in his ninth labor to acquire the belt of Ares from queen Hippolytê. Herakles defeats them and strips Hippolytê of the belt. The queen's sister Antiopê falls in love with Theseus and surrenders the city to him. Theseus then returns to Athens with her. Hippolytê then invades Athens where they set up camp on the ridge from the Areopagus to the Hill of the Muses; many defeated Amazons are buried there. Theseus has a son Hippolytos by Antiopê whom he is eventually forced to kill when, jealous over his impending marriage to MINOS's daughter Phaidra, she threatens to massacre the wedding guests (cf. MEDEA).

Other episodes are minor. The Amazons had fought at TROY three times, the last when they came to the aid of the Trojans under their queen Penthesileia. As ACHILLES killed her he fell in love with her and had intercourse with her body (NECROPHILIA). Pindar states that Amazons founded the sanctuary at Ephesus, where they established a shield DANCE and a circle dance that included rattling their quivers and beating the ground in unison (an allusion to the popular term, "ground-beaters," for women in "a tergo" inter-course). Eventually, the Amazons were driven from Themiskyra to Albania along with the Gargarensians. Inhabiting neigh-boring regions, they and the Amazons would meet every year for two months for sex. The girls that were born were reared as Amazons, and boys were sent back to the Gargarensians who distribu-ted them by lot to adoptive parents.

Amazons occur regularly in Greek art from the seventh century BCE on, both in vase painting and in sculpture, especially a group of five Amazons dedicated at Ephesus, the result (it was said) of a contest between Polykleitos, Phideias, Kresilas, Kydon, and Phradmon (Pliny, *HN* 34.53; Ridgway 1974). Scholars have assigned these five sculptural types to these sculptors, as if Pliny's contest was real. They are probably mostly Roman inventions.

While Amazons properly belong to Greek mythology, Vergil includes the Amazon-like Camilla, queen of the Volsci and servant of Diana (*Aen.* 7.803 ff., 11.532 ff.). And an embassy of 300 Amazons reportedly met with ALEXANDER THE GREAT at Hyrcania where he and queen Minythyia had sex for almost two weeks in order to produce exceptional children (Diodorus Siculus 17.77.1–3; cf. Plutarch, *Alex.* 46.1–2).

Real women warriors also existed in antiquity: Harpalykê of Thrace (Vergil, *Aen.* 1.317), Sophonisba queen of Numi-dia (Livy 30.12–15); Telesilla the poet of Argos (Pausanias 2.20.8–9, 2.28.2, 2.35.2); Pheretima queen of Cyrene (Her-odotus 4.159 ff.), and the famous Zeno-bia of Palmyra. In addition, female gladiators fought in the arenas until Septi-mius Severus banned them, ca. 200 CE (Mantas 1995). Women who live their lives as men are known today in the Balkans (Grémaux 1989).

von Bothmer 1957; Herodotus 4.110–117, 9.27; Isocrates 4.68, 70, 4.42, 7.75, 12.193; Diodorus Siculus 4.16, 4.28; Plutarch, *Thes.*

26–28; Pausanias 1.2.1, 1.15.2, 1.17.2, 1.25.2, 1.41.7, 2.32.9, 5.10.9, 5.11.4, 5.11.7, 5.25.11, 7.2.7.

Amphidromia/Lustratio, the legitimizing and naming ceremony (in Greece and Rome, respectively) held about a week after the birth of a child. In Greece, on the fifth or seventh day, the father, naked, carries the child around the household hearth and the women of the household purify themselves. The family decorates the doorway of their home to announce the birth of the new child: a wreath of olive leaves for a boy, sheep's wool for a girl (Plato, *Tht.* 160e). In Rome, the women also purify themselves and the house, and offer sacrifice; the ceremony for boys occurs on the ninth day, for girls on the eighth day.

Anacreon (fl. 536/5 BCE), lyric poet in Samos and Athens. It was said that he and Polykrates, tyrant of Samos, were in love with the same boy, Smerdies of Thrace, and that Polykrates cut the boy's HAIR (PMG 347). Anacreon was also said to have been the erastes of Kritias of Athens, the grandfather of the tyrant Kritias. Anacreon PMG 358, may suggest that there was an early connection, because of SAPPHO, between the island Lesbos and female homoerotic DESIRE (LESBIANISM; cf. Dover 1989: 183):

> Throwing me a purple ball
> Gold-haired Eros
> Calls me to play
> with a bright-sandaled girl –
> But she's from well-built
> Lesbos: she spurns my hair
> (it is white)
> and gapes after another.

"Gapes" (*kháskein*) may carry the conno-tation of FELLATIO (*lesbiázein*, "to do it Lesbos-style," meant to fellate [ETHNI-CITY]; the stretched mouths of the women fellating men, **108**). "Another" (*allên*) is feminine, referring either to "another person," a woman, or "another type" (referring to "hair," *komên*, i.e. pubic hair). If the latter, the girl from Lesbos is looking for a younger man (to fellate).

A group of Attic red-figure vases, called Anacreontic or "Booners" (**145**), portray "Anacreon" and "male symposiasts reveling in extravagant Eastern garb – long, flowing robes, turbans and headbands, earrings, and even parasols," suggesting refined sensuality (*habrosinê*; Kurke 1997: 132).

Analingus, oral stimulation of the anus. Three grafitti from POMPEII may refer to it: "Popilus canis cunnum linget Reno," "Popilus licks Renus's cunt [= anus] like a dog" (*CIL* 4.8898); "Priscus Extalio cunnum," "Priscus [licks] Extalius's 'cunt' " (*CIL* 4.8843); and "Fortunata, linge culum," "Fortunata, lick ass," CIL 4.4954.

Krenkel 1981.

Animals The sexual behavior of animals is often depicted in art (**251**) and often cited in philosophical and moralistic discussions as a model of "natural" sexual behavior in humans (cf. Plato, *Laws* 836c; HOMOEROTICISM).

Bears

ARTEMIS uses a bear to rear ATALANTA and to chase girls in the ARKTEIA. KALLISTO turns into a bear after she becomes PREGNANT by ZEUS. Polyphonê rejects APHRODITE and is driven mad with passion for a bear (Antoninus Liberalis 21).

Bovines

Bovines were powerful and potent. The Minoans leaped huge bulls, the *Bos primigenius* (Younger 1995); and in classical times there are several representations of bovines mating. ZEUS, in the disguise of a bull, carries off EUROPA. Pasiphaê (MINOS) DESIRES to mate with a bull.

Chickens

Pullus (Lat. chick) is slang for a male eromenos or male prostitute (Ausonius, *Epigr.* 70.5); cocks serve as LOVE GIFTS.

Crows

Crows were thought to mate for life. Because of their mutual affection, the Greeks said to the bride at a MARRIAGE *ek korí korí koronê*. This puzzling expression sounds something like the Greek word for crow (*kórax*) as well as an onomatopoetic version of the crow's caw (Aelian, *NA* 3.9; Edmonds 1967: 519). Crows accompanied HERA/JUNO.

Dogs

The Greek word for dog, *kúôn*, was used for the penis (DOGKNOT). Two main types of dogs are depicted, house dogs (small, fuzzy, curled tails) and hunting dogs (medium sized, long muzzles, droopy ears). On Greek tombstones and in vase paintings house dogs are usually associated with women and young children. Hunting dogs are always associated with males from adolescence on. On Attic vases, dogs often accompany youths courting other youths and boys (referring to the penis?), and may offer interpretive analogues for the main scene; for instance, a youth embraces a boy while a dog jumps at a caged hare (**164**, see HARES, below), and a man and youth engage in intercultural sex while holding a leashed dog and a hare (**159** [pl. 7]). Also see **122** (SEXUAL ACTIVITIES) and **36** (BODY FUNCTIONS). Similarly, Roman erotic depictions of men and women often include a house dog (**180, 230**). The dogs of the Subura accompany PROSTITUTES (Horace, *Epod.* 5.58; Tibullus 2.4.32), and they had a reputation for licking genitals (the *skúlax*, "bitch," was the position assumed for CUNNILINGUS: PETRONIUS 74.9, 75.110; cf. Martial 1.83.1–2).

Fish

Some fish were considered APHRODISIACS. One, the wrasse, was thought not to stop copulating even when caught (Athenaeus 7.281e–f).

Hares

Hares were thought to grow another opening in their body each year (Barnabas, *Epistle* 10.6); to "eat the hare" meant to have anal sex with boys.

Horses

There was a popular connection between women, horses, and unbridled desire (Castriota 1992: 53).

Pigs

The Greek word *hús* (pig) denotes the vagina (*Greek Anth.* 11.329.104: don't indulge your tongue, the "sow" has a formidable "thorn" [= clitoris]). ARISTOPHANES (*Acharnians* 790–2) mentions maidens "sacrificing to APHRODITE" a girl's "piggy" when it "blooms with the first hair."

Lions

Lions were thought incapable of copulation (Servius 3.113; Mythographi Vaticani 1.39; Palaephatus 14; Hyginus 185), thus the humor of **337**; ATALANTA and Meilanion are changed into lions for having had intercourse in the sanctuary of ARTEMIS.

Ravens

Ravens were thought to conceive by FELLATIO, and to bear their young orally (Martial 14.74; Juvenal 2.63 scholiast; cf *Kama Sutra* 82).

Snakes

Snakes were sacred to Asclepius, the healing god. Women reported getting PREGNANT by snakes (Dittenberger 1915–1924: 3342, p. 326, 129 ff.; Lucian, *Alexander* p. 665; Gellius 6.1.2–5). AUGUSTUS's mother, Atia, fell asleep during a nocturnal ceremony in the temple of APOLLO, and a snake visited her; when she awoke, she purified herself (as if after sex), and saw "an indelible mark in the shape of a serpent on her body" (Suetonius, *Augustus* 94.4; cf. Cass. Dio. 45.1).

Anteros In a PAIDERASTIC relationship EROS symbolizes the pursuit of the lover (cf. Plato, *Symp.* 203c.3–4), while Anteros personifies the flight of the eromenos (in heteroerotic relationships, Peitho takes the place of Anteros). The conception of Anteros dates apparently to the early fifth century BCE (**72**; cf. **142**, **309**). Plato discusses the twin concept of Eros and Anteros (*Phaedrus* 255b–e):

> When the erastes is present, the pain of both ceases, but when he is away, then the eromenos longs as he is longed for (*potheí kaí potheítai*) and has, as his image of LOVE, Anteros, which he terms not love but friendship, and his desire is like the desire of the other, but weaker (*asthenésteros*).

There was an altar to Anteros in Athens, probably near the Acropolis, set up by metics to commemorate an incident (Pausanias 1.30.1): Timagoras, a metic, was in love with an Athenian named Meles who spurned him, saying something like "go jump off a cliff," which Timagoras did, and Melas, being regretful, did the same.

Anthesteria, a three-day festival in Athens in early March in honor of DIONYSUS. On the first day, new wine was brought to the sanctuary of DIONYSUS in the Marshes; on the second day, there was a drinking contest and small jugs, *chóes*, were given to CHILDREN (AGE GRADES); on the third day, offerings were made to the dead. During the second day, the *basilínna*, the wife of the *árchon basileús* (the magistrate in charge of religion), sacrifices in the sanctuary and then processes to the Boukoleion, the archon's office near the agora. There, the god came to her and they spent the night together. As basilinna, the daughter of the PROSTITUTE NEAIRA profaned the mystery of her "MARRIAGE" with Dionysus.

See also: HIEROS GAMOS

Simon 1983: 92–9.

Antinoös (ca. 110–30 CE), a fourteen-year-old youth from Claudiopolis in Bithynia, probably met HADRIAN in 124, and became his companion eromenos until he drowned in the Nile in October 130 CE at the probable age of twenty. The cause of his drowning is not known, but at age twenty he was fast approaching adulthood. Hadrian mourned him excessively, deifying him, founding temples to him (Pausanias 8.9.7–8) and the city of Antinoöpolis near where he drowned, and commissioning statues of him in various guises (as Osiris at Tivoli, DIONYSUS at Delphi; Herakles at Chalkis, **246** [pl. 16]; Kleiner 1992: figs 207–10).

Antony (ca. 82–30 BCE), Marcus Antonius, Roman politician and general. After serving in JULIUS CAESAR's campaigns, he was his colleague in the consulship of 44, when Caesar was assassinated. He joined the first triumvirate with Octavian (AUGUSTUS) and Lepidus. After defeating Caesar's assassins, Brutus and Cassius, at Philippi (42), Antony met CLEOPATRA and spent the winter in Alexandria as her paramour. He returned to Rome in 40 to renew the triumvirate and MARRY Octavian's sister Octavia, his fourth wife; she bore him two daughters, Antonia maior and Antonia minor, mother of CLAUDIUS.

Antony's earlier wives had been Fadia, Antonia, and Fulvia, who bore Antony two sons, Antyllus and Iullus Antonius. Antyllus was once betrothed to Octavian's daughter JULIA MAIOR, but was put to death after the capture of Alexandria; Iullus married a niece of AUGUSTUS, but was convicted of ADULTERY with JULIA MAIOR in 2 and committed suicide.

After the establishment of the second triumvirate (37), Antony returned to Alexandria and married CLEOPATRA without DIVORCING Octavia (POLYGAMY); they had three children, Alexander, Ptolemy, and Cleopatra. After Octavian defeated Antony and Cleopatra at Actium (31) he pursued them to Alexandria. Before Octavian could enter the city, Antony committed suicide. After Cleopatra's suicide, Octavian had both buried side by side; Octavia magnanimously raised their three children.

Aphrodisiacs and Anaphrodisiacs, PLANTS and ANIMAL parts to stimulate or depress erotic DESIRE, respectively. Pepper and crushed nettle seeds could be smeared with oil on DILDOES and inserted into the anus or vagina (PETRONIUS 17). Generic dishes included the food *lastrauokákabos* (Athenaeus 1.9b–c) and the drink *satúrion* (PETRONIUS 1 and 4: nasturtium juice and nettles). FLAGELLATION with nettles and spanking with SANDALS also promoted desire.

Aphrodisiacs

(in general: barley, beans [fabae], wild bulbs [Athenaeus 1.5c], crayfish [Athenaeus 3.105c]), lily, mint, onions [OVID, *Rem. Am.* 797–8], saffron, savory)

mêlon ("apple")

A round fruit like the quince or pomegranate (the apple is introduced in late classical times). Eris throws a gold mêlon to disrupt the wedding of Peleus and

Thetis (TROJAN WAR); Meilanion throws three mêla down for ATALANTA to pick up. Brides eat a mêlon before consummating their MARRIAGE.

Eruca

Eryngô (cf. *ereúgomai*, to ejaculate; Horace, *Sat.* 2.8.51; Pliny, *HN* 19.8; Martial 3.75.3), a kind of colewort or rocket, sacred to PRIAPUS (Columella 11.3.29, 10.109.372). Phaon uses the *eryngô* plant on SAPPHO 2.

Lettuce

APHRODITE conceals Phaon (SAPPHO 2) amongst wild lettuce (Athenaeus 1.69b–f, 2.69d). HERA uses lettuce to conceive Hebe.

Pomegranate

Associated with MARRIAGE and fertility. Persephonê ate the seeds which compel her to remain half the year in Hades (*Homeric Hymn to Demeter* 412); Aphrodite planted the pomegranate tree in Cyprus (Athenaeus 3.84c)

seafood

Sea animals commonly decorate erotic scenes (284); oysters were especially popular.

Anaphrodisiacs

(in general: vitex)

Cucumber

According to the proverb ("munch a cucumber [*síkuon*], woman, and keep on weaving your CLOAK," Athenaeus 3.73d; perhaps punning on *boubálion*, cucumber=cunt, Hesychius s.v.), cucumbers inhibited intercourse because they are difficult to digest (Athenaeus 3.74c).

See also: MEDICINE

Richlin 1997: 236–7.

Aphrodite/Venus, goddess of love and sex (**236 [pl. 31], 237 [pl. 32]**). Born from the genitals of Ouranos in the guise of sea foam, she came ashore in Cyprus (whence her name Cypris). The Greek goddess came in two forms, Aphrodite Ourania (Heavenly Aphrodite) and Aphrodite Pandemos (Common Aphrodite), supposedly to distinguish love from lust.

Although Aphrodite was married to HEPHAESTUS, she has a long-term affair with Ares, with several children, including EROS and ANTEROS. Domodocus SINGS of her and Ares (Homer, *Odyssey* 8.266) and they appear frequently together in wall paintings at POMPEII (**336**). Aphrodite's alter ego was Peitho, who represented a person's consent to sex. Aphrodite's most notable temple was at Palaipaphos; there the faithful consulted an oracle (Suetonius, *Titus* 5), indulged in bathing, a procession to the sanctuary of ADONIS-APOLLO (at Rantidi?), and temple PROSTITUTION.

Since Venus was the mother of Aeneas, she was the personal protectress of the Roman nation, as well as the personal deity of JULIUS CAESAR. In Rome there were the temples of Venus and Roma designed by HADRIAN, Venus Genetrix in the Forum of Julius Caesar, and Venus Erycina near the Colline gate with an altar to Lethaeus Amor (OVID, *Rem. Am.* 549–54). Venus was also the patron goddess of POMPEII.

She was also depicted in several popular statues: the Aphrodite of Knidos (**18 [pl. 28]**) by PRAXITELES; and the Crouching Aphrodite by Doidalses of Bithynia (**19**; cf. **160**). The "Venus di Milo" was dedicated in the GYMNASIUM in Melos probably in the second century by Bakkhios son of Satios (inscription above her niche) and sculpted by "andros son of Menides of Antioch on the Meander" (inscription on the base). She holds a *mêlon* (a round fruit) in the left hand resting on a pillar, thus punning on the name of the island and referring to her victory in the judgment of Paris. Armed Aphrodite (*Aphrodítê hoplisménê* or *stráteia*) had a shrine atop Acrocorinth and a wood statue in SPARTA (Pausanias 2.5.1, 3.15.10).

Apollo, son of ZEUS and LETO, brother of ARTEMIS, a young (beardless) god of art, prophecy, and youths. The god's main sanctuaries were at Delphi where the stone that Kronos swallowed was kept, and Delos where he was born. Apollo oversaw the transition of youths into adulthood (AGE GRADES; HERMES). Apollo's first temple in Rome (449 BCE) was to Apollo Medicus (Sosianus), the healing god. AUGUSTUS built a temple to Apollo Palatinus near, and attached to, his own house.

Several stories concern Apollo and his loves (DAPHNE; HYAKINTHOS; LOVES OF THE GODS; cf. HERMES). As Helios, the sun god, he enters Leukothoê's bedroom disguised as her mother, Eurynomê (TRANSSEXUALITY), and rapes her (OVID, *Met.* 4.217–35); "Leukothea" is also the name of the month at Teos when ephebes became adult.

Aristogeiton and Harmodius, male lovers (Aristogeiton the erastes, Harmodios the eromenos). Hipparchos, brother of the tyrant Hippias, had tried to seduce Harmodios; at the Panatheneia of 514 BCE, he publicly removed his sister from participating in the weaving of Athena's peplos. The two lovers then plotted to assassinate the tyrants at the Panathenaic procession (citizens could appear armed then). They killed Hipparchos but Hippias escaped. Harmodios was killed immediately; Aristogeiton was soon captured and put to death. After the establishment of the democracy (510/509), the Athenians commissioned Endoios for a statue of the two Tyrannicides, which the Persians sent to Susa in their sack of Athens (480). After

the Athenians regained the city (479) they commissioned Kritias and Nesiotes for a replacement; ALEXANDER THE GREAT returned Endoios's group when he took Susa (325). Representations of the Tyrannicides abound (**144**). A well known drinking SONG was composed by Callistratus in their honor (Edmonds 1967: 567).

Herodotus 5.55, 6.109 and 123; Pausanias 1.8.5, 1.29.15; Thucydides 5.54.3; Brunnsåker 1971; Lavelle 1986; Robinson and Fluck 1937.

Aristophanes (ca. 447/6–386/80 BCE), Athenian poet of Old Comedy. Between 427 and 386 he wrote at least forty-four comedies, of which eleven survive. He comments continually on Athenian life, morals, and politicians, especially the demagogue Cleon (428 to 422). His ridicule of Socrates in the *Clouds* was partly responsible for the animosity toward him.

In every play Aristophanes uses sex and sexuality in at least three major ways: sexual INVECTIVE (to lampoon citizens of the state, often by calling them CINAEDI), commenting on sexual and gender roles (to highlight social absurdity), and jokes about BODY FUNCTIONS (commenting on our common humanity). For instance, in the *Lysistrata* alone, women observe that their primary social role is to be sexually used by men and to bear sons (10–20: "we are only good for one thing," 580–90; cf. 650–60); but women have sexual appetites (33–5: "give up sex? What a thought!"; 230–40: "our legs up, the 'doggy crouch' for pleasure"; 710–30: "we want men, and we need to get back to our beds!").

Aristophanes's major contribution to the history of SEXUAL ATTITUDES is his myth concerning the origin of the human species (Plato, *Symp.* 189e–192e, here much abridged):

Originally, there were three kinds of humans, not merely the two sexes, male and female, as now; but a type of both, an HERMAPHRODITE. Each was round, having the back and sides in a circle, four hands and four legs, and two faces on one neck that looked away from each other; and there were two sets of genitals (turned outwards). It walked about upright, like now, and whenever it wanted to run, it did cartwheels, like tumblers.

Now these three races had considerable strength and they assailed the gods. So ZEUS said, "I shall cut each in half; that way they will be weaker but, being twice as many, more useful to us. And they shall walk upright on two legs."

He cut them in half, and he commanded APOLLO to turn the face around to face the cut. And Zeus moved the genitals to the front, so they could have sex with each other. With a man and a woman, they could embrace and beget the species. And with a man and a man, they might lie together, get relief, and then return to their day-to-day affairs.

Thus, LOVE is ingrained in humans because of our original nature, and we try to make the two of us into one and in this way heal our soul. For each of us is a *symbolon* [an object cut in two, the pieces held by different parties]. And each of us is constantly searching for his other half, his other symbolon. The men who are half their original male-female are women-lovers, and the individual women are men-lovers, and ADULTERERS arise from these breeds. But the women who are searching for other women, these are the *hetairístriai* (LESBIANS). And those that are from the male-male pursue males, whether these are boys (fragments of males; PAIDERASTIA) or love and gratify men, lying with them and embracing them (MALE HOMOSEXUALITY). These are the best boys and youths since they are the most manly by nature, and they do not do this through shamelessness but because of courage, virtue, and manliness.

Now men such as these rise in politics, and when they become adults, they turn their affections to the boys next in line and are disinclined to get MARRIED and raise CHILDREN, but they do this by law. But they would prefer to dwell with each other, and not get married. Men like this are natural erasteis and eromenoi, each delighting in his own kind.

And when one individual half of the original happens upon his or her mate, and becomes a whole again, they fulfill each other in friendship and love, not wanting to be separated from each other, but to live out their lives with each other.

Arkteia, an Attic festival to ARTEMIS and Iphigeneia that took place at Brauron, on the Athens Acropolis, and at Mounychion, Piraeus. A variant on the Iphigeneia myth has Agamemnon sacrificing her at Brauron and Artemis substituting a bear for her, while another myth tells of a bear in the sanctuary playing with a girl and blinding her, and being killed by the girl's brother, for which the Athenian girls must atone by serving as bears (*ark-teuésthai*) before MARRIAGE.

The festival at Brauron was held every four years, when girls (5–10 years old) and women held footraces, sometimes dressed as bears. The sanctuary contained a temple to Artemis and the tomb of Iphigeneia. Through it runs a stream into which girls and women dedicated objects, including the COSTUMES of the girls and maternity clothes of women (Kahil 1977).

From all three sanctuaries come fragments of small vases (6th–5th century BCE) that depict girls, maidens, and women running NUDE, in short chitons, or in saffron CLOAKS (*krokotoí*; PLANTS); some of the girls run with both arms out, palms extended as if imitating bears; one fragment depicts a woman with a frontal bear face and a nude male with bear head, presumably KALLISTO and her son Arkas. As elements of an AGE-GRADE festival (cf. Aristophanes, *Lys.* 641–7), the short chitons might symbolize the girlhood to be left, (nude) racing the transition and pursuit of marriage (ATHLETICS), and the krokotoi the marriageable young women.

Sourvinou-Inwood 1987, 1988, 1990; Pinney 1995; Scanlon 2002: ch. 6.

Artemis/Diana, daughter of ZEUS and LETO, virgin sister of APOLLO. As goddess of the hunt of large animals (Pan for small animals) and of pubescent girls, she oversees their transition through adolescence (AGE GRADES; ARKTEIA) even, as Artemis Locheia, into CHILDBIRTH. She protects the maidens who are devoted to her and takes revenge on the males who pursue them (ATALANTA; KALLISTO) or who insult her (Actaion, Niobê, Tityos). She also presides over youths: for instance, in Piraeus the spring ephebic naval procession; and as Artemis Orthia at SPARTA, the boys' transition to adulthood (*agogê*). In the Daedalic period, Artemis appears NUDE in Crete and Sparta (8).

Aspasia (b. ca. 460/55–20 BCE), Athenian PROSTITUTE from Miletus. As Perikles's pallakê (ca. 445), she bore him Perikles II, who was legitimized in 430. They had a loving relationship: he was seen KISSING her. She was indicted several times on various charges (procuring free women, entering a temple, and influencing Perikles politically; Demosthenes 59.85–6, 113–4; Isaeus 6.49–50). After his death in 429, she became the pallakê of the demagogue Lysikles.

Aspasia was well known for her rhetorical skills: she conversed with Socrates (Cicero, *Inv.* 31.51), taught rhetoric, and wrote a funeral oration and dialogues on love (Plato, *Menex.* 236b schol., 235e). Aeschines and Antisthenes wrote dialogues entitled "Aspasia."

Aristophanes, *Achar.* 527–30; Xenophon, *Oec.* 3.15; Diodorus Athenaeus, FGrH 372 F40; Plutarch, *Per.* 24.3, 5, 6; 25.1; 32.1–3; 34; Diogenes Laertius 6.16; Harpocration, s.v. Aspasia; Athenaeus 13.583f; Bloedow 1975.

Astrology People born when the sun, moon, and planets were in the constellations Capricorn, Aquarius, Taurus, or Cancer were prone to secret vices, to unnatural intercourse, or to become pathics (Firmicus Maternus 5.2.4, 5.3.11 and 17, 5.6.8., 6.30.15; Vettius Valens 1.1, 2.16, 2.36 and 38). Men born under the conjunction of Venus, Mercury, and Saturn frotted to ORGASM between women's breasts (Manetho 4.312; cf. **262**).

Krenkel 1981.

Atalanta is exposed as an infant and suckled by a bear; as an adult, she lives as a virgin hunter dedicated to ARTEMIS (Pausanius 3.24.2). Meleager falls in love with her during the Calydonian boar hunt and she defeats Peleus in wrestling (ATHLETICS); eventually she agrees to a footrace with Hippomenes, also called Meilanion, who drops three gold "apples" (*mêla*) given him by APHRODITE (PLANTS) which she stops to pick up (cf. **150**). They have sex in a sanctuary and are turned into lions (ANIMALS); CYBELE uses these for her chariot. After her death she becomes a man (Plato, *Resp.* 620b; TRANSSEXUALITY).

Aeschylus, Sophocles, and Euripides wrote plays about her. Vases commonly depict her wrestling match (**45, 123**), but rarely her footrace (**71, 165**). OVID (*Ars Am.* 3.775–6) uses Meilanion and Atalanta as paradigms for the rare frontal SEXUAL POSITION.

Scanlon 2002: ch. 5.

Athena/Minerva is born adult and fully armed from ZEUS's head, a virgin goddess of wisdom, crafts, and war. Zeus consents for HEPHAESTUS to marry her but allows ATHENA to reject the proposal. Hephaestus ejaculates on her thigh (ORGASM). She brushes the SEMEN to the ground with wool, and Earth bears the child Erichthonius ("fleece-earthy"; Apollodorus 3.14.6; Hesychius S1791). To the Romans, Minerva is part of the Etruscan Capitoline Triad (with Jupiter and Juno) and presides over medicine; her cult on the Aventine was especially honored by flute-players (OVID, *Fasti* 3.827, 6.651 ff.).

Athletics and sex both concentrate on the BODY, and in antiquity the one had to forego the other (ABSTINENCE). Ancient authors use sports vocabulary to discuss SEXUAL ACTIVITY (cf. **322**; ARISTOPHANES, *Peace* 894–905; Garcia Romero 1995). DOMITIAN called sex "bed wrestling" (*klinopálê*). AUGUSTUS refused to attend NUDE Greek athletic contests, and he forbade women from seeing them too.

The GYMNASIUM was eroticized, EROS its patron deity; even the athlete's sweat, KONISALOS, was erotic. Discus-throwing was particularly erotic and dangerous: APOLLO kills HYAKINTHOS with a discus, Hermes Krokos, Perseus Akrisios, Peleus Phokos, and Oxylos Thermios or Alkidokos.

At SPARTA boys and girls exercised together nude (Propertius 3.14.1–4; OVID, *Heroides* 16.149–52), which was meant to arouse desire for sex and MARRIAGE. Men and their families came to athletic games to obtain suitable husbands for their daughters (Xenophon of Ephesus 1.2; Achilles Tatius 1.18). Unmarried women and the priestess of DEMETER could watch the Olympic games (Pausanias 5.6.7, 6.7.2; cf. Pindar, *Pyth.* 9). Cleisthenes of Sikyon announced the eligibility of his daughter AGARISTE at the Olympic games ca. 576 BCE. In mythology, footraces act as metaphors for marriage (cf. ATALANTA; cf. Libys of Cyrene who made his daughter stand at the finish line, (Pindar, *Pyth.* 9.111–20)). Victorious athletes also attracted male suitors. Kallias falls in love with the pankratist Autolykos (Xenophon, *Symp.* 1.9–10), and the runners Timestheus and Antikles

had many lovers (Aeschines, *In Tim.* 156–7). Pindar often refers to the erotic qualities of athletes; he compares the boy boxer Hagesidamos to Ganymede (*Ol.* 10.95–105, cf. *Ol.* 1).

Athletic contests often marked AGE GRADES. In Crete, the verb *ekdromein*, "to complete the race course," meant "to become a citizen."

The quadrennial Heraia games for women at Olympia (Pausanias 5.16.2–3; Scanlon 2002: ch. 4; Serwint 1993) were reorganized in the 580s. The *thíasos* (association), "Sixteen Women of Elis," oversaw the games, which probably took place before or after the men's games, so entire families could go to both (Pausanias 6.20.7). They consisted only of a footrace in the Olympic stadium; the winners received a bull to offer for sacrifice and a feast, an olive wreath, and the permission to dedicate their painted portraits, probably in the niches in the columns of the temple to HERA (O'Brien 1993: ch. 6 and appendix; cf. Nossis, *Greek Anth.* 6.353 and 354, 9.604 and 605). At Sparta the "Daughters of Leukippos" (LEUKIPPIDAI) organized a footrace for women in honor of DIONYSUS (cf. Theocritus 18; Hesychius E2823). The COSTUME for women's footraces may have been the short chiton, according to the depictions of women runners. Plato recommends that unmarried girls should compete in footraces (and nude if under thirteen; *Laws* 833c–834d). From the Roman period we hear of women's games at many cities (Lee 1988; 1994).

Scanlon 2002; Instone 1990; Spiro 1900.

Atreus, House of Tantalus, king of Argos, seduces GANYMEDE and cuts up his own son PELOPS to set before ZEUS. Zeus restores Pelops, who fathers Atreus and Thyestes.

ARTEMIS gives Atreus a gold lamb to sacrifice to her, but he keeps the fleece, for which she kills his wife Kleola. Atreus marries Aeropê, and fathers Agamemnon and Menelaus. Whoever has the gold fleece will become king of Mycenae, so Aeropê obtains it for Thyestes in return for sex. Atreus and Thyestes then agree that if the sun reverses its course, Atreus will be king; when Zeus wills it, Atreus ascends to the throne, serves Thyestes's children at a banquet, and kills Aeropê. Thyestes curses the house of Atreus.

The Delphic oracle commands Thyestes to beget a son on his remaining daughter, Pelopia (INCEST). Atreus marries Pelopia, and accepts her son, Aegisthus, as his own. Atreus imprisons Thyestes and orders Aegisthus (now seven) to kill him. Aegisthus fails, and Thyestes demands he bring Pelopia to him. When Thyestes reveals himself she kills herself. Thyestes then has Aegisthus kill Atreus, for which Agamemnon kills Thyestes.

Agamemnon marries Clytemnestra and they have Iphigeneia (ACHILLES), Orestes, Electra, and Chrysothemis. Clytemnestra and Aegisthus kill Agamemnon and his pallakê Cassandra when they return from the TROJAN WAR. Clytemnestra sends Orestes to Krissa and marries Electra to a peasant. When Orestes returns to Mycenae, he and Electra murder Clytemnestra and Aegisthus. Orestes is acquitted of matricide in Athens because mothers do not contribute genetic material during CONCEPTION, and therefore he is not truly related to her.

Attis, youthful consort of CYBELE. The gods castrate HERMAPHRODITIC Agdistis, from whose genitals sprout an almond tree from whose fruit Nana conceives Attis. To prevent his marrying, Cybale has him castrate himself (**294**), which her priests, the Galli, imitate. Attis is killed by a boar (cf. Atys, Herodotus 1.34–45). His festival, rare in Greece (Piraeus, *IG* 2².4671) but common in Italy, took place near the spring equinox. In art he appears EFFEMINATE, wearing a Phrygian COSTUME, cap and trousers.

See also: ADONIS

Pausanias 7.17.10–12; Catullus 63; Ovid, *Fasti* 4.221–44.

Augustus (63 BCE–14 CE), *princeps* Gaius Octavius (27 BCE–14 CE), adopted son of JULIUS CAESAR. As triumvir (43–37 BCE) he MARRIES Scribonia (40) as ANTONY marries his sister Octavia; soon after, he DIVORCES her (she complains about his ADULTERIES) to marry LIVIA. After Antony and CLEOPATRA commit suicide (31), he celebrates peace (28), transfers nominal power to the Senate (27), and receives the title *Augustus* (Supreme Leader).

Since JULIA is his only child, a daughter, his heirs descend from the women in his family: his sister Octavia is the grandmother of CLAUDIUS; Livia is the mother of TIBERIUS from her first marriage; Julia is the grandmother of CALIGULA and great-grandmother of NERO. Partly because of this situation, Augustus enacts various LAWS concerning adultery, marriage, and luxury.

OVID claims that Augustus owned erotic TABELLAE (*Tristia* 2.521–8); Suetonius relates how he enjoyed boys, especially dark Syrians and Moors, but did not have sex with them, though Plutarch (*Ant.* 59.4) claims he had a *deliciae*, a boyfriend. He did, however, like deflowering maidens, even though he was called EFFEMINATE and rumored to have had sex with Julius Caesar to gain his adoption.

Augustus righteously punished actors (THEATER) for immorality, refused to attend Greek ATHLETIC games, and forbade women from seeing them.

Suetonius, *Augustus*.

B

Bacchanalia, rites in honor of DIONYSUS, which the Roman senate outlawed in 186 BCE. Livy's story centers around Aebutius (not yet twenty), whom his mother and evil stepfather wish to initiate; Hispala his mistress warns him and also tells the consul Spurius Postumius Albinus that, as a slave, she had been initiated. The rites had been only for women for three days each year. A Campanian priestess, Paculla Annia, had recently introduced reforms: men were initiated, and the rites were held at night for three days every month; men were having sex with each other and those who refused were murdered. Within the last two years, according to Hispala, all males initiated were under the age of twenty; and these were so compromised (presumably through anal intercourse) that they could not go into military service. Postumius informed the Senate, which ordered (*senatus consultum de bacchanalibus*, CIL 1.196; ILS 18) a thorough investigation, arrested the participants, and tried and executed them without appeal. Aebutius and Hispala were rewarded.

See also: MAENADS

Livy 39.8–18; Gruen 1996: 34–78.

Baths There were public and private baths in both the Greek and Roman periods. Private baths are located in residences (POMPEII, House of Menander). Public baths consist of small *balnea* and elaborate Roman imperial *thermae*. Balneae are simple buildings with individual bathtubs of stone or terracotta (Athens: Travlos 1971 s.v.).

Thermae had changing rooms (*apodyterium*), baths of cold WATER (*frigidarium*), hot (*caldarium*), and warm (*tepidarium*). Rome had enormous and luxurious baths (Diocletian's) with mosaics and sculpture, and recital halls, libraries, meeting rooms, galleries, and gardens (Cicero, *Cael.* 61–7).

While bathing was beneficial, keeping the water clean was a problem, for it often kept circulating. Mixed bathing was usually not practiced (cf. Pausanias 4.35.9), although occasionally it was allowed (under ELAGABALUS) along with nude bathing (Pliny, *HN* 33.54.153; Quint. 5.9.14; Martial 3.51, 68 and 72, 7.35, 11.47; Juvenal 6.419; *Hist. Aug. Hadrian* 18; Cass. Dio. 69.8.2; CIL 6.579). Slaves were not allowed to bathe in the baths.

In Athens, bath house attendants either provided PROSTITUTES or sexually serviced the men themselves (Ehrenberg 1951, citing Aristophanes, *Knights* 1401, *Frogs* 1279f). Praxilla (Edmonds 1967: 570–1 no. 19; Aristophanes, *Thesm.* 528 schol.) wrote a SONG that has both prostitute and bath attendant, "wash the good and bad in the same sink." Bathing scenes are common on Attic vases (Sutton 1981: 46–8; cf. the erotic scenes of 37, 136), including preparations before MAR-RIAGE (the bride on 160, the groom on 103).

Roman baths were excellent places for CRUISING (PETRONIUS) and for lovers to meet (OVID, *Ars Am.* 3.639–40). The BROTHEL in POMPEII (the Lupanar, VII.12) is located directly accross the street from the Stabian Baths; and there may have been a brothel above the Sub-urban baths. Agrippina minor was said to have frequented the baths looking for quick sex. Prostitutes circulated in and outside the baths; in the more elaborate ones, bathers could rent private rooms for sex. Special slaves (*drauci*; Martial 1.96) sexually serviced men customers.

Fagan 1999.

Baubo, an old nurse, entertained DE-METER at Eleusis when she was disconso-late, searching for her daughter Persephonê abducted by Hades; she got her to laugh by producing her son Iak-khos from under her skirt, thereby expos-ing herself. Baubo probably originates as a folkloric *daímon*, spirit, of the vagina (cf. *baúbon*, DILDO). She is usually repre-sented in terracottas as a female body without head or breasts, her frontal face depicted on her stomach atop two legs with vagina emphasized (**264**).

Beauty Contests. At Olympia, women could "win the gold" (wreath?) at a beauty contest (Athenaeus 13.609e–f). Women's beauty contests were also held at Tenedos and Bisilis (Athenaeus 13.610a; Homer, *Iliad* 9.129 and *Odyssey* 6.292 scholiasts A and D), and possibly on Lesbos (Al-caeus fr. 130.32 Lobel-Page).

Male beauty was considered to connote good character. Similarly, the ugly man was reckoned poor in spirit, like Thersites (Homer, *Iliad* 2.211 ff.; ACHILLES). Nireus was remembered as the most beautiful man who went to TROY (*Iliad* 2.673),

and Pindar praises the beauty of young ATHLETES (*Ol.* 8.19–20, 10.100 ff.; *Pyth.* 4.123; *Nem.* 3.19; *Isthm.* 7.22–22b).

Cities conducted several men's beauty contests. Tanagra judged ephebes in honor of Hermes Kriophoros; the winner was declared "most beautiful in form," and carried a ram on his shoulders around the city walls (Pausanias 9.22.1). Elis held a beauty contest in honor of ATHENA, and the winner, beribboned by his friends, received weapons as prizes (Athenaeus 13.609f–610a). At the Athenian Panathe-naia, OLD men, chosen for their beauty, bore olive branches as *thallophoroi* (Xe-nophon, *Symp.* 4.17; *Etymologicum Mag-num* s.v.).

The *euándria* and *euéxia* were held at the Panathenaia and Theseia in Athens and other cities like SPARTA, Rhodes, and Sestos (Crowther 1985; Reed 1987). Athenaeus (13.565f) states that these were beauty contests, but Xenophon (*Mem.* 3.3.12–13) implies that they involved strength. During the Theseia the *euándria* is listed before the regular ATHLETIC events and seems linked to contests invol-ving armor, trumpeting, and heraldry (*IG* 2^2. 956 [= *Syll.* 3 667], 957, 958); the winner received a shield and 100 drach-mas and his tribe got an ox (*Suda*, s.v.; Andocides, *In Alc.* 4.42).

The *euéxia* was perhaps a contest of stamina (Crowther 1977). In Tralles it was held along with footraces, javelin throwing, and archery; in Samos, Beroia, and Chalcis it is listed after footraces and before the *philopónia* (ability to with-stand pain), *lithóbolos* (stone throwing), and *eutáxia* (military formations).

Beds and Couches Late Bronze Age beds have been retrieved at Akrotiri, THERA. Consisting of a narrow wood frame stretched with cowhide, they are wide enough for one person only. Greek and Roman beds (Grk *lékhos*, *eunê*; Lat. *lectus* [for sex], *torus* [for sleeping]) and couches (*klinê*; *cubile*) are well known. All facsimile couches are also for single individuals: Hellenistic stone couches from Macedonian tombs; Etruscan terracotta sarcophagi in the shape of couches (**194** [**pl. 1**]); and Roman couches reconstructed using surviving metal inlays (Williams 1905).

The Greek couch for the SYMPOSIUM consisted of a wood frame raised high (over 1m); the frame is tightly laced and supports a thick mattress with blankets. Facsimiles of couches and beds (see below) indicate the length, 2m or more, long enough for two symposiasts (**28**). The couches were arranged in a square, head to foot, the diners reclining on their left arm and eating with their right hand. It is on these couches that male symposiasts and hetairai are often depicted having sex (PROSTITUTION).

The actual sleeping bed for men and women is rarely depicted. Vase paintings give us glimpses of marriage beds (**85**), and it resembles the symposium couch. At the time of the actual wedding, a separate bed (*parábustos*) was placed in the bedroom so the couple could get some sleep – each bed was too narrow for the couple to sleep side-by-side. The masonry beds in POMPEII's Lupanar are also single beds.

A wider couch or bed must have been occasionally available. Odysseus's bed is wide enough for him and Penelopê (*Odyssey* 23.191–206). A wall painting (**326**) from a possible BROTHEL in Pompeii (IX.5.14–16) depicts a double wide but low bed with a high headboard and a single massive pillow (cf. the *capsae* depicted in the Surburban baths, **291**).

Greek bedrooms are difficult to identify archaeologically. Houses in Pompeii had rooms on the ground floor flanking the atrium that could serve as bedrooms; many of these could hold two beds. Pompey and Cornelia were notable for sleeping together (Lucan, *Pharsalia* 5.735–815; Myerowitz 1992: 141, 157 n. 10), but Pliny the Younger's wife Calpurnia had her own room (*Ep.* 7.5.1), as was usual.

Richter 1966.

Bestiality, SEXUAL ACTIVITY between humans and ANIMALS, usually easier to imagine than to accomplish (Johns 1982: 110–1). There are several depictions (man and doe **56**; woman and donkey **83**; woman and horse **217** [SEMIRAMIS?], **218**; pygmy and crocodile **216**; cf. **215**; ETHNICITY).

Kronos as a horse rapes Phillyra and she bears the CENTAUR Chiron. ZEUS has intercourse as a swan with LEDA (**210**), as an eagle with Asteriê, and as an eagle he abducts GANYMEDE and as a bull EUROPA. POSEIDON as a horse mates with DEMETER in Arcadia, and she bears him the horse Arion or the local goddess Despoina of Lycosura (Pausanias 8.25.4 and 8.42.1); as a bull he rapes Kanakê.

The goat god Pan attacks the shepherd Daphnis (**118**), has frontal intercourse with a nanny-goat (**245**), and attempts to rape a HERMAPHRODITE (**340**). SATYRS mostly rape MAENADS (**83**, **295**), but they also appear mounting a male donkey (**46**) and a mule (**48**).

PRIAPEA (**53**) threatens a thief with anal penetration by a donkey. Pasiphaê (MINOS) has intercourse with a bull and bears the Minotaur (cf. NERO), and Polyphonê has two sons by a bear (ANIMALS).

Juvenal (6.333 ff.) satirizes a woman for being penetrated by a donkey; and Apuleius 10.22 describes his hero, as a donkey, having sex with a woman. Copulation with a snake produced great sons: Aristodama as the mother of Aratus (Pausanias 2.10.3), Olympias the mother of ALEXANDER THE GREAT, the mother of Scipio, and Avia the mother of AUGUSTUS.

Birth A WOMAN's early adulthood, when she is producing CHILDREN, was the time when she was most at risk of dying (Becker 2003; cf. OVID's understated remark that childbirth shortens youth, *Ars Am.* 3.81–2). Most children were delivered by female MIDWIVES. Several PLANTS eased labor.

According to the Hippocratic writings, uterine contractions were really the child within struggling to break the membranes that held it (Hanson 1992: n. 59). After the birth of a girl, a mother's lochial flows were meant to continue for forty-two days after delivery, but for only thirty days after the birth of a boy (Hanson 1992: 52–3). There are few representations of childbirth (23, 24; cf. Van Straten 1981: 124 s.n. 15.118).

For divine help, Greek WOMEN supplicated ARTEMIS and EILEITHYIA (Callimachus, *Greek Anth.* 6.146; Van Straten 1981: 73). One woman, Kleo, writes on a votive tablet to Asklepios that she was PREGNANT for five years, and was delivered healthily, although of what the inscription does not specify (Van Straten 1981: 77 assumes it was a son). Roman women prayed to JUNO Lucina. For the Romans, when the baby came head first, the spirit Porrima, "forwarder," was helping; when there was a breech birth and the child came feet first, Postverta, "turner," was said to be interfering. Women also offered keys for successful PREGNANCIES.

See also: CONCEPTION; MEDICINE

Bisexuality, the ability to DESIRE and to derive sexual pleasure from both males and females equally. For the bisexuality of women, see LESBIANISM. Desire for both adult women and adult men was probably rare, although "where there is beauty, I'm ambidextrous" (*amphidéxios*; Plutarch, *Erotikos* 766f–767a).

Men, especially in the upper classes, were expected to desire both women and boys or youths (Plutarch, *Erotikos* 749c; cf. *Lyc.* 17.1 and 18.4; *Alc.* 4.1–4 and 6.1–2; and *Sull.* 2.2–4, 8–13, 147–17, 326–9). An early Greek SONG begins with two stanzas that mirror this concept: "Wish I could be an ivory lyre and pretty boys would carry me in their DIONYSUS DANCE. Wish I could be a beautiful gold jewel and a beautiful woman, pure of thought, would wear me" (Athenaeus 15.695c–d). A MARRIAGE contract (dated

92 BCE) from Egypt stipulates that the husband cannot have a second wife nor keep a pallakê or a boy.

Martial wrote several epigrams that lampoon men for being passive with men and active with women. Athenagoras was nicknamed Alfius (alpha) as a boy (i.e. bent-over in "a tergo" passive anal intercourse) but, as a man, was nicknamed Olfius because of the smell of his mouth after CUNNILINGUS (9.95+95a; cf. *Greek Anth.* 12.187.1–6). He also presents a word game in which all sexual activity is deemed inappropriate for Sextillus except FELLATIO and cunnilingus (2.28).

Bisexuality, in the sense of oscillating between women and youths, was also common for men; Martial 11.43 (cf. 11.22.9f, 12.96.9 ff.) stipulates the difference between the two: "Wife, with harsh words you berate me caught jammed up a boy, and you say you too have an ass; please don't give a masculine name to your two 'things' – think rather that you have two cunts." CATULLUS's great love was for "Lesbia" and PROPERTIUS's for "Cynthia," but when jilted by these women, both turned to boys, Catullus to "Iuventus" and Propertius to "Lygdamus."

There is evidence too for eromenoi youths in a PAIDERASTIC relationship turning to women presumably as that relationship begins to decline (cf. Persaios of Kition buys a flutegirl but hesitates to bring her to the home he shares with his lover Zenon; von Arnim 1903–: I fr. 451).

See also: HOMOEROTICISM; MALE HOMOSEXUALITY

Bodies

Body types

Ideal body types changed over time; I concentrate here on sculpture. Daidalic bodies (seventh century BCE) are thin, the head triangular and large, the torso triangular and constricted at the waist (BODY MODIFICATION), thighs thick. Archaic bodies (sixth century) become increasingly more naturalistic, the ideal age about 18–22. In Severe Style sculpture (early fifth century), the ideal age drops to below sixteen. Polykleitos's "Doryphoros" (mid-fifth century) and figures in the Parthenon's frieze seem again aged 18–22, their bodies mathematical in proportion. The Partheon's pediments (ca. 440–432) contain older and bulkier figures. Late Classical male torsoes (fourth century) elongate with thin legs; the face acquires a set of modular features expressive of character (cf. Philostratus, *Gym.* 31–40; Serwint 1987). PRAXITELES creates the first in-the-round statue of a nude woman, in her mid-to-late twenties, full figured (see below). Hellenistic artists (3rd–1st century) become interested in all sorts of body types (cf. **171–4**; Lucilius 56).

From the late Republic on there is a Roman tendency to portray people realistically, although Julio-Claudian elites added their portrait heads to classical body types (BODIES "BY GOD"). Beginning with HADRIAN, eyes are drilled to give a gleam to the pupil; under the Antonines and Severans, the HAIR is drilled. In the Constantinian period, people become toy-like.

Men's and women's bodies

These were socially constructed along pairs of opposites: MEN were hot, dry, hard, and associated with the right side of the body; WOMEN were cold, moist, soft, and associated with the left side of the body; children had masculinate bodies, although a boy's body is sometimes called feminine (below).

Women's bodies

Women's bodies (WOMEN) were compared to containers with channels for circulating liquid like those in sponges or fleece (Hippocrates, *Morb. mul.* 1.1, 1.16). The comparison to fleece rationalizes the full figure of PRAXITELES's "Knidia" and women's primary work of producing textiles (cf. ATHENA's use of fleece to wipe up HEPHAESTUS's SEMEN, the name for the child, "Erichthonius," "fleece-earthy," and the term for the "fetal sack" [*ámnion*, "sheepskin"]).

To facilitate the maturation of a girl's body into that of a woman, and to facilitate the circulation of her fluids, her body needed to be "broken down" (*katarrhégnutai*) by regular intercourse and BIRTHING (Hanson 1992: 38–9; cf. Aelian, *HN* 3.9). Women were not supposed to exert themselves, since this could evaporate their moisture. A woman got naturally dry only in OLD AGE.

Men's bodies (MEN)

Since the "boy is similar to a woman" (Aristotle, *Gen. An.* 728a18–22), his body had to be helped to become a man's body (ATHLETICS; GYMNASIUM; PAIDERASTIA), firm and hot. Men got wet only with OLD AGE. Men out of training suffered from fatigue (Hippocrates, *Regimen* 2.66), which caused a "melting" within the body, sweat and damp (Hanson 1992: 51–3; cf. ETHNICITY [Skythians]).

See also: BODY FUNCTIONS; BODY MODIFICATION; BODY PARTS; MEDICINE

Hanson 1992; Dean-Jones 1989, 1991, 1992, 1994; Jones 1987; Richlin 1997.

Bodies "by God", the realistic portrait heads of elite Roman men and women added to classical Greek body types (**243** [**pl. 42**], **244**; Kleiner 1992: figs 48, 50, 106; d'Ambra 1996; Lapatin 1997: 156). The Polykleitan male body emphasizes male reason through mathematical proportions and self-control through restrained modeling. The PRAXITELEAN APHRODITE empowered the sexuality of the Roman matron and also alluded to Venus's dual political function as mother of Aeneas, and the Roman race, and as protector of the Julio-Claudian family. Painters (PORNOGRAPHOI, Athenaeus 13.567b) painted PROSTITUTES as goddesses.

Body Care From earliest times, men and women explored a variety of ways to keep their bodies clean, healthy, and attractive, including mirrors and different kinds of utensils like tweezers and razors to remove unwanted HAIR and earpicks to clean the ears, and personal attendants (*therápainai*) like barbers and perfumers. In addition, the Romans added more specialists like *alipilarii* (people who plucked the hair from the armpits and other parts of the body), *paratiltriae* (children entrusted with the cleansing of bodily orifices), and *picatrices* (young girls who arranged the pubic hair).

For men, too much attention paid to their body could make them EFFEMINATE (AUGUSTUS; INVECTIVE; JULIUS CAESAR).

See also: BODIES; COSMETICS

D'Ambrosio 2001; Dayagi-Mendels 1989; Carter 1998: 73–4; Papaefthimiou-Papanthimou: 1979.

Body Functions were considered humorous (cf. ARISTOPHANES *passim*). Feces, urine, and other human eliminations (sweat [KONISALOS] and ear wax) are also ingredients in MAGIC spells and in MEDICINE.

Constipation

Vespasian's countenance looked like he was constipated, which elicited a joke: one of his courtiers, when asked to pay attention, said he would when the emperor had finished relieving himself (Suetonius, *Vespasian* 20).

Ejaculation

It was a necessary function, evacuating SEMEN as a waste product. Too much ejaculation, however, threatened an imbalance of humors (Hanson 1992: 57).

Erections

Erections were thought to be caused by air inflating the penis and blowing the semen out (ORGASM; Aristotle, *Problems* 30). Males with erections are explicitly erotic, mortals and gods (ZEUS and POSEIDON). Their erections are usually not large (cf. **65, 79**; Johns 1982: 52; Dover 1989: 126–8), but the erections of Pan, PRIAPUS, and SATYRS usually are (cf. Shapiro 1992: 54). In PETRONIUS 11, Ascyltos had an enormous penis; Vespasian appreciated men with large penises, citing Homer, *Iliad* 7.213 (Suetonius, *Vespasian* 23); and ELAGABALUS had agents search out men with enormous penises (*vassati*; *Hist. Aug. Elagabalus* 17.5.3).

Excretions

Harpies (bird bodies and women's heads) torment Pheneus by snatching and excreting on his food (Apollonius 2.188 ff.). A black-figure eye-cup by the Amasis Painter (**36**) links excreting and sex.

Farts

EURIPIDES likens ZEUS's thundering to farting (*Cycl.* 323–9). Lucan once farted in a public latrine (pl. **37**) loudly and odorously; as everyone fled, he quoted a line of NERO's, "you might think it sounded beneath the earth" (Suetonius, *Lucan*). To ARISTOPHANES, a person sleeping soundly farts without waking (*Clouds* 8–10; *Knights* 115–7). CALIGULA had planned an edict to allow farting at dinner, since he had heard of someone who almost died by trying to hold it in (Suetonius, *Caligula* 32).

Urination

Depictions of people urinating are not uncommon (**92**). ARISTOPHANES describes rain as ZEUS urinating (*Clouds* 373). NERO was said to have urinated on the statue of the Syrian goddess Atargatis (Suetonius, *Nero* 56; cf. Juvenal 6.311 ff.). Vespasian imposed a tax on public latrines, and, when Titus objected, he held up some coins and asked him if he smelled any offensive odor – after all, "it comes from urine" (*e lotio est*; Suetonius, *Vespasian* 23).

See also: BODIES; BODY MODIFICATION; BODY PARTS; MASTURBATION; MENSTRUATION; ORGASM; PHALLUS; SEMEN

Body Modification, deliberately shaping the body for cultural and personal purposes and for social identification. In Greece, body modification was not much practiced, but Egypt had a long history of tattooing, branding, and piercing (Montserrat 1996: 61–79).

In the Greco-Roman world such body modifications identified barbarians, slaves, and criminals (who also could have their ears or noses cut off); men who had their ears pierced were EFFEMINATE.

Body sculpting

Body building, developing and defining musculature through exercises, is not directly known, but Hellenistic sculpture of the "Baroque" style (second century BCE) may refer to it (**171, 178**). Earlier examples of "strong men" are known, implying some kind of body building (Crowther 1977): the sixth-century Bubon, whose huge stone (Olympia Museum) carries the inscription that he lifted it with one hand over his head and threw it.

Bronze cuirasses from the Archaic through the Roman period are shaped to display taut pectoral muscles and a defined abdomen, regardless of the age or physical shape of the soldier (Flory 1994; cf. **21, 242**).

Another kind of body sculpting was also practiced by waist compression (see below), by compressing a woman's breasts with the STROPHIUM, and by restricting the growth of CHILDREN in jars (DWARVES).

Genital mutilation
(Aldeeb Abu-Sahlieh 2001)

Castration

This involved the removal of the testicles, sometimes the entire penis. Voluntary self-castration was practiced by the priests of CYBELE, using a Samian potsherd (Pliny, *HN* 35.165; cf. Lucilius 306–7). Castration was performed on boys, sometimes men, to turn them into EUNUCHS, loyal servants, entertainers, and sexual pathics (CINAEDI). Castration could also be a punishment (PERIANDER). Domitian and Nerva forbade it (Cass. Dio. 67.2.3 and 68.2.4).

Clitoridectomy ("female circumcision") and female infibulation

Neither procedure (the removal of the clitoris; narrowing the vaginal opening with suture [CHASTITY BELT]) is medically necessary. Ptolemaic mummies of women have provided evidence for both procedures (cf. Meinardus 1967: 389–90; Hunt and Edgar 1970: 1.31–3; Brunner 1991; Wilcken 1978: text 2, 1.16; Thompson 1988: 232–3). Both Strabo (17.2.5) and Philo (*Questions Genesis* 3.47) attest to these practices occurring in a girl's fourteenth year, prior to MARRIAGE. Adramytes, king of Lydia, was the first to "eunuchize women" (Athenaeus 12.515d–e).

Clitoridectomy may have gone into decline by the time of Muhammed; he did not circumcise his daughters, and the Koran does not speak of this practice. Clitoridectomy is practiced today, however, by Muslims and Coptic Christians, especially in sub-Saharan Africa.

Male circumcision

(ABSTINENCE; CHASTITY BELT; DOGKNOT; *Sweet 1985*)

This involved the removal of the foreskin or the entire skin of the penis and/or scrotum. These procedures are not medically necessary. Circumcision was known in pharaonic Egypt (de Wit 1972); in Israel it originated with God's covenant with Abraham (Genesis 17), requiring him to circumcise himself and his descendants and slaves.

For Jews, Christians, and Muslims who abide by Abraham's covenant, circumcision is performed when the boy is eight days old. In classical antiquity, circumcision was practiced by Jews, Egyptians (by Roman times, only priests, Josephus, *In Ap.* 2.141), and by Arabs, Ethiopians, Phoenicians, and Colchians. Converts to Judaism were also circumcised (Tacitus, *Hist.* 5.5; Juvenal 14). The first Christians debated whether circumcision was required of new converts (Acts 10–11, 15; Galatians 2.3).

Circumcision, however, concerned the emperors. Domitian taxed Jews severely and had a ninety-year-old man's genitals examined to see if he were a Jew (Suetonius, *Domitian* 7.1, 12). HADRIAN forbade circumcision (*Hist. Aug. Hadrian* 14.2; *Digest* 48.8.3.5). Antoninus Pius restored the right of circumcision to Jews but not to converts (*Digest* 48.8.11.1; Smallwood 1959). Today, male circumcision is a common practice, with the USA having the highest rate (60 per cent of all males in 1996) and western Europe and Britain having the lowest rates (2 per cent and less).

Male epispasm/recutitio

(Hall 1992)

This was a procedure to restore the foreskin either by attaching a weight on the skin of the penis (a heavy ring; CHASTITY BELT, and *male infibulation* below) and slowly lengthening it (Soranus 2.34; cf. Martial 7.85, 9.27) or by cutting the skin around the penis and pulling it forward to cover the glans as a new foreskin (Celsus 7.25.1–2). Circumcized Jews, who then hellenized and participated in Greek-style nude events or went to a Roman BATH, either covered their penis to hide their circumcision or underwent restoration (1 Corinthians 7:18; 1 Maccabees 1:15; Josephus, *Ant. Jud.* 12.241; *Talmud*, Sanhedrin 44.1, Shabbath 19.2, Yebamoth 72.1).

Male infibulation

A piercing of the foreskin with a pin, ring, or thread (Oribasius, *Perí krikóseôs*). A metal *fibula* (like a large modern safety pin) would prevent a full erection. Male SINGERS, THEATRICAL entertainers, and gladiators and ATHLETES were often infibulated to maintain ABSTINENCE (CHASTITY BELT; Martial 7.85, 14.215; Galen 9:12 Kühn; cf. Aristotle, *Gen. An.* 7.1); the fibula was also used to keep slaves chaste (Martial 9.27). Juvenal satirizes women who paid to have fibulae removed from entertainers they desired (6.379 schol.).

A heavy fibula could also lengthen the penis (**253**; cf. Celsus 4.25.3).

Piercing

Ears were pierced from the Bronze Age (Younger 1992) throughout the Greek and Roman period (as surviving earrings attest; JEWELRY), but there is little evidence for the piercing of other body parts.

Tattooing

Staining patterns into the skin, probably with dark ink. Tattooing, temporary or permanent, may have been practiced from early times, as demonstrated by Neolithic terracotta figurines (Talalay 1991, 1993: 161–8), Early Bronze Age marble statuettes from the Cyclades (Preziosi and Weinberg 1970; Hendrix 2003), and Minoan and Mycenaean terracotta figurines and wall frescoes (Younger 1998–2000). Tattooing is also known from Egypt (Bianchi 1988), the Near East, and, recently, Neolithic Europe (Fowler 2000).

In the classical period, we have little evidence for tattooing (Fellman 1978); the Pistoxenos Painter painted thirty-eight vases with tattooed Thracian WOMEN, twenty-seven of which present the death of ORPHEUS (Zimmerman 1980; Robertson 1992: 157).

Waist compression

A constricting of the waist to wasp-thinness using a laced corset or a tall belt which pushes organs up into the lower chest cavity and produces a pronounced chest and shelf-like hips. The practice begins in the Greek Late Bronze Age (**1, 3, 4**; Younger 1995, 1998–2000). The tall belt appears in Late Geometric vase painting and Daedalic sculpture (cf. **15–17**). The practice apparently dies out by the Archaic period.

See also: BODIES;   BODY   FUNCTIONS; BODY PARTS; COSMETICS; HAIR

Body Parts

Breasts

(female; for the male chest see BODIES; BODIES "BY GOD," BODY MODIFICATION: body sculpting)

The female breast is an emblem for motherhood; Clytemnestra offers her breast to Orestes (Aeschylus, *Libation Bearers* 896–8), Menelaus sees HELEN's breasts and does not kill her, and NERO kisses the breasts of his mother before attempting to assassinate her (Suetonius, *Nero* 34). It is also an eroticized body part (cf. Aristophanes, *Acharnians* 1199–1200; Euripides, *Hecuba* 558–70). Males touch the breasts of a female (**27, 296, 310, 336**; cf. **136**), and when having sex (**304**); and a woman touches the breast of another (**141**; LESBIANISM). In explicitly sexual Roman wall paintings, the woman often wears the STROPHIUM (**299, 341**), perhaps to heighten feeling, or call attention to the breasts.

One fetish has the man rubbing his penis to ORGASM between a woman's breasts (ASTROLOGY).

Maternal and erotic aspects combine in the stories of the father nursing at his daughter's breast (Kimon and Pero, Val. Max. 5.4.1; Mykos and Xanthippe, Hyginus 254.3), and the story of Etruscan JUNO offering HERAKLES her breast to suck as a sign of her permission to enter Olympus (de Grummond 2002: 67, fig. 11). Drinking from breast-shape cups (*mástoi*) might also combine the maternal and erotic (cf. Athenaeus 11.487b; Hesychius s.v.). Votive mastoi and breasts, usually of terracotta, were dedicated at many sanctuaries (Van Straten 1981: 107–38, 144).

Finger

The second (or middle) finger was "infamous" or "shameful" (*infamis, impudicus digitus*; Persius 2.33; RELIGION). When the finger is extended and the other fingers are contracted, the gesture resembles the erect penis, and was shown to CINAEDI: "Cestus complains to me of being teased with your finger, Mamurianus" (Martial 2.28, 6.70; cf. CALIGULA).

For the "ficus" or "fig," the tip of the thumb lies between the first and second (middle) finger of the clenched hand (cf. Italian, *mano fica*); the gesture represents the clitoris in the vulva (OVID, *Fasti* 5.433; Johns 1982: 73–4, fig. 57).

Feet

Antiphannes (101 K-A) finds pleasure in a woman rubbing his feet. Vitellius used to carry around one of MESSALINA'S SANDALS (Suetonius, *Vitellius* 2). The Severan Philostratus and Alciphron wrote letters that praise feet and footprints (Benner and Fobes 1949; Levine 2002).

Genitals

Female

Female genitals are rarely mentioned outside medical texts, and the clitoris, *landica*, even more rarely (Martial 3.72.6; cf. PRIAPEA 12.10–15 and 78.5; POMPEII graffiti CIL 4.10004, 11.6721[5], *Euplia laxa landicosa*). Some male authors refer to the vagina as a *glottokomeíon*, a tongue-case (Aristophanes, *Peace* 883; Lysippus 5 K-A; Timocles 2.13 K-A) or *bulga*, a bag (Lucilius 61). Forms of the word for myrtle were used for the clitoris (*múrton*) and the labial lips (*murtócheila*; Rufus, *Onom.* 112; see below); this in turn elicited a homeopathic amenagogue, "soda and meal mixed with myrtle oil" (Ps.-Theod. Prisc., *Add.* p. 340.16).

CUNNILINGUS was often considered foul, either because of MENSTRUATION or because of the vaginal secretions from Bartholini's glands just inside the labia; the smell was likened to that of salted fish (Ausonius 82.1–6; Martial 1.77, 2.84, 3.81 and 96; 4.43, 7.95, 11.47 and 61, 12.59 and 85).

Representations of the female pubic area (Johns 1982: 72) are not uncommon (**82, 147**; cf. **263**). Women dedicated votive plaques of the vulva (**268 [pl. 18]**; Mulas 1978: 26) to APHRODITE, Asclepius, and ZEUS Hypsistos on the Athens Pnyx, a women's cult (Van Straten 1981: 108–13, 115–21, 135); one plaque (no.

11.4) is inscribed: "Philouménê delighting in (*kharizoménê*) Aphrodite, rejoice all you passers-by!" She may have been a PROSTITUTE.

The vagina was occasionally used to decorate other objects (lamp **213**), but more frequently it appears along with PHALLOI (**231, 241 [pl. 20]**).

Male
(BODY FUNCTIONS; MASTURBATION; ORGASM)

Male genitals were commonly mentioned and represented, and were granted apotropaic power (PHALLOI); votive genitals, however, are not common (van Straten 1981: 108–42). A form of the word for "myrtle" was used for the penis tip (*múrrinon*; Pollux 2.174). In Greek and Roman imperial art, males are usually nude, their genitals displayed (male infants too), as if they demonstrate CITIZENSHIP, eventual or attained.

The penis was thought to have a mind of its own, a *mentula* (Latin, "little mind"); the Greeks may have felt it needed "reining in," therefore the term *kunodesmê*, a dog leash or DOGKNOT.

Hymen

Although the Greeks and Romans did not recognize the hymen (WOMEN), they did view the uterus (below) as obstructed (Hanson 1992: n. 58; HYMENAEUS).

Uterus

Hippocratic and popular anatomy thought that the mouth of the uterus, the inner mouth of the vagina, was closed off prior to menarche and/or first penetration; it was this inner mouth whose lips were expected to purse tight after CONCEPTION; and it was this obstruction that Soranus was denying (1.16–17; Hanson 1992: n. 58).

The uterus was believed to "freely move about inside the abdomen, as though it were an animal with a life of its own" (Van Straten 1981: 124 n. 194 quoting Aretaios). It tended to gravitate toward cool and wet areas, but could be lured back to its proper place by sweet smells applied to the vagina. The cause of uterine displacement (or suffocation) was laid to the womb being too dry, insufficiently irrigated by SEMEN, or made too hot by excessive, unfeminine exercise (Hanson 1992: 36, 38–9).

Terracotta uterus votives dedicated at sanctuaries (especially Asklepios) resemble small jars or bleeding-cups (Hippocrates, *Vetere Medicina* 22) with stacked horizontal ridges; Italian votives have a lateral appendage, probably the bladder (Van Straten 1981: 123–5, 129–32; **267** [**pl. 17**]).

See also: BODIES; BODY MODIFICATION; HAIR

Boy-Love is expressed by Roman adult males towards slave boys, young male PROSTITUTES, and young non-citizen males; it did not have the socializing or moralistic aim of Greek PAIDERASTIA (Cantarella 1992: 98). Lucilius 63 warns against being "all burnt out, fucking boys" (*pedicum ... iam excoquit omne*). Polybius (31.25.2–6) attributes Rome's lax morals to the introduction of boy-love, hetairai, MUSIC, and SYMPOSIA in the time of the Scipios.

Roman LAWS and attitudes forbade homosexual activity between free-born CITIZEN males. Haterius's famous remark, quoted by Seneca the Elder (LAWS), implies that the active male participant in SEXUAL ACTIVITY is a citizen but the passive male participant is not; this is repeated by several authors (Plutarch, *Quaest. Rom.* 101 Martial 3.95, 5.46, 7.62, 9.67, 11.43, 12.96). Plautus lists those who are not available to a citizen man: "he can love anyone he wants as long as he avoids married women, widows, virgins and freeborn youths" (Plautus, *Curculio* 35–40).

Roman male homoeroticism thus seems based on a disparity of status. The boy-friends of the poets CATULLUS ("Iuventius," 99), Tibullus ("Marathus," 8, 9), and PROPERTIUS ("Lygdamus," 4.8) were probably some type of non-citizen, their SLAVES, or hired PROSTITUTES (Iuventius means youth; Marathus and Lygdamus are Greek names). Horace recommends "a slave girl or slave boy" "when your crotch is about to burst" (*Satire* 1.2.116–9 [cf. 2.3.325]). It is possible too that most Roman boyfriends (*deliciae*, "delicacies" or "trifles;" AUGUSTUS) were Greek. All Martial's boys (*pueri*) have Greek names and are young; their facial HAIR marked the end of their attraction (4.7), even if depilated (2.62, 3.74, 6.56, 9.27, 14.205). HADRIAN's ANTINOOS was not Roman and probably not a citizen. The penetrated youths on the Warren cup (**288, pl. 43**) are probably prostitutes. Acquiring their attentions demanded money; Cato observed that pretty boys were more expensive than land (Polybius 31.25.3).

See also: BISEXUALITY; HETEROEROTICISM; HOMOEROTICISM; MALE HOMOSEXUALITY

Lilja 1983; Williams 1999.

Brothels Building "Z" near the Sacred Gate in Athens is probably the brothel owned by Euktemon (ca. 350–300 BCE; Isaeus 6.19; cf. Alexis 206 K-A). The building contains ten small rooms surrounding a central court (Knigge 1988: 89–94; Lind 1988). POMPEII had several brothels and cells for individual PROSTITUTES.

At Ephesus, an inscription refers to a latrine (cf. **pl. 37**) and a *paidiskeíon* (brothel); Tacitus (*Ann.* 6.1) derives *sellarii*, a word for male prostitutes (TIBERIUS), from the place where they congregated, a *sellarium* or public latrine. At Thessalonike a building has also been identified as a brothel (Agence France-Presse 1998), perhaps because of its large

and circular room with twenty-five latrines. At Ephesus, a rock-cut sign also
leads clients to the brothel: two SANDALED
feet turn left below two WOMEN. Ashka-
lon produced a brothel with mosaics,
erotic pottery, and a number of fetus
skeletons in the drains connected with
the building (Faerman 1998).

Rome had many brothels (forty-five in
the fourth century CE) and prostitutes'
cells in the Subura (McGinn 2002: 27).

And individuals could set up temporary
brothels in their homes (Val. Max. 9.1.8;
cf. CALIGULA'S on the Palatine, Suetonius,
Caligula 41.1).

Brothels can be inferred from scenes on
Greek vases where women are seated in a
domestic setting and men are standing,
apparently visiting (Webster 1972: 216,
219–23, class B; cf. **69**, **96**, **121** [**pl. 13**]).

McGinn 1998b.

C

Caeneus, originally a Lapith girl, Caenis. POSEIDON fell in love with her, and requested of her anything; she asked to be a man; he added immortality as well. At the centauromachy at Pirithoös's wedding CENTAURS hammered Caeneus into the ground; this demise is frequently represented.

See also: TRANSSEXUALITY

Ovid, *Met.* 12.189–209; Apollonius 1.57 scholiast; Homer, *Iliad* 1.264 and 2.746 scholiast; Hyginus 14.4; Pindar fr. 150 Bowra.

Caligula (12–41 CE), emperor Gaius Julius Caesar Germanicus (37–41), son of Germanicus and Agrippina maior, nicknamed "Little Boots" by his father's soldiers. In 32, he joined TIBERIUS on Capri where he would disguise himself in a wig and long robe and act and DANCE on stage. He married Junia Claudilla, who died in childbirth. He then seduced Ennia Naevia, wife of Macro the commander of the Praetorian Guard, through whom he reportedly had Tiberius poisoned in 37. He was then proclaimed emperor. An illness later that year may have caused his mental instability. He was assassinated in 41; the main conspirator was Cassius Chaerea, to whom Caligula would hold out his hand, using the middle finger for him to KISS (BODY PARTS). While killing him, some assassins thrust their swords through his genitals (cf. DOMITIAN).

It was said that he banished *spintriae* (male prostitutes) from Rome, since he could not drown them all at sea, but he also taxed all PROSTITUTES, both female and male (Justin Martyr, 1 *Apology* 27; the tax was rescinded in 498 CE). He also set up a BROTHEL in the palace of married women and freeborn youths. It was said he stole PRAXITELES's EROS from Thespiai (Cicero, *Verr.* 2.4.135; Plutarch, *Erotikos* 748a; Pausanias 9.27.3).

Caligula boasted that his mother was born of AUGUSTUS's INCEST with his daughter JULIA MAIOR, and he was reported to have had committed incest with all his sisters. He raped Drusilla when still a boy. Even after she MARRIED he lived with her as husband and wife until she died in 38. Caligula married several women, often only for brief periods and after having DIVORCED them from their husbands (Livia Orestilla married to Gaius Piso, Lollia to Gaius Memmius). Caesonia was his great love, however, neither beautiful nor young; when she bore him Julia Drusilla, he declared her his wife. After his death, both Caesonia and their daughter were killed.

Caligula also had sexual affairs with men, including Marcus Lepidus and the pantomime Mnester.

Suetonius, *Caligula*; Cass. Dio. 59.

Castor and Pollux, the *Dioskouroi* ("sons of ZEUS"), sons of LEDA and Tyndareus of SPARTA (Castor) and/or Zeus (Pollux). Their main cult was in Sparta, but after they participated in the Battle of the Sagra at lake Regillus (484 BCE), the Temple of Castor was built in the Roman forum. After THESEUS abducted HELEN, they retrieved her and, in revenge, abducted his mother Aithra. They also carried off the two LEUKIPPIDAI; their two cousins, Idas and Lynkeus, pursued them and died fighting – Castor was also killed. According to the wishes of Pollux, the two brothers share his immortality, living half their time in Hades and half on Olympus. In Homer (*Iliad* 3.237 ff., *Odyssey* 11.300 ff.) they are mortal heroes. The two are often connected with the constellation Gemini (Euripides, *Helen* 140) and, as the *leukopôloi* (white colts) with horses.

Catullus, Gaius? Valerius (84?–54 BCE), Roman poet. Catullus's 116 poems were preserved in only one manuscript, now lost; they are heterogeneous in subject, consisting of MARRIAGE SONGS (some imitating SAPPHO I, especially 51), minor epics, and elegiacs.

Most of his love poems are addressed to a married woman he calls "Lesbia" (presumably as intelligent and/or creative as SAPPHO); she is usually identified with CLODIA. They share countless KISSES (5, 7, 12), but she breaks him as the passing plow breaks a flower at the edge of a field (11.17–8). Catullus also has an affair with a youth, "Iuventius" (24, 81); and with him too he shares countless kisses (48, 99) and he also is unfaithful (Richardson 1963); his identity is unknown, but it is unlikely he was Roman or even free-born (BOY-LOVE).

Other poems mention male-male relationships (Manlius Torquatus, who is getting married, and his slave-boy *concubinus*, 61). Other poems deride men for being CINAEDI or *pathici* (16, 29, 33).

Centaurs, half-horse (hindquarters and body), half-human (torso and head). The first centaur was Centaurus, the offspring of Ixion and a cloud in the image of HERA, whom he was trying to rape. Two centaurs were more human, Pholus who could stay sober (Apollodorus 2.5.4) and Chiron, who is usually portrayed with human frontal legs. Chiron is the tutor of ACHILLES, Actaion, and Asklepios; his precepts were the subject of a poem ascribed to Hesiod (Pausanias 9.31.5). Female centaurs are rarely depicted.

Centaurs live in the mountains of Arcadia and on Mt Pelion. Invited to the wedding of Pirithoös, king of the Lapiths, and Hippodameia, they become drunk and try to rape the women and youths. The centauromachy, including the death of CAENEUS, was a popular theme in Greek art.

Chastity Belt, a sheath that prevents intercourse by covering the male genitals (chastity belts for WOMEN are unknown in classical antiquity). For men, there is both a large *fibula* (like a modern safety pin), that pierces the foreskin and covers the penis, and a *theca*, a metal pouch, or leather bag (*aluta*) that encloses the genitals (Martial 7.35, 7.82). Hellenized Jews could use the *theca* to hide their circumcised penis.

Women, in the eastern Mediterranean, could have the vaginal opening narrowed by suturing or by a ring (Strabo 17.2.5).

See also: ABSTINENCE; BODY MODIFICATION

Dingwall 1925.

Children Within a week or so after BIRTH children could be accepted by their father into the family; in Rome first daughters and all sons were accepted. If not, they were killed or exposed for adoption (Aristotle, *Politics* 1334a2–12; Hanson 1992: n. 164); girls ran a greater risk of being killed or exposed.

To produce an heir, one could also adopt. In Greece, CITIZEN MEN could adopt other citizen men to whom they could also MARRY their daughters. Roman men could adopt citizen men by themselves (*adoptio*) or with their entire family (*adrogatio*); it could also be done after death via a will (AUGUSTUS). With adoption, the adoptee became legally the same as a natural son, taking a new name and rank. In the later empire, WOMEN could also adopt.

Childhood tended to end at age eight, at which time boys went to school and girls were given more duties at home. Between 14 and 16, boys began their military training; at this age Greek girls would marry men at least ten years older, while Roman boys could themselves marry.

Since infant mortality was high, some couples raised multiple "families." Twins were regarded with suspicion; in mythology, a god fathers the more important son (HERAKLES and Pollux), and the mortal husband fathers the lesser (Iphikles and CASTOR). Empedocles believed that twins developed from a superabundance of sperm (SEMEN), but since CONCEPTION was thought to occur over several days, successive intercourse was also thought to be the cause. Multiple children interfered with inheritance: the dowries of too many daughters depleted the estate; too many sons divided it. One son was best (Hesiod, *Works* 376).

States were concerned to stabilize the population according to available agricultural land and military commitments (Hanson 1992: 58–9 and n. 162). Plato thought an ideal state of 5,040 men would maintain itself (*Laws* 737c–8a); Aristotle disagreed (*Politics* 1265a39–b12).

See also: AGE-GRADES; AMPHIDROMIA; MEDICINE; PAIDERASTIA; PREGNANCY; MIDWIVES

Cinaedi, a derogatory term for EFFEMINATE, penetrable men in both Greek and Latin. The word probably derives from the Greek *kineín*, "to move" and later "to fuck" (*kinêtêrion*, "fuckery," BROTHEL). Cinaedi also DANCED (Lucilius 254–8), wiggling their buttocks (Plautus, *Poen.* 1317).

Kínaidos supplanted *katapúgôn* in the fourth century BCE; the two terms are thus aligned with Latin *pathicus* ("qui muliebria patitur," *Digest* 3.1.1.6, "a pathic is one who has sex like a WOMAN"). But if Catullus 16 is taken literally *cinaedus Furius* likes to FELLATE and Aurelius is the penetrable pathic (similarly Martial 1.96: the lips of the effeminate quiver when they see penises).

The term was applied so generally that it loses force (cf. ARISTOPHANES's plays *passim*, and INVECTIVE, Cicero, *Fam.* 8.13.3, 8.14.4). Cinaedi could also have sex with women (Richlin 1993: 533; JUVENAL). On two Hellenistic MOULDMADE BOWLS a cinaedus has equestrian sex with a woman (**190, 191**). Davidson (1998: 167–82) thus argues that the cinaedus lacked sexual self-control (cf. Plato, *Gorgias* 493–494e).

It is possible to characterize the cinaedus as a type of person. He has a medical pathology. One of Aristotle's *Problems* asks why effeminate men like to be anally penetrated (4.26): "in some men the passages to the testicles are blocked, and the moisture [that produces sexual DESIRE] flows instead" into the lower intestine. Soranus (*On Chronic Diseases*) thinks men who play the passive role have a mental disease. Cinaedi also exhibit certain behaviors. They stick together (*magna inter molles concordia*, Juvenal 2.44–50). They can be recognized by their distinctive dress and long HAIR, and by the gesture of scratching their head with the middle finger (Seneca, *Controv.* 7.4.7; cf. Plutarch, *Pomp.* 48.7; Juvenal 9.130–3; BODY PARTS).

In Rome, the pathics were so numerous that emperors from CALIGULA on sought to clear the city of them (cf. Juvenal 9.130–3; Romans 1.26–7); in a city of a million, they may have numbered 10,000 or more (Williams 1999).

See also: CINAEDOLOGOI; MALE HOMOSEXUALITY; SOTADES

Taylor 1997.

Cinaedologoi, performers of sexual and satirical verses in SONG and action, thought to be CINAEDI themselves (PETRONIUS 23.3). The verses were invented by SOTADES.

Strabo 14.1.41; Aristid. Quint. 1.13; Athenaeus 7.296e, 7.283a, 14.620d–f; *Suda* s.v. Sotades.

Circe, daughter of Helios, and MEDEA's aunt. She transforms Odysseus's men into swine (a sexual metaphor for vaginas; ANIMALS). With HERMES's help and the PLANT *moly* Odysseus remains immune and forces her to restore his men. They live together for a year before he resumes his journey.

OVID tells two more stories: after Glaucus spurns Circe for Scylla, she turns her into a sea monster whose lower body consists of several rows of dog heads; after king Picus of Latium spurns her for his wife she turns him into a woodpecker.

Homer, *Odyssey* 10 passim; Vergil, *Aen.* 7.19–20; Ovid, *Met.* 13.900–14.74, 14.320–96.

Citizenship Freeborn Athenian men were made citizens at two separate occasions, when they graduated from being ephebes (AGE GRADES) and when they took office or spoke first in the assembly. Graduating from being an ephebe may have involved NUDITY, since "Philokleon" could see their genitals (Aristophanes, *Wasps* 578). Upon entering office, men were scrutinized (*dokimasía*, Winkler 1990: 54–64) and asked several questions, including had they PROSTITUTED themselves for money (Aeschines, *In Tim.*; Lysias 16, 25, 26, 31; Cratinus, *Cheiron* fr. 9 Koch; Xenophon, *Mem.* 2.2.13; Deinarchus 2.17). Citizens could be disenfranchised for prostituting themselves, for procuring, and for refusing to DIVORCE an ADULTERESS.

Roman citizenship by 218 BCE was granted to Italian communities with the right of intermarriage (*connubium*) with a Roman citizen. From then on, Roman citizenship was granted on occasion until Caracalla extended it to all (212 CE).

Class Distinctions along economic, political, and ETHNIC lines bring sexual distinctions: who can MARRY whom, who can have intercourse with whom. Thus, for instance, the separation in the Roman world between the elite (*superiores*) and commoners (*humiliores*) also carried differences in punishments for sexual crimes (BODY MODIFICATION; HADRIAN; LAWS). In the Athenian democracy, class distinctions were not marked by great differences in dress (Xenophon [*Ath. Pol.*] 1.10–12); Greek art, however, may have rendered the citizen male NUDE and the non-citizen clothed (Hollein 1988).

Claudius (10 BCE–54 CE), emperor Tiberius Nero Germanicus (41–54). Rumored to be an illegitimate child fathered by AUGUSTUS, he suffered from paralysis and perhaps epilepsy. After the assassination of CALIGULA, he was acclaimed by the Praetorian Guard.

Claudius was uxorious. Of his two fiancées, the second was Livia Medullina Camilla, who died on their wedding day. His first wife was Plautia Urgulanilla, whom he DIVORCED for ADULTERY. His second wife Aelia Paetina bore him a daughter; he divorced her for lewdness and murder by poison. His third wife Valeria MESSALINA bore him Octavia, later the wife of NERO, and Britannicus, probably poisoned by Nero; Messalina was accused of treason and committed suicide. His fourth wife was his niece Agrippina minor, whom he MARRIED illegally with the senate's consent. She urged Claudius to adopt her son Nero from a prior marriage; four years later Claudius died, probably poisoned.

Suetonius, *Claudius*.

Cleomachus of Pharsalus fought in the Lelantine War fighting for Chalcis (late eighth century BCE). Plutarch tells the story (*Erotikos* 760e–761b):

> He asked his eromenos if he would watch the fight. 'Yes,' said the youth (*neaniskos*) and helped him put on his helmet with a KISS. Cleomachus then attacked the enemy and routed their cavalry but was killed. His tomb is in the agora of Chalkis, and the Chalcidians from that time on welcomed PAIDERASTIA.

There are at least two more versions of the story. Plutarch says that Aristotle identified another soldier, Anton from the Thracian Chalcidike, who fought for the Chalcidians, and was kissed by his eromenos, Philistos. A poem commemorates him (PMG 130). An inscription in Athens refers to a third version of the story: on the obverse, "Here a man beloved by a boy (*paidós*) swore an oath to join the strife of war which brings tears. I am consecrated to Gnatios whose life was lost in war, son of Heroas"; and on the reverse the eromenos's lament: "Gnathios, always hasten[ing am I to greet you]" (Friedländer and Hoffleit 1948: 63–4, no. 59 dated ca. 500 BCE).

Cleopatra VII (68–30 BCE), queen of Egypt (51–30 BCE), daughter of Ptolemy Auletes, and wife of her young brother, Ptolemy XIII (INCEST). Since both were minors at their accession, Rome had stewardship with Pompey as their guardian. Soon afterward, Cleopatra fled to Syria until JULIUS CAESAR came to Egypt in pursuit of Pompey (48); she was then introduced to Caesar, hidden NUDE in a package (popularly, a rolled rug). Caesar restored her to the throne, and had her MARRY a younger brother, Ptolemy XIV,

then eleven years old. She bore Caesar a son, Ptolemy Caesar ("Caesarion," 47–30), and followed him to Rome; when he was assassinated (44), she returned to Egypt, had Ptolemy XIV poisoned, and ruled nominally with her son.

After ANTONY's victory at Philippi over Brutus and Cassius (42), Cleopatra became his mistress, bearing him three children, Alexander, Ptolemy, and Cleopatra. At Alexandria for the winter, he treated her as a queen independent of Rome. He left the next year (40). A renewal of the first triumvirate gave him control of the eastern provinces, in return for which he married Octavia, the sister of AUGUSTUS. After the establishment of the second triumvirate (37), he returned to Alexandria and married Cleopatra without divorcing Octavia.

In the "Donations of Alexandria," Antony made her queen over the kings of the east (34). In response, Octavian induced the senate to strip Antony of his powers and to declare war against Cleopatra. When the eastern forces refused to fight at the "battle" of Actium (31) Cleopatra fled to Alexandria, Antony in pursuit, and Octavian pursuing both of them. Before Octavian could enter the city, Antony committed suicide (30). After Cleopatra tried in vain to seduce Octavian, she committed suicide by the bite of an asp. Octavian had Caesarion killed and buried Antony and Cleopatra side by side in a grand funeral; their children were magnanimously raised by Octavia.

Cloak, a military garment and blanket used to mask a couple having sex. Greek vases depict two people sharing a single cloak; they usually stand, holding it up behind them. Men and women share a single cloak, usually reclining on a couch. Two men also share cloaks (57). Several vases depict only women sharing a cloak (LESBIANISM), usually two women (47 [pl. 8], 53), occasionally three. One vessel (58) connects three scenes: two women sharing a cloak, a man and veiled woman face each other, and two men engaged in intercrural intercourse (PAIDERASTIA).

The earliest textual reference may be SAPPHO (PMG 54), who mentions EROS wrapped in a purple cloak (khlámun). In Plato's *Symp.* 219b ALCIBIADES shares a cloak (chlaínan) with Socrates while on military duty, though they did not have sex (Athenaeus 5.219b). The poet Sophocles has sex in a cloak with a boy, who then runs off with it (Athenaeus 13.603e–604d). And in PETRONIUS 1, Ascyltus catches Encolpius and Giton having sex under a cloak.

Sex and the military cloak may have been linked only in Greece, although Suetonius tells an odd anecdote about Otho (2) that "he used to roam at night and whatever man he found drunk or incapacitated he would toss into the air in a military cloak" (*vagari noctibus solitus atque invalidum quemque obviorum vel potulentum corripere ac distento sago imposito in sublime iactare*). Unless Otho was strong enough to toss a man into the air by himself, the expression *in sublime iactare* may be a sexual circumlocution for rape.

Koch-Harnack 1989: 109–85.

Clodia (fl. 50 BCE) was MARRIED to Q. Metellus Celer. It is widely believed that, while still married, she had an affair with the poet CATULLUS and to have been his "Lesbia" (Gudeman 1890).

After Metellus's death in 59 (reputedly poisoned by Clodia), she had an affair with M. Caelius Rufus whom she later prosecuted (Bauman 1992: 69–73) and perhaps poisoned as well. She never remarried. She was wealthy; her estate on the Tiber was situated so she could watch men swimming and plan her affairs with them.

One of Clodia's three brothers was Publius Clodius Pulcher, who, in 62, dressed as a woman and attended the all-women's festival of the Bona Dea to meet

Pompeia, JULIUS CAESAR's wife (Cicero, *Att.* 1.13.3, 16.2.5; Suetonius, *Caes.* 6.2; Plutarch, *Caes.* 9–10); Juvenal may have had this incident in mind when he describes (2) how a *pathicus* puts on women's clothes to attend the Bona Dea. As well as having sex with "all parts of his body," Cicero charges Clodius with PROSTITUTION in his youth and INCEST with his sisters (*Har. Resp.* 27.38).

Cicero, *Cael.* 3.6; *Dom.* 92; *Fam.* 1.9.15; *Q fr.* 2.3.2; *Sest.* 16.19; cf. Velleius Paterculus 2.45.1; Plutarch, *Cic.* 29.2.

Commodus (161–92 CE), Lucius Aurelius, Roman emperor (co-ruler 177, and sole ruler 180–192), son of Marcus Aurelius. From 190 to his death by strangulation, Commodus appears to have been insane. He was said to have become IMPOTENT and thereafter performed FELLATIO and CUNNILINGUS (Cass. Dio 77.16.1; he was seen wearing women's clothing, and drinking from a cup with a PHALLUS-spout (**181** [pl. **21**]). He also kept certain men whom he named after the genitals of both sexes.

Hist. Aug. Commodus 7.

Conception. Ancient thinking concerned at least the following six major issues.

Is there a female seed?

No: Aristotle, some Pythagoreans, and others believed that only sperm (SEMEN) contributed to the formation of the embryo. In Aeschylus's *Eumenides*, APOLLO asserts that there is no female seed; the father is "the one who mounts and plants" (658–66).

Yes: according to the Hippocratics and others, both parents produced genetic material (*pangenesis*). Fathers produced sperm; women produced a secretion into the womb that sometimes leaked out of the womb when its opening was wide; it was, however, weaker and more watery than the male semen. These two secretions made up the embryo, baked solid by the heat of the womb. Herophilos dissected women and saw "female testicles" in the ovaries and "spermatic ducts" in Fallopian tubes.

A female seed would explain a child's resemblance to his mother. At the same time, if the mother provided the location of conception (the womb), the nourishment to the seed and to the embryo during development (the menses, as Hippocratics believed), then the womb was at least the site for a struggle over character (*Regimen* 1.1.28; cf. *Nat. pueri*).

What is the best time to conceive?

The Hippocratics, Aristotle, and SORANUS (2.35) believed that the best time to conceive was immediately following MENSTRUATION. Aristotle thought that a woman menstruating cannot conceive (*Gen. An.* 727b12–23).

What factor(s) determine the sex of the offspring?

(For tests to discover the sex of the fetus, see PREGNANCY.) Since Aristotle did not think that women contributed genetic material, then the sex of the offspring was established by which testicle the seed had come from or in which side of the uterus the embryo developed: right for males, left for females (Hippocrates, *Superfetation* 31; *Pop.* 6.4.21; *Aphorisms* 5.48). Aristotle also thought the child's sex was determined at the end of conception.

The Hippocratics thought that each parent can produce a strong or a weak seed, and that sex was determined by the greater quantity of strong or weak seed. If both parents produce equal amounts of strong seeds, they create a manly boy; if they both produce weak seeds, they create a feminine girl. Permutations were discussed in detail.

What is the length of conception?

To the Hippocratics, three days; to Aristotle, as many as seven days. Soranus is vague: conception lasted as long as the material inside the womb was a seed and continues while the embryo develops. The mother was thought to know when conception had taken place, since the womb closed on the seed (BODY PARTS [uterus]). Males articulate faster; they could be determined in the ABORTED fetus at 30 or 40 days. Females could be discerned in the fetus at 42 or 90 days (*Nat. puer.* 13.3 and 18).

What is the role of menstrual blood in conception?

To the Hippocratics, menstrual blood provided an indication of the general health of the woman, the cessation of its flow was the proper time for conception, and a developing child used all the menses that continued to be produced for nourishment. Aristotle thought the menstrual blood that remained after menses had abated provided material to the sperm for shaping the fetus.

Is a woman's sexual desire or pleasure necessary for conception?

To the Hippocratics, all conception requires pleasure, but not all pleasure resulted in conception. Aristotle noted, however, that conception can occur in some women who do not experience pleasure during intercourse. Soranus comments on women who conceive through rape, that at least "the emotion of sexual appetite [i.e. DESIRE] existed in them too, but was obscured by mental resolve," making a distinction between desire for intercourse (necessary for conception) and pleasure during intercourse (good for conception).

See also: BIRTH; CONTRACEPTION; MEDICINE; MIDWIVES; PREGNANCY

Dean-Jones 1994; Hanson 1992; Hippocrates; Lloyd 1978: 318–21; Van Der Eijk, 1999.

Contraception (*atókia*) and ABORTION often relied on the same methods: PLANTS (the squirting cucumber), strenuous activity (the "Laconian leap," DANCE), and intervention (sponge suppositories; Athenaeus 1.18d). Conception could be avoided through the rhythm method and through *coitus interruptus*, whereby the man's ORGASM either does not take place at all or takes place outside the vagina (on the woman's BODY: "I will spill upon your dewy garden," Archilochus 196A West = S478 Page = Campbell 1976: 463: 15–16; cf. Lucretius 4.1269–76; Hippocrates, *Nat. puer.* 4.3, 5 [VII: 476]; Genesis 38.10). The conception of Erichthonius (ATHENA) refers both to coitus interruptus and to intervention. Anal intercourse could also substitute for vaginal intercourse, especially on the first night of MARRIAGE if the bride was afraid (Martial 11.78.5–6; cf. PEISISTRATOS, PRIAPEA 3.6–7).

See also: MEDICINE

Cosmetics Agents to color the skin and to hide blemishes and perfumes to counteract BODY odor ("let no smelly goat wait in the wings," *ne trux caper iret in alas*, OVID, *Ars Am.* 3.193) were used by both MEN and WOMEN from the earliest times (cf. Carter 1998: 73–4; Papaefthimiou-Papanthimou 1979).

Greek and Roman women used *psímthion* (white lead) to whiten the skin, *phúkos*, a rouge made from PLANTS (alkanet and mulberry), and soot and kohl (antimony sulfide) to darken the eyebrows and highlight the eyes. Women and men used tweezers and razors to remove unwanted HAIR and earpicks to clean the ears, and other utensils and servants for BODY CARE.

OVID mentions cosmetics and adornment frequently (*Ars Am.* 3.129–32 [wear little jewelry], 197–8 [clean your teeth, wash], 199–214 [clay *creta* for whitening the skin, rouge, soot, saffron for the eyes, and *oesypum* made from unwashed wool oil]). He wrote a treatise on the subject, *Medicamina faciei femineae*; even though fragmentary its 100 lines list over twenty ingredients for face packs, cleansing aids, and skin colorants.

Using too many cosmetics, however, was thought dishonest (Ovid, *Rem. Am.* 354): "Her hair, her teeth, her clothes, her face are laid aside at night hidden in a hundred caskets. The woman is all sexual orifice wrapped in deceit" (Martial 9.37).

d'Ambrosio 2001; Dayagi-Mendels 1989; Green 1979; Paszthory 1990; Varone 2001b; Wyke 1994.

Costume, when specifically erotic and sexual, usually entails some baring of the flesh. When HERA sets out to seduce ZEUS, she puts on APHRODITE's girdle of lappets that both conceal and reveal (Homer, *Iliad* 14.294). Greek art depicts males either NUDE or partially so, wearing a CLOAK (*himation*) that reveals their genitals (cf. **135**). Women wear the tunic (*peplos* or *chiton*); when sleeveless it can slip off the shoulder (cf. APHRODITE, and sometimes ARTEMIS, as on the Parthenon's east frieze); from the fifth century BCE, women can appear nude in vase painting and, from the mid-fourth century, in sculpture. Roman art portrays few males nude (NERO, **243 [pl. 42]**), and the usual assortment of nude Aphrodites, sometimes with the portrait heads of real women (BODIES "BY GOD"). In the THEATER, actors wore special costumes whose padding emphasized buttocks and breasts, and special shoes that gave them height. From vase paintings, male actors could also wear very short *chitons* that reveal exaggerated PHALLOI.

See also: JEWELRY; SANDALS; STROPHIUM; TRANSVESTISM

Courtship begins in antiquity as a man's pursuit of a youth or boy (PAIDERASTIA), since most MARRIAGES are arranged until the fourth century BCE at the earliest; the man presents himself as a suitable lover and presents LOVE-GIFTS. Until romantic LOVE begins to color marriage (no earlier than the late fifth century BCE), early heterosexual courtship would have involved a man courting a hetaira (PROSTITUTION).

Couvade, a man experiencing the symptoms of giving BIRTH. At the shrine of APHRODITE and Ariadnê in Amathous, Cyprus, a young man goes through couvade in an annual ceremony (Plutarch, *Thes.* 20; Leitao 1998): according to the story, THESEUS and Ariadnê were driven by storm to Cyprus, where she, PREGNANT, disembarked while he remained with the ship. Local women brought her forged letters from Theseus to cheer her, but she died without giving birth. When Theseus returned, he honored her by initiating the ritual couvade to complete her pregnancy.

Cruising, the process whereby men seek each other out for casual sex (also PROSTITUTION). In Athens, men cruised on the Hill of the Muses and in the Ceramicus cemetery (Wycherley 1957: 222–3; Aristophanes, *Frogs* 422), and in Rome it was around the Colosseum and in latrines (BROTHELS). SOLON reportedly passed LAWS to keep GYMNASIA and boys' ATHLETIC contests (the Hermaia) from becoming cruising grounds (cf. Aristophanes, *Peace* 762–3).

Cunnilingus, oral stimulation of the female genitals. To lick (Greek *leíkhein*, Latin *lambere*) was the most common term, abbreviated simply as "L" (Ausonius, *Epigr.* 87.7; Varro, *Sat. Men.* 48 B, 70 Cèbe); thus, the lambda on SPARTAN shields was a joke (Eupolis 1 Edmonds 1957; cf. Photius s.v. lambda). To perform cunnilingus was to do it "Phoenician style" (ETHNICITY) and to do it from the

rear was to assume the *skylax* (puppy) position (Hesychius s.v.).

Cunnilingus was thought appropriate for IMPOTENT men, especially in OLD AGE (Martial 6.26, 11.25, 11.47), or for eunuchs (3.81).

The practice was considered vile. "We are more revolted by cunnilingus than by FELLATIO" (Galen 12:249 Kühn). The common Latin phrase *nihil negare* "to deny [him/her] nothing," conveys its unspeakable nature. For instance, "I deny nothing to you, Phyllis: deny nothing to me" (Martial 11.50.12). When the tyrant Agathocles was dying, his wife lamented, "What did I not do to you? what did you not do to me?" (Polybius 12.15.104).

Since the vagina was thought to have a strong smell, like salted fish (Ausonius, *Epigr.* 82.1–6; BODY PARTS), cunnilictors were accused of having bad breath. So Martial (9.95+95a) accuses Athenagoras (cf. *Greek Anth.* 12.187.1–6). Quintus Remmius Palaemon, an intellectual, was accused of "defiling his mouth" with women; a man who was KISSED by him, quipped, "whenever you see somebody in a hurry [*festinare*, "coming"], must you kiss him?" (*ligurrire*, "to lick;" Suetonius, *de Grammaticis* 23). In fact, nothing could disguise their bad breath (Aristophanes, *Eccles.* 647; Martial 3.77).

Cunnilingus on MENSTRUATING women was considered especially vile (cf. Galen, 12:249 Kühn; cf. Aristophanes, *Peace* 883–5). Seneca characterizes a certain Natalis for having "a wicked as well as a stinking tongue" (*tam improbae linguae quam impurae*) and "a mouth in which women purged themselves" (*in cuius ore feminae purgabantur*; *Ep.* 87.16; cf. *Ben.* 4.31.2–5).

Cunnilingus on PREGNANT women was the subject of jokes. Since Nanneius did it and heard "the babies wailing within, a shocking sickness paralyzed" his tongue (Martial 11.61.1–14). Ausonius (*Epigr.* 86.1–2) says of the schoolteacher Eunus, "while licking the strong smelling cunt of your pregnant wife, you hasten to teach *glossae* (languages, tongues) to your not-yet-born children."

There are few depictions of heterosexual cunnilingus (**139, 219, 220, 291** VII), and one of woman-woman cunnilingus (**291** IIII).

Krenkel 1980, 1981.

Cybelê/Magna Mater (Great Mother), a Phrygian goddess related to Rhea (Herodotus 1.80). As the Mother of the Gods, she had several sanctuaries (*Mêtrôa*; Pausanias 7.17.9, 7.20.3, 8.46.4, 9.25.3), but her main temple was at Sardis, where she was also worshipped as ARTEMIS. Other Mother goddesses are also known in Campania (an enthroned Mother with infant[s]) and the Matres of the Celts. Cybelê was worshipped along with her young lover ATTIS, a god of vegetation (cf. ADONIS), and both were thought to convey immortality on their believers. Her cult was officially brought to Rome in 205/4 BCE, but remained for the most part in a temple on the Palatine served by eastern priests. Under CLAUDIUS the worship of ATTIS was opened to CITIZENS.

Cybelê's priests, called Galli (from the Gallus river in Phrygia, whose water made men mad), worked themselves into a frenzy and cut off their testicles with a sherd of Arretine pottery on 24 March, the *dies sanguinis* (Day of Blood); henceforth they wandered and begged as mendicants. According to a story, Dionysios of Syracuse (probably Dionysios II, tyrant 367/6–45 BCE) rapes the Lokrian virgins (his father had married a Lokrian); their fathers revenge themselves upon his wife and children by raping, murdering, and defiling them; Dionysios then spent his life as a mendicant priest of Cybelê, presumably therefore also castrated (Athenaeus 12.541c–e). In reality, he was ousted from Syracuse in 345 and spent the remainder of his life in Corinth.

See also: ATALANTA

D

Dance representations begin in the Bronze Age ("Dance in the Grove" fresco from Knossos). Late Geometric pottery portrays lines of dancers. Archaic Attic and Corinthian pottery feature *kómoi*, MEN who dance drunkenly, wear padded COSTUMES to emphasize the buttocks and belly, and display exaggerated PHALLOI (Seeberg 1971; cf. AGARISTE).

Other vigorous dances (Pollux 15.102) include the Lacedaemonian *bíbasis* (Mantas 1995); boys and girls leap and kick their heels back to touch the buttocks. The dance was also recommended as an ABORTIFACIENT. Another dance, *ekláktisma*, required women to throw their feet higher than their shoulders. Young women also danced while singing "Maiden SONGS" (*parthénea*).

Roman female dancer-PROSTITUTES (*comessationes, saltatrices*), especially those from Cadiz (ETHNICITY), performed erotic dances (*cordax*), wiggling the buttocks, appearing sometimes NUDE (Cicero, *Verr.* 2.3.9.23; cf. Lucian, *Conviv.* 16.35.46).

Roman "dance stories" (*salticae fabulae*) were popular, written by celebrated authors like Statius and Lucan (Juvenal 7.82–92; Lucan, *Lucani vita*). OVID was not pleased when some of his works were danced while he was in exile (*Tristia* 2.519–20; cf. Richlin 1992b: 175).

The male pantomime danced the sexual myths of WOMEN like LEDA and PROCNÊ (Juvenal 6.63, 7.92; Beare 1955). Roman culture stigmatized dancing as EFFEMINATE (Richlin 1983: 92–3, 98; Pliny, *Pan.* 54.1), but pantomimes were DESIRED by both women and men (cf. Bathyllus: Juvenal 6.63–6; Tacitus, *Ann.* 1.54.3).

See also: MUSIC; THEATER

Daphnê, a companion of ARTEMIS. Both APOLLO and LEUKIPPOS 3 fell in LOVE with her, but she shunned MEN. Leukippos dressed as a maiden (TRANSVESTISM) to join the virgin huntresses, but was discovered and killed. Daphnê also refused Apollo and fled praying for help; ZEUS turned her into the laurel tree, Apollo's prophetic PLANT.

Sophocles, *Trachiniae*; Ovid, *Met.* 1.452 ff.

Deformity, a physiological malformation of the BODY. Deformed infants were exposed by law in SPARTA. In Rome, DWARVES, hunchbacks, and other malformed people, including the obese, were thought amusing (see Pliny's list, *HN* 8), even erotic (cf. Galba's father: Suetonius, *Galba* 3).

Deianeira, won by HERAKLES with his victory over the river Akheloös. Herakles gives her to the CENTAUR Nessos to carry her over his river (WATER). Nessos tries to rape her and Herakles kills him with an arrow. Dying, Nessos tells Deianeira to take some of his blood as a LOVE-charm (MAGIC). When Herakles brings his mistress Iolê home, Deianeira daubs Herakles's CLOAK with Nessos's blood; it immolates him (MEDEA). Deianeira commits suicide.

Demeter/Ceres, goddess of grain, worshipped with her daughter Persephonê. In mourning the disappearance of her daughter (abducted by Hades), Demeter causes no agricultural growth. At Eleusis, disguised as an OLD woman, she is given hospitality, during which she is entertained by BAUBO. ZEUS relents and Persephonê comes back to her mother.

In Arcadia, Demeter mates with POSEIDON as a horse (BESTIALITY), and bears Arion and Despoina; horse-headed Demeter was worshipped at Phigaleia (Pausanias 8.25.4 and 8.42.1, 4).

Demeter's Mysteries are celebrated in October; several PLANTS associated with the THESMOPHORIA (pennyroyal, pomegranate, pine, vitex) promote women's ability "to regulate their reproductive lives" (Nixon 1995: 88). Another festival, the Haloa in December, ensured the successful germination of sown seed; it was celebrated by women only, including PROSTITUTES at their own SYMPOSIUM with PHALLIC food (cf. 97).

Homeric Hymn, *Demeter*.

Desire, erotic yearning for someone one does not possess: *póthos* (Greek) for the attainable and *hímeros* (Greek) for the unobtainable; *desderium* (Latin); EROS. Desire can be increased by challenges, such as injunctions against having sex with certain people (CITIZEN youths, and the daughters and wives of citizens), and by physical barriers like CLOAKS (**78, 116, 146**) and the confines of the house (Davidson 1998: 127–36).

Uncontrollable desire was the source of most character flaws: "moderation in all things," especially drinking (cf. Athenaeus 2.36b–c, 37a–b) and sex. Socrates advises Kritoboulos not to KISS ALCIBIADES's son: "it'll take you a year to recover" (Xenophon, *Mem.* 1.3.13). Lust is "the fiercest kind and the most despotic" (Plato, *Laws* 783ab); happy is he who rejects bodily pleasures and seeks wisdom (*Phaedo* 82c, 83b and d, 64d, 81b, 114e). Aristotle (*Rhet.* 2.6.4) says that people should not "have sex with those one mustn't, where one mustn't, and when one mustn't; such activities derive from a lack of self-restraint" (*akolasía*). "Ancient authors attributed the crises of the late Republic to political ambition and to male bodies out of control, guilty of, in Livy's words, 'luxus, avaritia, libido, cupiditas, abundantes voluptates' (luxurious living, avarice, lust, immoderate desire, excessive pleasures)" (Joshel 1992: 117; cf. Horace, *Carm.* 3.24.52–4). Seneca advises that, if one avoids lust, one can avoid all other forms of desire (*Helv.* 13.2–4).

Prolonged sexual indulgence, was thought to cause physical changes: those "who indulge in sex over a long time, their vessels swell up and they become enlarged" (Galen 8:451–2; cf. Tardieu's medical examinations of male prostitutes in early nineteenth-century Paris which confirmed "a certain deformation of one part of the body, the proof of habitual prostitution," Symonds 1891: section IV).

Restraint (Grk *sôphrosúnê*, Lat. *disciplina*) needed constant maintenance; good WOMEN on Greek tombstones are praised for their self-restraint. "The Roman discourse on chaos often joins loose women with male failure to control various appetites" (Joshel 1992: 118–19).

See also: HETEROEROTICISM; LOVE; MALE HOMOSEXUALITY; PAIDERASTIA

Griffiths 1990.

Dido, legendary Phoenician queen of Carthage (founded 814/13 BCE). Wooed by a local king, she falls instead for Aeneas. A storm forces the two of them out hunting into a cave where they have sex. Dido assumes they are now MARRIED; Aeneas disagrees – there were no torches. Aeneas is ordered on to Latium, and, as he departs, Dido commits suicide.

Vergil, *Aen.* 1 and 4; Ovid, *Heroides* 7.

Dildo (*olísbos*), a device, shaped like an erect penis but longer, for insertion into a BODY orifice. Ancient dildoes were made of leather and stuffed with some material (*Suda* s.v.). They are rarely mentioned in literature (Cratinus F354 K-A 294, "hateful are WOMEN who use dildoes," imitating Herodotus 8.96.2; Aristophanes, *Lys.* 107–10; Herodas 6; Athenaeus 3.86e; Pollux 7.96; and Edmonds 1957–61: no. 320.13).

MEN could also use dildoes for anal penetration (never depicted); in PETRONIUS 16, Oenothea pushes a leather dildo, smeared with oil, pepper and crushed nettle seeds, into Encolpius's anus as an APHRODISIAC.

In art, dildoes tend to be long (about 2ft); most have just the one end shaped like a penis, but double-ended dildoes are occasionally shown (**111**). Except for a few examples in minor Roman sculpture (**215, 224, 262, 280**), all depictions of dildoes are of women using them on Greek red-figure vases of the early fifth century BCE (**82, 91, 108**).

Some scholars have identified these women with dildoes as LESBIANS (Licht 1963, ch. 3; Kilmer 1993: 26–30), but this is unwarranted. Since most illustrations of women with dildoes show them alone, it is not certain who is the object of their DESIRE, or if a partner is desired at all.

Dionysus/Bacchus/Liber, god of ecstatic behavior, FERTILITY, and wine. Although the name Dionysus appears in Mycenaean Linear B documents, the Greeks imagined he was introduced to Greece in the Archaic period. The god is accompanied by SATYRS, silens, and MAENADS; he rides a panther, holds a wine goblet, and is associated with ivy; he appears mainly to WOMEN, often as a bull (AGE-GRADES; ATHLETICS).

Dionysus was conceived by Semelê as ZEUS killed her with his lightning presence; Zeus then sews the child into his thigh until his BIRTH (whence his epithet "twice born," Apollodorus 3.4.3; OVID, *Met.* 3.289–312; contrast the stories told by Homer, *Iliad* 14.323–5, and Hesiod, *Theogony* 940–2). As a boy, sailors capture him for their captain Akoites ("bedmate-less"). During the voyage, Dionysus transforms the sailors into dolphins (OVID, *Met.* 3.605–91). When he returns from Egypt, AMAZONS oppose him; he pursues some to Ephesus and others to Samos. After THESEUS abandons Ariadnê, Dionysus marries her; they have a son, Oinopion.

In Euripides's *Bacchae*, king Pentheus of Thebes wants to root out the BACCHANALS in which his mother is participating. Dionysus garbs him like a woman (TRANSVESTISM) to watch them; they tear him apart (DAPHNE).

Dionysus was worshipped at Athens in four major festivals, including the rural Dionysia in December, in which men carrying large PHALLOI and dressed as satyrs DANCED the komos; and the City Dionysia in late March to early April. Both Dionysia had THEATER.

See also: PRIAPUS

Divorce, dissolution of MARRIAGE. In Greece, a husband could divorce his wife by sending her back to her former guardian; a wife could divorce her husband in front of the chief magistrate; and the wife's former guardian could annul the marriage. In all cases, the wife would retain the dowry. In actual fact, only three divorces by wives are known, and none was successful; in one, ALCIBIADES, divorced by his wife, abducted her back. In Rome, divorce resulted when one partner left the house, taking their belongings (including the dowry for the wife); CHIL-DREN went with the father. No official notice was necessary, although, under AUGUSTUS, there had to be seven witnesses to the divorce if ADULTERY was the cause. Marriage *cum manu* would have ended with a formal reversal of the legalities.

The earliest no-fault divorce occurred in 235 BCE when Spurius Carvilius Ruga divorced his wife, although he loved her greatly, for barrenness (Val. Max. 2.1.4; Gellius 10.15). In the late Republic and early empire, divorce was common when political alliances changed (JULIUS CAESAR).

Dogknot (Grk *kunodesmê*), the Greek and Etruscan method of using a leather thong to tie the foreskin closed over the penis (Photius s.v.; Pollux 2.171; Hesychius s.v.), to double the penis back onto itself (**79**), or to tie the penis vertically to a thong about the waist (**196**). The procedure was practiced in the GYMNASIUM (**87, 126**), perhaps to protect the penis during exercise, to prevent the penis from getting an erection, or to preserve a reputation for ABSTINENCE. But in some representations of the dogknot an erection would have been expected (**73, 125, 157**), including PAN's (**176 [pl. 15]**).

See also: BODY MODIFICATION

Keuls 1985: 68–70; Sweet 1985; Scanlon 2002: 234–6.

Domitian (51–96 CE), Titus Flavius, emperor (81–96). In 83 and 90 Domitian had four VESTAL VIRGINS executed for immorality. His rule became more tyrann-

ical until his wife Domitia had him stabbed in the groin (cf. CALIGULA).

Domitian forbade senators from DANCING and acting in the THEATER, and banished actors from the public stage (they could act in private). He also forbade the castration of males (BODY MODIFICATION) and lowered the price of eunuch-slaves to make the practice less lucrative. Perhaps because he did not approve of circumcision, he taxed Jews severely.

Domitian was said to have promised Clodius Pollio a "night," but his SEXUAL ACTIVITY otherwise was with WOMEN. He seduced many, including Longina, wife of Aelius Lamia, who, when someone praised his singing voice, replied "I practice ABSTINENCE." Domitian DIVORCED his wife Domitia for ADULTERY with the pantomime Paris, but took her back and had a pupil of Paris killed by cauterizing his genitals or anus (cf. the death of Edward II). Apparently he liked rough sex, for he called it "bed-wrestling" (*klinopálê*).

Suetonius, *Domitian.*

Dwarves, small people, unusually proportioned, and sometimes DEFORMED. Romans intentionally created dwarves (*nanni*) by confining CHILDREN in small cages (Ps.-Longinus, *De subliminibus* 44.5; Seneca, *Controv.* 10.40; cf. Victor Hugo, *By Order of the King*, 2nd introduction). Dwarves were thought sexually humorous (**212**) and appropriate for oral sex (Martial 9.7.1–10, 11.61.1–14; Suetonius, *Tiberius* 44). A man could have a fetish for a dwarf woman (Hesychius s.v. nannaristes).

Krenkel 1981.

E

Effeminacy, a set of denigrated behaviors in MEN that are thought appropriate in WOMEN. The charge of effeminacy is usually the core of INVECTIVE. Philip II of Macedon apparently encouraged his effeminate friends (Athenaeus 6.260e–261a, here abridged): "What shameless thing did they not do? Did not adult men shave and depilate themselves, and, even the bearded, did they not consort with each other? There were even two or three male PROSTITUTES (*hetairouménous*), and these made their services available."

HAIR was a special locus for effeminacy (OVID, *Ars Am.* 3.433–6). JULIUS CAESAR (Suetonius 45.2) was deemed "overnice" in regards to his body, carefully trimmed, shaved, his superfluous hair plucked, his bald spot combed over and covered by his laurel wreath. AUGUSTUS (Suetonius 68) reportedly singed his leg hair to make it softer. NERO (Suetonius 51) arranged his hair in tiers of curls, letting it grow long for his trips to Greece. And Otho (Suetonius 12) had his superfluous hair plucked out, wore a wig, shaved every day, and smeared his face with moist bread.

Effeminate pathics, CINAEDI, were abhorred (cf. Plutarch, *Erotikos* 768e); they were known for having a soft, feminine appearance and comportment (Plautus, *Aul.* 422; Catullus 25; PRIAPEA 64.1). In Latin, these men are often called *molles mares* ("soft males"), somewhat close to the American "pansy"; thus, Crispa is

maligned as being penetrated in both cavities (*molitur per utramque cavernam*, Ausonius 79.7). Scipio libels Publius Sulpicius Galus (Gellius 6.12.3–4):

> He, who, day in day out, anoints himself and is concerned with his make-up in front of a mirror, who shaves his eyebrows, who has his beard plucked and hangs around among depilated women; he is not only lusting after wine, but also after males.
>
> (cf. Juvenal 2)

It was thought that men who spent too much time around women became literally feminized. The Athenian Ktesippos was proverbial for having sold his father's war monument to pay his PROSTITUTES: "brilliant among the women but not the men" (Athenaeus 4.166a quoting Timokles). A Republican orator described an effeminate young man "walking limply, like a rather soft woman in order to please women" (*incedentem ut feminis placeat femina mollius*, Seneca, *Controv.* 2.1.6).

But effeminacy was the mark of urbanity. Lucius Torquatus ridiculed the orator Hortensius for being a *gesticularium*, a gesticulator, and called him "Dionysia," the name of a popular *saltaricula* (female dancer). Hortensius replied calmly in an effeminate voice (*voce molli atque*

demissa) that he would "rather be Dionysia than you, Torquatus, who are uncul-
tured, uncharming, and un-Dionysus-like
(i.e. dull)" (*Dionysia malo equidem esse
quam quod tu, Torquate, ámousos, ana-
phróditos, aprosdiónusos*, Gellius 1.5.2–3;
Williams 1999: 155–7).

Eileithyia, usually a pair of goddesses of
childbirth, daughters of ZEUS and HERA,
partners of ARTEMIS. They are attested in
Linear B. They either were born at Amni-
sos in Crete (Apollodorus 1.2.6) or came
with the Hypoboreans to Delos (Pausanias 1.18.5). In vase painting they are
often shown flanking the figure giving
BIRTH (25).

See also: JUNO

Ekdysia, a festival at Phaistos in honor of
LETO, who changed a maiden, "LEUKIPPOS
2" (reared as a boy) into a youth. It was
"customary before MARRIAGE to sleep
next to the statue of Leukippos" (Antoninus Liberalis 17). The festival was probably for youths about to become citizens
(AGE GRADES). The verb *ekdúô* (to un-
dress) describes taking the oath of CITI-
ZENSHIP in several Cretan cities; at Lyttos
this festival took place in September/
October (cf. OSCHOPHORIA) and had another name, the Periblemaia, "putting
clothes on." Becoming a citizen apparently involved changing clothes, perhaps
from those of youth to the clothes of a
citizen (cf. the Roman custom of assum-
ing the *toga virilis*), or shedding feminine
clothes that had been assumed for the
occasion.

See also: TRANSVESTISM

Leitao 1995.

Elagabalus (203–22 CE), emperor Marcus
Aurelius Antoninus Bassianus (218–22
CE). Before he became emperor he was
priest of Helios-Baal at Emesa in Syria,
whence comes his nickname "Heliogaba-

lus." After Macrinus had Caracalla assassinated (217), Elagabalus's mother
claimed that Caracalla was his father; the
soldiers of the local legion saluted him
emperor and killed Macrinus near Antioch. Elagabalus arrived in Rome the next
year (219).

Elagabalus first MARRIED Cornelia
Paula, but DIVORCED her soon after; he
then married a VESTAL VIRGIN, Aquilia
Severa (221). He adopted his cousin
Alexienus and gave him control of admin-
istration, but soon regretted this decision,
and plotted to have him killed. The
soldiers, however, stood by Alexienus and
assassinated Elagabalus (222); Alexienus
then ascended the throne as Alexander
Severus. His historians say that Elagabalus was killed in a latrine (BROTHELS); his
corpse was hurled into the Tiber.

Elagabalus is reported to have had
committed many sexual crimes: he
had promiscuous sex with MEN; never
had intercourse with the same WOMAN
twice except with his wives; searched the
empire for men with large genitals (*ono-
beli*, like an ass; *vassati*, hung); opened
brothels in his house for his friends (cf.
CALIGULA); ordered that real ADULTERY be
represented on the stage (cf. NERO); gave
money to PROSTITUTES, both male and
female, appearing to each in their own
COSTUME (to women with protruding
bosom, to males like a boy exposed for
anal penetration); opened the BATHS to
both men and women simultaneously;
bathed in the public baths with the
women, and would depilate himself with
them; would shave the pubic HAIR of his
lovers with his own razor; went out with
painted eyes and rouged cheeks; prostituted himself; and asked physicians to
construct a vagina in his body.

Elagabalus also raised common men to
high rank because of their large genitals.
He loved a certain Hierokles so much, he
was said to have kissed his anus, and to
have staged his own adulterous affairs so
Hierokles would beat him. Elagabalus
was also married as a wife (NERO) to

Aurelius Zoticus, an ATHLETE from Smyrna; Hierokles, jealous of this man, administered a potion to make him IMPOTENT. After an embarassing night, Zoticus fled Rome, and this saved his life; Hierokles did not survive Elagabalus's assassination.

Aelius Lampridius, *Elagabalus*; Cass. Dio. 80; Herodian 5.

Eos, predatory goddess of dawn. She abducts the TROJAN prince Tithonos (VIOLENCE), and bears him Memnon. Tithonos begs ZEUS for immortality so he can live with her, but he forgets to ask for eternal youth; he shrivels up like a cicada and she locks him in a room and throws away the key. Eos abducts Kephalos, the son of HERMES, and she bears him Phaêthon. Kephalos had also once married Procris daughter of Erechtheus; he suspects her of ADULTERY and accidentally kills her when she spies on him hunting (Ovid, *Met.* 7.688a–865). And Eos abducts Orion as he goes hunting; for his acquiescence ARTEMIS kills him.

Eros/Cupid, the son of APHRODITE (Plutarch, *Erotikos* 756e–f; contrast Hesiod, *Theogony* 120; Plato, *Symp.* 178b; Plutarch, *Erotikos* 765e quoting Alcaeus). Eros comes in several aspects, Heavenly (Ouranios) and Common (Pandemos; Plutarch, *Erotikos* 764b), Eros and ANTEROS (LOVE returned) with MEN (Peitho with WOMEN), Eros and Philia (friendship) with men and youths, and Pothos (yearning for the attainable) and Himeros (for the unattainable).

A famous shrine to Eros was at Thespiai (Scanlon 2002: 264–6), which held the Erotidaia games (ATHLETICS; Athenaeus 13.561e; scholion to Pindar, *Ol.* 7.154c). The sanctuary had both a cult image (a rough stone) and a statue of Eros that PRAXITELES sculpted (Cicero, *Verr.* 2.4.135; Plutarch, *Erotikos* 748a; cf. Schauenburg 1981); it was stolen by CALIGULA (Pausanias 9.27.3; Pfrommer 1980).

Another shrine was at the Athens Academy. PEISISTRATOS set up a statue to Eros and his eromenos Kharmos later set up the inscribed altar (Scanlon 2002: 89; Athenaeus 13.609d; Friedländer and Hoffleit 1948: 108–9, no. 112).

In literature, Eros is a violent god who loosens the limbs (Sappho's *lysimelos*, PMG 130; cf. Homer, *Iliad* 3.442, 14.295; *Odyssey* 18.212), is disarming (cf. Sappho's "crafty Eros," PMG 130), arrives suddenly, brings torments (Alcman 36 Diehl; ANACREON fr. 45), and, shooting people with his bow and arrow (Euripides, *Iph. Aul.* 548–9), drives people to passion (Paris and HELEN).

As a god of maturation, Eros is associated with GYMNASIA. Athenian vase paintings depict him there and with ATHLETES (**72**); terms like "struggling" or "wrestling with Eros" allude to his agonistic nature (Anacreon fr. 369 Diehl; Lucian, *Dial. deor.* 7.3; cf. Aristophanes, *Peace* 894–905, quoted in SEXUAL POSITIONS). The SACRED BAND at Thebes and SPARTAN warriors worshipped him (Athenaeus 13.561, 602).

Eros is the god most frequently depicted (cf. **7**, **19**, **161**; Greifenhagen 1957; Shapiro 1992; Albert 1997). By the late fifth century, Eros supports romantic love (**85**), "expressing both the emotion felt by the bride and the feeling she engenders in the groom" (Sutton 1992: 26–27). By the Hellenistic period Eros is duplicated as *erótes* to mimic human activity. On the impressed sealings from Delos (second century BCE; Stampoulides 1992) Eros is armed like Ares, has labors like HERAKLES, is punished, plays MUSICAL instruments, and is an athlete, a charioteer, and a horse rider. In Roman art Cupid and cupids (*amorini*) abound (**305 [pl. 33], 249, 238 [pl. 34], 309**); the Cupid-seller is known in at least three works and may refer to a popular story (**313, 342, 233**).

In spite of the plethora of guises, Eros/Cupid has no mythology until the story of

"Cupid and PSYCHE" (end of the fourth century BCE; 308).

Ethnicity Bizarre sexual behavior is attributed to people close by (INVECTIVE) as well as far removed (cf. Romm 1994), where stories could not be gainsaid (cf. the Greek saying, *tó pórrô dusélenkton*).

Aiskhropoioi

A people or sect in India known as "Perverts." The term is commonly used of FELLATORS, but they also pierced the penis (BODY MODIFICATION) and filled the hole with objects that increased its size and its ability to stimulate.

Campanians

Campanians were fond of oral sex; the disease *campanus morbus*, a skin condition of the face, was thought to have been a SEXUALLY TRANSMITTED DISEASE.

Egyptians

They CIRCUMCISED MALES (**120**) and females (BODY MODIFICATION; Reinhold 1980).

Etruscans

They "dine in company with their women, lying back under the same CLOAK" (Athenaeus 1.23d quoting Aristotle; **194 [pl. 1]**). Etruscan women were also powerful (Bonfante 1994). Etruscan male PROSTITUTES were common (Plautus, *Cist.* 562–3, *Curculio* 481; Seneca, *Ep.* 114.4; **198, 204**).

Lesbians

Lesbian women might also be LESBIANS (SAPPHO). To have sex "Lesbian-style" (*lesbiázein*), however, was to FELLATE (Aristophanes, *Frogs* 1308, *Wasps* 1346).

Libyans

Nasamone wives were all used in common; when a man wanted a woman, he set up a pole in front of her house (Herodotus 4.172). Gindane women wore leather bands around their ankles corresponding to the number of their lovers (4.176). The Machlyes and Auses did not practice marriage, but the women were common to all; intercourse was casual, like animals; the men met every three months to determine whom each child most resembled (4.180; cf. AMAZONS).

Lydians

Lydian men rape the wives and daughters of other men (Athenaeus 12.515f). Lydian women prostitute themselves to earn the money for their dowries, and they choose their own husbands (Herodotus 1.93).

Negroes

Negroes in Athenian art are depicted in two main ways: men stand by palm trees, perhaps guarding incense trees (Group of the Negro Alabastra, ARV^2 267–9, 1641); and plastic drinking mugs take the shape of, on one side, a negro male head and, frequently, a female head on the other side (ARV^2 1529–52 *passim*); it is possible that the mugs refer to them as immoderate drinkers (Davidson 1998). In Roman art, negro men have large penises and erections (**231, 234 [pl. 14]**; Clarke 1998: 120–9). A Knidian jug associates a negro's head and three couples in vaginal frontal intercourse (**276**). A graffito from POMPEII was written by a woman: "White women have taught me to avoid/hate black women; but I am able, and not unwillingly, to love them" (*CIL* 4.1512–47; cf. OVID, *Amores* 3.11.35; Vergil, *Ecl.* 2.56). One of the ways a man could convince himself to break off with a female lover is, if she is dark, to think of her as a negro (*si fusca est nigra vocetur*;

OVID, *Rem. Am.* 327). Greeks and Romans found negro pygmies humorous (**214, 215**; Clarke 2001).

Oscans

The Oscans of Capua contributed the word *obscenus* (Horace, *Sat.* 1.5.62: *qui Osci dicebantur, ore inmundi habiti sunt, unde etiam 'obscenos' dictos putant, quasi 'Oscenos'*); probably they performed FELLATIO (cf. Festus 31; Horace, *Sat.* 1.5.54).

Phoenicians

To perform cunnilingus was to have sex "Phoenician style" (*phoinikízein*, Hesychius s.v. *skêma aphrodisiakón*; Lucian, *Apophras* 28; *Greek Anth.* 11.329.1–4), perhaps during MENSTRUATION (cf. Galen 12.249 Kühn; Aristophanes, *Peace* 883–5).

Satyr-islanders

The men in these mythical islands in the Atlantic had tails like SATYRS and, since they would attack the women and not men, sailors would throw them foreign women (Pausanias 1.23.5–6).

Siphnians

They were known for anal intercourse (Photios s.v. *siphniázein*).

Scythians

They lived in a wet and chilly climate, where the land itself was feminine (*tethelusménoi*), and the men had large, fleshy woman-like BODIES (Hippocrates, *Aer.* 15.17). All Scythian wives are used promiscuously. Among the Massagetae of Sogdiana, if a man wants a woman, he hangs his quiver before her wagon and goes in to have her (Herodotus 1.216).

Tarentines

The Tarentines rape the wives and daughters of other men (Athenaeus 12.522d–e).

Hall 1989; Miller 1997.

Eunuchs. Castrated MEN, their testicles and sometimes penises removed. Eunuchs were suitable as sexual pathics (CINAEDI), as loyal servants, and as entertainers. There were several Greek and Latin words for castrated men: *bagoas* (from the Persian), *eunuchi*, and *spadones* are generic terms; *castrati* have their penis and testicles removed; *thlibiae* have their testicles extracted, and *thliasiae* have them crushed.

Eunuch priests are castrated to be pure: Semites of Hierapolis-Bambyce, the priests (Megabyzi) of ARTEMIS at Ephesus (Strabo 14.23), the priests of Hekate at Lagina (Butler 1998), and the Galli of CYBELE. Martial characterizes the Gallus Baeticus as "still a male with your mouth" (3.81.1–6).

SEMIRAMIS was reported to be the first to have eunuch slaves (Claudian, *In Eutrop.* 1.339; Ammianus 14.6). Babylon had to send the Persian king 500 eunuch youths yearly (Herodotus 3.92). ALEXANDER enjoyed sex with Darius's eunuch (Curtius 6.53, 10.1.25). From the sixth century BCE eunuchs were common in Greece. Periander seized 300 Corcyrean boys and shipped them to Lydia to be castrated. From the first century Rome also had eunuchs imported from Syria and Egypt (Cicero, *De or.* 70.232) and Delos (PETRONIUS 23).

See also: BODY MODIFICATION

Euripides (ca. 485–07/06 BCE), Athenian playwright of some ninety plays, of which nineteen survive. Several plays, both surviving and lost, turn upon sexual themes. The *Aeolus* (date unknown) concerns INCEST, *Alkestis* (438) a wife's willingness to die for one's husband, *Cretan Women* (438) BESTIALITY between a woman and a bull, MEDEA (431) jealousy, *Hippolytos* (428) a stepmother's passion for her chaste stepson, *Electra* (415?) the repressed sexuality of the heroine, *Iphigenia at Aulis* her upcoming MARRIAGE/death, *Chrysippus* (409?) LAIOS's passion for the boy, and the *Bacchae* (408–6) the TRANSVESTISM and voyeurism of Pentheus. His plays also often take WOMEN as central characters.

Europa, daughter of Agenor of Tyre, is abducted by ZEUS in the shape of a white bull which comes swimming to her while she is playing on the shore. She climbs on his back and he takes her swimming across the sea to Crete (WATER). There Europa bears him two sons, MINOS and Rhadymanthus, and in later accounts Sarpedon. After her death Europa was worshipped as the handmaid of Zeus at the Hellotia in Corinth and Crete. In art, the abduction of Europa is occasionally portrayed (**62**).

See also: BESTIALITY

Ovid, *Met.* 2.844–75.

F

Faunus, a Latin divinity. Faunus acts much like Pan (not goat-like but wearing a goatskin). In Augustan literature, Faunus protects fields and livestock, appears to WOMEN in dreams, and can produce terror; like PRIAPUS, he can bring harm and induce strong erotic DESIRE. In mythology, Faunus turns himself into a snake and has intercourse with his daughter (INCEST; Macríbrus, *Sat.*1.12.24; cf. Lactantius 1.22.9 ff.; Servius 7.47 and 8.314).

Fellatio/Irrumatio, oral stimulation of the penis. The Greek terms include "lick" (*laikázein*; Martial 11.58.12), "to do something shameful" (*aiskhropoieín*), "to shut a person up" (*arrhetopoieín*); and *lesbiázein* (to do it Lesbos-style [ETHNICITY]).

In Latin *fellatio* conveys the action of the mouth, while *irrumatio* conveys the action of the penis, thus a type of rape or face-fucking (CINAEDUS). To Martial irrumatio is virile (2.82, 2.83, 4.17, 4.50, 7.55), and a woman fellatrix has a hot mouth (*bucca calda*; 2.28.4). Latin also had vaguer terms: "to lick" (*lambere*, Martial 9.27.14), "to offer the mouth" (*os praebere*), "to offer head" (*caput praebere*; cf. *capiti non parcere*, Cicero, *Har. Resp.* 27.59), and "to devour a man's middle" (Catullus 80.6).

Fellatio was thought unclean (Martial 9.63; cf. CUNNILINGUS), more so for MEN than for WOMEN (Martial 2.50). The mouth was defiled (*os impure*), lips white (Catullus 80); the breath was so bad (Martial 10.22, 12.55), that smelly food could not disguise it (Martial 3.77.5–10). Cicero charges ANTONY with an *incesto ore* ("unchaste mouth," *Phil.* 2.2.5) and Q. Apronius with bad breath (*Verr.* 2.3.9, 23; INVECTIVE). KISSING a fellator is to be avoided (cf. Catullus 79.4; Martial 6.55.5, 6.66.1–9, 12.85).

Good fellators are congratulated at POMPEII: for example, "Myrtis, you suck well" (*Murtis bene felas*; CIL 4.2273 + p. 216; Varone 2001a: 77) and "Secundus is an excellent fellator" (*Secundus felator rarus*, CIL 4.9027; Varone 2001a: 140). Chrysippos raises fellatio to divine heights: in a painting depicting HERA fellating ZEUS, "Hera stands for matter, that receives seminal *logoi* (principles) from the deity" (Origen, *Cels.* 4.48; Theophilus, *Ad Autolycum* 3.3 and 8).

Fellatio could substitute for vaginal intercourse, preserving VIRGINITY (cf. Martial 4.84.1–4) and acting as a CONTRACEPTIVE. It might not be considered "sex" at all: "She's chaste a thousand times. She doesn't put out, but she doesn't deny men anything either" (Martial 4.71.5–6). Fellatio was considered an appropriate activity for OLD WOMEN:

"even an old wife, Simylos, sucks" (*Greek Anth.* 5.38 [37]; cf. Horace, *Epod.* 8; Martial 4.50.2).

There are few depictions of fellatio, all HETEROEROTICISM: terracottas (**221**); metal tokens (**275**); wall paintings (**291** III and VII, **311**; cf. Parrhasius's painting, "ATALANTA fellating Meleager," SEX IN ART).

Catullus refers to auto-fellatio: "to eat himself with his head lowered" (*demisso capiti se ipse vorare*, 88.8). Gymnastic entertainers like pantomimes might have employed it. Athenaeus (14.622a–d) quotes the Hellenistic writer Semos (fl. 200 BCE) about erotic performers, including *autokábdaloi*, probably "self-fellators" (SEXUAL POSITIONS).

Greek ASTROLOGICAL conceits called the palate "heaven" (*ouranós*; Athenaeus 8.344b; *Greek Anth.* 5 104.3–4; cf. *Greek Anth.* 11.328.9) and both the star Sirius and the penis a "dog" (*kúôn*; cf. DOG-KNOT). Thus, Menophila's "heaven has the Dog as well as the Twins (the testicles)" (*Greek Anth.* 5.105; cf. PRIAPEA 62).

Krenkel 1981.

Fertility, the capability for a man and woman to conceive a child. MEN often assumed that since intercourse could result in CONCEPTION, every act of intercourse should do so, unless the woman was deliberately using CONTRACEPTIVES or having ABORTIONS. WOMEN, however, who did not conceive readily, might resort to MAGIC and divine propitiation (cf. Euripides, *Ion*); at the Asklepieion at Epidaurus, women consulted about reproductive problems and dedicated votives (Hanson 1992: n. 149). Women would also offer keys (PREGNANCY) and tie small pieces of cloth on the branches of special bushes (this last is still practiced; I have seen three such bushes). FLAGELLATION was also thought to induce fertility.

See also: APHRODISIACS; BIRTH; CHILDREN; IMPOTENCY; MEDICINE; STERILITY

Richlin 1997: 239–40.

Flagellation, whipping or caning the body for sexual pleasure. Flagellation is rare (Johns 1982: 114; but **199**, VILLA OF THE MYSTERIES), but SANDAL-slapping was common. Unsuccessful Arcadian hunters flogged a statue of Pan to restore his powers of FERTILITY (Theocritus 7.106–8). And during the Lupercalia, young men ran around the base of the Palatine, whipping women who wished to CONCEIVE.

Food and Drink. Different foods, both PLANTS and ANIMALS, could cause (bulbs and crayfish) or reduce (cucumber) sexual DESIRE (APHRODISIACS). Matro called the anchovy the hetaira of Triton, and the eel the white-armed goddess that had lain with ZEUS (Athenaeus 4.135a–c). Cookies in the shape of genitals were made by Greek women during the ADONIA and ANTHESTERIA, and by Romans (Martial 14.69).

Wine was a common aphrodisiac, but too much could dull men's ability to perform (Shakespeare, *Macbeth* 2.3), cause them "to kiss women no one would want to" (Aristotle, *Problems* 30; cf. OVID, *Rem. Am.* 806–10), even to do something "shameful" (CUNNILINGUS; FELLATIO; Aristotle, *Problems* 10.3; Apuleius, *Met.* 2.11.2; Juvenal 6.300–1). Drinking cups in the shape of a PHALLUS, thus directly associating wine and sex, were made by both Greeks and Romans (**49, 55, 90, 181 [pl. 21]**; cf. Iuvenal 2.95; COMMODUS).

Henry 1992.

Frottage, rubbing the body for sexual pleasure. Rubbing the feet was pleasureable (Athenaeus 12.553a–c quoting Antiphanes; cf. Pliny, *HN* 13.22; PETRONIUS 70.8; BODY PARTS). Men who are born under the conjunction of Venus, Mercury and Saturn like to frot to ORGASM be-tween women's breasts (Manetho 4.312; **262**).

Krenkel 1981.

G

Ganymede, son of Tros (or Laomedon) of TROY. ZEUS fell in LOVE with him (Homer, *Iliad* 22.230–5) and, either in his own shape (**22?**) or as an eagle (**235 [pl. 27]**; OVID, *Met.* 10.150–61), swooped him up to Olympus to be his eromenos cupbearer (PAIDERASTIA; Apollodorus 3.12.2; Pausanias 5.24.5; THEOGNIS 1345–8). His name in Etruscan, "Catmite," becomes the Latin *catamitus* and the English "catamite."

Gnathaina and Gnathainion, two famous, high-priced hetairai (PROSTITUTES), grandmother and granddaughter, apparently early to mid-third century BCE. Gnathaina charged 100 drachmes for herself but 500 for her granddaughter, and she wrote a poem in 323 lines, a Rules of Conduct (*nómos sussitikós*) for her clients (Athenaeus 13.581c, 584c, 585b).

The comic poet Diphilus talked about her cold wine cellar; she kept it cold, she said, by stoking it with his plays (Athenaeus 13.579e–580c). When a youth from the Pontus (land of Skythians and rustics; ETHNICITY) was having sex with Gnaethaena, he asked for her ass, presumably for "a tergo" anal intercourse; she replied, "you ask me for my ass when you should be driving pigs to pasture!" (*hús*, slang for cunt; Athenaeus 13.580f; ANIMALS). When she was OLD Gnaethaena asked an adolescent butcher,

"how do you weigh (*hístes*) your meat" (the verb also means to stand); he replies, "bent over (*kúbda*) for three obols" (SEXUAL POSITIONS).

Of Gnathainion, it was said that she had equestrian sex with a coppersmith: "I didn't want to embrace a man so covered in soot, but for a lot of gold I obliged to take in only what stuck out farthest from his body" (Athenaeus 13.581e–f).

Davidson 1998.

Gods and Goddesses Few sexual encounters between the gods themselves formed themes in literature and art. HERA seduces ZEUS (Homer, *Iliad Il.* 14.294); Parrhasius painted a picture of her FELLATING him; and they had anal intercourse (Origen, *Cels.* 4.48). HEPHAESTUS has an ORGASM on ATHENA's thigh and he catches Ares and APHRODITE having sex (they are often depicted together in Roman wall paintings: **310, 336**).

Male gods (and the female EOS) have sex with mortals (HETEROEROTICISM; LOVES OF THE GODS; PAIDERASTIA).

See also: APOLLO; ARTEMIS; CYBELE; DEMETER; DIONYSUS; EROS; FAUNUS; HERMES; JUNO; POSEIDON; PRIAPUS

Gymnasia, "places to be NUDE" (*gymnós*), buildings for male ATHLETIC and military training. By the fourth century BCE, a portico surrounds an open space with rooms for state-sponsored schools, BATHS, and latrines; racecourses are attached. Protecting gods included EROS for bonding, HERMES as god of transitions (AGE GRADES), and HERAKLES for strength (Athenaeus 13.561d).

The gymnasium was early associated with PAIDERASTIA (Plutarch, *Erotikos* 751f–752a; Cicero, *Tusc.* 4.70; cf. *Greek Anth.* 12.192; THEOGNIS). In Thebes, the gymnasium of IOLAUS, his sanctuary, and tomb, were CRUISING grounds.

SOLON is said to have enacted several LAWS to protect boys in the gymnasium from undesirable men like slaves, freedmen, male PROSTITUTES [*hetaireukótes*], peddlers, drunkards and lunatics (Miller 1991: 126–38; *SEG* 27.261). Gymnasiarchs had to be over forty years old, less likely to molest youths. Although gymnasia had daylight operating times (Aeschines, *In Tim.* 1.10; cf. 1.135; Aristophanes, *Peace* 762–3), cruising could still take place ("in the past," says Just Logic, "boys modestly swept away the marks of their genitals in the sand when they stood up"; Aristophanes, *Clouds* 974–8). ALCIBIADES invited Socrates to exercise with him (Plato, *Symp.* 217b–c).

H

Hadrian, Publius Aelius, philhellenic emperor of Rome (117–38 CE). In 100 he MARRIED Trajan's great-niece Sabina, though he found her disagreeable and made certain they had no children. To celebrate Rome's birthday he designed and dedicated the temple to Venus and Roma in the Roman Forum, 21 April 121.

He met ANTINOOS (246 [pl. 16]), a Bithynian youth of fourteen, during a tour of Asia Minor (probably 124), and kept him with him for the next 5–6 years. On his tour of Egypt and the Levant in 129–30, Hadrian established the colony Aelia Capitolina at Jerusalem, a capitolium on the Temple Mound, and banned circumcision (BODY MODIFICATION); in Egypt, during a boating party on the Nile, Antinoös drowned. Hadrian deified him and founded the city Antinoöpolis in his honor. Sabina died in 136/7, perhaps POISONED, and Hadrian deified her.

Hair grooming, depilation, and shaving, was common throughout antiquity.

Head hair

The Minoans related hair lengths to AGE GRADES (Rehak 1999). Classical youths and maidens cut their hair and dedicated it to HERAKLES (youths) and ARTEMIS (maidens) (Euripides, *Hipp.* 1425–7; Van Straten 1981: 89–90, fig. 29; cf. Pausanias 1.37.3; Theophrastus, *Char.* 21.3; *IG* 12.5.173). In Athens and in SPARTA wives wore their hair short. Athenian men kept their hair short and thus thought Spartan soldiers, who wore it long, EFFEMINATE (Ephraim 1992). Romans also considered long hair unmasculine (Musonius Rufus fr. 21). Bald men could be thought erotic (140), though JULIUS CAESAR apparently did not (Suetonius, *Caesar* 51).

Women's hair styles fluctuate over time, but like COSTUME changes they may parallel economic and political trends (cf. OVID, *Amores* 2.14). For dyeing the hair, henna and *sapo* were used to stain the hair from black to strawberry blond (Ovid, *Ars Am.* 3.137–55, 163–4, 167–8, 245–50; *Amores* 1.14; Pliny *HN* 28.191; cf. Aristophanes, *Eccles.* 735; Martial 8.83.20).

Facial hair

Few Minoan men wore beards (Betts 1981); Mycenaean men and men in classical Greece regularly wore beards (PAIDERASTIA). Roman men shaved, at least until the time of HADRIAN.

Body hair (not head, facial, or pubic hair)

Men's body hair is usually not depicted until the late fifth century BCE (66; but mid-sixth-century *kouroi* from Anavyssos and Merenda [NMA 3851 and 4890] have small dots around the nipples which may represent hair roots). In literature, however, references to chest hair occur early (cf. Homer's "shaggy breasts"). Greek vase painting from the late fifth century and Hellenistic sculpture depict body hair (POLYPHEMUS from Sperlonga); Roman art does not. OVID recommends that women shave their legs (*Ars Am.* 3.194). The Romans had specialists, *alipilarii*, who plucked the hair from the armpits and other parts of the body. And women's body hair is never depicted.

Depilation was considered EFFEMINATE for men (Martial 2.62, 3.74, 6.56, 9.27, 14.205; Tara 1985; CINAEDI). Melted rosin in oil was used to burn off leg hair, and tweezers or specialists (*ustricles*) were used to make BODIES hairless (Suetonius, *Augustus* 68).

Pubic hair

Women could practice pubic depilation ("we pluck and trim our doorways like good spiders; the flies come strolling in," Aristophanes, *Lys.* 150–7; cf. Athenaeus 6.269b–c). One way was to singe the hair with an oil lamp (**70, 115**; cf. **66**). Not all women did this (**163**), however, nor did all men like it (cf. Lucilius, *in bulgam penetrare pilosam*, "to penetrate a hairy bag," 61 Warmington): "a hairy cunt is fucked much better than one which is smooth; it holds in the steam and wants cock" (*futuitur cunnus pilossus multo melliur quam glaber; eadem continet vaporem et eadem vellit mentulam*, POMPEII graffito CIL 4.1830). A young female specialist, *picatrix*, arranged pubic hair.

Greek men may also have singed their pubic hair (ARISTOPHANES, *Thesm.* 279–95, 550–62). Archaic kouroi often display pubic hair either trimmed straight across and shaped into two horizontal clumps (the bronze "Striding God from Artemisium," NMA X 15161; the "Omphalos" Apollo, NMA 45) or trimmed at the top with a three-point ogive or trilobe arch

(Samos Museum 6; "Anavyssos" kouros NMA 3851, painted red; "Aristodikos" NMA 3938).

Ehrhardt 1971; Kilmer 1982; Harrison 1988; David 1992; Levine 1995.

Helen of Troy, daughter of ZEUS and LEDA (or Nemesis), sister of Clytemnestra and CASTOR AND POLLUX, wife of Menelaus of SPARTA. First abducted by THESEUS, he at fifty, she at twelve, and rescued by her brothers; by Menelaus she has a daughter, Hermionê. When Paris of TROY visits Sparta, he abducts her and takes her back to Troy. After the war, Menelaus, intending to kill her, drops his sword at the sight of her breasts (*Little Iliad* fr. 19 EGF) and brings her back to Sparta (*Od.* 4.120–305). The first SEX MANUAL was reputedly written by Helen of Troy's maid, Astyanassa. At Sparta Helen was worshipped as a goddess, and, with Menelaus, from at least the eighth century BCE at the Menelaion, a large altar on the river bluffs east of the city. Theocritus (18.22–5) refers to maidens running a footrace in honor of Helen.

The sixth-century poet Stesichorus reportedly wrote a poem blaming Helen, but went blind until he wrote another in which a phantom (*eídolon*) went to Troy while the gods sent her to Egypt (cf. Herodotus 2.112–20; Euripides, *Helen*). Schoolboys composed defenses of Helen (Gorgias, *Isocrates* 10).

Hephaestus/Vulcan, son of HERA, god of fire and metal working. Upon his BIRTH, Hera throws him out of Olympus because of his DEFORMED feet. When he returns he MARRIES APHRODITE, but catches her having sex with Ares; he throws a net over them and invites the other gods to ridicule the snared couple. He is the father of Erechthonius of Athens by his ORGASM on ATHENA's thigh.

Hera, daughter of Kronos and wife and sister of ZEUS (COSTUME; INCEST). Mentioned in Mycenaean texts, Hera is the major classical female deity, worshipped primarily in Dorian cities (especially Argos, Samos, Olympia [ATHLETICS]). As goddess of MARRIAGE (HIEROS GAMOS; THEOGAMELIA), she was patron of brides and of WOMEN's lives. At Argos, a statue of Hera was bathed every year in the Nauplia spring to restore its VIRGINITY. By Zeus, she is mother to Ares, Hebe, and EILEITHYIA, is sole parent of Typhon and HEPHAESTUS (Hesiod, Theogony 927–8; cf. Pindar, Pyth. 2.42), and she nurses the Hydra and Nemean lion and suckles HERAKLES (BREASTS).

See also: JUNO

Herakles, one of twins, he the son of Alkmenê and ZEUS (CHILDREN). He first MARRIES Megara, but Hera causes him to murder her and their children. He marries again, DEIANEIRA, who mistakenly immolates him. Brought to Olympus, he marries Hêbê. One of his labors was to fetch the belt of Ares from Hippolytê, queen of the AMAZONS. He rapes Augê, priestess of ATHENA Alea at Tegea, and fathers Telephos the founder of Pergamum. Herakles has two eromenoi, Hylas and IOLAUS. While on the Argonaut expedition Hylas fetches WATER and is abducted by nymphs. Because of a misdeed, Zeus or APOLLO has Herakles sold to Omphalê queen of Lydia for several years. He becomes her lover but must wear women's clothing and do women's work (OVID, Heroides 9.53–118; Fasti 2.318–24; Plutarch, Quaest. Graec. 58 = 304cd; TRANSVESTISM). Because of his strength, Herakles is co-patron of GYMNASIA.

Hermaphroditus, the son of HERMES and APHRODITE. The WATER nymph Salmacis near Halicarnassus fell in love with Hermaphroditus, but he rejected her; she prayed to be united with him. When he entered the water to BATHE, she entwined herself around him and they became one (OVID, Met. 4.285–399).

The conventional image of Hermaphroditê assumes a female with male genitals (contrast PRIAPUS, with a male body but often dressed like a woman). Some depictions are straightforward (254, 256), but a famous Hellenistic statue (175 [pls 35, 36]) plays with the viewer expecting a beautiful woman but discovering "she" has male genitals. In Roman paintings satyrs accost Hermaphroditê and recoil in surprise (340; cf. 333).

Scythians robbed the temple of APHRODITE of Ashcalon, and she punished them with androgyny (Herodotus 1.105, 4.67). ARISTOPHANES's myth assumes hermaphrodites. Cults of Hermaphroditê are known in Athens (fourth century BCE), Cos, and elsewhere.

Real hermaphrodites (TRANSSEXUALS) were known from Greece (Phlegon of Tralles, Mirabilia). In Rome, the decemviri ritually killed hermaphrodites from 207 to 92 BCE (Livy 27.11.4; cf. Augustine Trinity 6.8); by Pliny's time, hermaphrodites were thought only to have a physical abnormality (HN 11.262).

Ajootian 1997; Brisson 2002.

Hermes/Mercury, son of ZEUS and Maia, a messenger god. He has three sons, Eudorus, Pan, and HERMAPHRODITUS by APHRODITE. He oversees adolescence (AGE GRADES); he thus is co-patron of the GYMNASIUM and is honored at the boys' festival Hermaia in Athens (ATHLETICS). He and Aphrodite have a sanctuary together on the south slopes of Mt Dikte in Crete (Lempesi 2000–; PAIDERASTIA). As patron of commerce, Mercury is often apotropaically equipped with a large PHALLUS (HERMS) on shop signs (269) and as tintinnabula (258).

Phoebus APOLLO and Mercury dispute the girl Khionê (Ovid, Met. 11.301–7). Mercury causes her to fall asleep and rapes her. At night, Apollo, disguised as an OLD woman, also rapes her (LOVES OF THE GODS; TRANSSEXUALITY). Khionê bears twins (CHILDREN): by Hermes,

Autolycus, a thief, and by Apollo, Philammon, a MUSICIAN.

Herms, tall pillars with male genitals and topped with a head, often of HERMES. As markers of boundaries, they are placed at crossroads and thresholds. Hipparchos introduces them in Athens (Plato, *Hipp.* 228d; Van Straten 1981: 143), where a special group was kept in the Stoa of the Herms at the northwest entrance to the agora (Pausanias 1.24.3). In the night before the departure of the Athenian expedition to Syracuse (mid-June, 415 BCE; ADONIA), these herms were mutilated (ALCIBIADES; Plutarch, *Alc.* 18).

Roman herms had PHALLOI and the bearded head of PRIAPUS or portraits of real people (cf. the herms of Caecilius Jucundus in POMPEII).

Hero and Leander, Hellenistic lovers. Hero was priestess of APHRODITE in Sestos on the European side of the Hellespont. Leander met her at a festival and they fell in love. He swam across the Hellespont from Abydos on the Asiatic side to meet Hero at night; she lit a lamp to guide him, until a storm put it out and he drowned (Vergil, *G.* 3.258–63; OVID, *Heroides* 18–19; Musaeus, *Epyllion*; also Marlowe, *Hero and Leander*). Two paintings at POMPEII (House of the Vettii) depict the story.

Heteroeroticism, the erotic attraction between MEN and WOMEN. Modern scholarship has often discounted ancient heteroerotic DESIRE in favor of males exerting sexual power over social inferiors (including women) and an erotic desire for boys (BOY-LOVE; MALE HOMOSEXUALITY; PAIDERASTIA); but many men in antiquity expressed erotic desire for women (Davidson 1998). By the fourth century BCE such desire was "normal" (SEXUAL ATTITUDES). ARISTOPHANES's myth assumes man-woman desire (**195 [pl. 2]**); Chrysippus calls men who desire only

women *gynaikománes* (Athenaeus 11.464d–e). OVID prefers women (*Amores* 3.2.40; cf. *Ars Am.* 2.683–4); CLAUDIUS was uxorious. Plutarch probably prefers women, and thinks MARRIAGE satisfying (*Erotikos* 766–7).

A few woman poets write of their desire for men (SULPICIA 1; SULPICIA 2; cf. SABINUS AND EMPONA). Women's unrequited love for men was a common theme (Euripides, *Hippolytos*; Ovid, *Met.* 8.45–150). Hedyla, a woman poet, wrote of the love Scylla had for Glaukos (Athenaeus 7.295f–296b), and Myrtis wrote of Ochnê's for Eunostos (Plutarch, *Quaest. Graec.* 40). A POMPEIIAN woman writes, "Victor, take care, for you fuck well" (*CIL* 4.2260+p. 216; Varone 2001a: 83–4).

Hieros Gamos, "sacred wedding," an ancient (Menander fr. 265 Körte) and modern concept of a divine MARRIAGE and its mortal celebration through re-enactment. A Hieros Gamos between ZEUS and HERA was celebrated at Athens (THEOGAMIA; cf. ANTHESTERIA) and Knossos; the Daedala at Plataiai celebrates Zeus's marriage to a log dressed as a bride, but Hera interrupts it.

Hippolytos, son of THESEUS and Hippolytê (or Antiopê), queen of the AMAZONS (Euripides, *Hippolytos*; OVID, *Heroides* 4). After her MARRIAGE to Theseus, Phaedra falls in love with Hippolytos who, preferring to remain a companion of ARTEMIS, spurns her advances. She then hangs herself (WOMEN), leaving a note accusing him of rape. Theseus curses his son, who leaves for Troizene in exile, but POSEIDON sends a bull from the sea to frighten the horses of his chariot and crash it. Hippolytos is killed, and either becomes the constellation Auriga or was removed as Virbius to the sanctuary of Diana at Aricia (Vergil, *Aen.* 7.765–82).

Hippolytos was also worshipped along with APHRODITE on the Athens Acropolis

(Euripides, *Hipp.* 31–3); at Troizene, maidens ready for marriage bewail his death and dedicate their HAIR to him (Pausanias 2.32.1; AGE GRADES).

Homoeroticism, the erotic attraction between members of the same sex, either male-male (MALE HOMOSEXUALITY) or female-female (LESBIANISM). I discuss here the attitudes to homoeroticism (SEXUAL ATTITUDES).

PAIDERASTIA is not mentioned in Homer or Hesiod, although Patroklos and ACHILLES have a strong friendship; it was commonly accepted at least from the beginning of the sixth century BCE until the mid-fourth century. Condemnation of it is only against over-indulgence. Lesbianism is attested in the writings of SAPPHO I (ca. 600 BCE) and is assumed by Plutarch to be like paiderastia in SPARTA (*Lycurgus* 18.9). PLATO's middle dialogues warn that paiderastia should not replace a LOVE of philosophy. His last dialogue, however, declares homoeroticism "contrary to nature" (*pará phúsin*; *Laws* 636b–c, 838e, 839a, 841d; cf. *Phaedrus* 250e–251a), and, for political reasons, AESCHINES agrees (*In Tim.* 185).

In Republican Rome homosexual rape of any freeborn male was against the LAW (Val. Max. 6.1.5, 7, 9–12). Philo, a Hellenized Jew, denounces non-procreative sex and paiderastia for EFFEMINACY (*Special Laws* 1.325, 3.34–6, 113; *On Abraham* 134–7). Plutarch's *Erotikos* argues for and against paiderastia, but eventually prefers HETEROEROTICISM. Musonius Rufus links male homoeroticism to a lack of self-control (fr. 12). Lucian notes a female homoerotic attraction, even though "unnatural" (*Dial. meret.* 5). Maximus of Tyre asks if the love "of the Lesbian [SAPPHO I] could be anything else than Socrates's way of love?, he of men, she of women" (24.7). Artemidorus interprets same-sex acts between men as "according to nature" (*katá phúsin*) but same-sex acts between women as "contrary to nature" (*Oneir.* 1.78 and 1.80).

In the third century CE, Christian writers uniformly condemn non-procreative sex in general, including, therefore, homoeroticism. St Jerome regulates against temptation in his order: "No one should sleep with another. No one should hold another's hand" (*Regulae Sancti Pachomii* 94, rule 104). The edict of Constantius and Constans (342 CE) criminalizes gender inversion ("When a man marries [*nubere*] in the manner of a woman [*muliebre*], or a woman is about to renounce men"); the Theodosian Code (438) agrees. The Justinian codes prescribe death for both men involved in same-sex acts (533) and make "crimes against nature" capital crimes against God and state (538).

See also: BISEXUALITY

Hyakinthos, god of vegetation (and probably adolescence [AGE GRADES]) primarily in Dorian cities. APOLLO kills his eromenos Hyakinthos with a throw of a discus which the jealous Zephyrus blows off course (Euripides, *Helen* 1459–61; Apollodorus 3.116; Lucian, *Dial. deor.* 16.14.2; Philostratus, *Imag.* 1.24; Libanius, *Progymn. narr* 2). An iris springs from his blood (OVID, *Met.* 10.215; 13. 396).

Hyakinthos was worshipped primarily as a bearded god (Pausanias 3.19.3–4) at Amyklai south of SPARTA; there, a three-day festival centered about his tomb. At Knidos, ARTEMIS was worshipped as "Hyakinthotrophus," the rearer of Hyakinthos. In Athenian art, Hyakinthos is a beardless youth (60; cf. 161).

Hymenaeus, late mythological figure connected with MARRIAGE. In SAPPHO's marriage songs, "Hymenaeus" is sung as a refrain. Pindar (fr. 128c. 7–8 Snell-Maehler) tells how Hymenaeus, a groom, dies on the night of his marriage, perhaps a metaphor for the breaking of the hymen (BODIES; BODY PARTS); similarly in Sophocles's *Electra*, Hymen is Electra's destined groom who hangs himself after she hangs herself (WOMEN). In Euripides (*Phaetho* 233–5) he is the son of APHRODITE, and CATULLUS (61) sees him as the god of marriage.

I

Impotency, the inability for men to maintain an erection to ORGASM (STERILITY; Hanson 1992: 46; Hippocrates, *Aphorisms* 5.62–3). The impotent elderly (OLD AGE; but cf. Nestor and Phoenix, Athenaeus 13.556c–d) could perform CUNNILINGUS and FELLATIO ("he cannot get an erection; now he licks," Martial 6.26.1–3; cf. 11.25.1–2).

Cures included APHRODISIACS (cf. PETRONIUS) and homeopathic medicine (one's own rusted blood for Iphiklos, Graves 1960: 1, 234 [§72c]). Theodorus Priscianus (2.11 Rose 133) recommended "pretty girls and boys, and reading NOVELS that lure the mind to sexual pleasures (*ad delicias*)."

See also: CONCEPTION

Krenkel 1981.

Incest, sexual activity between close relatives. In Greece, incest was forbidden between half-siblings born of different mothers (but see CONCEPTION), and between aunts/uncles and their nephews/nieces. Romans forbade incest between siblings and between aunts/uncles and nephews/nieces (Thoas 1980). In myth, incest is not rare: Cinyras and his daughter Myrrha (ADONIS; OVID, *Met.* 10.298 ff.), Thyestes and his daughter Pelopia (ATREUS), and OEDIPUS and his mother Jokasta.

INVECTIVE makes use of incest, especially with sisters (CALIGULA). Cicero was thought to have committed incest with his daughter Tullia. CLAUDIUS, who had illegally married his niece Agrippina minor, forced Torquatus to commit suicide for incest with his sister Iunica Calvina (Seneca, *Apocol.* 8.2–3). NERO was rumored to have had incest with his mother Agrippina minor (Suetonius, *Nero* 28). Important women, too, were charged with incest with their brothers: Elpinikê with Kimon, and CLODIA with Publius Clodius.

The pharaohs of Egypt commonly MARRIED their full sister, and the Ptolemies of Egypt continued this custom (Montserrat 1996, 80–105; Ogden 1999).

Krenkel 1981.

Invective, the practice of libeling persons and races. Sexual invective was routinely applied to important people (Seneca, *Controv.* 1.2.23), as if they were "so powerful that … " they were automatically imagined as trespassing all moral boundaries.

Typical invective included sexual profligacy, INCEST, FELLATIO, CUNNILINGUS, PROSTITUTION, MASTURBATION, EFFEMINACY for MEN and masculine behavior for WOMEN. Stock charges included "unspeakable" crimes (that is, fellatio and/or cunnilingus), using one's "entire body" for sex, and performing cunnilingus on MEN-STRUATING women.

For various sexual charges, see, for example, AUGUSTUS, CALIGULA, COMMO-DUS, JULIUS CAESAR, Marc ANTONY, NERO, Philip II, and the false story about Diony-sios of Syracuse (CYBELE). Cicero charged Publius Clodius Pulcher (CLODIA) with using all parts of his body for sex, prostitution, and incest with his sisters (*Har. Resp.* 27.59; cf. *Cael.* 3.6). With similar crimes Suetonius charges Nero (*Nero* 29), and the *Historia Augusta* Commodus (7.5.11) and ELAGABALUS (17.5.2).

Cicero also charges Sextus Cloelius with cunnilingus on menstruating women (*Dom.* 10.25) and he accuses Q. Apro-nius, Verres's henchman, of having bad breath, the sign of a FELLATOR or CUNNI-LICTOR, *Verr.* 2, 3, 9, 23). Seneca (*Ep.* 87.16) condemns Natalis, "in whose mouth women purged themselves" (cf. his similar charge against Mamercus Ae-milius Scaurus, *Ben.* 4.31.2–5).

Rivals for thrones often charged each other with illegitimacy. So Alexander termed Philip Arrhidaios and Demetrios (son of Philip V) Perseus.

See also: ETHNICITY

Krenkel 1981.

Iolaos, eromenos of HERAKLES, and son of his brother Iphikles. At his tomb and sanctuary at Thebes male lovers ex-changed vows (Pausanias 9.23.1; Plu-tarch, *Mor.* 761d, *Pel.* 18.4; Diodorus Siculus 4.24.4, 4.29.4) and celebrated games in his honor.

Iphis is a girl whom her mother disguises as a boy in order to avoid having her exposed as her father ordered (LEUKIPPOS I). At thirteen "he" is betrothed to and falls in love with Ianthê (LESBIANISM), but as the wedding draws closer, Iphis begins to feel her love is unnatural (*pro-digiosus,* OVID, *Met.* 9.666–797). She then calls out to the gods for help and they transform her into a man to MARRY Ianthê.

See also: TRANSVESTISM; TRANSSEXUALITY

J

Jewelry was worn more by WOMEN than MEN. Bronze Age Aegean women wore large circular earrings, necklaces, hairpins, and sometimes anklets (Younger 1992). Greek and Roman women also wore earrings and necklaces, in addition to armbands and fingerrings.

Women's necklaces were important; Bronze Age women finger them prominently in wall paintings. Polyneikes, son of OEDIPUS, obtains the necklace of Harmonia, daughter of APHRODITE and Ares, in order to bribe Eriphylê to urge her husband Amphiareus the seer to join his expedition against Thebes (cf. LUCIAN, *Dial. meret.* 5).

Men rarely wore jewelry, apart from fingerrings, sealstones, and hairbands. Some sixth-century male sculptures (*kouroi*) wear fillets around their neck; DIONYSUS in the classical period sometimes wears anklets, as do occasional warriors (Ares Borghese, **124**; Palagia 1998: 19). Demetrios Poliorcetes dedicated a pair of anklets at Delos (McCudy 1932).

See also: BODY MODIFICATION; COSTUME; HAIR

Julia maior (39 BCE–14 CE), daughter of AUGUSTUS and Scribonia. Her first husband (in 25), Marcus Claudius Marcellus, son of Augustus's sister Octavia, died in 23. In 21 she married Agrippa (**290**); she bore him three sons, Gaius and Lucius Caesar, and Agrippa Postumus, and two daughters, Agrippina maior and Julia minor. Agrippa died in 12; Julia married TIBERIUS the next year. When he retired from Rome to Rhodes in 6, she stayed behind. In 2 she apparently committed adultery with Iullus Antonius, son of Marc ANTONY (Lacey 1980). Antonius committed suicide, and Augustus banished her from Rome. She died of malnutrition late in 14 CE.

OVID's "Corinna" was said to have been Julia (*Amores* 2.13, 2.17; Sidonius Apollonaris 23.159); and she was said to have been the lover of an Olympic victor, Demosthenes (*Greek Anth.* 6.350; Scanlon 2002: 51, 355 n. 29).

Julius Caesar, Gaius (100–44 BCE), Roman politician, general, and Pontifex Maximus (from 63). At nineteen, Caesar was sent to the court of Nicomedes IV Philopator (king ca. 94–75/4) of Bithynia on a military mission; it was rumored that they were lovers (Plutarch, *Caes.* 1; Cass. Dio. 43.20.2 ff.).

At sixteen Caesar married Cornelia, the daughter of Lucius Cornelius Cinna; she died in 69. He then married Pompeia, granddaughter of Sulla. As the wife of the Pontifex Maximus, she oversaw the Bona Dea festival (to which no man is admitted) in December 62 when Publius Clodius Pulcher (CLODIA), dressed as a woman, attended the festival to win her to his cause (Plutarch, *Caes.* 9–10; Cicero, *Att.* 1.13.3, 16.2.5). Caesar DIVORCED her: "Caesar's wife must be above suspicion."

In 59, Pompey married Julia (age fourteen), Caesar's daughter, and Caesar married Calpurnia, daughter of L. Calpurnius Piso Caesoninus who became consul the next year. In 54, Julia died, but, though the alliance dissolved, Caesar remained married to Calpurnia.

In 48, he pursued Pompey to Egypt where he spent the next six months, putting CLEOPATRA VII on the throne. After he left for Asia Minor, she bore a son, Ptolemy Caesar ("Caesarion"), whom he acknowledged. On 15 March 44, Caesar was assassinated.

Caesar was known to have seduced many women, including queen Eunoê the Moor wife of Bogudes. About his sexual versatility, Curio remarked that he was "every woman's man and every man's woman," a comment also made by Callisthenes about ALCIBIADES. Suetonius describes Caesar as "overnice," carefully trimmed, shaved, his superfluous HAIR plucked, bald spot combed over and covered by his laurel wreath.

Caesar established the *lex Julia triorum liberorum*, whereby citizens who have three or more children receive tax breaks from the state.

Suetonius, *Caesar.*

Juno, Roman goddess of WOMEN, wife of Jupiter (ZEUS). The name "Juno" also stood for the spirit that gives women their power. As Interdux she brings the bride to her new home; as Cinxia she guards the bride's girdle; as Opigena she brings on childbirth (BIRTH); and as Lucina she delivers CHILDREN.

The Sabine women as Roman wives founded the temple to Juno Lucina on the Esquiline where MARRIED women celebrated the Matronalia on 1 March (OVID, *Fasti* 3.167–258; Pliny, *HN* 16.235). Women not PREGNANT wore fresh flowers in their HAIR; pregnant women wore their hair unbound so their womb would be unbound.

See also: EILEITHYIA; HERA

Juvenal (ca. 55/60–128 CE), satirist. SATIRE 2 rails against hypermasculine philosophers who, CINAEDI themselves, preach against them; their "disease" begins with TRANSVESTISM and ends with their MARRYING "husbands." In Satire 6, a wife complains about her husband's boys and mistresses (272–3); and two women go drinking, have equestrian sex (*inque vices equitant*), and then urinate against a statue of *Pudicitia* (Chastity; 311 ff.). In Satire 3.186–8 a man dedicates locks of HAIR from his boyfriend (*amatus*). In Satire 5.56–66 Virro treats his guests to inferior food and service, while an expensive slave boy serves him. In Satire 9 the male PROSTITUTE Naevolus has anal sex with Virro by whose wife he is the father of Virro's legitimized children. In Satire 11, handsome slave boys in the good old days were modest and decent instead of hanging around the BATHS offering themselves for money.

K

Kallisto, an Arcadian nymph. After she becomes PREGNANT by ZEUS disguised as ARTEMIS, Kallisto delivers the boy Arkas and is turned into a bear (or shot) by the goddess (**167, 168**).

See also: ARKTEIA; LESBIANISM; TRANSSEXUALITY

Ovid, *Met.* 2.409–40, 4.217–33, 11.310, 14.654–771; *Fasti* 2.155–92; Apollodorus 3.101; ps.-Eratosthenes, *Catasterismi* 1.1.1–11.

Kalos-names, inscriptions painted on sixth and fifth-century BCE Attic vases that proclaim "So-and-so *kalós*" ("handsome") or, rarely, "So-and-so *kalê*" ("beautiful"). It is uncertain who decided to paint the inscriptions and what they mean. The women named in the *kalê* inscriptions were probably PROSTITUTES, and thus the named youths are probably eromenoi (PAIDERASTIA). The most common kalos-name is Leagros, an aristocrat and eventual general (ca. 525–465).

Davies 1971; Dover 1989, 111–24; Dunn 1998; Robinson and Fluck 1937; Shapiro 1987.

Kissing, a standard greeting among friends in antiquity, and an expression of LOVE. As emperor, Tiberius forbade kissing as a greeting (Suetonius, *Tiberius* 34.2). There was a kissing contest at Thebes (PHILOLAOS), and kissing appears on several Greek vase paintings (**38**), some Hellenistic and Roman terracotta figurines (**180**), and a couple of wall paintings from POMPEII (CUPID AND PSYCHE, **304**; and POLYPHEMUS and GALATEA, **323**).

Konisalos (Greek), the mix of sweat, dust, and oil that a male ATHLETE scrapes off his body after exercise, and the name of a sexual DANCE. The mixture was thought to contain the essence of the athlete's exertions, and it therefore had MAGICAL and MEDICINAL properties (Aristophanes, *Lys.* 918; Galen 12:283 Kühn), including allowing an athlete to ABSTAIN from sex (Sanson 1988: 122–8).

Homer uses the term for the dusty swirl of battle (*Iliad* 3.13); eventually it carries sexual connotations, characterizing a type of PRIAPUS deity (Plato Comicus, *Phaon* 2.31 schol.) and a dance that mimes sexual acts between men (THERA; Hesychius K3521–2; Strabo 13.1.12; cf. Synesius, *Ep.* 32). Timocles (fourth century BCE) wrote a play, "Konisalos."

L

Laios, king of Thebes, father of OEDIPUS. As the first PAIDERAST, Laios abducts Chrysippus, son of PELOPS, and takes him to Thebes (or the Nemean Games). PELOPS's wife Hippodameia kills Chrysippus, but in EURIPIDES's play *Chrysippus*, the boy commits suicide.

Laïs 1 (ca. 422–392BCE), PROSTITUTE of Corinth. Born in Hykkaron, Sicily (near the Palermo airport), Laïs was brought to Corinth at seven years old. She was said to have been the courtesan of ALCIBIADES when quite young (Athenaeus 13.574e). She fell in LOVE with Olympic victor Eubotas of Cyrene (408/7), who AB-STAINED from sex with her but promised to MARRY her after his victory; when he won, he did not want to break his promise to her; so he "had a sculpture of Laïs made, and had it sent back to Cyrene, thus 'favorably' [*khariéntos*] ful-filling his oath" (SEX IN ART; Aelian, *VH* 10.2; Clement of Alexandria, *Stromata* 3.6.50, 4.51.1). The Socratic philosopher Aristippos of Cyrene paid Laïs for two months each year at the Dionysia in Aigina; he "merely possessed her, and was not possessed by her." Her tomb at Kraneion was decorated with the sculp-ture of a lioness attacking a ewe, referring to the SEXUAL POSITION *léaina*, which she favored (SEXUAL ACTIVITIES; scholiast, Aristophanes, *Wealth* 179).

Laïs 2 (fourth century BCE; or fl. 338, Pliny, *HN* 35.79), PROSTITUTE also of Corinth. Apelles was struck by her beauty when she was about twelve years old, and painters painted her breasts. She (or LAÏS 1) was the subject of a scornful play, the *Antilaïs* by Epicrates (first half 3rd cen-tury?). She gave herself freely to Diogenes the Cynic (400–325); she also consorted with Demosthenes (Gellius 1.8). At the end of her life, she fell in LOVE with a certain Pausanias (or Hippolochos, Plu-tarch, *Erotikos* 767f) of Thessaly and WOMEN there beat her to death in a temple to APHRODITE (cf. the death of ORPHEUS); her tomb was near the Peneios river with an epigram attesting to her beauty. A now-lost Roman relief depicting Laïs and Pausanias in bed was once attributed to the sculptor Polykleitos and wielded some influence on Renaissance artists (Bober 1995).

Other stories are linked to a Laïs: no longer beautiful in old age, she became a pimp (Claudian in Eutropius I 90 ff.; p. 77B) and a drunk. Several Hellenistic epigrams work a literary topos (which may have started earlier; cf. **153**), that, now old, she no longer wants to look at herself in a mirror and so dedicates it to Aphrodite (*Greek Anth.* 6.1 by Plato; and 18, 19, 20 by Julianus; Athenaeus 12.544 and 13.570 ff.; Stewart 1995).

Lamps (225–227 [pls 23–25]) of clay, sometimes bronze, from the late Hellenistic period on carry erotic motifs, which cease by the sixth century CE. The motifs either assume a part of the lamp (handle as PHALLUS or vagina) or, more commonly, appear in relief on the central disc. The workshop of Perithoös (fl. third century CE) was popular for its erotic scenes (Parlama and Stampolides 2000: 178).

The erotic images of lamps include phalloi, the rare vagina, couples reclining together, couples KISSING, and EROTES/amorini. The sexual images include sexual intercourse ("a tergo," equestrian, facing) and ORAL-GENITAL stimulation; MASTURBATION and ORGIES are rare (SEXUAL ACTIVITIES). BESTIALITY appears as commonly as oral-genital scenes; aside from LEDA and the Swan, there are several featuring negro pygmies and crocodiles, and horses (or mules) having intercourse with women (Clarke 2001; SEMIRAMIS).

Laws and Regulations

Greek

In Athens (fourth century BCE), a CITIZEN man speaking for the first time in the assembly underwent the *dokimasía*: did he know where the tombs of his ancestors were? Had he squandered his patrimony? Had he been anally penetrated for money? (AESCHINES, *In Tim.* 1.19–32; Dover 1978, 13–109; Winkler 1990: 45–70). Citizens convicted of PROSTITUTION (*hetairêsis*) could be disenfranchised. INCEST was prohibited.

According to one of Draco's laws (621 BCE), a man catching a man in the act of ADULTERY with his WOMEN (wife, daughter, mother, sister, pallaké) could kill him (Lysias, *Eratosthenes*; Demosthenes 23.53); a husband could punish a man convicted of adultery in any way except by dagger (Demosthenes 59.66). Husbands had to DIVORCE adulterous wives. Women adulterers were

barred from public rituals (Aeschines, *In Tim.* 1.183).

The Women's Police (*gynaikonómoi*) regulated women's movements in Athens (*Politics* 1299a, 1300a, 1322b35, 1323a; Timokles 32.3 K-A; Philochorus 103) and elsewhere (Andania, first century BCE: *IG* 5¹.1390.26; SPARTA, third century CE: *IG* 5¹.170; Gambreion: *SIG* 1219.17). The concept may go back to SOLON (Plutarch, *Sol.* 21).

Roman Republic

An early law (*de adtemptata pudicitia*, ca. 200 BCE? cf. Plautus, *Curculio* 35–38 [193 BCE]) prohibited molestation of freeborn women and boys on public highways (Gaius, *Institutes* 3.220–4; Ulpian, *Edicts* paragr. 192; *Digest* 47.10.15.15–23).

Persons of ill repute (*infames*) were forbidden (by the *lex Julia municipalis*, Lewis and Reinhold 1959, 1: 416–20) to address courts on behalf of others: women and sexually penetrated men (*qui corpore suo muliebria passus est*; cf. *Digest* 3.1.1.5).

Stuprum was a crime: a man raping a freeborn Roman male or female (see the comment by the Augustan orator Haterius: "debasement [or, loss of virtue] is a crime [*stuprum*] in the freeborn, a necessity for a SLAVE, and a duty for the freedman" [*inpudicitia in ingenuo crimen est, in servo necessitas, in liberto officium*]; Seneca, *Controv.* 4.10). The earliest instance of criminal *stuprum* occurred in 326: a creditor wanted to have intercourse with a young Roman CITIZEN enslaved for debt; the consuls imprisoned the creditor (Val. Max. 6.1.9; cf. Livy 8.28; Dionysius of Halicarnassus 16.9). Ca. 226, C. Scantinius Capitolinus, a tribune, was indicted for having raped the son of a curule aedile and was fined (Plutarch, *Marc.* 2.1–4; Val. Max. 6.1.7).

The *lex Scantinia* (Lilja 1983: 112–21; Williams 1999: 119–24) might be named for this C. Scantinius Capitolinus, or have been proposed by his relative the pontifex Publius Scantinius (fl. 216 BCE; Livy 23.21) to expiate Capitolinus's crime. Earlier references to the law are vague (Cicero, *Fam.* 8.12 and 14, 50 BCE; *Phil.* 3.6; Suetonius, *Domitian* 8.3). In Juvenal 2.43–8, it definitely has something to do with prohibiting citizens from being penetrated. Ausonius 92 (394 CE) states it also concerned the *semivir*, "semi-man," perhaps a EUNUCH or an EFFEMINATE male. Quintilian (*Institutes* 4.2.69) gives the penalty, 10,000 sesterces.

Augustan Rome

The *lex Julia de adulteriis coercendis* (18 BCE) defined ADULTERY (*adulterium*) as involving a MARRIED woman, and *stuprum* involving a widow or unmarried freeborn woman; by the time of the *Digest* (48.6.3.4 and 5.2), raping any freeborn (boy, man, or woman) was a capital crime. The *lex Julia de maritandis ordinibus* (18 BCE) defined legitimate marriages; established incentives for marrying and begetting CHILDREN; and prohibited members of the senatorial families to marry into the families of freedmen. The *lex Papia Poppaea* (9 CE) exempted men from taxes if, as citizens, they fathered three children, as Italic four, and as provincial five. Freeborn women who had given birth to three children were allowed to inherit after their husband died (*ius trium liberorum*).

Early imperial Rome

DOMITIAN and Nerva forbade castration (Cass. Dio. 67.2.3 and 68.2.4; Suetonius, *Domitian* 7; Martial 6.2); HADRIAN may have forbade circumcision (*Hist. Aug. Hadrian* 14.2; *Digest* 48.8.3.5); Antoninus Pius (135) restored the right of circumcision to Jews but not to converts (*Digest* 48.8.11.1; Smallwood 1959; BODY MODIFICATION).

Third-century Rome

In Rome, male-male sex (*arrhenomixía*) was apparently forbidden by law (Sextus Empiricus, *Outlines of Scepticism* 1.152; early third century CE). Alexander Severus (222–35) taxed male PROSTITUTES (*Hist. Aug. Severus Alex.* 24.1–5, 39.2). Philip the Arab (224–9) forbade male prostitution (*Hist. Aug. Elagabalus* 32.6; Aurelius Victor, *Liber de Caesaribus* 28.6).

Fourth–sixth-century Rome

An edict of Constantius and Constans (342 CE) declares that "When a man marries (*nubere*) in the manner of a woman (*muliebre*), or a woman is about to renounce men," the appropriate laws are reaffirmed (cf. the later Theodosian Code, 438). Valentinian, Arcadius, and Theodosius (390 CE) ordered Orientius, the vicar of Rome, to burn publicly all pathics (Riccobono 1940–3/1992, 2: 556–7; also Theodosian Code 9.7.6); he gave them two months to leave the city. In Gaius, *Institutes* 4.18.4 (published 533; restated in 544, *Digest Novel* 141), the *lex Julia de adulteriis coercendis* makes any sex between men punishable by the death of both. In 538, Justinian decreed (*Novel* 77) that those who commit "crimes against nature" answer both to God and to the law (Procopius, *Anecdota* 11.34–36).

Leda, wife of Tyndareus king of SPARTA. ZEUS in the form of a swan has sex with her (**214**), and she gives birth to HELEN and Pollux from an egg, and, from an almost simultaneous union with Tyndareus, CASTOR and Clytemnestra. The egg was preserved in Sparta (Pausanias 3.16.1).

See also: BESTIALITY; CHILDREN

Lesbianism, WOMEN's erotic attraction to or DESIRES for women. The modern term (from SAPPHO's Lesbos) may be first attested in a tenth-century CE scholion on Clement of Alexandria (Cassio 1983; Hallett 1989; Dover 1989: 183; ANAKREON). In OVID, Heroides 15.199–202, Sappho denies her homoerotic desires for Lesbides (Lesbian women; see LUCIAN). The classical Greek verb lesbiázein ("to do it Lesbos-style") meant to FELLATE (ETHNICITY; SEXUAL ACTIVITIES; Aristophanes, Frogs 1308 and Wasps 1346; RE XII.2: cols. 2100–2).

PLATO coins the unique word hetairístria (Symp. 19e) for a passive lesbian, and from it Pollux 6.188 derives hetairistês for a masculine Lesbian. The common classical word for lesbian, however, in both Greek and Latin, was tribás, from tríbein, to rub, FROT, or MASTURBATE (Martial 7.67, 7.70; Lucian, Amores 28; Phaedrus 4.15; Ptolemy Tetrab. III 18f. 44r 33; Manetho 4.358; Krenkel 1989; Jocelyn 1980).

There is no myth or depiction of a goddess loving a woman (Shapiro 1992: 60), although some male gods assume female shape to seduce women (LOVES OF THE GODS; TRANSSEXUALITY). Depictions that represent female homoeroticism should derive from everyday life, the most explicit being 61 [pl. 10], a woman rubbing the vagina of another; a stele from Thessaly (11) and a vase-painting (73) depict two women who use the MARRIAGE gesture of anakalypsis; and in an ORGY a woman performs CUNNILINGUS on another (291 VII). Depictions of women with DILDOES have been thought to depict lesbians (Licht 1963, ch. 3; Kilmer 1993: 26–30), though this is doubtful (Johns 1982: 102; Rabinowitz 2002).

Other depictions of women's homoerotic desire portray women in scenes which, if they were men, would be considered homoerotic (MALE HOMOSEXUALITY; PAIDERASTIA). Two or more women share a CLOAK; a young woman offers flowers and a leather purse to another (12 [pl. 9]; PROSTITUTION).

The earliest textual references to women's homoerotic desire include SAPPHO's poetry (late seventh century BCE, below), ANAKREON 358 (?), and Alcman's Parthénea, in which maidens express their admiration and love for each other. ARISTOPHANES's myth acknowledges lesbian love. PLATO's late work, Laws 636e, denounces lesbian sex. Nossis (early third century BCE) calls herself another Sappho (Greek Anth. 7.718). Plautus, Truculentus 262, refers to sex between a matron and her female SLAVE. MARTIAL (7.67, 7.70) describes the tribade Philainis who fucks (pedicat) boys and, "with a harder erection than a husband," pounds eleven girls in one day (cf. 1.90; Juvenal 6.311 ff.). Plutarch (Lyc. 18.9) writes that, in SPARTA, "Sexual relations of this type [male PAIDERASTIC] were so highly valued that respectable women (kalás k'agathás) would have love affairs with maidens (parthénôn)." In theory, however, female homoerotic relationships should be different from those between men (Rabinowitz 2002; cf. Mure 1857: 586–7; Myerowitz 1992: 153, 157 n. 18; Vicinus 1994).

The sources written by men consider only the masculine "invert" woman and her unnatural desire (IPHIS AND IANTHE); although "born to be passive" (pati natae), some women "rival men's lust" (Seneca, Ep. 95.20.2; Hallett 1989: 266 and passim). In 36 BCE a man found his wife in bed having sex with another woman, and he killed them both; the lawyers termed the other woman ándra (man) (Plutarch, Ant. 24.5; Strabo 660). The woman whom the mannish woman desires was somewhat invisible, like a youth eromenos. In ARISTOPHANES's Lysistrata (Lys. 83–92), Lysistrata fondles the Spartan woman Lampito, who likens herself to a sacrificial calf, then they fondle silent Boeotian and Corinthian women.

Sappho, however, expresses a tenderness between women (PMG 126: "you enflame gentle companions [hetaíras] in their breast"), a passion (fr. 47, 48), and mutuality (94; Zweig 1992: 89 n. 12). Nossis's poems celebrate the sexuality of women: Polyarkhis dedicates a gold statue to APHRODITE, "having profited by dispensing her own body" (*Greek Anth.* 9.332); and "nothing is sweeter than love. Whom Kypris has not loved does not know what kind of flowers those roses are" (*Greek Anth.* 5.170, a metaphor for the vagina's lips). Similarly, some women used MAGIC to attract women (Faraone 1999: 147–8, SM 42). A woman wrote a hexameter graffito in POMPEII (*CIL* 4.1512–47): "a white woman has taught me to hate black girls, but I will love them even unwillingly. Venus Pompeiana in the flesh wrote this" (*candida me docuit nigras odisse puellas ... sed ... non invitus amabo. Scripsit Venus fisica pompeiana*; cf. Ovid, *Amores* 3.11.35).

Leto, a Titan, the mother of ARTEMIS and APOLLO, whom she delivers on Delos (*Homeric Hymn to Apollo*). Artemis is born first, fully a maiden, and helps her mother deliver Apollo (cf. 8). In Phaistos and Athens she seems to have been the patron goddess of ephebes (AGE GRADES; LEUKIPPOS 1; *IG* 2² 1237.123–5).

Leukippidai, Phoibê and Hilairia, the White-Horse Maidens, daughters of a certain Leukippos. Phoibê was priestess of ATHENA and Hilairia of ARTEMIS, both virgin goddesses. CASTOR AND POLLUX abducted them (**107**) but were pursued by the sisters' fiancés, Lynkeus and Idas, who, along with Castor, were killed. Phoibê and Hilairia were granted immortality along with Castor and Pollux.

In SPARTA, the *thiasos* (religious organization), "The Daughters of Leukippos," organized a footrace for maidens in honor of DIONYSUS, and they wove his robe.

Leukippos 1 A Cretan maiden turned into a youth by LETO. Galateia married Lampros of Phaistos and became PREGNANT; Lampros ordered his wife to expose the child if it were a girl. During his absence

Galateia bore a daughter but told her husband that she had delivered a son, named Leukippos, and kept the child's true sex a secret. When the girl matured, Galateia prayed to Leto to change her daughter into a son and Leto did. Her festival is called the EKDYSIA. In OVID'S version (*Met.* 9.731–5, 762–3), the mother appeals to Leto because the father was arranging a MARRIAGE between Leukippos and a young woman Ianthê (IPHIS), whom Leukippos as a girl found attractive (LESBIANISM).

See also: AGE-GRADES; TRANSSEXUALITY; TRANSVESTISM

Antoninus Liberalis 17; Leitao 1995.

Leukippos 2 Son of Oinomaos and brother to Hippodameia (PELOPS). Leukippos fell in LOVE with DAPHNE, but she shunned men to remain a companion of ARTEMIS. Leukippos therefore put on women's clothes to join her company (TRANSVESTISM). One day, Daphnê went bathing with her girl comrades, but Leukippos was reluctant to strip, so they undressed him, saw that he was a man and killed him (Pausanias 8.20.2–4; OVID, *Met.* 1.462–567). As a story about AGE-GRADES, "His was a failed initiation" (Leitao 1995: 148).

Leukippos 3 Son of Xanthios of Lycia. APHRODITE causes him to fall in LOVE with his sister with his mother's help (INCEST). But the girl's father and her fiancé wait outside the chamber to catch the man seducing the girl. She hears them, runs out, and they kill her; her screams bring Leukippos out of the chamber and he kills his father. He is driven into exile and goes to Phaistos (LEUKIPPOS 1; Parthenius, *Amat. Narr.* 5).

Livia Drusilla (58 BCE–29 CE), wife of Octavian-AUGUSTUS and mother of emperor TIBERIUS by a prior MARRIAGE. She had a prominent role in politics, which earned her enmity; she was reportedly complicit in the deaths of several members of the family in order to ensure her son's ascension. Horace praises her as a chaste wife (*Carm.* 3.14.5). CALIGULA executed her will, calling her an "Odysseus in a gown" (*Ulixes stolatus*); and CLAUDIUS deified her.

Once she happened upon a group of NUDE prisoners about to be executed; when their guard asked her forgiveness, she replied that she had just thought them statues, which saved their lives (Cass. Dio. 58.2.4). OVID generalizes (*Tristia* 2.308–14), that "stern-browed matrons" often see naked women ready for sex and VESTAL VIRGINS see PROSTITUTES' bodies for sale. Proper women are expected to "turn a blind eye."

Love In early antiquity people felt love (EROS), but they did not base long-term partnerships on it; love was more accepted as a passion outside MARRIAGE, especially between males (BOY-LOVE; PAIDERASTIA; Plutarch, *Erotikos*). In the late fifth century BCE, romantic love starts becoming important; in fourth-century plays, its conflict with social, economic, and political concerns is a major aspect of plot (THEATER); and by the Hellenistic period, and certainly in the Roman period, some couples arrange their own long-term relationships based, at least partially, on love.

Love was thought destructive; OVID (*Amores* 1.1, 2.18, and *passim*) refers to it as war. When erotic madness seizes a man, MAGIC cannot restore him; pictures of his beloved are burned into his mind like wax paintings. Love before marriage was to be avoided, though love could develop during marriage (Plutarch, *Erotikos* 754c–d, 755d, 759b, 767d, 769f).

There were several well known SONGS about unrequited love, mostly about spurned women (Athenaeus 14.618c; HETEROEROTICISM): the mythical poetess Eriphanis composed a song about her unreturned love for Manalkas as she wandered the mountain woods in misery; Stesichorus wrote a song about Kalykê who threw herself over the Leucadian cliff (SAPPHO 2); and another song concerned the maiden Harpalykê who died after Iphiklos rejected her.

Male poets treated their own rejection, CATULLUS by Lesbia, PROPERTIUS by Cynthia, and OVID by Corinna; songs like the *paraklausíthyron* lament the man's being shut out by his mistress's closed door (Plutarch, *Erotikos* 753b; cf. Horace, *Carm.* 3.10).

Love-Gifts given by the lover to the beloved (COURTSHIP; PAIDERASTIA). These usually consist of FOOD, money (in leather bags) or luxury objects, useful items, and pets. The nature of the gift is often gendered. Gifts of food are the most common, especially meat (joints of meat, seafood like fish and octopus, and birds to women and cocks and hares [148 (pl. 3)] to youths). Useful items like toiletries are offered to women, and hounds to youths and house dogs to boys. Wreaths and flowers are also common love-gifts.

Loves of the Gods In the late sixth/early fifth century BCE, a new iconography arises on approximately 400 vases portraying the gods and objects of their desire; presumably new stories also develop. Most of the "loves" are actually rapes: the deity desires a maiden or youth who usually consents, albeit unwillingly. The purpose of these rapes is not the sexual intercourse, which is almost never shown (80), but rather its result, the male children; after the birth of these heroes, their mother usually has no more significance.

A few beloveds refuse (DAPHNE) and a few of these are respected (CAENEUS). Occasionally, the deity's DESIRE is returned (ADONIS; GANYMEDE).

In almost all cases the desiring deity is male, but EOS and Salmacis (HERMAPHRODITUS) also rape; APHRODITE rapes Phaêthon the son of Eos and Kephalos. And while there is no instance of a female deity raping another female, Jupiter (ZEUS) disguised as ARTEMIS rapes KALLISTO (*nec se sine crimine prodit*, OVID *Met.* 2.433); Phoebus APOLLO rapes Leukothoê disguised as her mother (4.217–35), and disguised as an old woman he rapes Khionê (HERMES; 11.301–17); and VERTUMNUS disguised as an old woman convinces Pomona to MARRY him.

See also: DEMETER; DIONYSUS; HYAKINTHOS; PELOPS; POSEIDON; TRANSSEXUALITY; VIOLENCE

Ovid, *Metamorphoses*; Shapiro 1992.

Lucian (ca. 120–70 CE), author from Commagene, but probably writing in Athens. In "Dialogues of the Courtesans" (*Dial. meret.*) 5 Leaina lets the "dreadfully mannish" (*deinôs andrikê*) Megilla make LOVE to her; "there are women like that in Lesbos, with masculine faces, who don't want sex with men, but only with women, as though they themselves were men." Leaina herself is neither mannish nor interested in women; she acts like an eromenos in a PAIDERASTIC relationship, but she is persuaded by Megilla's gifts (a linen dress and a necklace [JEWELRY]). Megilla calls herself by the masculine "Megillus," and she shaves her head. Her regular partner is Demonasa, who is called "wife," and acts like Leaina.

Lucretia, Roman heroine, whose death in 509 BCE brought about the fall of the Etruscan monarchy. The sons of king Tarquinius Superbus bet their kinsman Collatinus who has the best wife, and to settle the question they go see what their wives are doing. The princes' wives are enjoying themselves at a banquet; Collatinus's wife, Lucretia, at home in Collatia, spins by lamplight with her maids. Prince Sextus Tarquinius is inflamed by Lucretia's beauty and industry, and returns when the household is asleep; he wakes Lucretia, declaring his love and threatening to kill her if she does not have sex with him. She relents only when he threatens to make her seem unchaste (he will murder her and a SLAVE and leave the slave's body next to hers). After the rape, she sends for her husband, her father, and Lucius Junius Brutus. She tells them what Sextus Tarquinius did: "My body only is violated; my mind is guiltless. But no unchaste woman will live with Lucretia as a precedent." And she kills herself with a knife. Brutus swears on her blood to destroy the monarchy; he displays her body in the forum, and incites the men to take up arms, and exile the king. The Republic begins with the election of two consuls, Brutus and Collatinus (Livy 1.57–60).

For a predecessor, see the story of Aristodemos (ca. 735–15 BCE), who was told by the Delphic oracle to sacrifice his virgin daughter if the Messenians are to obtain their freedom (Pausanias 4.26.4, 6.3.4).

See also: VERGINIA

Joshel 1992.

M

Maenads, real WOMEN made ecstatic by DIONYSUS during winter biennial celebrations in the mountains. In art maenads commonly wear long HAIR and fawn skins, carry a *thyrsos* (branch topped with pinecone), and eat small animals (**35**). Sleeping maenads arouse SATYRS (**100**). Maenads could be murderous (cf. Corinna, "Minyaiê"; EURIPIDES, *Bacchae*). Olympias, the mother of ALEXANDER THE GREAT, was a devotée of Dionysus and practiced maenadism (Henrichs 1978). The celebrations declined in the Hellenistic period.

See also: BESTIALITY

Henrichs 1978.

Magic, a manipulation of people and things through supernatural means. CIRCE (Homer, *Odyssey* 10.275 ff.) conjures ghosts and turns men into animals (cf. a graffito at POMPEII; Varone 2001a: 125). By Greco-Roman times, witches and sorcerers are common characters in comedy; they prepare spells, potions, and charms that protect the body, especially the genitals, from evil (**210**). *Agogê* spells induce people to desire someone (Horace, *Ep.* 5.11–82), fall out of love with them (Horace, *Ep.* 17), or keep rivals away (Betz 1986; Faraone 1999); most are heteroerotic (but see LESBIANISM; PAIDERASTIA). Greek love magic is used "by men

to instill erotic passion in women and by women to maintain affection in men" (Faraone 1999: 27). This spell keeps a rival away: a) "May Philematio fall under the power of ... I consecrate to the infernal gods her face, her hair, her mind, her breath, her vital organs; may he be hateful to her and she to him." b) "Even as he remains with idle testicles, so may she remain with empty cunt" (Varone 2001a: 127–9). The inyx-wheel, invented by APHRODITE (Pindar, *Pyth.* 4.214) and used generally by women (**161**), also creates a spell.

Love potions (DEIANEIRA; POISON) may have caused CALIGULA's madness and sleeplessness (Suetonius, *Caligula* 50.2). Vitellius's father mixed the spit of a freedwoman he loved with honey and used it on his throat and jaws (Suetonius, *Vitellius* 2).

Since Greek letters had numerical value, a number could render a name ("Ephesian letters"); for instance, "The number of the woman I love is 545" (*phílô hês arithmós phi-mu-epsilon*; Varone 2001a: 130).

See also: RELIGION

Male Homosexuality, the erotic attraction between two adult males. ARISTOPHANES's myth conceives of male-male desire as an essential aspect of human nature. In both Greece and Rome male HOMOEROTIC

72

attraction took several forms: PAIDERAS-TIA or "BOY-LOVE," male PROSTITUTION, the EFFEMINATE CINAEDUS, and male-male relationships among adults (discussed here).

In Greece adult male homosexual relationships are uncommon (cf. Plutarch, *Erotikos* 770b–c; Athenaeus 13.607e concerning Zenon and Persaios). Plato's *Symposium* celebrates the victory of the playwright Agathon (born ca. 445 BCE) in 416; he is now about thirty years old and still the eromenos of a certain Pausanias (177c). Aristophanes also jokes about Agathon (*Thesm.* 35; cf. Plato, *Prt.* 315e; Xen, *Sym.* 8.32; Robinson and Fluck 1937). Plutarch (*Erotikos* 770c) records that Euripides, having kissed the adult Agathon, remarked, "even the autumn of the fair is fair." Another adult homosexual pair is the erastes PHILOLAOS of Corinth and his eromenos Diokles (late eighth century); they moved to Thebes and lived out their lives together.

Nearly adult relationships are implied by Theopompos (FGrH 29) who has the Athenian mountain Lykabettos say, "On me, young men (*meirákia*) who are too old (for paiderastic relationships) give themselves to their agemates" (cf. **198**). No Greek art depicts adult men having sex, but one vase (**109**) shows bearded SATYRS having sex with each other.

Greek military campaigns provided opportunities for situational homosexual activity (cf. Athenaeus 1.25c). The SACRED BAND of Thebes consisted of pairs of lovers, most of them paiderastic couples, but could have included older pairs as well. And a few pieces of sculpture depict what could be pairs of adult lovers (**13 [pl. 12], 14**; cf. Flory 1994).

In the Roman period, there are more adult male-male sexual relationships. Cicero had a sexual relationship with his slave Tiro (Pliny, *Ep.* 7.4). Haterius's famous remark (Seneca, *Controv.* 4.10) implies sexual activity between adult men, even if one is the freeborn patron and his partners are unwilling slaves or freedmen

clients. After his wife's death, Galba preferred "men, adult and strong" (Suetonius, *Galba* 12, 22). Vitellius had an on-off sexual relationship with his freedman Asiaticus (Suetonius, *Vitellius* 12).

Romans apparently thought that male-male sex is "more violent than that with women, and thus more tiring" (Musonius Rufus in Lutz 1947: 71–7; cf. Cantarella 1992: 203). OVID disagrees in order to emphasize his love of women (*Ars Am.* 2.683–4).

Martial satirizes the MARRIAGE of Decianus, as wife, to a rugged, hairy man (1.24); and mentions how "Bearded Callistratus married rugged Afer like a virgin marries a man; the torches shone, the wedding veil covered his face … even a dowry" (12.42). Juvenal (2.117–142) describes another such marriage: "Gracchus gave a dowry of 400,000 sesterces to a horn player; marriage documents were signed, greetings exchanged, a banquet." These passages describe real marriage rites (Williams 1999: 245–52; Boswell 1994). NERO marries the endowed Pythagoras as his wife (at age twenty-seven) and the eunuch Sporus as his husband (age twenty-eight).

There are few Roman depictions of adult men having sex (**291 VII**).

Roman and Christian prohibitions against male homosexual acts (SEXUAL ATTITUDES) do not specify the ages or status of the participants (Romans 1.26; edicts of Constantius and Constans, Theodosius, and Justinian). It is possible, then, that criminalized male homosexual acts were those between two citizens – it was hardly ever a crime for an adult citizen man to penetrate a male slave or non-citizen.

See also: BISEXUALITY; HETEROEROTICISM; LAWS; LESBIANISM

Marriage, a partnership between a man and a woman recognized by the community, especially for the bearing of legitimate CHILDREN (for partnerships between

men, see MALE HOMOSEXUALITY). HERA/
JUNO and DIONYSUS/BACCHUS preside
over marriage.

Greece

General remarks

The word for marriage is *gámos*, the
groom *gambrós*, the bride *númphê*, husband *anêr* ("man"), and wife *gunê* ("woman"). Marriages were arranged between
families for economic and political mo-
tives until the late fifth century when
romantic LOVE becomes a factor (Rabinowitz 1992: 51).

In the early period, the aristocratic
father of the bride could hold contests
among suitors (Athenaeus 13.555b; cf.
PELOPS; AGARISTE). Variations on "Bride
Contests" included victors in battle having the right to choose WOMEN (and/or
boys) as spoils (Homer, *Iliad* 1; Plato,
Resp. 468c), or the groom having to
wrestle (Peleus and Thetis) or race (ATA-
LANTA) the bride.

The groom was usually ten years older
than the bride and more mature and
experienced. They saw little of each other
and had little in common (Xenophon,
Oec. 12–13; Lysias 1.6–14), at least at
first. Plutarch asserts "time and companionship produces a mutual loyalty in the
wedded couple" (*Erotikos* 767d; cf. 769f;
Mor. 142f). For love in marriage see
SABINUS; SULPICIA 2.

Marriage was a communal celebration
(Homer, *Iliad* 18.490 ff.). Athenian vase
paintings of the late fifth century, however, romanticize the marriage (**143**),
make the groom younger and the bride
older, and include "allegorical figures such
as EROS and APHRODITE, eye contact and
tender glances" (McManus 1990: 231).
The "Athenian bride was perhaps inspired
by this refined erotic vision to accept her
sexual and social role in society" (Sutton
1992: 25, 26–7). The compulsory emphasis on love today as the basis of marriage
probably does much the same thing.

Eligibility

A citizen man and slave woman probably
could live together without marriage and
produce children (cf. Clairmont 1993: no.
2.406). An Athenian man living with a
metic woman could be fined 1,000
drachmes; a metic man found living with
a proper Athenian woman could be sold
into slavery. Marriage was forbidden between relatives closer than first cousins
and between aunts/uncles and their ne-
phews/nieces, or between siblings or half-
siblings by the same mother (Ptolemies,
however, married full sisters, nieces, and
the widows of their brothers; see INCEST).
Marriage between half-siblings by the
same father (CONCEPTION) guaranteed
that household property remained intact.

Women were marriageable at the conventional age of fourteen (Xenophon,
Oec. 7.5) or fifteen (Demosthenes 27.4,
29.43), men after they had served in the
military and were in their late twenties or
early thirties (Hesiod, *Works* 696–8; Plutarch, *Erotikos* 754c–d).

Betrothal

Before the wedding, sometimes several
years before (Demosthenes's mother was
betrothed at age five), the bride's father
and the groom settled the marriage contract with a handshake (*enguê*); the woman was not consulted. A dowry (*proíka*)
was important; the husband would man-
age the dowry but it had to remain intact
(cf. Athenaeus 13.558f). The groom gives
the bride's family a gift (*hédnon*), assuring
his intent to marry. To ensure the legiti-
macy of the marriage and eventual children, the groom had to obtain the assent
of his kinship group (phratry).

Wedding

The wedding took place over three days;
it was mostly a social event with no legal
registration and with little religious significance. The preferred time of year in

Athens was at the full moon (good for conception) during the month of Gamelion (roughly January) when ZEUS and HERA married.

The first day, *proaúlia*, was occupied with preparations, celebrations and sacrifices (*protéleia*) to ensure a safe transition (women and men could die on their wedding day; see CLAUDIUS; HYMENAEUS). Brides dedicated toys and other objects (hairnets) (Friedländer and Hoffleit 1948: 102 no. 104). They spent that night in their respective in-law's house, she with a little boy, he with a little girl.

Either late the first day or early the second day the bride and groom BATHE with special WATER (in Athens, from the Enneakrounos) from special jars, the *loutróphoros* (these, in stone, mark the tombs of the unmarried; cf. Montserrat 1996: 80–105); the special water was to ensure FERTILITY (cf. Aeschines, *Ep.* 10.3–8).

On the second day, *gámos*, the bride and groom dress in their own houses. The rest of the day is spent celebrating with guests. "At nightfall, the bride's father gave his daughter to the groom in full view of the guests" (Pherecydes FGrH 3.33); when the groom looks at her to take her by her wrist (*cheír' epí kárpo*; **93** [**pl. 41**]), the bride signals her acceptance, "drawing aside the veil of her bridal dress" (*anakálypsis*; Euphorion 107 Powell 49). A procession lit by torches then brings the bride to her new home (the mothers provide the torches; cf. Euripides, *Iph. Aul.* 732. A "wedding without torches" is illegitimate; cf. Vergil, *Aen.* 2).

At the new home, the groom's mother welcomes the bride. At the hearth, figs, nuts, or coins are poured over the couple (*katachúsmata*, also poured over newly purchased slaves; Plutarch, *Erotikos* 753d). The bridal chamber (*thálamos*) contains a marriage BED (*lékhos*) and, next to it, another bed, the *parábustos*, for sleeping. During the night, outside the house, the guests sing *epithalámia*, often rather rowdily (Edmonds 1967: 505), to accompany the pair consummating their marriage ("so that the voice of the maiden being violated [*biazoménê*] will not be heard"; Theocritus schol. Wendel 1914: 331).

The third day, *epaúlia*, sees further celebrations. The bride's father brings gifts and perhaps the dowry in a procession led by children (Eustathius, *Iliad* 24.29).

Eventually, the groom gives a feast to his phratry to announce that he is now married. And the bride dedicates her wedding pottery (in Athens, at the spring of Nymphê on the south slope of the Acropolis).

Status of the wife

With her marriage the wife passes into the guardianship of her husband (her father could initiate DIVORCE). If she does not bear him children she can be divorced and returned to her father's household or supplanted by a pallakê (a mistress approved by the phratry for bearing legitimate children; see PROSTITUTES).

End of marriage

Marriages end either in divorce or with the death of a spouse. If the wife dies, the husband can marry again; if the husband dies, the wife then passes into the guardianship of a son or of her nearest male relative, along with her dowry, to be married again if appropriate. If she has no male relative, the state can marry her to an appropriate man. The husband can stipulate in a will who is to marry his widow, although in practice it may have been rarely carried out (Demosthenes 27, 36).

Rome

General remarks

The word for marriage is *matrimonium*, for the groom *maritus*, the bride *nupta*, husband *vir* ("man"), and wife *uxor* ("wife"). The purpose of marriage was ostensibly to produce legitimate children, but by the early empire marriages were also for compatibility and sexual companionship.

Marriage was the citizen man's duty (SEXUAL ATTITUDES); every five years censors held a review of married and unmarried men and urged bachelors to marry and produce children. By the *lex Julia de maritandis ordinibus* (18 BCE) AUGUSTUS defined legitimate marriages and established financial incentives for marrying and begetting children (LAWS).

Roman marriage could be very simple; Cato of Utica married, for his second time, Marcia only in the company of an *augur* (to give the blessing). Marriages lasted while there was "marital affection." Some couples were in love with each other (cf. Pliny, *Ep.* 4.7, 4.19, 7.5), so much so that the wife chooses to die with her husband: Paxea with Pomponius Labeo (Tacitus, *Ann.* 6.29), and Arria Maior with Caecina Peto (Pliny, *Ep.* 3.16).

Eligibility

The legal age for a formal marriage was based on puberty, conventionally set as low as twelve for girls and thirteen or fourteen for boys, although less formal marriages could occur at any age (PETRONIUS 25.1–3 and 7, 26.1–3: Giton "marries" Pannychis, aged seven).

People of the same status had the right to marry (*connubium*), but by the late Republic freedmen could marry the freeborn. The senatorial class, however, could not marry below their rank (De Felice 2001: 49–60), nor could guardians marry their wards, or provincial officials women from that province. Following CLAUDIUS, uncles could marry their nieces.

Betrothal

This occurs with the consent of the father and the bride. The betrothal is made public in the company of friends and family. Marriage contracts are possible, stipulating such items as no extra-marital affairs (Hunt and Edgar 1970: 1, no. 2).

Types of marriage (Treggiari 1991)

Usus creates a common law marriage: the citizen couple (freeborn or freed) cohabits without interruption for a year. There were several types of common law marriage (Evans-Grubbs 1993; De Felice 2001: 53–60): *concubinatus* ("live in"), a long-term relationship between a high-status man and a low-status woman, especially between a master and his former slave; and *contubernium* ("tent-mates"), a relationship without children (Treggiari 1981).

Cum manu, the woman passes into the guardianship of her husband; this marriage was traditional until the late Republic. It took two forms: *confarreatio*, the couple offer a barley cake (*farreus panis*) to their ancestors in the presence of the Pontifex Maximus and the Flamen Dialis; and *coemptio*, the groom makes a legal purchase of the bride from her father, putting a gold ring (earnest money) on the bride's ring finger (third finger of the left hand; a nerve runs from there to the heart, Gellius 10.10).

Sine manu, the bride does not pass into the guardianship of her husband; this marriage was popular from the late Republic on. The couple gives mutual vows, emphasizing their equality. Since the *sine manu* marriage could become the same as *usus*, the couple lives apart three nights every year (XII Tables 6.6, Thatcher 1901: 9–11).

Wedding

Marriage takes place following betrothal and a ceremony of celebration. The traditional wedding is complex. The night before the wedding, the bride sleeps with her HAIR in a red net. On the day of the marriage, the bride dresses in a hemless tunic (*tunica recta*) secured by a wool belt with a double knot of HERAKLES (the "square" knot); over the tunic she wears a saffron cloak (*palla*), saffron SANDALS, and a metal collar around her neck. On her head she wears six pads of artificial hair as VESTAL VIRGINS do, and over her hair an orange veil (*flammeum*) and wreath. An animal sacrifice in the presence of an augur secures good fortune. Ten people drawn from both families serve as witnesses to the wedding (and sign the contract, if there is one). The couple exchanges vows in the presence of the augur, ending with the pledge, *ubi tu Gaius, ego Gaia* (whither you go Gaius, thither I go Gaia). After a feast, the groom takes the bride to their new home in a night procession accompanied by three children whose parents are still living and led by flautists and torch bearers. When they reach their home, nuts are thrown on them; the groom lifts the bride over the threshold. The chief bridesmaid leads the bride to the marriage bed where the groom removes her saffron cloak and unties the knot of the belt while the guests retire.

Status of the wife

With marriage *sine manu* the wife is more or less equal to her husband. With marriage *cum manu*, however, the husband is her guardian. If she commits ADULTERY, drinks, handles POISON, or copies his keys, he could, in consultation with her relatives, put her to death (Dio. Hal. 2.25; Plutarch, *Rom.* 25).

End of marriage

Marriage ended by divorce or the death of a spouse; however the marriage ends, all children inherit. If the wife dies first any dowry goes back to her family; the husband retains all other gifts. If the marriage ends for any other reason, all gifts not given over to the children go back to the givers.

Remarriage was required for divorcees and widows under fifty, though the latter could wait ten months before remarrying. Upon the death of her husband the widow became the ward of her sons or of her nearest male blood-relative; in the later empire, under HADRIAN, a woman who had three children could be the legitimate heir (*ius trium liberorum*); and by the *senatus consultum Orphitianum* under Marcus Aurelius, mothers could inherit and pass their inheritance on to their children.

See also: AGE GRADES; HIEROS GAMOS; THEOGAMIA

For Greek marriage: Just 1989/1994, Oakley 1995, and Oakley and Sinos 1993; for Roman marriage: Rawson 1991.

Martial (Marcus Valerius Martialis, ca. 40–104 CE), epigrammatist and satirist. Martial chides a husband for spending money on EFFEMINATE boys when he has a wife (12.97), and upbraids a wife for being jealous of her husband's affairs with slave boys (12.96). To Martial, proper WOMEN should not be ADULTEROUS, independent, or bossy, and, when old, they should have no DESIRE for sex. He does, however, want women to enjoy sex (12.91).

While Martial may prefer women to MEN, over fifty epigrams deal with sexual relations with boys (slaves or prostitutes); Martial prefers *pueri* (boys) with a pale complexion, bright eyes, soft hair, red lips. All his *pueri* have Greek names and are young; facial HAIR marks the end of their attraction (4.7; cf. 2.62, 3.74, 6.56, 9.27, 14.205; Obermayer 1998). Two satires, 7.67 and 7.70, describe women with voracious appetites for other women (LESBIANISM).

Masturbation, manual stimulation of the genitals. The words for masturbation are Greek *tríbein*, and Latin *frico* or *masturbor* ("beat with the hand," Adams 1982: 208–11).

Self-stimulation

Aristotle discusses how, "even before they produce SEMEN, boys obtain sexual pleasure by rubbing their genitals; this pleasure derives from air passing through the channels [in the penis] through which semen later passes" (*Problems* 30). PRIAPEA 63.17 refers to a woman masturbating. Diogenes the Cynic, caught masturbating in the agora, comments "if only one could satisfy one's hunger by rubbing one's stomach" (Plutarch, *Mor.* 1044b). A graffito from POMPEII concurs: "when my worries oppress my body, with my left hand, I release my pent up fluids" (*multa mihi curae cum [pr]esserit artus has ego mancinas, stagna refusa, dabo*; *CIL* 4.2066; Varone 2001a: 94). Masturbation can release deep emotions; PETRONIUS 11, describes how the viewer of a beautiful painting by Apelles can only masturbate to express his admiration.

There are several representations of men masturbating (SATYR: **203**; Greek and Roman men: **36**, **129B**, **132**; an OLD philosopher: **228**), and at least one of a woman masturbating (**139**).

Stimulating another

OVID suggests that men can bring women close to ORGASM with the hand (*Ars Am.* 2.707–24) and a graffito from Capua (*CIL* 10.4483) states, "I shall rub your cunt" (*cunnum tibi fricabo*); a woman masturbates a youth on a Greek vase (**129A**).

See also: FELLATIO; SEXUAL ACTIVITY

Krenkel 1979a.

Medea, a witch, daughter of king Aeëtes first of Corinth and then of Colchis, granddaughter of Helios APOLLO, and cousin to CIRCE. When Jason and the Argonauts come to Colchis for the golden fleece, Medea, in love with Jason, enchants the dragon guarding the fleece; aboard the Argo, she cuts up her brother and tosses the pieces into the sea for her pursuing father to retrieve. When they arrive at Iolkos, Medea cuts up king Pelias in a fraudulent attempt to rejuvenate him. They then flee to Corinth, where Jason opts for an opportune marriage with king Kreon's daughter Glaukê; Medea gives her a POISONED gown for her wedding that immolates both her and her father. She then murders her two sons by Jason and flees to Athens in a chariot of the Sun drawn by dragons. As the guest of king Aegeus, she plots to kill his son THESEUS, but fails. Her own death is not related.

Medea appears first in Hesiod, *Theogony* 992–1002 and prominently in Euripides, *Medea* (431 BCE), Apollonius, *Argonautica*, and Seneca, *Medea*, and in a lost tragedy by OVID. In art, she appears regularly with a bowl and stirring rod for mixing potions (cf. Circe's chest of herbs); after 440 she is always depicted dressed in an oriental costume, perhaps in Euripides's play as well.

See also: AMAZONS

Medicine began with observing BODY FUNCTIONS and interviewing patients; much gynecological information came from PROSTITUTES. Medical practitioners included MIDWIVES and doctors employed at public clinics and sanctuaries, especially those of the healing god Asklepios. The two most important Greek clinics were those at Epidaurus and Cos; Rome's major clinic, on the Tiber island, dates to 291 BCE.

The WOMAN medical practitioner Elephantis (first century BCE), wrote on ABORTIFACIENTS (Pliny, *HN* 28.51) and COSMETICS (Galen 12:416 Kühn). MEN medical practitioners include Hippocrates of Cos (ca. 469–399 BCE) under whose name is assembled the Hippocratic cor-

Plate 1 Etruscan terracotta sarcophagus (6th c. BCE; Villa Giulia; **194**).

Plate 2 Etruscan marble sarcophagus lid (late 5th c. BCE; BMFA; **195**).

Plate 3 Red-figure hydria (early 5th c. BCE; Villa Giulia 50635; **148**).

Plate 4 Chieftain Cup from Haghia Triada (ca. 1550 BCE; HM; **5**).

Plate 5 Red-figure kylix by Makron (early 5th c. BCE; Toledo; **104**), exterior.

Plate 6 Red-figure kylix by Douris (early 5th c. BCE; BM E768; 77), interior.

Plate 7 Red-figure pelike (early 5th c. BCE; Mykonos; **159**).

Plate 8 Black-figure dinos (late 6th c. BCE; Vatican 35605; **47**).

Plate 9 Tombstone, Pharsalos (early 5th c. BCE; Louvre; **12**).

Plate 10 Red-figure kylix, Apollodorus (early 5th c. BCE; Tarquinia; **61**).

Plate 11 Red-figure bell krater, Louvre G521 Ptr (late 5th c. BCE; Vatican 9098; **101**).

Plate 12 Marble tombstone from Piraeus (late 5th c. BCE; Piraeus; **13**).

Plate 13 Red-figure kylix, Peithinos (early 5th c. BCE; Berlin, Charlottenburg; **121**).

Plate 14 Mosaic from El Jem (2nd c. CE; El Jem A16; 234).

Plate 15 Marble statue of Pan from Athens, Olympieion (4th c. BCE; NMA; 176).

Plate 16 Marble statue of Antinoös from Chalkis (early 2nd c. CE; Chalkis; 246; photo by Paul Rehak).

Plate 17 Terracotta uterus (2nd-1st c. BCE?; University of Kansas; **267**).

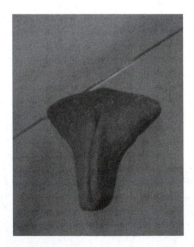

Plate 18 Terracotta vulva from Città Castellana (2nd-1st c. BCE?; Città Castellana; **268**).

Plate 20 Mosaic from Sousse (2nd-3rd c. CE; Sousse; **241**).

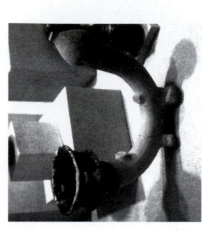

Plate 21 Phallus-shaped drinking vessel from Pella (3rd c. BCE; Pella; **181**).

Plate 19 Entrance mosaic from the House of Jupiter the Thunderer, Ostia (1st-2nd c. CE; **240**).

Plate 22 Red-figure kylix (mid 5th c. BCE; Villa Giulia 50404; **158**).

Plate 23 Discus lamp from the Cave of Pan, Attica (1st c. CE; NMA; **225**).

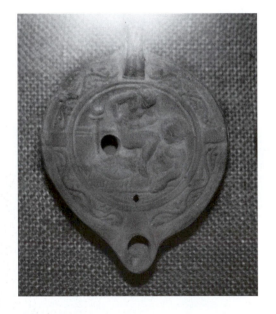

Plate 24 Discus lamp from Sparta (1st c. CE; Sparta; **226**).

pus, SORANUS of Ephesus who wrote a *Gynocology*, and Galen of Pergamum (129–99 CE). There are two major genres of medical texts, catalogues and monographs. The authors of monographs replaced folkloristic accounts of the body with philosophical descriptions of mechanical processes. The Hippocratic writers of catalogues, however, "maintained popular medical traditions" (Hanson 1992: 33–5).

The major theories (beginning with Alkmaion of Croton, fifth century BCE) held that health is a proper balance of opposites (hot and cold, dry and wet, hard and soft, right and left) and of "humors" (blood, yellow bile, black bile, and phlegm). This holistic account is also gendered: MEN are hot, dry, hard, and associated with the right side of the BODY; WOMEN are cold, moist, soft, and associated with the left side of the body.

Much medical thinking was constructed upon analogy. For instance, SEMEN, like mucus, must originate in the head and pass to the genitals; and because women MENSTRUATE, their bodies, like sponges, must contain pockets for storing this liquid.

Feces, urine, and other human eliminations were also ingredients in medicines. Uterine bleeding could be stopped by drinking goat urine and applying feces (Pliny, *HN* 28.247, 254, 255). Galen, however, abhors the practice of drinking sweat (KONISALOS), urine, or menses, and he contradicts Xenocrates (fl. 54–96 CE) who had written that human excrescence (including earwax) could be beneficial when applied or swallowed (12:249 Kühn).

Men

Biography (AGE GRADES)

Greece

After BIRTH, if he is accepted by his father (in Athens, AMPHIDROMIA) or by his tribe (SPARTA) and not exposed, he is given his paternal grandfather's name (his full name was conventional: "NAME, patronymic ('son of NAME'), demotic ('from the town NAME')" [in Athens]). He is enrolled in his father's kinship group (phratry), and schooled at home (or by the state in Sparta) until age 6–8, when he is sent to the state-run school in a GYMNASIUM, where (in Athens), he studies literature, arithmetic, and MUSIC and begins physical training. At age twelve he begins military training, and, if customary, becomes involved in a PAIDERASTIC relationship. At age eighteen he enters the military as a cadet (ephebe), and patrols the border forts (Athens). At twenty he is on military reserve. In Athens he could attend the assembly, but at age thirty he is allowed to speak, propose legislation, and hold office. It is at about this time that a man MARRIES (perhaps earlier in Sparta). At age sixty, he is released from military service.

Rome

All boys were to be raised by LAW, and each boy is purified on the eighth or ninth day (AMPHIDROMIA). At age fourteen he could marry, and by age sixteen he replaces his boyhood *toga praetexta* (with purple border) for the plain *toga virilis*. Serving in the military was necessary before launching a political career (*tribune, quaestor, aedile, praetor,* and *consul* in that order, the *cursus honorum*).

Greece and Rome

Males went through three main periods when chances of dying were great (Becker 2003): perinatal (1 month), weaning (2–4 years) and late adolescence (15–20 years), especially in war and from reckless behavior (Varone 2001b: 166). After late adolescence, men's average age at death was mid-forties, though many men lived to seventy. Death at an age much older than that was remarkable (cf. AUGUSTUS; EURIPIDES).

Men's bodies

Men's BODIES were socially constructed to be hard, dry, hot, active, unadorned, and unpenetrated; they were to strive for naturalness (no BODY MODIFICATION); male NUDITY was an ideal condition for the CITIZEN, especially fit for artistic expression, public exhibition (e.g in the Greek GYMNASIUM and the Roman BATH), and physical scrutiny for signs of EFFEMINACY.

Greek art favors muscular male bodies. Romans emphasized endurance (cf. gladiators voluntarily enslaving themselves, Brown 1992: 186). Men were not to pay excessive attention to grooming or to elaborate dress (cf. ALCIBIADES; JULIUS CAESAR).

Male nature, masculinity, and work

EFFEMINACY in men was of great concern in both Greece and Rome: the heat that kept them "cooked," hot, and dry, could always cool (Brown 1988: 10); being around WOMEN could also feminize a man. Apparently women threatened a man's masculinity: "You ask why I don't marry you, Galla? You're too eloquent. My penis makes too many grammatical errors" (Martial 11.19; cf. Juvenal 6.185 ff.). Men therefore could not be penetrated like women (cf. CINAEDI) and could not be watched like women (thus, men in the THEATER and arena are suspect; Seneca, *Q nat.* 7.31.2–3; Juvenal 2.143–8). Hypermasculinity (HAIRINESS, Juvenal 2.41), however, was associated with hypersexuality, which could include unrestrained sexual activity of all sorts, including being penetrated.

Appropriate work for a man consisted of "the market and urban affairs" (Stobaeus, *Flor.* 3.696f quoting Hierokles),

that is, all outdoor work (Xen., *Oik.* 7.22), and property (Aristotle, *Politics* 1277b.24f) and food acquisition (Columella cited in Wyke 1994: 140). In rural areas, "men tend to have 'erect' tasks (scythe, arboriculture, bee-keeping, fishing, hunting)" (Scheidel 1995: 212); cf. compare Aristotle's distinction between erect citizens and bent-over slaves (*Politics* 1254b.25–30).

Status

Men were the heads of their family and the state. Maintaining this dominance was precarious and produced anxiety (cf. Gardner 1989 re: Aristophanes, *Lysistrata*, *Ecclesiasuzae*). Men felt that it was necessary to have frequent sexual access to their wives, slaves, PROSTITUTES, and non-citizens of both sexes (cf. the LAWS of SOLON; Val. Max. 6.7.1–3; Zweig 1992: 77–8). Sexually, it was a man's right to have intercourse: ORGASM was necessary to eliminate waste (cf. BODY FUNCTIONS). Sexual activity was natural and occurred naturally; OVID advises men (*Ars Am.* 2.703–32) that they will know what to do by instinct: "*natura* will take its course."

See also: ABORTION; BIRTH; CONCEPTION; MAGIC; MENSTRUATION; PLANTS; SEXUAL DIFFERENTIATION

Hanson 1992; Dean-Jones 1994.

Menstruation, a WOMAN's monthly passing of blood from the womb, stored there in preparation for CONCEPTION. Menses was thought to provide nourishment for the developing fetus and to transform into milk for the nursing child (Hanson 1992: 38–9). The vaginal passage needed to be kept unblocked for its free flow. Otherwise, the blood finds other exits (nosebleeds, hemorrhoids); trapped menstrual blood could be fatal after six months (Hippocrates, *Morb. mul.* 1.2). Normal menstruation was two

Attic *kotyls* of blood per month (about 18 fluid ounces, 6–7 times greater than that measured today). Menstruation should come at the same time every month, especially with the moon's waning.

Menstruation was considered foul. CUNNILINGUS of menstruating women was especially obscene (Galen 12:249 Kühn); OVID advises the lover who wants to fall out of love to observe the woman performing something "obscene," presumably waste elimination, especially menstruation (*Rem. Am* 437–40). Menstrual blood was thought to be not only emotionally but also physically powerful, so strong it could dissolve the bitumen that clung to boats in the Dead Sea (Josephus, *Bell. Jud.* 4.8.4; cf. Pliny, *NH* 28.70–82; Richlin 1997).

See also: BODY FUNCTIONS

Hanson 1992; Dean-Jones 1989; Jones 1987.

Messalina (ca. 20–48 CE), Valeria, the third wife of CLAUDIUS. She would use a BROTHEL in which to have so much sex she would outdo even the PROSTITUTES (Juvenal 6.114 ff.). In 48, when Claudius went to Ostia, Messalina illegally MARRIED C. Silius, the consul designate; "she took the auspices, put on the veil, made sacrifices to the gods, had a public banquet, and spent the night consummating their wedding." Messalina was accused of treason, and committed suicide.

Joshel 1997.

Midwives, specialists in assisting the BIRTH of CHILDREN (Greek *maía*; Latin *obstetrix*). SORANUS and Galen give midwives high respect (MEDICINE), though they are not much mentioned by the Hippocratics. Slave midwives fetched high prices. A few midwives were given expensive tombstones in fourth-century Athens (Clairmont 1993: no. 2.890). Male midwives may be possible (*maioi, IG* 12.5.199).

See also: CONCEPTION; PREGNANCY; WOMEN

Hanson 1992: nn. 146, 147; Pomeroy 1975: 84.

Minos, legendary king of Crete, son of ZEUS and EUROPA. Minos is married to Pasiphaê, daughter of Helios APOLLO the sun god (and therefore sister of CIRCE and aunt to MEDEA); they have three children, Androgeos, Phaidra, and Ariadnê. Androgeos is killed in Attica, either treacherously or while capturing the Marathonian bull. To avenge his death, Minos exacts an annual tribute from Athens of seven youths and seven maidens. To legitimate his rule, Minos prays to POSEIDON for a bull to sacrifice, but the bull is too handsome to do so. Poseidon (or APHRODITE, Hyginus 40.1) then causes Pasiphaê to DESIRE the bull. Daidalos constructs a hollow bronze cow for her to fit into (cf. LOVES OF THE GODS, [Zeus and Io]) and have intercourse with the bull; she bears the Minotaur, a bull-headed man.

To house the monster, Daidalos creates the maze-like Labyrinth; and in it the Athenian tribute is put for the Minotaur to eat. When THESEUS arrives in Athens, he volunteers to lead the tribute to Knossos and he substitutes at least two youths for the maidens (OSCHOPHORIA; TRANSVESTISM). Ariadnê falls in love with Theseus and gives him the "clue" (usually a ball of yarn) for getting out of the Labyrinth. When Theseus escapes he takes her with him but abandons her on the island Dia, traditionally Naxos. She then becomes the bride of DIONYSUS, who takes her to Lemnos; when she dies, he buries her at Argos. Eventually, Theseus marries Phaidra, who falls in love with his son HIPPOLYTOS (AMAZONS) and hangs herself.

Ariadnê abandoned by Theseus, and Pasiphaê and the bull (**306**), are popular subjects in POMPEIIAN wall painting;

NERO even presented a live staging of Pasiphaê and the bull (Suetonius, *Nero* 12).

See also: BESTIALITY

Apollodorus 2.1.4, 3.1.2–4, 5.1.6 and 9; Pausanias 1.20.3, 1.22.5, 2.23.8, 5.19.1, 9.40.3–4, 10.29.3–4.

Mould-made Bowls (182–193, 277–280) were produced from the Hellenistic into the Roman period in a variety of fabrics. The scenes in relief occasionally depict couples having sex in different positions; two bowls depict enigmatic CINAEDUS scenes, perhaps taken from THEATER (190, 191). Some bowls include inscribed exhortations and both scenes and exhortations repeat on different bowls (188, 189, 193), implying that they were conventional (PORNOGRAPHY; SEX IN ART).

Music has the power to stimulate (cf. OVID, *Amores* 2.1). From antiquity there are fifty-one extant musical scores (West 1992: 277–326). In the Aegean Bronze Age only men play instruments, especially the concert lyre (*kithára*) and the double oboe (*auloí*); both instruments are known in classical times. In Greece only men played the kithara, while men at the SYMPOSIUM, WOMEN at home, and the young at school played the tortoise-shell lyre (*lúra*).

The lyre and auloi were played at Greek SYMPOSIA, at the Roman THEATER, as well as at all sacrifices and processions. Auloi were considered exciting: when ALEXANDER THE GREAT heard Timotheus playing, he rushed for his weapons (Dio Chrysostom 1.1–2). Auloi also had erotic connotations; they are played by PROSTITUTES (101 [pl. 11], 67, 68, 94, 112, 132, 202), and occasionally by eromenoi; in other scenes they are played by a man about to have intercourse with a woman "a tergo" (279.4), by an ithyphallic DWARF (239), and by EROS while a TRANSVESTITE HERAKLES serves Omphalê (324); and they were not thought suitable for citizen Romans to play (Lyne 1980: 200).

The men who play the kithara are elaborately dressed (West 1992: 54–5). They, and the men who sang to the kithara, were considered EFFEMINATE (Plato, *Symp.* 179d; Dover 1989: 73–5; ORPHEUS). The diners in Athenaeus (1.14b) note that Homer did not consider these musicians masculine enough either to take to war or to imagine them a threat with the women at home. Kitharists are also the objects of HOMOEROTIC DESIRE (Aeschines, *In Tim.* 1.41; Athenaeus 13.603a–b).

See also: DANCE; SONG

Younger 1998.

N

Narcissus, son of the river Kephissos in Boeotia. Narcissus falls in love with himself when he sees himself reflected in a pool (**298**). OVID (*Met.* 3. 342–407) adds Echo, who loves him but can only repeat his words; he spurns her and she fades away leaving only her voice.

Neaira (fl. late fourth century), Corinthian hetaira. Neaira begins as a BROTHEL SLAVE (a customer was the speech-writer Lysias). She is bought by two men for 3,000 drachmes, and purchases her freedom for 2,000, raised partly from a certain Phrynion, whom she has to serve as part of her manumission agreement. A certain Stephanos takes her to Athens, where Phrynion has her indicted for breaking their agreement. The Athenian court upholds her freedom but she must serve both Stephanos and Phrynion. Some charges against her concern her daughter, who had impersonated a proper Athenian woman and had married Athens' *árchon basileús* (religious magistrate); as such she was the *basilínna* (ANTHESTERIA). Apollodorus, her speech-writer, gives a succinct definition of women: "We have hetairai for our pleasure, pallakai to serve us, and wives to bear us legitimate children" (**122**). Neaira was the subject of a comedy by Timocles.

See also: PROSTITUTES

Demosthenes 59.

Necrophilia, sex with a corpse. Periander, tyrant of Corinth, killed his wife and had sex with her corpse, as did ACHILLES with the AMAZON queen Penthesileia.

Nero (37–68 CE; **243** [**pl. 42**]), Claudius Caesar, emperor (54–68). In his first year as emperor, he shaved his first beard and stowed the HAIR in a gold box, which he dedicated in the Capitolium. To preserve his SINGING voice, he would lie on his back with a lead plate on his chest, give himself enemas, vomit, and ABSTAIN from certain FOODS. While he sang, no one could leave: thus, women were said to give BIRTH. In the arena, he had boys DANCE the story of Pasiphaê, complete with a bull mounting a wooden heifer in which a woman was concealed. He would banquet in public in the Naumachia, waited on by PROSTITUTES, and for his boat parties, he would have booths set up with prostitutes, including noble women.

It was rumored that he and his mother Agrippina had an INCESTUOUS relationship: when they rode in a litter together, they would get out with their clothing stained. Eventually, he attempted to POISON her three times (she had ready antidotes). When he could not kill her by rigging a ceiling to drop on her, he contrived to have a boat she was in collapse on her. She escaped, being a strong swimmer. Nero then had a freedman kill her. Afterwards he felt hounded by her ghost and by the Furies.

Nero's first wife was Octavia, whom he DIVORCED for barrenness, banished, and finally had put to death for ADULTERY by bribing his praetorian prefect to confess to raping her. He then MARRIED Poppaea Sabina, but kicked her when she was PREGNANT (NOVELS, Chariton); she and the daughter she bore both died. He then proposed to Antonia, daughter of CLAUDIUS, but she refused, and he had her killed. Finally, he married Statilia MESSALINA, whose husband he had killed.

Nero also married three men (Cass. Dio. 62.13.1–2; Orosius, *Hist.* 7.7.2). In 64, as the "wife" to a certain Pythagoras, Nero wore a bridal veil, took the auspices, gave a dowry, and, after a torch-lit procession, had a special wedding bed prepared (Tacitus, *Ann.* 15.37.4). The next year, Nero castrated (BODY MODIFICATION) a boy, Sporus, had him don the bridal veil and provide a dowry, and married him as his husband, giving rise to a popular joke: "it would have been better for us all had Nero's father taken a similar wife." Another man he married as his "wife" was a freedman Doryphorus; on their wedding night Nero imitated the screams of a maiden being deflowered.

In his last year, he composed verses set to lascivious tunes (*lasciveque modulata*) and sexual gestures to mock Galba's revolt; later, to advance against Galba, he had prostitutes shear their hair and carry AMAZON axes and shields. Eventually, deserted by all except a few (including Sporus), he committed suicide.

Suetonius, *Nero.*

Nocturnal Emissions, a man's involuntary ORGASM during sleep. Galen recommends that athletes place a lead plate (ABSTINENCE; NERO) under the thigh to chill the genitals (12:232 Kühn).

See also: ABSTINENCE

Novels, long fictional narratives with significant erotic content. Predecessors include the story of Panthea and Abradatas in the *Cyropaedia* of Xenophon of Athens, and the plays of New Comedy (THEATER). The novel as a genre begins at the end of the Hellenistic period with a papyrus account of SEMIRAMIS; and the *Milesian Tales* by Aristides (ca. 100 BCE; OVID, *Tristia* 2.413–14, 443–4; cf. the boy from Pergamum and the widow of Miletus in PETRONIUS 85–7 and 111–2; HERO AND LEANDER). Most ancient examples, however, date from the first to the third century CE.

Theodorus Priscianus, a doctor, urged IMPOTENT men to read novels (along with "the services of pretty girls and boys too," 2.11 Rose 133). The emperor Julian (361–3 CE) forbade the reading of erotic literature (*Epist.* 89(301b)); and Macrobius (early fifth century) thought fiction bad for the soul (*In somn.* 1.2.6–12).

Many scholars see the novels' plots and characters as unrealistic. Feminist scholars find them misogynistic (Elsom 1992: 245). The Near Eastern geographical settings are unpersuasive; and the exotic ethnicity of the authors may be fictional. Thus, the ancient novel is much like the modern romance (Montague 1992: 232–5). Although women may have written novels (Hägg 1983: 95–6), most scholars wonder if women read them, arguing therefore for a male readership and male authors.

In Greek

Plots are basically the same: a young man and young woman are in LOVE, get separated, have the "usual adventures" (false deaths, enslavement, magic, mistaken identity, kidnapped by pirates, shipwreck, rivals' lust), and reunite happily. Rhetorical devices abound: ecphrasis (a painting tells a story), learned digressions (Achilles Tatius on homosexual and heterosexual love [2.35–8]), and the conscious use of spare (Attic) or florid (Asian) writing styles.

Here are short descriptions of four works:

Achilles Tatius (late second century CE) of "Alexandria": *The Story of Leukippê and Klitophon*. Klitophon is engaged to his half-sister; he dreams she castrates him. When Leukippe and her mother come to visit, Klitophon falls in love, and they arrange to have sex. The mother dreams of Leukippe's deflowering by a sword, and interrupts their tryst. They elope and have the usual adventures. In one episode, Klitophon watches bandits pretend to sacrifice Leukippe by disembowling her (she has a false belly which spills animal viscera). Later, Klitophon watches pirates pretend to behead her and throw her body overboard. They reunite in Ephesus, Leukippe still a virgin but Klitophon has been seduced by a married woman (5.27).

Chariton (probably early second century CE), "Aphrodisias": *The Story of Khaireas and Kallirhoê*. Set in the early fourth century BCE. The couple fall in love and MARRY; soon she is PREGNANT. In an argument, Khaireas kicks her in the belly and she is presumed to be dead (NERO); she is buried, but tomb robbers carry her off and sell her in Miletus where she marries Dionysios the tyrant. Eventually Kallirhoê recognizes Khaireas; he rescues her and brings her back to Syracuse.

Heliodorus (early third century CE), "Ethiopian" living in Emesa: *Ethiopian Tale of Theagenes and Kharikleia*. Kharikleia is born white to an Ethiopian couple (TABELLAE) and exposed; she is adopted. Theagenes falls in love with her; they run away and have the usual adventures until they reach Meroê where, just about to be sacrificed, Kharikleia is recognized by her parents and is saved. She and Theagenes MARRY.

Longus (probably late second or early third century CE): *The Pastoral Story of Daphnis and Khloê*, told as one long

ecphrasis. The two heroes gradually fall in love and become sexually aware, urged on by EROS, Pan, and the Nymphs. The couple experiences the usual adventures, and Daphnis is seduced by an adult woman (3.17–18). This story of sexual awakening has influenced artists (Chagall) and composers (Ravel). Other stories about Daphnis have him pursued by Pan (**118**; Theocritus 3; *Greek Anth.* 9.338) and the nymph Ekhenais (Aelian, *VH* 10.18; Timaeus, FGrH 566 F83; contrast Theocritus 1.64–142).

In Latin

Before PETRONIUS, there are no long prose works of fiction. Sisenna's translations of Aristides's *Milesian Tales* and the Menippean SATIRES adapted by Varro may have been influential. Seneca's *The Pumpkinification of Claudius* continues the genre of prose fictional narrative. Roman novels mock the Greek: the love is hardly virtuous, and the adventures are usually crass.

Apuleius (ca. 125–70 CE), of Madaurus: *Metamorphoses* (*The Golden Ass*). Lucius, eager to learn MAGIC, is transformed into a donkey and goes through the usual adventures. In one, a woman seduces him (BESTIALITY). Lucius's owner proposes to make money by having him copulate in public with a condemned murderess. Lucius escapes. Eventually, Isis turns him back into himself. The *Metamorphoses* includes the story of CUPID AND PSYCHE.

Reardon 1989.

Nudity, going about (in public) with little or no clothing. ATHLETIC nudity may date to the Bronze Age (**2**). Thucydides (1.6.4–5), however, says, "athletes wore a belt (*perizôma*) across their middle; and it is but a few years since that practice ceased" (cf. Plato, *Resp.* 452c). Thucydides's "few years" amount to about three centuries: in 720 BCE Orsippos of Megara (*IG* 7.52; cf. Pausanias 1.44.1; Sweet 1985) dropped his perizoma running in the Olympics, and may have tripped on it, fallen, and died. Afterward, all competitors contested nude.

Male public nudity reportedly originated in Crete and was introduced to SPARTA by Lykourgos (Plato, *Resp.* 425c–457b, 458d). Spartan *gymnopaidíai* (nude boys events) began after their defeat at Hysiae (668 BCE; Xenophon, *Hell.* 6.4.16; Plutarch, *Lyc.* 15.1–2); boys and MARRIED men cut their HAIR and chanted that they had been justly punished. After their successful battle at Thyrea (ca. 547), the gymnopaidia celebrates victory; only the boys are nude and wear their hair short, while the men don a feather crown (cf. Tyrtaeus 10.26–7; Papalas 1991).

Greeks themselves were aware that "athletic nudity was unique to their culture" (Lucian, *Anacharsis* 36–7). Males, presumably proper CITIZENS, are commonly depicted nude or CLOAKED so their genitals are exposed; only a few males in sculpture wear tunics (20). It may be that nudity in art distinguished the citizen male from the non-citizen (Hollein 1988; contrast Xenophon [*Ath. pol.*] 1.10–12). When making the transition from adolescent to citizen adult, youths changed clothes (cf. LEUKIPPOS I; TRANSVESTISM) and may have appeared nude briefly (AGE GRADES). Nudity is also intertwined with PAIDERASTIA (Murray 1980: 205–6).

Nude females are rare until the late fifth century (8; Scanlon 2002: app. 5.1). The legendary beauty of Spartan women (Homer, *Odyssey* 13.412; Aristophanes, *Lys.* 79–83; Athenaeus 12.566a; Strabo 10.13) was associated with their practice of training nude (Plutarch, *Lyc.* 14.1–3, 15.1.9–10, 17.1; Aristotle, *Politics* 1270b1–7). Nude ATALANTA (71), hetairai, (PROSTITUTES; 112, 149), BATHING WOMEN, and women about to be raped (114) are common on red-figure Attic pottery. The first nude woman in sculpture is about to be raped (9), and the first nude woman in the round is the "Knidia," an APHRODITE (18 [pl. 28]).

Nudity appears in Etruscan tomb paintings (Crowther 1980–1981), but Romans distinguished between their own gladiatorial combats and athletic games and those "in the Greek fashion" (i.e. nude). From 186, however, Greek games were frequent in Rome. Still, there was opposition to athletic nudity: "crime begins with citizens exposing their body" (*flagiti principium est nudare inter civis corpora*, Cicero, *Tusc.* 4.70 quoting Ennius); AUGUSTUS would not attend Greek games (Suetonius, *Augustus* 45.2). After the Neronian games (60 CE) athletes were commonly nude (Tacitus, *Ann.* 14.20).

Outside the Roman arena, nudity was either a mark of the heroic emperor (243 [pl. 42]) or of subservience and availability. PROSTITUTES stood nude at their cells (OVID, *Tristia* 2.308–14; Pliny *HN* 29.8.26); LIVIA DRUSILLA saw nude criminals. Nudity must also have been common at the BATHS.

Females' rare appearance nude connotes men's power (women in danger of being raped), men's voyeurism (bathing women), and men's demand for available sex (prostitutes, Aphrodite). Its ubiquitous appearance for males connotes the "heroic, divine, athletic, and youthful," their reliance on their body in war, and their confidence in themselves as CITIZENS (Bonfante 1989: 549–61).

O

Oedipus, legendary king of Thebes. An oracle has warned king LAIOS and queen Jokasta of Thebes that their son will murder his father and marry his mother. When the child is born, they order it exposed, but it eventually is passed to the childless king and queen of Corinth. When consulting the Delphic oracle, Oedipus is ordered out as a parricide and committer of INCEST. Thinking to avoid his father and mother, he flees towards Thebes. On the way he kills Laios. He then MARRIES the now husbandless queen and fathers two sons and two daughters. A plague breaks out and Oedipus, swearing he will find the cause, begins to discover the truth. Jokasta hangs herself and Oedipus puts out his eyes with her dresspins. Oedipus goes to Athens to gain asylum from king Theseus, where his death bequeaths a lasting blessing upon the city.

Old Age While the elderly (sixty and above) were considered wise and venerable, socially they were pathetic (cf. Hesiod, *Theogony* 603–5). Over the age of fifty they should restrain from engendering CHILDREN (SOLON; PLATO, *Resp.* 459d [over fifty-five]). Old men reportedly suffered from ABSTINENCE and IMPOTENCY; Dionysius of Heraclea was impotent with a hetaira, saying, "I cannot stretch the bow, let another take it" (Athenaeus 10.437e–f quoting Homer, *Odyssey*

21.152). Old women were thought too unattractive for sex (OVID, *Ars Am.* 3.69–80; cf. Keuls 1985: 54). Both were thus eligible for ORAL-GENITAL SEX (Aristophanes, *Lys.* end; Cass. Dio. 77.16.1; Martial 6.26.1–3, 11.25.1–2, 11.61.1–14; Athenaeus 6.246 a–b; cf. 67). Old men could also MASTURBATE (228). Some old men, however, were still sexually active (Nestor and Phoenix, Athenaeus 13.556c–d; cf. Plutarch, *Quaest. conv.* 3.6.4).

Krenkel 1981; Houdijk and Vanderbroeck 1987.

Oral-genital Sex, the penis (FELLATIO) or the vagina (CUNNILINGUS) stimulated by the mouth. "The lips, the tongue, and the whole interior of the mouth constitute an erogenous area of nearly as great significance as the genitalia" (Kinsey 1967: 587). The mouth can stand for the anus and vagina, and the tongue for the penis and clitoris. With sexual arousal, smell and taste diminish (Kinsey 1967: 616), leaving touch, which, for the tongue, is great; compare Ausonius 83: "Eunus licks and smells two different things."

Circumlocutions expressed oral-genital sex: "to defile every orifice of the body" (Suetonius, *Nero* 29); to have an "impure mouth" (Latin *os impurum*); "to do something unspeakable" or "shameless." Thus, Galen called it "a shameless activity against nature" (*pará phúsin aiskhrourgían*, 5:29–30 Kühn; cf. Euripides, *Bacchae*

1062, referring to "shameless" activity among the MAENADS).

See also: RECIPROCAL POSITION FOR ORAL-GENITAL INTERCOURSE

Orgasm, pleasurable and intense contractions of muscles in the genital region, rarely mentioned in literature (cf. a POMPEII graffito, *oblinge mentulam, mentulam elinges, destillatio me tenet*; get my cock hard, lick my cock, I'm coming! [*CIL* 4.760; Varone 2001a: 120–1]). Since orgasm eliminates waste with SPERM, ejecting it makes men cheerful, although it also chills the body and makes some depressed (Aristotle, *Problems* 30, 31.23). OVID considers mutual orgasm an attainable goal (*Ars Am.* 2.703–32). The male orgasm is occasionally depicted (**154, 202, 280, 307**).

The moment of orgasm may be depicted: MEN, and sometimes WOMEN, stretch out an arm as if in great excitement (Vorberg 1965: 230). Thus, the males have their arm outstretched: two youths in anal intercourse (**204**); males MASTURBATING (**139, 228**); man in "a tergo" intercourse with a woman (**7, 63, 201, 284, 316**); a woman in equestrian intercourse with a man (**328**); and a woman FELLATING a man (**222, 311**). And a woman stretches out her arm in frontal vaginal intercourse (**339**).

Orgies, SEXUAL ACTIVITY involving more than two persons. Some Greek vases depict SATYRS in orgies that could reflect human behavior (**109**; cf. **79**).

The most popular activity at an orgy involves a "man-woman-man" group: one man has intercourse with the woman "a tergo" while she bends forward to fellate the other man (cf. Martial 10.81; **67, 84, 122, 199, 229, 274.**10; cf. **223, 311**). A version has Hostius Quadra, while being anally penetrated by a man and performing cunnilingus on a woman, exclaiming "I'm acting like both a man and a woman" (*simul et virum et feminam*

patior; Seneca, *Q nat.* 1.16.7; cf. Williams 1999: 255–9).

Some orgies involve only typical man-woman sexual activities (**42+43, 112, 205, 232**). A kylix (**122**) emphasizes fellatio and includes a dog (ANIMALS). Another kylix (**67**) emphasizes pain (including burning, caning [FLAGELLATION], and SANDAL slapping). A stamnos (**132**) carries an odd version of the "man-woman-man" group (the second man MASTURBATES), while two men with erections and a sandal accost a flutegirl.

Rarely do MEN have sex with both men and WOMEN at an orgy (**108**). On one vase, besides four HETEROEROTIC couples, two men have facing anal intercourse (**54**) while under them a woman also lies supine, her legs also lifted high – is the penetrator alternating between the man above and the woman below? (cf. **201**). Only one vase depicts an orgy among only men (**110**): two nude youths bend over and touch their bottoms together while a youth inserts his erect penis between them – a version of intercrural intercourse.

A black-figure kylix (**52**) in Florence carries complicated mixed orgies. On one side men and women have sex in strenuous positions (twice the woman is upside-down); on the other side men only have sex, including the homosexual version of the "man-woman-man" group. Intensifying the scene are a man defecating and another urinating (BODY FUNCTIONS). A kantharos (**108**) by the Nikosthenes Painter presents a youth about to have equestrian intercourse with another youth; a youth prepares to insert a double-ended DILDO into a woman's anus as she fellates another youth (another version of the "man-woman-man" group); and youths push women.

No women-only orgies are depicted (but see MAENADS; SYMPOSIA).

See also: LAMPS; MOULD-MADE BOWLS; SEX IN ART; SEX MANUALS; VOYEURISM

Orpheus, mythological Thracian MUSI-CIAN, son of APOLLO. Eurydicê, having MARRIED Orpheus, dies from a snakebite; Orpheus enchants Hades with his SING-ING and is allowed to retrieve Eurydicê if, on the journey back, he does not look back. He does and loses her. In grief, Orpheus sings laments and turns PAIDER-ASTIC and EFFEMINATE (*hóti malthakí-zesthai edókei, háte ôn kitharoidós*, PLATO, *Symp.* 179d; cf. Maas and Snyder 1989: 118–20). When he introduces this practice to Thrace, the women (or BAC-CHANTS) murder him (**131**; cf. LAïS 2). His head, now reciting prophecies, floats to Lesbos.

Ovid, *Met.* 10.1–11, 84; Vergil, *G.* 4.453–525.

Oschophoria, an Athenian festival cele-brating DIONYSUS, the vintage, and the return of THESEUS from Crete in late October. The name derives from *óskhos*, a vine-branch with grapes or to the medical term *oskhé*, scrotum. A proces-sion was led by two boys in female dress referring to the two youths who had accompanied Theseus disguised as mai-dens (TRANSVESTISM); as *oschophóroi* they may have carried vine-branches and grape clusters (cf. the race *staphylodrómoi* for APOLLO Karneios at SPARTA), perhaps a metaphor for their hidden male genitals.

See also: AGE GRADES

Simon 1983: 89–92.

Ovid (Publius Ovidius Naso; 43 BCE–17/ 18 CE), Augustan poet. Ovid was MAR-RIED three times (at age sixteen, divorced at eighteen; at age twenty-eight, widowed soon after; and then for a third time). After completing the *Metamorphoses*, he was suddenly banished in 8 CE by AUGUS-TUS to Tomis in the Crimea; Ovid gives two reasons (*Tristia* 1.3, 2.345–6; *Pont.* 3.3.57–8): his amatory poems and an "error." The *Ars Amatoria*, however, had been published ten years previously, in 2

BCE, the same year JULIA MAIOR was banished for ADULTERY, and his *Amores* was republished. Augustus, however, did not censor erotic poetry (*Tristia* 2.361–470, 497–546). In 8 CE, L. Aemilius Paulus was executed for plotting against Augustus, and his wife, Julia maior's daughter, was exiled. Perhaps Ovid was personally involved either with her or the plot. Ovid's wife and daughter did not accompany him.

Eleven works have survived, including the *Amores* (in 14 and 2 BCE); *Heroides* or rhetorical letters from famous women (some are probably not by Ovid); *Medi-camina Faciei* or art of makeup (incom-plete); *Ars Amatoria*, the "Art of Love"; *Amoris Remedia*, "Falling out of Love"; and the *Metamorphoses*. Except for the *Metamorphoses* in hexameter, everything is elegaic.

Ovid is best known for the *Ars Ama-toria*, a manual of seduction (PORNOGRA-PHY), its pendant *Amoris Remedia*, and the *Metamorphoses*, stories about mytho-logical transformations: male gods trans-form in order to rape women and the women transform into plants or beasts. Ovid speaks almost exclusively of LOVE and sex between MEN and WOMEN, and he himself preferred women (*Amores* 3.2.40): "I hate embraces that don't wear out both partners; that's why I'm not touched by BOY-LOVE" (*Ars Am.* 2.683–4; but see MALE HOMOSEXUALITY; SEXUAL ATTITUDES). The *Metamorphoses* occa-sionally mentions male homoeroticism (NARCISSUS; ORPHEUS [Makowski 1996]), and *Heroides* 15.199–202 denies SAP-PHO's love of women. His poems are cited in POMPEIIAN graffiti.

Ovid's poetry has been the subject of feminist analysis (Keuls 1990; Janan forthcoming). His women, fleeing rape, are more attractive in their fear (cf. *Amores* 1.5), and, transformed into a tree or animal, they lose their power of speech – compare women's modern sense of powerlessness. The concept of attractive fear is a topos; Achilles Tatius describes a painting of Andromeda (3.7; cf. **289**, the movie "King Kong"): "Her face bore a mix of beauty and fear that only increased her charms."

Myerowitz 1992.

P

Paiderastia, the eroticized socialization of an adolescent boy into Greek male society by an adult man (contrast Roman BOY-LOVE), especially in the sixth and fifth century BCE (ARISTOPHANES; HOMOEROTICISM; SEXUAL ATTITUDES). The adolescent (11–18) was the erômenos (beloved, or paidiká, "kid"); the man (late 20s–early 30s) was the erastês (lover) perhaps the boy's maternal uncle (Bremmer 1983; IOLAUS). In SPARTA, he was called the espnêlas (inspirer) and the boy the parastátês (bystander, comrade, cup-bearer like GANYMEDE and PELOPS for ZEUS and POSEIDON).

For Crete and other Dorian states, Ephoros (Strabo 10.4.21) describes the process (quotation abridged): through COURTSHIP,

> the philêtôr (lover) wins the good will of the beloved, his friends and family; he tells the boy's friends that he is going to abduct him three or four days later; if the abductor is the boy's equal or superior in rank, the friends turn the boy over to him to lead away. The boy is worthy of being loved not because of his beauty but because of his manliness and decorum [andreíai kaí kosmiôtêti]. The abductor takes him to the country; and those present at the abduction follow. After feasting and hunting for two months, they return to the city. The man gives the boy a military habit, an ox, and a drinking-cup [these are required by LAW]). The boy sacrifices the ox to Zeus and provides a feast, at which he relates the facts about his intimacy with his lover, whether it pleased him or not, the law allowing him this opportunity so that, if force was applied, he might be able to avenge himself and be rid of the lover. It is disgraceful for those who are handsome or of good families to fail to obtain lovers, the presumption being that their character is responsible for such a fate.

Afterwards, the boy is called kleínos (famous or called) and wears distinctive clothing. The relationship leads to the boy's induction into the man's mess (andreíon or syssítia), a basic unit of the military and a crucial step towards CITIZENSHIP. Cretan lovers may also have sacrificed to HERMES and APHRODITE at their sanctuary at Kato Symi on the south slopes of Mt Dikte in Crete (Lembesi 2001–; Flory 1994). The gift of military gear is also known from Thebes (Plutarch, Erotikos 761b) and from Athenian vases (Bremmer 1990: 142).

Parastateis also "enjoy honors at choral DANCES and at races" (AGE GRADES; THERA). ATHLETICS and NUDE military training for the boys took place in the GYMNASIUM where Socrates seeks to fill "the souls of boys and youths with wisdom, virtue" (Plato, *Symp.* 205e–211b). He discusses philosophy with attractive adolescents, like Charmides whose body excites him (*Chrm.* 155d), and gives advice to Hippothales on how to speak to his paidika (*Lysis* 204b–206a, 207a). Several epigrams deal with trainers taking advantage of the boys in the gymnasium (*Greek Anth.* 12.34, 12.222).

Athenian vase paintings of the sixth and fifth century show courting scenes in which the erastês gives LOVE-GIFTS of hares, cocks, dogs, and meat, and makes a gesture of fondling the boy's genitals (the "hands up-and-down" position, Beazley 1947). Some of the love-gifts are also metaphors (Shapiro 1981a), dog for penis and hare for the erômenos (Ausonius 70.5; ANIMALS). A few paiderastic MAGIC (*agogê*) spells are extant (Faraone 1999: 147–8): "make the heart and soul of Ammoneios burn for Serapiakos" or "May Juvinus lie awake on account of his affection for me, Porphyrios" (cf. Theocritus 7).

In Athens, the adult man socialized the boy into adult citizen male society and the adolescent expressed his gratitude by granting his erastês "favor" (*kháris*), sexual license, even intercrural intercourse (SEXUAL ACTIVITIES). Only the erastês was meant to experience LOVE (EROS); the erômenos should experience "friendship" (*philía*; but see Johns 1982: 101; DeVries 1997; Halperin 1997: 45–54). Socrates advises that the relationship should be casual if the erômenos cannot restrain himself (Plato, *Symp.* 231a–256d). ALCIBIADES was eager to gratify (*kharízein*) Socrates, who therefore maintained his self-control (*sôphrosúnê*; Plato, *Symp.* 219b–d). The danger concerned the adolescent being sexually compromised and his citizenship thwarted (PROSTITUTES).

The relationship would continue from its inception when the boy was young (eleven years old, STRATON) to the time when he begins to get facial HAIR (Plutarch, *Erotikos* 770b–c) and is inducted into the military, at age eighteen. The erastês could waste money on an erômenos (*Greek Anth.* 5.19.1, 5.208.1; Plutarch, *Mor.* 88f); Socrates warns, "give a boy a kiss, and you'll be his SLAVE," completely "paiderasticated" (*katapepaiderastekénai*, Xenophon, *Mem.* 1.3.11–12; Lysias 3). The relationship rarely continued (MALE HOMOSEXUALITY). Both partners were expected to MARRY, the erastês soon after his paiderastic relationship ceased. The erômenos thus could be the erastês of another erômenos (PEISISTRATOS).

Paiderastia clearly corresponds to anthropologically attested practices in other cultures that violently wrench the boy away from the mother-dominated household, remove him from society, teach him "how to be a man," instill in him his masculinity (in some cultures by FELLATIO), and reintegrate him in society as a citizen (von Gennep 1909/60; Greenberg 1988; Herdt 1997; Leitao 1995: 149–56).

Several scholars (Percy 1996; Scanlon 2002) assume that, because Homer and Hesiod (eighth century) do not mention it, paiderastia must postdate them. But there are mentions of paiderastia belonging to the late eighth and seventh century: an inscribed pithos from Phaistos ("this belongs to Erpetidamos the boy-lover," *Erpetidámo paidopílas hóde*; Catalano 1971); and the stories of PHILOLAOS and CLEOMACHUS. In addition, NUDITY is introduced in the Olympic games in 720. As a rite of passage and a socialization of young males into adulthood, paiderastia must originate in early tribal society, no later than the Middle Bronze Age (ca. 1900–1700; Branigan 1998), and perhaps earlier (Bremmer 1980; Sergent 1986; Cantarella 1992: 3–8). The Minoan "Chieftain Cup" (5 [pl. 4]) is probably a paiderastic gift (Koehl 1986).

By the fifth century, paiderastia was a conservative hold-over amongst the elite in Athens and elsewhere; there is a shift downwards in age, the erastês from adult to youth and the erômenos from youth to boy. By 450 representations virtually cease (Shapiro 1992: 71). In the late fourth century PLATO and others speak out against it (SEXUAL ATTITUDES).

In the military, paiderastia was considered essential (Plato, *Symp.* 178e–179a). Courage (*andreía*) inspired LOVE (an inscription from the Athens Acropolis, *SIG* 1266: "Lysitheos declares he loves Mikion best of all in the city, for he is manly"). An early fifth-century tombstone (Thebes Museum 28200) commemorates the death of the ephebe Mnesiphrios and his lover's grief. Pairs of lovers were courageous fighters (10). The Theban general, Epameinondas (fl. 370–62 BCE), who established the SACRED BAND, loved two youths, Asopichos, a formidable warrior, and Kaphisodoros who died with him at Mantineia; they were buried together (Plutarch, *Erotikos* 761d). A military campaign encouraged situational homosexual sex; the Achaeans reportedly came back from the TROJAN WAR with "wider asses than the city gates" (Athenaeus 1.25b–c, quoting Eubulus).

Pairs of lovers could be violent. Athenaeus remarks that they "are hostile to the interests of tyrants, who thus forbade paiderastic relationships; some even burnt down the gymnasia, considering them forts inimical to their own palaces," referring to the tyrants Polykrates of Samos and Aristodemos of Cumae, and to the tyrannicides ARISTOGEITON AND HARMODIUS, all late sixth century (Athenaeus 13.602d; Dio Hal. 7.9.3–4); Plato refers to paiderastia causing civil strife in Miletos, Boeotia, and Thurii (*Laws* 636b).

An abused erômenos could be dangerous if insulted (Plutarch, *Erotikos* 768f). Krateas killed his erastês Archelaos (Plato, *Alc.* 141d) and Pytholaos killed Alexander of Pherae (Plutarch, *Pel.* 35). When his lover refused to restore him to his homeland, Hellanokrates of Larissa killed him; and when Periander tyrant of Ambracia asked his erômenos at a SYMPO-SIUM if he was PREGNANT yet, the youth killed him (Aristotle, *Politics* 1311a–b).

See also: BISEXUALITY; HETEROEROTICISM; LESBIANISM

Dover 1989; Kilmer 1993.

Peisistratos (ca. 605–527 BCE), tyrant of Athens (ca. 560–27). The erômenos of SOLON (Plutarch, *Sol.* 1.4), he dedicated a statue of EROS in the Academy to which his own erômenos Kharmos added an altar (Athenaeus 13.609d); Kharmos becomes the erastês and father-in-law to Peisistratos's son Hippias by his first MARRIAGE (ARISTOGEITON). Peisistratos married (for the second time) Megakles's daughter, but had "unnatural" intercourse with her (anal intercourse?).

Herodotus 1.59–65, 6.131.

Pelops, son of Tantalus and eponymous hero of the Peloponnese. Tantalus cut up Pelops for ZEUS to eat, but he refused it; DEMETER, however, ate Pelops's shoulder. Zeus revived him by boiling him in a cauldron (cf. MEDEA) and Demeter gave him an ivory shoulder. Pelops became the cup-bearer (erômenos) of POSEIDON (Pindar, *Ol.* 1.40–5; PAIDERASTIA).

When Oinomaos, king of Elis, received suitors for his daughter Hippodameia, he killed them in a chariot race. Pelops, who had a winged chariot, bribed the king's charioteer Myrtilos (with the right of first night with Hippodameia) to sabotage the king's chariot, killing him. Pelops then married Hippodameia, but before their first night, they all went for a ride in the winged chariot; over Cape Garaistos in Euboea, Pelops kicked Myrtilus out and he drowned. In Hippodameia's honor the Heraia games were established (ATHLETICS). Pelops's children include ATREUS and Thyestes, and Chrysippus, the erômenos of LAIOS.

Petronius, probably Titus Petronius Niger (ca. 10–66 CE), author of the *Satyrica*. As

NERO's "arbiter of elegance," he "passed his days in sleep, and his nights in 'business'" (Tacitus, *Annals*, 16.18–20). Ordered to commit suicide, he first sends Nero a list of his debaucheries and participants, and then slits his veins and slowly dies at Cumae (Pliny, *HN* 37.20).

The Satyrica, written ca. 61, is an incomplete NOVEL which SATIRIZES extravagance, new-comers, and sexual mores. Encolpius, the narrator, and Ascyltos are friends, about twenty years old, in south Italy; they are also sexual partners, refering to each other as *frater* (brother; Martial 10.65). A youth, Giton, is attracted to both men and has sex with them as a passive erômenos (PAIDERASTIA).

The story begins with Encolpius meeting Ascyltos, both of them having had a close encounter with a BROTHEL. Ascyltos then attempts to rape Giton, and they quarrel over the boy. In Book 2, our three heroes go to the country estate of Lycurgus, who had been Ascyltos's lover when he was a boy; there they meet Tryphaena and Lichas who owns estates. Encolpius beds Tryphaena, thus incurring Lichas's DESIRE for him. Since Lycurgus and Ascyltos have taken up their affair again, Encolpius leaves with Giton for Lichas's estate. There, all parties, plus Lichas's wife Doris, begin affairs in various combinations. Finally, Encolpius and Giton loot a shipwreck and join Ascyltos at Lycurgus's home, which they then rob before escaping to the city. In Book 3, they come upon some WOMEN celebrating PRIAPUS, one of whom, Quartilla, follows them back to their inn, where she implores Encolpius to cure an illness she has by having sex with her. He refuses and she has them abducted and carried to her palace. In Book 4, Quartilla's maid, Psychê, attempts to rouse Encolpius to erection by binding his hands and feet and making him drink the APHRODISIAC *satyrion*, which she also pours on Ascyltos. A CINAEDUS tries to seduce first Encolpius, then Ascyltos. As an entertainment, Quartilla brings in a seven-year-old girl, Pannychis, for Giton to MARRY. When the two go to consummate their union, Encolpius and Quartilla are tied facing each other, so that they begin to have sex while the cinaedus has anal intercourse with Encolpius. As Giton and Pannychis consummate their marriage they fall out of bed, during which diversion our three heroes escape back to their inn. In Book 5, the three youths go to the BATHS, meet Trimalchio, and attend his banquet (Books 6–10). In Book 11, our three heroes escape to their inn where Giton first has sex with Encolpius then Ascyltos, and is asked to choose between the two; he chooses Ascyltos and Encolpius moves out. He tries to assuage his loss by viewing paintings in the stoas, where he meets an old philosopher, Eumolpus, who tells him a story: he was lodging in a family's house in Pergamum and had taken a fancy to the son; by pretending sternly not to be a BOY-LOVER, he was granted the duty of accompanying him to the GYMNASIUM; eventually he seduced the boy who, however, liked the sex so much he demanded more and more of it until the old man was exhausted. In Book 12, Encolpius finds Giton in a bath now ready to return to him, and so they retire to the inn. Eumolpus also arrives and begins to lust after Giton; he relates that earlier he had met up with Ascyltos in the bath and a man who had seen that he had an enormous penis took him home. Encolpius locks Eumolpus out of the room in order to enjoy Giton. Ascyltos arrives, but Eumolpus who owns a ship gets Encolpius and Giton to sail with him to Tarentum. The ship is wrecked and the three are the only survivors. The novel ends abruptly.

Phalloi, isolated, erect penises as a symbol of power and fertility. Their purpose was usually apotropaic, to promote health and increase by warding off evil, and humorous (MAGIC; RELIGION). Roman boys wore phallus amulets around their neck and chest, "to prevent harm from coming to them" (Varro, *Ling.* 7.97; cf. **210**). Phalluses decorate transition points like bridges and entrances to houses (**240 [pl. 19]**), and common household objects like LAMPS; as tintinnabula with bells they act like windchimes (**256–261**).

The phallus appears as a separate object (miniature, **26**; colossal, **41, 177**); carried in procession (**51, 119, 158 [pl. 22]**), as a sacred stone (Friedländer and Hoffleit 1948: 43–4, no. 40), as dedications in sanctuaries (Van Straton 1981: 101 no. 182, 108–13, 115, 120, 136; cf. Johns 1982: 52–68, 92), on HERMS, as a defining part of Pan (**265**) and PRIAPUS (**247, 249**), as street and shop signs (**269, 270**) and graffiti, and as parts of vases (**31, 49, 55,** cf. **90**). It often accompanies the "evil eye" (**239, 271, 272, 273**), itself an abstract vagina (cf. the blinding of OEDIPUS for breaking sexual taboos, and the blinding of POLYPHEMUS for his inhospitality; cf. HELEN; SODOM; TIRESIAS).

In THEATER, there were two groups of phallus-bearers for DIONYSUS, the *ithyphalli* and *phallophoroi* (Athenaeus 14.622b). Ithyphalli wear drunken masks and long robes. Phallophoroi wear no masks, but are garlanded and wreathed; they enter the orchestra from all sides, chanting, poking the audience with their phalluses.

Pheidias and Pantarkes, Athenian sculptor (fl. 465–25 BCE) and his erômenos, of Elis, victor in the boys' Olympic wrestling (436 BCE). Pheidias reportedly inscribed *Pantárkês kalós* (KALOS-NAMES) on the finger of ZEUS at Olympia and carved between his feet, in relief, Pantarkes as an athlete crowning himself.

Pausanias 5.11.3, 6.10.6, 6.15.2; *Suda* s.v. Rhamnousia Nemesis; Clement, *Protr.* 4.47, 53; Taplin 1986–7.

Philolaos and Diokles, Philolaos, a Theban aristocrat, lawgiver, and erastês, and his erômenos of Corinth, victor of the Olympic footrace in 728 BCE. "Diokles left Corinth for Thebes, and there both of

them lived out their lives." Their tombs were near each other (Aristotle, *Politics* 1274a–b); and Diokles's tomb was the site of a boys' KISSING contest judged by adult men (Theocritus 12.27–38).

See also: MALE HOMOSEXUALITY; PAIDERASTIA

Phrynê (ca. 350 BCE), a well known PROSTITUTE and PRAXITELES's mistress and model for the "Knidia" and for another statue of APHRODITE at Delphi (Plutarch, *Mor.* 336c–d, 401a, d; Pausanias 10.15.1). To her Praxiteles gave his statue of EROS to dedicate at Thespiai (Pausanias 1.20.1–2, 9.27.3–5; Plutarch, *Erotikos* 753f). Phrynê charged 100 drachmes a session (Machon 376–86). At the Eleusinia, in full sight, she removed her CLOAK, let her HAIR fall, and walked into the sea. She was charged with impiety (introducing herself as a new god); when Hypereides's speech failed to impress the jury, "he introduced Phrynê, tore off her tunic, exposed her breasts. He filled the jurors with religious awe and stopped them from condemning to death Aphrodite's representative" (Athenaeus 13.590de, 591f). After the Macedonians destroyed Thebes, she said she would pay for rebuilding the fortifications, if they could be inscribed: "ALEXANDER knocked it down, but Phrynê got it back up" (Athenaeus 13.591b).

Plants were used to stimulate or diminish DESIRE, to prevent CONCEPTION, to produce miscarriages and ABORTIONS, to alleviate MENSTRUAL pain, and to facilitate lactation. With such plants, WOMEN could regulate their reproductive lives. The efficacy of these plants is being confirmed by modern MEDICINE. Here is a select list.

aristolochia (birthwort) – emmenagogue, CONTRACEPTIVE, abortifacient, for labor pains.

chaste tree (*castus*) – emmenagogue, contraceptive, abortifacient.

cucumber, squirting – emmenagogue, contraceptive, abortifacient.

fennel – for lactation (in a tea).

figs – for anal warts and piles (poultice) resulting from frequent anal intercourse.

honey – contraceptive (pessary).

iris – emmenagogue, contraceptive, abortifacient.

lily – APHRODISIAC, emmenagogue, for childbirth, obstetric softening salve.

mint – aphrodisiac (in a tea), contraceptive (pessary), for lactation.

parsley oil – abortifacient.

pennyroyal (Menta pulegium; Greek blêkhôn) – emmenagogue, abortifacient, for contractions. It is an important ingredient in the Eleusinian drink kukeôn, which also included barley meal and water. The Hippocratic Corpus recommends pennyroyal for opening up the uterus, for cleansing it before intercourse, for hysteria, for expelling afterbirth, and for stimulating lochia.

pine – aphrodisiac, emmenagogue, contraceptive, abortifacient, for childbirth. The Hippocratic Corpus recommends an extract for cleansing uterine discharge, thrush, prolapse, hysteria, amenorrhoea, and for expelling afterbirth and stimulating lochia. Modern medicine has identified female hormones in pine.

pomegranate – emmenagogue, contraceptive, abortifacient (tincture, tea, and seeds); for childbirth (tea). The Hippocratic Corpus recommends its use for cleansing uterine discharge, thrush, prolapse, and hysteria; for expelling the fetus and afterbirth. Modern medicine has identified female hormones in the pomegranate. Persephonê ate the seeds which compelled her to remain half the year in Hades (Homeric Hymn to Demeter, 412); the seeds were thought to relate to sperm as the red juice did to menstruation.

raspberry leaf (powder, modern use) – for contractions (given in final three days).

saffron (stamens of the autumn crocus) – emmenagogue, contraceptive, abortifacient (Rehak, 1999).

silphium – contraceptive. A member of the ferula, celery, or fennel family, it grew in Libya and was in such great demand that it was wiped out around the first century CE.

vitex – anaphrodisiac, emmenagogue, for childbirth and lactation. At the THESMOPHORIA, women were advised to sit or lie on branches of vitex during the second day (Pliny, HN 24.59–63). Modern medicine has determined that vitex acts on the pituitary gland to bring hormones into sequence; it thus could be used to regulate menstrual cycles, induce labor.

Riddle 1992, 1997; Riddle et al. 1994; Nixon 1995: 85–8.

Plato (ca. 429–344 BCE), Athenian philosopher. His early dialogues (ca. 400–388 BCE) approve of sexual DESIRE (Crito). Socrates is concerned that one's beloved be kalòs k'agathós (good and virtuous; Prt. 309a–d; cf. Lysis 204b–206a, 207a), but he still finds himself aroused when he peeks inside Charmides's CLOAK (Chrm. 155d).

His middle dialogues (ca. 388–61) find no disgrace in honorably loving a lover or becoming wise (Euthydemus 282b), but ALCIBIADES, desirable though he may be, is more fickle than philosophy or virtue (Gorgias 481d–482d). Socrates agrees at first; it is better for an erômenos to grant sexual favors to a non-lover because he is not sick (ou nosei) with passion (epithumía). But eventually he argues that when the erastês is incapable of self-control, it is better to leave that passion unsatisfied (cf. Symp. 218c; Phaedrus 231a–256d). Honorable lovers and beloveds make the best CITIZENS; PAIDERASTIA inspires courage, each striving to do honor in the sight of the other (Symp. 178e–179a). There are two APHRODITES, one "heavenly" (ourania) for paiderastic love, and one "common" (pandêmos) for sexual desire for WOMEN and boys (Symp. 181b–185b). With heavenly love, boys can be taught virtue since virtuous males are "PREGNANT" in mind and long to bear wisdom (205e–211b). But women are pregnant in body only, and men who are similarly pregnant (i.e. desire only sexual pleasure) will be drawn to women, since, by begetting children instead of wisdom, they are only approximating the search for an ultimate good (Gould 1963: 53).

In his later dialogues (ca. 361–47), Plato stresses the unnaturalness of same-sex sex. A factor of contemporary urban society (*Laws* 836c), same-sex love lacks self-control (*akráteia*). Men's urinary tract is connected to the spinal cord and this transports *sperma*, a living thing with a desire (EROS) for getting out. Thus the penis (*aidoíon*) in men is self-willed (cf. Latin *mentula*, "little mind"). In women, the living thing is the womb, and its desire is for child-bearing (*Ti.* 91a–d). Thus, sex must be for procreation only, according to nature (*katá phúsin*; *Phaedrus* 250e–251a; *Laws* 838e, 839a).

Plutarch (45–125 CE), Lucius Mestrius, prolific Greek biographer and essayist. The biographies often contain interesting sexual anecdotes (ALCIBIADES; ALEXANDER; JULIUS CAESAR).

In Plutarch's essay, *Erotikos*, a rich young widow of Thespiai, Imenodora (thirty years old), LOVES a youth Bacchon (18–20 years old), who is also loved by two adult men. While Protogenes and Daphnaios argue for and against the MARRIAGE, Ismenodora abducts Bacchon and MARRIES him. Protogenes supports BOY-LOVE, claiming that it is superior to the love of women: marriage is for procreation only; sex is an animalistic necessity; love for women is feminine (*thêlun*), damp and housebound (*hugrón kaí oikourón*), soft (*málthaka*), and un-manly (*anándrois*). Boy-love, however, is the proper venue for friendship and love; it makes a man strong and protective; ADULTERY in a homoerotic relationship is unheard of. Daphnaios asserts that boy-love is "contrary to nature" (*pará phúsin*) and that marriage will often lead, as boy-love will not, to a mature respect between the partners. Boy-love involves violence and corruption (*metá bías kaí leëlasías*); when there is consent it implies a weak and EFFEMINATE beloved (*sún malákiai kaí thêlutêti*) who allows himself "to be covered and mounted like cattle" (cf. Plato, *Phaedrus* 250e; *Laws* 636c); and friendships such as these "are parted by a hair as eggs are" (cf. Plato, *Symp.* 190d–e).

Poison, a woman's weapon (MEDEA); in the fourth century BCE several wives were convicted of poisoning their husbands in a single trial (Livy 8.22; Fantham 1994: 227–8). NERO sponsored a poisoner, Lucusta, and used her products to poison Britannicus successfully and his mother and wife Octavia unsuccessfully (Suetonius, *Nero* 33–5).

Polygamy, having more than one spouse, especially of a husband MARRIED to more than one wife. Polygamy was common amongst the Macedonian and Ptolemaic royalty (ANTONY; CLEOPATRA; INCEST). Sons by the same father but different mothers (*amphimêtores*) caused problems with succession. Whichever son obtained the throne proclaimed his rivals bastards (ALEXANDER and his half-brother Philip Arrhidaios; Demetrios son of Philip V and Perseus).

Ogden 1996, 1999.

Polyphemus and Galatea, a Cyclops and a nymph. Galatea loved Acis, the son of a river god, but Polyphemus loved Galatea. The Cyclops sang of his LOVE for Galatea. Afterward, he caught the couple together; Galatea fled into the sea, but Polyphemus crushed Acis with a rock. Galatea then transformed her dead lover to a river god. The story was popular in Roman wall painting (**289, 312, 323**; cf. Theocritus 6; OVID, *Met.* 13.750–897).

Pompeii, a port-city south of Naples. Established by the sixth century BCE, it suffered substantial damage in an earthquake (62 CE) which was still being cleaned up when the eruption of Vesuvius, 17–18 August 79, buried the city in pumice; many of the 10–12,000 inhabitants were asphyxiated. Excavations at Pompeii began haphazardly in 1748 and systematically in 1861; about four-fifths of the city has now been excavated, plus tombs and villas (VILLA OF THE MYSTERIES) outside the walls. The city has a rectangular forum with Capitolium, civic buildings, temples to APOLLO, Isis, and Fortuna, GYMNASIA, THEATERS, and an amphitheater. Residential *insulae* (city blocks) make up the rest of the city. Houses receive addresses that give region, insula and doorway, and some houses have conventional names (I.7.11 = the House of the Ephebe).

Brothels

The *Lupanar* (VII.12.18–20; general views: Clarke 2003: figs 31–3) is the only specially erected BROTHEL in the Roman world. This two-storey building near the forum and across the street from the Stabian BATHS has five small rooms downstairs and upstairs (perhaps the private rooms of the PROSTITUTES; cf. Juvenal 6.127). A painting of PRIAPUS with a double PHALLUS decorates the entrance; inside, the rooms open off a short corridor, at the end of which is a latrine below another staircase. The rooms are small, ca. 3×4m, with a masonry BED (including pillow). Over each doorway is a sexually explicit heterosexual painting, three of intercourse "a tergo" (**316, 318, 320**) alternating with two of equestrian intercourse (**317, 319**). Over 100 erotic graffiti praise the women ("Murtis you suck well," *CIL* 4.2273; Varone 2001a: 77 [hereafter in this section, no *CIL* and just Varone]) and give prices ("Arpocras had a good fuck with Drauca for a denarius" [4.2193]). Several graffiti use the verb *pedicare*, to fuck a boy (4.2210; Varone 131), which may imply a male prostitute in the brothel.

More brothels (as many as twenty-five) were established within remodeled residences (McGinn 2002; **325**). If each brothel had four prostitutes, there would then be one prostitute per fifty men (half the population of 10–12,000). The brothel in house I.10.10–11 is the largest; another was the house of Amandus (IX.6.8C) with eight small rooms around

an atrium with graffiti on the outside walls listing prices of women household SLAVES (*vernae*) at 5–8 asses (4.5203, 5204, 5206). Other, small brothels were connected to taverns (*cauponae, popinae*). Cauponae at V.1.13, VI.11.5/15–16, and V.2.B-D have multiple rooms and graffiti naming prices for both women and men prostitutes (4.8454: "Felicula for 2 asses," 4024: "Menander for 2 asses, nice manners"). The caupona at VI.10.1 and the tavern at IX.5.14–15 had small rooms and erotic wall paintings (**299, 300; and 324, 326, 327, 328**).

In addition, there are more than ten rooms (*cellae meretriciae*) located either on the streets for individual women or within houses for household slaves. Several cells are located near the Lupanar (VII.11.12, VII.12.33; cf. VII.2.28) or cluster together (VII.13.15, 16, 19) to share business. One of these (VII.4.42) had a masonry bed and an erotic painting of a man with an erection walking toward a woman reclining on the bed (Warsher 1938–1957: VII.4 Parts 1–3). The room of a household slave-prostitute is identified by the paintings (**329, 330**) in cubiculum 43 in the House of the Centenary (IX.8.3/6).

Baths

There were two public BATHS in Pompeii, the Suburban baths (VII.16.B) near the Porta Marina, and the Stabian baths (VII.1.8) near the Forum. The apodyterium (dressing room) of the Suburban baths held shelves at shoulder height with bins (*capsae*) for one's clothes; above, wall paintings depicted men and women having sex in various combinations (**291**) perhaps to help patrons remember their capsa (Clarke 2003: 117, fig. 80). Perhaps the paintings also refer to a brothel upstairs; a graffito nearby (4.1751+pp. 211, 464; Varone 150) recommends "if you want a fuck, ask for Attica, 16 asses."

The Stabian baths are located diagonally opposite the Lupanar and near several cells. In the men's apodyterium there are stucco reliefs of a HERMAPHRODITE and amorini (EROS). A set of erotic graffiti was written in charcoal: "get my cock hard, lick my cock, [...] I'm coming!," *oblinge mentulam, mentulam elinges ... destillatio me tenet* (4.760+p. 196; Varone 120–1).

Venus

Venus was the patron goddess of the city; many houses had paintings and/or sculptures of her. The most popular is Venus at her toilet (248; cf. 238 [pl. 34]) or looking at herself in a mirror. In the House of the First Floor (I.11.15), cubiculum 14, Mars accompanies Venus admiring herself in a mirror (east wall) and THESEUS abandons Ariadnê (south wall; Pugliese Carratelli 1990–2003 II: Regio 1, part 2). In the House of Sallust (VI.2.4), cubiculum 34 held a painting of Mars taking Venus by the wrist as she removes her necklace and as amorini play with his armor.

A megalographic painting of Venus watching ADONIS borne aloft by amorini appears in the peristyle of the eponymous house VI.7.18; other rooms had erotic paintings (room 11: Venus admires herself in a mirror, HERMAPHRODITUS at the toilet, amorini and sea beasts frolic in the predelle, and Nilotic scenes occupy the upper zones). In the House of the Tragic Poet (VI.8.5), room 12 had paintings of amorini in a nest, LEDA playing with her children in a nest, Theseus abandoning Ariadnê, and Venus and Adonis; room 15 had paintings of Ariadnê abandoned and Venus fishing (Warsher 1938–1957: VI.8, parts II–III).

In the eponymous house II.3.3 (293 [pl. 30]) Venus rises from the sea on a shell, with Mars as a statue on a pedestal. Other rooms held APOLLO and DAPHNE, LEDA and the swan, and floating amorini. A mosaic fountain in the House of the Bear (VII.2.44–46) depicts Venus on a shell, while other rooms have paintings of NARCISSUS, Danaê, and Perseus.

Houses

The typical Pompeiian house consists of exterior blank walls, a large front entrance that leads through a passage into the *atrium* (central room) flanked by *cubicula* (bedrooms but flexible in function) and large closets (*alae*). At the back of the atrium is a large room, the *tablinum* or office of the houseowner, alongside which a corridor (*andron*) led to gardens at the back with a peristyle, more cubicula, and dining rooms (*triclinia*). There are also baths, latrines, kitchens, and servant quarters.

The living areas received wall paintings in four conventional styles: first style (late fourth century BCE on) imitates masonry; second style (late second/first century) introduces large outdoor scenes with simple perspective; third style (Augustan) separates monochrome (red, black, white) panels containing easel paintings of landscape and architecture with frilly borders; and fourth style (first century CE) uses theatrical settings, complicated zones, and large panel paintings, often mythological, inserted into the walls. The constant scatter of erotic scenes makes it clear that "a generalized eroticism" characterized sophistication (Kurke 1997: 118–19, cf. 132).

The House of Lucius Caecilius Jucundus (V.1.26; Pugliese Carratelli 1990–2003 V: 574–620; Warsher 1938–1957: I) was originally a standard house of the third or early second century BCE which absorbed the house to the north and situated there the service areas, a kitchen, and bath. Jucundus's father or uncle was probably the subject of the portrait HERMS placed before the tablinum. Paintings adorn the walls, third style in the atrium and its cubicula, fourth style in the rooms around the peristyle.

Black and white mosaics covered the floors (a dog in the entrance passage; geometric motifs elsewhere). In the atrium an altar (*lararium*) to the household gods was decorated with a relief of the earthquake of 62. The walls were decorated with panel paintings, including Ulysses and Penelopê and an amorino. On the north wall of the tablinum paintings of a SATYR fondling the breast of a MAENAD (**296**) and of a maenad carrying an amorino flanked a central panel that depicted Iphigeneia at Tauris (**pl. 38**). The south wall carried two more satyr and maenad panels flanking Hecuba and Andromachê lamenting the body of Hector. The decorative frames contained stylized candelabra, garlands, Pan pipes, peacocks, and swans.

The Doric peristyle surrounds a small garden with a marble fountain; on its walls were paintings of half-nude women, tondi with portraits of women, and the Judgment of Paris (TROJAN WAR). To the right of the winter triclinium was a sexually explicit painting (**297**), below which was a graffito (4.4082), "Natalis is a CINAEDUS." On the triclinium's "east wall we find the inevitable [Theseus abandoning] Ariadnê – one could say about Pompeii, 'so many houses, so many Ariadnês' " (Warsher 1938–57: I); but this Ariadnê is more erotic, half-draped, her chest high, right arm flung behind her head. On the west wall were floating figures, a maenad, and a Medusa. Next to the triclinium was a room decorated with paintings of Venus and Mars, DIONYSUS, EROS, and a wreathed Muse. One of the small rooms off the peristyle had panels portraying a hermaphrodite with Silenus and Mars with a semi-nude Venus with amorini, and another chamber had floating women with butterfly wings (CUPID; PSYCHE).

Finally, several graffiti come from the house, including one that attests to a liaison between Staphylus and Quieta (4.4087; Varone 46; this Staphylus may have also tarried with Romula in house VII.13.8; 4.2060; Varone 45) and a popular love SONG, that starts "whoever loves may they prosper."

The House of the Vettii (VI.15.1;) was built in the second century BCE and extensively remodeled after the earthquake of 62 CE. The main entrance passage contains, on the right, a mock lararium; the left jamb of the doorway to the atrium has a central panel of fighting cocks and the right has a tall panel of Priapus (**301**). The atrium is decorated in white, red, and black panels with small inset framed paintings and decorated predelle: floating female figures; Cupids and Psychês miming human activity; animal hunting scenes; fancy candelabra; children at windows. A large room in the southeast corner of the atrium had walls painted in three major zones: a red socle with flimsy architecture, peacocks, and garlands; a broad zone of white panels alternating with flimsy architecture and inset mythological panel paintings; and an upper zone of sturdier architecture, windows and doorways, in which figures or objects seem to look down into the room. The upper figures include ZEUS, LEDA and the swan, SATYRS, and MAENADS. The central mythological panels include Kyparissos; and Cupid and Pan wrestling while DIONYSUS, Ariadnê, Silenus and fauns watch. A small suite of rooms off the Via Abbondanza had (north wall) THESEUS abandoning Ariadnê and (south wall) a rare representation of HERO AND LEANDER (also in the House of the Painters, I.12.11).

The peristyle garden (**pl. 39**) was rich in marble tables, fountains, and sculpture (bronze infants holding grape clusters and geese that spurt water, marble infants, Theseus, Paris [TROJAN WAR], DIONYSUS, satyrs, an infant holding a duck, infants with their hands tied behind their backs [fountains], and double headed busts atop floral columns). The back walls of the garden porticus are painted in three zones: a red socle with panels containing vessels and PLANTS; a zone of alternating large black panels with central framed paintings (maenads and Pans) and narrower yellow panels with architectural vistas above floating figures; and a short upper zone of white panels.

The southeast triclinium (**pl. 40**) has predominantly yellow walls with large panels with framed mythological paintings (north, HERAKLES and the snakes; east, Agavê killing Pentheus [302]; south, the trampling of Dirkê) alternating with smaller paintings of architectural vistas; an upper zone of white panels again contains mythological and other figures in windows or doorways. The northeast triclinium has a similar scheme of decoration but with red walls and paintings (north, Daidalos shows Pasiphaê the bronze cow [306]; east, the supplication of Ixion; south, Dionysus greeting an almost NUDE Ariadnê) – above this last painting is a smaller scene of Pan exposing a HERMAPHRODITE. The northwest triclinium has broad red panels containing floating figures alternating with narrow black panels containing candelabra and flimsy architecture; black predelle stretch below each panel; below is a black socle of garlands and standing figures, and above are white panels with flimsy architecture and figures (satyrs, maenads, Pans) looking out. The floating figures include Dionysus and Ariadnê, Perseus and Andromeda, POSEIDON and Amymone, all basically nude. The socles contain SATYRS, MAENADS, AMAZONS, and priestesses. In the predelle are Cupids and PSYCHES miming human activities (**305**), APOLLO at Delphi, and the sacrifice of Iphigeneia. A small panel on the outside of this room depicts Silenus surprising a hermaphrodite.

In the service area, a fourth triclinium lay next to the kitchen. Black panels with either tondi with floating females or central framed paintings alternate with narrower white panels with architectural vistas. The framed paintings include drunken HERAKLES's rape of Augê (south wall) and ACHILLES revealed on Skyros (east wall).

The most famous room in the house is the small cubiculum "x," whose walls carried two sexually explicit paintings: (east wall) frontal intercourse (**303**) and (west wall) equestrian frontal intercourse (**302**). In the room, too, was found the marble Priapus (**247**) now displayed in the garden. Although Clarke (1998: 177) sees the room "as a gift for a favorite slave, most probably the cook," it most likely served as a *cella meretricia* (Richardson 1988: 325–6), perhaps for "Eutychis female household slave, Greek, for 2 asses, good manners" (a graffito inscribed in the entrance way, left wall; 4.4592; Varone 143–4); a graffito on an outside wall advertises "Isidorus male household slave from Puteoli licks cunt" (4699; Varone 81).

Graffiti

Most graffiti follow a formula: NAME *CINAEDUS* (4.4917, Varone 137), NAME *fellat/fellator, irrumo* NAME (4.4547), or NAME *linguit* ("licks cunt," 4.5178; "licks dick," 4.8512; Varone 139; or "lick ass," "Fortunata, linge culu < m >," 4.4954). Many graffiti also deal with fucking, using *futuere* for both males and females (4.3938: *Iarinus futuit Atheto hic*) and *pedicare* for adolescent males (*Vesbinus cinedus, Vitalio pedicavit,* "Vesbinus is a CINAEDUS, Vitalio fucked him," 4.2319b+p.216; Varone 137).

Another formula stipulates that "NAME was with NAME here" ("Prima with Sparitundiolus, Scutularius with Africana," 4.10151, 10153f, 10156; Varone 47). "Sabinus was with Primigenia here" (4.8260a; Varone 46); "Primigenia with Secundus" (4.5358; Varone 46), and "Secundus with Restituta a SLAVE" (4.1665; Varone 160). Secundus is also praised as a talented (*rarus*) fellator (4.9027; Varone 140). Romula also got around; she dallied with Staphylos at house VII.13.8 (4.2060; Varone 45), but, at the house of Fabius Rufus (VII, Ins. Occ., 19), she fellated her guy "here and everywhere" as well as had 300,000 men (Varone 70–1). A certain Auctus fucked Quintium in the tavern V.1.7 (4.4818) and in another tavern IX.1.27 someone "fucked Quintius' waggling buttocks here and saw to it he was in pain" (*Quintio hic futuit ceventes et vidit qui doluit*, 4.4977; Varone 75).

Homoerotic declarations of love include "The slave Helios loves you, Thrason master of Helios" (4.5037=3310; Varone 157) and "if only Damoetas would give it to me, I'd be happier than Pasiphaê; this is what Zosimus has written" (4.5007 [=3299+3300]; Varone 134). Unrequited love is expressed both by heterosexuals ("Marcellus loves Praenestina, but it's not returned," 4.3042; Varone 99) and by LESBIANS (*Chloê Eutychiae s < alutem >* : *non me curas, Eutychia. Spe firma tua Ruf amas*, "Chloê, health to Eutychia: you don't care about me. Stubbornly you love Rufa," 4.8321a; Varone 2001: 102). And one homoerotic expression (in Greek) smacks of disappointment: "If a boy has the fortune to be born beautiful, but does not offer his ass (*édoke pugiásai*), let him be in love with a beautiful girl but not get to fuck her" (*mê túkhoi beinêmatos*; Varone 131).

Three graffiti announce marital feelings: satisfaction ("L. Claudius Varus and Pelagia, his wife" [*coniunx*], IX.3.25 cubiculum, 4.2321; Varone 160) and bliss ("I wouldn't sell my husband for any price," 4.3061+p. 466 and [repeated] 3062; Varone 162).

Crescens declares his penis hard and huge (4.10085b; Varone 87) and Gaius Verlius Enustus, a soldier in the 1st praetorian cohort, declares himself to be "the greatest fucker" (4.2145; Varone 67). Secundus, perhaps the same as above, also "fucked boys screaming for it" (*Sucundus pedicavd pueros* [*lu*]*gentis*; 4.2048+p. 215; Varone 132). In the Great Palaestra (II.7) Floronius describes himself: "a

fucker (*binetas*); a soldier of the VIIth legion was here, and only a few women got to know him – just 6" (4.8767; Varone 66); and Quintus Postumius runs his boast like an election notice: "On 9 September, Quintus Postumius invited (*rogavit*) Aulus Attius for a fuck" (*pedicarim*; 4.8805; Varone 136).

In the Gladiators' Barracks (V.5.3; Varone 68–70) there was an ego war between Celadus Thrax ("the Thracian") and Cresces (*retiarius*, a gladiator with a net): "Celadus Thrax is just right for the girls" (4.4345); "Cresces gets some dolls (*puparum*) at night, others in the morning" (4.4353); "Celadus is the girls' heartthrob" (*suspirium*; 4.4397). In a similar graffito war Successus sends his greetings to two slaves, Felix and Fortunata (4.5373; Varone 163); in a tavern he declares his love for Iris, but Severus, whom Iris really loves, mocks him for it (4.8259; Varone 113–4); in the tavern next door, their rivalry is referred to (4.9848; Varone 113).

In an election notice on the Schola Armaturarum (III.3.6), a certain Martial is urging the election of Proculus for *aedile* (a city services official); under it is the INVECTIVE "Martial, you're fellating Proculus." And a mock notice to the left of a shop entrance urges support for Isodorus for aedile because he performs the best CUNNILINGUS (*Isidorum aed. optime cunulincet*, 4.1383; Varone 81).

One graffito may record the BIRTH of a CITIZEN, "Cornelius Sabinus is born" (4.8149; Varone 168), but others more likely deal with slaves or PROSTITUTES: "Ra[has gotten me pregnant" (*gravido me tenet Ra*[; 4.7080; Varone 167); "I don't care about your pregnancy, Salvilla, I reject it" (Latin, in Greek letters: *contemno, derideo Latona*(*m*) *tua*(*m*) *Salvilla*, 4.8384; Varone 100); and the simple declaration, "on 23 Jan. Ursa has given birth, a Thursday" (*X K*(*alendas*) *Febr*(*u*)*a*(*rias*) *Ursa peperit diem Iovis*, 4.8820; Varone 167–7).

The final set of graffiti here is in verse.

The KISSES I stole, you complain of, beautiful girl;
Take them back then, but I'm not the only one who loves you
"Whoever loves may they prosper ..."

> (VII, Ins. Occ. 19, House of Fabius Rufus Varone 53; SONGS)

A possible Locrian song or Fescinnine verse (4.1825+p. 212, 464; Varone 140):

Fucked, I say, fucked with legs apart [*atractis pedibus*] were the cunts of the women of Rome
and no other moans were heard than those of pleasure in the worst way.

Miscellaneous elegies:

Every lover's a soldier [*miltat omnis amans*; cf. OVID, *Amores* 1.9.1–2], and Desire has the fort –
Atticus, believe me, every lover's a soldier

> (Varone 55)

Who dissuades lovers can fetter the winds
and forbid the waters to run from their fountains

> (4.1649; Varone 62)

If anyone by chance desires to violate my girl
may LOVE burn him in the desolate mountains

> (4.1645+p. 463)

Here I've fucked at last a beautiful girl,
praised by many but a mudhole inside [*lutus intus*];

> (4.1516; Varone 119)

Here I have penetrated the mistress [of the house], her open buttocks [*resoluto clue*];
bad of me to write this verse!

> (VILLA OF THE MYSTERIES; 4.1781 + p. 464; Varone 74)

Finally, seven hexameters (4.5296 + p. 705; Varone 101):

Oh, if only I (fem.) could hold my gentle arms around you
and press my kisses on your tender lips. Go now, girl, confide your joys to the winds:
believe me, flighty is the nature of men. These things I've often meditated
lying awake in despair in the middle of the night: many has Fortune raised on high
then suddenly let fall headlong, oppressing them with worst trouble.
Likewise, though Venus in a moment unites the bodies of lovers,
the first light divides them and you (Venus) would separate their love.

Pornography, writings and depictions of explicit sexual activity in order to sexually excite their audience. *Pornográphos* is first used by Athenaeus (13.567b) to describe "the painters Aristeides, Pausias, and Nickophanes," who painted PROSTITUTES (*pórnai*; Krenkel 1970; SEX IN ART). Modern attitudes have considered pornography dangerous and corrupting. Sexually explicit material has been separated from "innocent" eyes: a separate volume in the publication of the Herculaneum finds, a "Secret Cabinet" in the Naples Archaeological Museum, and the Witt Collection in the British Museum (Johns 1982: 19–32). Modern legal analysis has grappled with the definition of pornography, especially in academic settings, in sex counseling, and in art and literature. And social critics, especially feminists, have debated whether pornography merely provides vicarious and harmless enjoyment, leads its audience to replicate the pornographic event and thus do some harm (rape), or objectifies persons (the participants) by reducing them to mere body parts (Richlin 1992a; Parker 1992: 99–100).

Was there pornography in antiquity? Can we know the intention of those who produced sexually explicit scenes and can we know if they actually did arouse their audience? (Parker 1992: 90–1; Jones 1982: 96). We do know the genres and their effects: SEX MANUALS; sexually explicit plays, verses, and entertainments (CINAEDOLOGOI; NERO; THEATER) performed by actors who emphasized the sexual content deliberately to cause sexual arousal; TABELLAE, which could be opened precisely when needed; erotic LAMPS (212–229) and other portable objects like cameos, mirrors (7, 230), MOULD-MADE BOWLS all with erotic scenes that could be considered at sexually appropriate moments, and literature that explores the pleasureable effects of erotic feelings (NOVELS; OVID).

Pornography depends on at least three basic premises: the sex act needs to be perceived, the audience needs to feel the sex act is being performed for them, and ORGASM needs at least to be anticipated. For the first premise, the mirror cover from Corinth (7) positions the couple so we clearly see the man's penis entering the woman's vagina; in Roman wall paintings the man tucks his near hand behind his back (326) or places it on his hip, so as not to interfere with our viewing the actual moment of penetration – such hand placements are tell-tale signs of modern pornography, the actor conscious of the camera.

For the second premise, modern pornography places the sexual activity in a staged setting (platforms, obvious sets), introduces a third party that stands for the audience (usually not intimately participating), and provides formulaic exclamations that are repeated theatrically to focus the audience's attention on the activity. In ancient depictions of sexual activity, a stage setting appears routinely: a curtain is drawn behind the participants isolating them, along with the audience, from the rest of the world (250, 317, 318, 320, 332, 338, 339). Roman art often introduces the third party, a personal servant or *cubicularius* (288, [1.43.6] 290). Repetitive exclamations are inscribed over the sex scene: on vases (74, "hold still;" 113, "let me!" and "stop!"), in paintings (314, "push it in slowly"), and on several mould-made bowls (188, 189, 193).

For the third premise, orgasm can be stated in literature, and it occasionally is in POMPEII graffiti. Paintings depict the man, and once the woman (339), with one hand outstretched as if conveying the tension and excitement of the activity (cf. 179).

Poseidon/Neptune, god of the sea, earthquakes, and horses, and father of POLYPHEMUS. As stallion he mates with an Erinys or with DEMETER Erinys as a mare to produce the horse Arion (Pausanias 8.25.4–5); with Black Demeter who has a horse's head, he fathers Despoina at Phigaleia (her major sanctuary is at Lycosura); and with the Gorgon Medusa he fathers the man Chrysaor and the winged horse Pegasus. Poseidon also has his eromenos "cupbearer" PELOPS.

Praxiteles (fl. 364–1 BCE), son of Kephisodotos of Athens, a sculptor. One of his famous works was EROS which he gave his mistress PHRYNE to dedicate in the sanctuary of Eros at Thespiai (Cicero, *Verr.* 2.4.135; Plutarch, *Erotikos* 748a; cf. Schauenburg 1981); it was stolen by CALIGULA (Pausanias 9.27.3). The Palatine Eros is probably a copy (Pfrommer 1980).

His most famous work, however, was the "Knidia" (18 [pl. 28]), a NUDE statue of APHRODITE and the first in-the-round statue of a nude woman. Kos had commissioned a statue of Aphrodite from Praxiteles, who made two versions, one clothed and the other nude, both based on his mistress, the hetaira Phrynê (or Kratina, Clement, *Protr.* 4.48, 51; PROSTITUTES). Kos took the clothed statue, Knidos bought the nude statue and set it up in a completely open rotunda (excavated and confirmed, Love 1972: 70–6). Several authors record an incident that a youth ejaculated onto the leg of the statue and stained it (Lucian, *Eikones* 4, *Amores* 15–16; Val. Max. 8.11.4; Pliny, *HN* 7.127 and 36.20–21; Tzetzes, *Chil.* 8.375; cf. the story of HEPHAESTOS and ATHENA). The statue inspired numerous copies as well as variations (SEX IN ART).

Ovid, *Ars Am.* 2.613–4; Pliny, *HN* 34.50; Lucian, *Amores* 13, *Eikones* 6; Lapatin 1997.

Pregnancy SORANUS did not distinguish much between CONCEPTION and the development of the fetus during pregnancy.

Others felt that conception was either instantaneous or lasted as long as three days. A popular belief was that intercourse always resulted in pregnancy, a generalization from Homer, *Odyssey* 11.248–50. If intercourse did not result in pregnancy, then "it was assumed that the woman had intervened (ABORTION; CONTRACEPTION) – or that her organs of generation were anatomically deficient or nosologically impaired" (Hanson 1992: 46).

In the first week, the seed (the fetus) either congealed or fell out. The male fetus quickened at three months, the female fetus at four months since its seed was watery (Hanson 1992: 53). During pregnancy the woman "becomes yellowish green, because each day the pure part of her blood always trickles down from her body and goes to the embryo as its nourishment. [S]ince there is less blood present in her body, she desires strange foods" (Hanson 1992: 34 quoting the Hippocratic corpus). Pliny thinks that pregnant WOMEN stink (*HN* 7.64): "A horrible smell fills the air; it drives dogs mad and infects their bites with an incurable POISON." Pregnancy was likened to cooking: the membrane that forms around the conceived seed looks like that on the surface of bread as it is being baked (Prisc. 3 [I:574–8] 1992; Hanson 1992: 133). For this reason, one could discover the sex of the fetus by taking some of the mother's milk, mixing it with flour to make a cookie of it, and baking it – if the cookie congeals and bakes properly, the fetus is a boy; if it stays liquid, it is a girl (Hanson 1992: 54).

Expectant mothers invoked the assistance of specialized goddesses EILEITHYIA and ARTEMIS, to whom they dedicated their maternity clothes (Euripides, *Iph. Taur.* 1462; Van Straten 1981: 99), even when they had died in childbirth (McClees 1920). Other dedications included terracotta models (wombs, pregnant women [**266**], women in labor, women giving BIRTH; Van Straten 1981: 99–100, 115). Occasionally, women offered keys for a successful birth (Aristophanes, *Thesm.* 973–6; Festus 39), and dedicated keys have been excavated in the sanctuary at Foce del Sele; the practice still continues (Van Straten 1981: 100).

See also: CHILDREN; FERTILITY; MEDICINE; MIDWIVES

Priapus and the "Priapea," apotropaic, bearded male god of gardens and FERTILITY, and the collection of eighty-six poems dedicated to him. Priapus was the son of APHRODITE and DIONYSUS (or ZEUS), born at Lampsacus. Coins of Lampsacus, dating to the end of the third century BCE, carry Priapus, whose cult had apparently spread to Rome by 90.

In the Augustan period, people placed statues of Priapus in gardens. These were originally wood branches or logs with a fork whose tip could be painted red to resemble a PHALLUS; other versions also existed (**247, 255, 301, 324**). Mutinus/Tutinus was a local priapic divinity in Rome, whose sanctuary housed a statue of a seated Mutinus with erect phallus. New brides, to become FERTILE, sat on the phallus, as if having equestrian intercourse. Coins of 90 BCE portray Mutinus somewhat like Priapus (i.e. a bearded HERM standing with erect phallus).

The god is also the patron of BROTHELS (315; cf. *Hist. Apoll. Tyr.* 33–6). Several Priapea poems record dedications made by PROSTITUTES (Hooper 1999: nos. 19, 27, 34, 40).

The Priapea is a collection of short poems purporting to be labels on the statues of Priapus in the garden or epigrams on his temple walls, warning thieves of punishments the god will inflict with his phallus or by BODY FUNCTIONS (urination, defecation). The two introductions (nos. 1 and 2) ascribe the poems to a single author, who could be Euphronius (fl. under Ptolemy Philopator, 222–204 BCE; Hephaestion 15.59). Seneca, however, attributes no. 3 to OVID (*Controv.* 1.2.22); no. 80 parodies *Amores* 3.7.1–2. Stylistically, the collection seems earlier than MARTIAL; most scholars prefer an Augustan date.

Most of the poems in the collection mention the large size of Priapus's phallus (no. 17: "no woman has ever been loose for me"), and what he will do with it to whom (no. 22: "if a woman, man, or boy thieve from me, one will offer me her cunt, his head, or his ass"). Some poems employ puns and riddles (no. 67: "The first syllable of Dido follows the first of Penelopê, and the first of Remus follows the first of Cadmus; what results, you will owe me, if you come as a thief into my garden"). Other poets have poems to Priapus: Theocritus 1.81, Tibullus 1.4, Horace, *Sat.* 1.8.

Richlin 1983.

Procnê and Philomela, daughters of Pandion, king of Attica. King Tereus of Thrace MARRIES Procnê and they have a son Itys. He falls in love, however, with Philomela, and, concealing Procnê, he reports her death to Pandion who then offers him his other daughter; Tereus rapes Philomela, and cuts out Procnê's tongue to silence her. She, however, embroiders her whereabouts into a tapestry, which Philomela sees and rescues her

sister. In revenge, Procnê kills her son and serves his cooked flesh in a dish to her husband. When Tereus discovers what he is eating, he pursues the fleeing sisters in an attempt to kill them but the gods intervene, changing all into birds. Procnê becomes a swallow, Philomela a nightingale, and Tereus a hoopoe. Itys is revived and turned into a goldfinch.

Ovid, *Met.* 6.524–85.

Propertius (54/47–2 BCE), Sextus, poet. Propertius expresses his LOVE for "Cynthia," (really Hostia, Apuleius, *Apol.* 10); love, he says, was his career (*militia*, 1.6.29). Book 3 purports to document the end of his affair with Cynthia, but poems 4.7 and 4.8 take up the theme again. In 4.8, he declares his love for Lygdamus (BOY-LOVE).

Prostitutes and Prostitution, selling the sexual use of one's body for gain.

Terminology

Greek *pornê* and Latin *meretrix*. *Pornê* comes from the verb *pérnêmi*, to sell; several prostitute names incorporate money (Obolê [the smallest Greek coin], Didrachmon [12 obols]). Slang words for prostitute (Latin *scortum*) were common, and certain professionals (flutegirl in Greece; mime in Rome; bath-attendant in both) were conventionally considered prostitutes.

Pornê and meretrix designated both the prostitute who worked primarily alone, a "streetwalker" (*peripolis*, or girl about town; Pollux 7.203), and the prostitute who worked with others in a BROTHEL; the hetaira (Greek and Latin) also could work alone or with others but she was more expensive and spent longer time with customers; she was also expected to be educated, witty, and politically astute. The *pallakê* (Greek) or *concubina* (Latin) was a live-in mistress (cf. male *pallakós/concubinus*), a kind of non-legal spouse with whom a man could have legitimate

CHILDREN (ASPASIA). Most prostitutes named in literature are resident aliens (metic hetairai) or SLAVES, sold into prostitution and owned by a brothel manager. Men and women, represented as penetrated, should all be prostitutes (except perhaps **198, 204**), since proper citizens should not be so portrayed (cf. Wells 1979: 18–9).

Pornai/meretrices

They were paid in cash, hetairai generally not; thus the classical depictions of MEN offering leather bags (Grk *phormískoi*) to WOMEN (**64, 107, 117, 146**) or youths (below) are probably depicting pornai and their male customers. Such bags probably contained coins (cf. Keuls 1985: 419, fig. 240); knucklebones, *astragaloi*, are also suggested (Pinney 1986; cf. Kalogeropoulou 1986: 124–5). In a Roman wall painting, PRIAPUS weighs his PHALLUS against a leather bag full of coins (**301**). The Latin word for this leather bag, *bulga*, is used by Lucilius 61, *in bulgam penetrare pilosam*, "to penetrate a hairy bag," paraphrased in a POMPEII graffito (*CIL* 4.1830; Varone 2001: 60).

Pallakai/concubinae

A prostitute whom a man could set up in a house, after a DIVORCE or his wife's death, and live with her as if married. The Greek man could also appeal to his kinship group (phratry) to have their children legitimized if he had no sons by his previous MARRIAGE (ASPASIA). A man abandoning his wife for a pallakê is rare (Isaeus 6.21).

Hetairai

The term hetaira is the feminine form of *hetaíros*, a man's (war) companion; women could refer to their female friends as hetairai (Athenaeus 13.571d quoting Sappho 12 Edmonds 1928). A tombstone (Clairmont 1993: no. 146) carries an inscription that mentions *hetairoi*, "male companions," of a woman Anthemis; perhaps she was a hetaira herself.

As "companions," hetairai are often shown acting like men, reclining at SYMPOSIA (**68, 152, 156**) and taking the lead in sex (**139**). During the festival "Haloa" in honor of DEMETER, hetairai held their own SYMPOSIUM at Eleusis; and prostitutes could be initiated into the Eleusinian Mysteries.

The hetaira emerges early in the sixth century BCE (contemporary with the invention of coinage). Her major function is to entertain; at symposia she plays lyres, SINGS, DANCES, converses, and has sex. Most depictions of hetairai occur in vase painting dating ca. 520–470, but depictions and descriptions of them continue into at least the Hellenistic period (Shapiro 1992: 53–4). The OLD hetaira becomes a topos in both art (**122?, 153, 174**) and literature (Aristophanes, *Eccles.* end; Anacreon 346 PMG); several Hellenistic epigrams in the Greek Anthology purport to be labels for mirrors dedicated by old hetairai (LAÏS I).

Hetairai are conventionally paid in LOVE-GIFTS, like eromenoi (Aristophanes, *Wealth* 149–59). Gift-exchanges (Kurke 1997: 108) create a special bond between giver and receiver. Hetairai are an invention therefore of an aristocratic society shying away from the new mercantile class that deals in "common lucre." The gifts "persuade" (cf. Peitho) the woman to "give favors" (*kharízomai*; Kurke 1997: 108): you've fallen in love, not with a *pornê* but with a hetaira, who "services those in need, as a favor," *khárin* (Anaxilas fr. 21 K-A). Compare korai statues (female statues, sixth century BCE), which appear contemporaneously and in the same aristocratic setting; they also offer "favors": flowers, pomegranates, tops.

In Socrates's conversation with the hetaira Theodotê (Xenophon, *Mem.* 3.11) she avoids telling him precisely how she manages to live so well; she lives by the kindness of friends (much as Blanche DuBois lives by the kindness of strangers), which she then repays in sexual favors. "All pornai can be labelled Theban Sphinx; nothing they babble is straightforward, but it's all in riddles, of how they love 'to love,' and 'be friends' and 'go with' you. And then it's 'If only I could have ...'" (Athenaeus 13.558d quoting Anaxilas). To make the "favor" seem independent of the gift some time should elapse (Davidson 1998: 120–7).

Male prostitution

CITIZEN men were occasionally called prostitutes as political INVECTIVE (Marc ANTONY, Cicero, *Phil.* 2.44–45; members of AUGUSTUS's family, Tacitus, *Ann.* 5.3.3). Men convicted of prostitution (AESCHINES) could not enter temples, make speeches, or initiate official proceedings (Demosthenes 30.61, 73). Presumably, if an Athenian citizen was a prostitute and did not pursue public office of any kind, "he was safe from prosecution and punishment" (Dover 1989: 29; cf. Demosthenes 22.30–1). Similar restrictions applied in other cities: a second century BCE inscription from Beroia (*SEG* 27.261, B:26–9) lists the persons prohibited from entering the GYMNASIUM; these include slaves, drunks, madmen, and those who have prostituted themselves (*hetaireukôtes*).

In Athens, most male prostitutes were slaves. Phaedo, an aristocratic Elean, had been enslaved when his city was captured and was put to work as a prostitute in a "cell" (*oîkêma*); he was bought by Socrates's wealthy friends (Diogenes Laertius 2.105). Male prostitutes worked in brothels (**288** [**pl. 43**]; cf. **208**), were paid in coin (**77** [**pl. 6**], **162**), and perhaps, like hetairai, in gifts (cf. **170**). Any depiction of male-male intercourse probably implies that the penetrated man is a prostitute (**69**). Male prostitutes, however, were not

just for men; women also paid for sex (Martial 7.75, 11.29, 11.62).

The city of Rome had thousands of young male prostitutes (CINAEDI) who acted EFFEMINATE, wore the woman's *stola* (Cicero, *Phil.* 2.44; PETRONIUS 81.5), and offered themselves in the regions known for prostitution in Rome. There was also a holiday (at least once) for male prostitutes (*CIL* 1.236; Griffin 1976: 102). Tacitus (*Annales* 6.1) discusses two special terms for young male prostitutes, *sellarii* and *spintriae*; he derives sellarii from *sellarium*, a public latrine where they congregated (**pl. 37**; BROTHELS; ELAGABALUS). Tacitus also tells us that spintriae were known for being passive. TIBERIUS attracted both types (Suetonius, *Tiberius* 43.1, *Caligula* 16.1); Vitellius was even nicknamed "Spintria" because as a boy he was rumored to have prostituted himself with Tiberius at Capri to obtain his father's political advancement (Suetonius, *Vitellius* 3.2).

History

Prostitutes may have been everywhere in the classical world, but brothels are hard to find (none in Ostia); few have been excavated. In POMPEII, brothels are clustered near the BATHS and city gates. In Rome prostitutes were everywhere (Dio Chrysostom), out at the city walls (Martial 11.61.2), in the arches of the Colosseum, and especially in the area of the Subura on the lower slopes of the Esquiline now traversed by the Via Cavour (PROPERTIUS 4.7.15; PRIAPEA 40; Persius 5.32f.; Livy 3.13.2; Martial 2.17.1, 6.66.2, 11.61.3, 11.78.11). Prostitution could be an extension of hospitality (ADULTERY; SODOM).

SOLON's legislation (594 BCE) reputedly concerned prostitution: *deikteriádes* (women who showed themselves in public; Plutarch, *Sol.* 23.1; cf. a LAW in Thasos, Henry 2002) had fixed prices (Xenophon [*Ath. Pol.*] 50.2; cf. Hypereides, *Eux.* 3) and paid taxes (*pornikón télos*) to special tax collectors (cf. Philonides fr. 5; Harpocration s.v.). They were confined to a licensed brothel, were not allowed on the street during the day, and had to have a special permit for leaving the city. Solon also prohibited prostitutes from attending religious ceremonies and entering temples; they had to be recognizable (dye their HAIR saffron, wear a special multi-colored garment; cf. the prostitutes in Syracuse, Athenaeus 12.521b); and they could not refuse a customer.

The purpose of these regulations may have been to provide the male citizen population plenty of cheap prostitutes so they could stay sexually satisfied without unnecessary rivalry over proper women and so their estates would not be squandered over high-priced hetairai. Athenaeus quotes from classical comedy about the easy availability of prostitutes and their client's dismissive attitudes (13.568d–569f), ending with Philemon's *Fratres* (abridged): there are

> women in various neighborhoods, ready and available for all. They stand naked, lest you be deceived; look at everything. The door is open; the price, one obol! Jump right in, and there isn't any dissembling or nonsense, [take her] as you wish and in whatever way you wish. You exit, and you can tell her to go to hell. She's a stranger to you.

Prostitutes were thought dirty (Anacreon PMG 346; Aristophanes, *Knights* 1397–1401; Menander, *Samia* 390 ff.). Even so, they could be thought better than wives since a prostitute "must get and keep a man by being amenable" (Henry 1992: 262, using Athenaeus 13.559a–b). But prostitutes were also necessary, especially on a military campaign; they accompanied Perikles in his expedition to Samos and dedicated a famous statue to APHRODITE there (Athe-naeus 13.572f; SEX IN ART [sculptures]); they also accompanied the "Ten Thousand" (Xenophon, *Anab.* 4.3 and 19).

Rome was introduced to Greek-style banquets, including slave girls as entertainers, presumably as prostitutes, in the early second century BCE (Livy 39.6.7–9). Being a prostitute and procuring for prostitutes made a man ineligible for holding office (LAWS). Although CALIGULA first wanted to ban *spintriae* from Rome and even to drown them in the sea, he taxed them and all prostitutes, both female (Suetonius, *Caligula* 16.40) and male (Justin Martyr, 1 *Apology* 27). The tax apparently was rescinded only well into the Christian period, 498 CE.

Alexander Severus (emperor 222–35 CE) had contemplated banishing male prostitutes from Rome, but Philip the Arab (244–9) apparently actually accomplished it (Aelius Lambridius, *Alexander Severus* 24). Marcus Claudius Tacitus (275–6) outlawed brothels in the capital, but it could have hardly been carried out during his short reign.

Temple (or sacred) prostitution

This has been identified in the Near East, especially Mesopotamia, although the terminology is obscure. Middle Assyrian lead figurines depicting intercourse have been found in the temple of Ishtar at Asshur; Ishtar (Inana) was the Assyrian goddess of physical love, and was herself sometimes referred to as a prostitute and her temple as a tavern (Black and Green 1992: 151; also Leick 1994: ch. 13). Shamhat the prostitute in tablet 1 of the "Epic of Gilgamesh" has sex with Enkidu and wants to take him with her to the temple of Anu and Ishtar. A fifth-century Phoenician inscription from Kition (BM 125.080) refers to dogs (*keleb*) in the precinct of Astarte there; since Deuteronomy 23:18–19 bans female prostitutes (*qedeshah*) and dogs (*klmb*) from the temples, it has been supposed that "dogs" are male prostitutes (Brunet 1985).

Herodotus 1.199 describes temple prostitution in the cult of "Aphrodite" (Mylitta) at Babylon: all "women were required at least once to have intercourse with a stranger within the temple precinct." He mentions "similar rituals in Cyprus," at the sanctuaries of Aphrodite at Amathous and Paphos (Paleopaphos). The *Acts of St Barnabas* refers to a religious procession and "lewd" doings near the Aphrodite sanctuary at Paleopaphos; Justin (*Epit. Hist.* 18.5, quoting Pompeius Trogus) says "the Cypriots send their young women before marriage to the seashore to get money by prostitution" (cf. Ennius, *Euhemerus* 134–8; OVID, *Met.* 10.238–46). Strabo (6.2.6) claims temple prostitution not only for the Paleopaphos sanctuary (his text mirrors Herodotus's closely) but also for other sanctuaries of Aphrodite, at Corinth, Locri Epizephyrii, and at Eryx, Sicily (cf. Diodorus Siculus 4.83).

At Corinth there were "more than a 1,000 sacred prostitutes, whom both men and women dedicated to the goddess," Aphrodite (Strabo 8.6.20; cf. 12.3.36; cf. Athenaeus 13.573f–574c). Where these prostitutes practiced is not known, probably not at the small temple to Aphrodite on the top of Acrocorinth (elevation 575m; Pausanias 2.4.7).

Several scholars have taken these ancient references at face value (MacLaughlan 1992; Strong 1997). But Herodotus is vague and later classical references were written long after the period they claim temple prostitution existed. Herodotus also does not mention temple prostitution in Corinth, nor does Pausanias when he mentions the temple on the acropolis – this last point seems telling, since Pausanias is interested in peculiar religious practices. An alternative interpretation of the concept of "sacred" prostitution is to see the Greek verb for having sex, *aphrodisiázein*, "to do Aphrodite," as implying that all intercourse is sacred.

Prices, normal

Greece

Prostitutes charged 1–2 drachmes (Aristophanes, *Thesm.* 344–5), although less was proverbial (as in "two-bit whore"); 2 drachmes was the maximum legal fee for hiring a flutegirl (Hyperides, *Eux.* 3; *Suda* D 528). Slave prostitutes were able to keep some of the money they earned to buy their freedom (NEAIRA).

Prices differed according to the sex act and position, length of time, and exclusivity of access. Special entertainers, such as the harpist Habrotonon (Charisius, *Arbitration*), charged 10–12 drachmes (cf. Menander, *Samia* 392), and high-class prostitutes like PHRYNE cost as much as 100 drachmes for a session (see below).

In some instances, the customer signed a contract with the owner of the prostitute. Simon had a contract with the owner of Theodotus, a boy from Plataea, for 300 drachmes, but the boy broke the contract by seeing someone else (Lysias 3.21–6). Diabolus had a contract with the mother of Philainion for 20,000 drachmes (Plautus, *Asin.* 746–96). Lead tablets from Dodona record a mother's question of ZEUS: should she give her daughters to Theodoros and Teisias (Licht 1926: 1: 1). One could always buy a slave for sex; Nikaretê sells her daughter Neaira to two men for 30,000 drachmes.

Rome
(Varone 2001a: 143–7, 153–4)

The typical price seen in the POMPEII graffiti (*CIL* 4) is two or three asses. Both male and female prostitutes advertise FELLATIO at this price (and one prostitute, "Glyco," probably female, advertises CUNNILINGUS). "Felix" advertises fellatio for one as on tomb 4 outside the Noceria gate, the lowest price mentioned (cf. Juvenal 3.66, 6.365; Martial 1.34.8). "Maritimus" advertises cunnilingus for four asses. "Florus" may be advertising himself for something special (to be pene-trated?) at ten asses. Two inscriptions at one locale, *CIL* 4.7339, refer to Felix and Florus selling sex, perhaps together, as Constans and Priscus seem to have done (*CIL* 4.4690; Varone 2001a: 153).

A few female prostitutes advertise themselves for more than three asses; Euplia offers fellatio at five asses, but the unnamed household slaves of insula IX 6 do not specify what they offer for eight asses – it might be for vaginal intercourse: in the Lupanar, Arpocras celebrates his "good fuck" (*bene futuit*) with Drauca for a denarius (sixteen asses [*CIL* 4.2193]).

Living/working conditions

The common male and female prostitute could be the child of a prostitute, a SLAVE, a prisoner of war, or kidnapped. They worked in brothels for an owner or by themselves in cells (Grk *oikêmata*, Lat. *cellae*; cf. Aeschines *In Tim.* 1.74) or at festivals (Montserrat 1996: 106–34). Other professionals did prostitution on the side, especially bath-attendants and *cubicularii* (chamber servants). Since many prostitutes could not refuse a client, they worked long hours, day and night; at night they lit LAMPS by open doors of their cells (Plutarch, *Erotikos* 759e–f; Juvenal 6.127 has the pimp send his prostitutes home at the end of the day, a literary foil to point up the "hard work-ing" MESSALINA). PREGNANCIES were to be avoided (CONTRACEPTION), unless the prostitutes wanted children to raise as prostitutes (NEAIRA). ABORTIONS may also have been common; the brothel at Ashka-lon produced a number of fetus skeletons in its drains (Faerman 1998).

Fights over prostitutes were common (in a dispute, the men could draw lots as to who would have sex with the prostitute first). A papyrus (Zilliacus 1941: 4.1024) records the murder of a prostitute in the fourth century. Philoneos, tired of his slave-concubine, was going to sell her to a brothel; she then POISONED him and a dinner companion, and was tortured and executed. Philoneos's wife may have put her up to it (Antiphon, *Against the Step-mother*). In sex, too, especially ORGIES, prostitutes could be subject to abuse. They could be beaten with SANDALS (**132, 139**), burnt with oil lamps (**67**), or caned and whipped (**199**). Prostitutes must have teamed up on occasion. The clusters of prostitutes and their cells at Pompeii suggest either single ownership or a mu-tual attraction for business and company.

The goddess Aphrodite/Venus was the patron of prostitutes. An elegaic quatrain by Nossis (*Greek Anth.* 9.332) records the dedication by Polyarkhis to Aphrodite of a gold statue, "having profited a lot from dispensing her own glorious body" (see BODY PARTS [genitals, female]).

Hetairai and expensive (and famous) prostitutes

The *megalomísthoi*, hetairai for "big fees," were not only well known during their lifetime but some became legendary; several had plays written about them (LAÏS I, Sinope, Mania, GNATHAINA, Naïs, THAÏS; Athenaeus 13.567c), and Anti-phanes the Younger and Aristophanes of Byzantium both wrote treatises on "He-taeras" (Athenaeus 13.567a, 583d and f, 587b). The finest houses in Alexandria belonged to the hetairai Mnêsis and Potheinê (Polybius 14.11.3–4).

The earliest hetaira we know, aside from the concubine SEMIRAMIS, is Doricha (or RHODOPIS) of Naukratis (ca. 600 BCE), whom SAPPHO's brother Kharaxos appar-ently bought, much to the poet's anger. In the fifth century there were Thargelia of Miletos who helped win Thessaly over to the Persians (490; Plutarch, *Per.* 24), ASPA-SIA the mistress of Perikles, Habrotonon from Thrace, the mother of Themistokles (Plutarch, *Erotikos* 753d), and Theodotê, whom Socrates visited and the mistress of ALCIBIADES (Athenaeus 13.574e). In the fourth century there were LAÏS, PHRYNE, and NEAIRA. "Klepsydra," the Water-Clock (fl. 350 BCE), timed her sex sessions; Eubulus wrote a comedy about her (Asclepiades, FGrH 157 F1). Some hetairai had shrines erected in their honor, like Pythionikê, mistress of Harpalus (Athenaeus 13.595a–e), and Belestichê, became the mistress of Ptolemy II (Plutarch, *Erotikos* 753e).

Bagnall 1991; Davidson 1998; Edwards 1997; Flemming 1999; Garrett 1990; Hooks 1985; Krenkel 1979b; Kurke 1997; McClure 2002; McGarry 1989; McGinn 1989, 1998, 2002; Oden 2000; Wells 1979.

Psychê, Greek for soul. She/it does not have a mythology until at least the fourth century. Earlier, the soul might have been conceived as a flying animal, butterfly, bird or bat (cf. Homer, *Iliad* 23.101, *Od.* 24.6) or as an *eídolon*, an apparition. Psychê first appears as female in the late fifth century. By the end of the fourth, she is linked to EROS. In the Hellenistic period, Eros plagues her with tortures. She is also the stereotype of the innocent bride (Apuleius, *Met.* 4.28).

Psychê is often depicted with butterfly wings (**197.1, 308;**). She may also appear in the Great Frieze of the VILLA OF THE MYSTERIES, holding a mirror up to the adornment of the bride, as she does to APHRODITE (de Grummond 2002: 77–8, n. 41, figs 22, 25).

R

Reciprocal Position for Oral-genital Intercourse ("69"), depicted only for a man and woman (52, 220; cf. OVID, Ars Am. 2.703–32).

Religion, in antiquity, had two major sexual aspects: FERTILITY (of people, livestock, and agriculture) and the power to avert evil (apotropaicism). Fertility was ensured by propitiating divinities of agriculture (ADONIS; ATTIS; DEMETER; CYBELE), of husbandry (ARTEMIS; FAUNUS, Pan, and Silvanus), of human procreation (APHRODITE; CYBELE; DIONYSUS; EROS; Fortuna; HERA), and of human BIRTH (EILEITHYIA.) Fertility was symbolized by the concept of plenty (*cornucopia*, a horn filled with fruits, flowers, and vegetables, and an arrangement of farm animals, both portrayed in the Ara Pacis east panels), by a mother nursing her offspring (mother and child [*kourotróphos*], mother animal and human child [goat Amaltheia nursing baby ZEUS, wolf nursing Romulus and Remus, hind nursing Telephos]), and by the concept of sexual power (PHALLOI; BODY PARTS [vagina]; BODY FUNCTIONS [ejaculation]; dedications of terracottas depicting body parts [genitals, uteruses, breasts]).

Apotropaic images include HERMS, phalloi, PRIAPUS, the eye (or "evil" eye), the male and female genitals (Johns 1982: 75), and various gestures: *mano fica* (Italian for "hand," "cunt"; the fist clenched with the tip of the thumb inserted between the first and second finger, representing the penis or clitoris lodged in the vagina [Johns 1982: 73; **273**]); "the finger" (middle finger raised, other fingers pulled into the hand, the hand held up, palm in [**134**]; Martial 2.28; CALIGULA would hold out his "finger" for suitors to kiss [Suetonius, *Caligula* 56.1]); and the "horns" (hand up, the first and little fingers raised, the others pulled into the hand; **200**). Laughter (BAUBO), insults (INVECTIVE), SONGS, and DANCES (NUDITY) are other types of apotropaic actions (Corbeill 1996). Initiates into the Mysteries endured insults hurled at them as they processed to Eleusis (Winkler 1990: 188–209; Zweig 1992: 85), and Roman soldiers sang ribald songs and jeered at their generals during their triumph (Pliny, *HN* 28.39).

Rhodopis (fl. early sixth century BCE), the earliest attested hetaira (PROSTITUTES). From Thrace, she had once been a fellow SLAVE with Aesop (Herodotus 2.134–5). She was brought to Naukratis in Egypt; Kharaxos, SAPPHO's brother, bought her and set her free, and perhaps MARRIED her (*Suda*). Rhodopis dedicated iron spits at Delphi. Sappho, however, calls her brother's lover Dorikha (cf. Athenaeus 13.596b).

Popular opinion also held that the smallest pyramid at Giza was built for her, although Herodotus says that was beyond even her means. According to Strabo (17.33) and Aelian (13.33), when Rhodopis was BATHING at Naukratis, an eagle snatched up one of her SANDALS and carried it to Memphis where it dropped it into the lap of pharoah Psammetichos; the king, struck by its beauty, searched for her, made her his queen, and erected the pyramid as her tomb.

S

Sabinus and Empona In the reign of Vespasian, a Gaul named Sabinus had participated in an unsuccessful uprising; he escaped into a cave and gave out that he was dead. His wife Empona hid with him for nine years, giving BIRTH to two sons, before she was caught and taken to Rome where she taunted Vespasian with her happiness and was executed (Plutarch, *Erotikos* 700c–771c; Tacitus, *Hist.* 4.67; Cass. Dio. 65.16).

Sacred Band, Theban fighting force of 150 pairs of lovers maintained by the state. Gorgidas (or Pammenes) established the unit probably in 379/8 BCE; it fought so successfully that it was employed thereafter, including Epameinondas's victories over the SPARTANS at Leuctra in 371 and at Mantineia in 362. The men worshipped EROS who bound them together (Athenaeus 13.561, 602). The force was so feared that Philip II ordered ALEXANDER to eradicate it at Chaironeia in 338 (Plutarch, *Alex.* 9.2); the colossal stone lion there probably marks their mass grave.

Plutarch, *Pel.* 18.2–4, *Mor.* 618d, 805e, *Erotikos* 760c–763c.

Sandals, the most common form of ancient footwear. Socrates went barefoot (Plato, *Symp.* 221b2; Aristophanes, *Clouds* 358–63) for simplicity's sake; and the chorus in Aeschylus, *Prometheus*

Bound, rushes impulsively to action, without strapping them on (135).

Wearing sandals, however, was a mark of sexual readiness (Aristotle, *Problems* 4.5; cf. RHODOPIS, and Vitellius's fetish for MESSALINA's sandal, Suetonius, *Vitellius* 2); they ensured that the feet stay warm (male) and moist (female), conducive to the proper expenditure of sexual fluids. The Greek verb, *baínein*, "to walk," implied sexual intercourse particularly between men (Henderson 1991: 19 n. 70).

It is possible that the juxtapositions barefoot/impulsive and shod/sexual had further ramifications (cf. the story of OEDIPUS who wears only one sandal when he meets his father and kills him). Dio Chrysostom attributes Socrates's condemnation to his barefootedness and his corruption of minors (66.25, 26), and several vase paintings show couples in erotic situations, the adult men shod, the PROSTITUTE women (**63**) or eromenoi youths barefoot (**65, 121 [pl. 13]**).

SAPPHO mentions sandals, beautifully decorated, as emblems of MARRIAGE (PMG 39; cf. Oakley and Sinos 1993: 33). Prostitutes' sandals could have an exhortation "follow me" (*akoloúthi*) spelled out in nails on the sole, so that their footprint would advertise the way to the nearest BROTHEL (Clement, *Paid.* 2.11; Licht 1963: 338; Daremberg 1877–1919: vol. 3, 1828 fig. 4068). In Greek art, spanking with sandals is commonly depicted (SEX IN ART; VIOLENCE [sadism]; Kilmer 1993: 108–10 and 121–4; *Greek Anth.* 5.202, 503), and removed sandals are prominent in depictions of Roman sexual activity (**292, 331, 341**).

Levine 2002.

Sappho 1 (fl. Olympiad 42 = 612–19, or 45.2 = 598 BCE), daughter of Skamandronymos (or others) and Kleïs of Mytilene (or Eresos). She had three brothers, Larikhos, Kharaxos, and Euryguios (of whom we know nothing). Larikhos was "wine-pourer" (*oinokhooúnta*) in the city council of Mytilene (Athenaeus 10.424e). Kharaxos bought and freed RHODOPIS, for which Sappho reportedly rebuked him (Herodotus 2.135). OVID adds that at six years old she lost a parent (her father since PMG 102 mentions her mother), and had a daughter, Kleïs (*Heroides* 15.51). Of the three poems that mention Kleïs [PMG 98 and 132, and 82 Edmonds 1928], only 132 calls her a "child" (*pais*), which can also describe one's beloved (DuBois 1995: 148). The *Suda* gives the name of a husband, Kerkolas of Andros (his name sounds fabricated: *kerkós* = animal's "tail" and *andrós* = "of a man"). In appearance, Sappho was reportedly small and dark (OVID, *Heroides* 15.31–41; schol. LUCIAN, *Eikones* 18). She died old in Mytilene (PMG 121; *Greek Anth.* 7.14).

Sappho wrote nine books of poetry. They and other sources name several women close to her: the *Suda* counts three companions (hetairai), Atthis (PMG 49, 82, 96, 131, 133), Telesippa, and Megara, and four pupils (*mathetés*), Anagora of Miletos, Gongyla of Kolophon (PMG 95), and Euneika of Salamis (cf. Max. Tyr. 24.7); add Damophyla of Pamphylia (Edmonds 1928: 156–7). Sappho herself exalts her LOVE for Anaktoria (PMG 16), praises Mnasidica and Gyrinna (82), and wearies of Gorgô (144).

Sappho's poems divide into two major types: personal poems addressed to her girlfriends/girl friends, and MARRIAGE SONGS. A couple of poems blend the genres: her famous poem ("He seems to me like a god," PMG 31) is probably a wedding song but, appropriating the groom's feelings, Sappho describes DESIRE for the bride directly; a fragmentary poem (91) remembers the good times Sappho and Anactoria had, now that Anactoria has gone away to Sardis, perhaps to be married.

Sappho was well known in her own lifetime (SOLON wished to learn her poems [Stobaeus 3.29.58 quoting Aelian]; cf. Athenaeus 13.605e). She enjoyed high esteem as a wise poet (Plato, *Phaedrus* 235b; *Anth. Plan.* 310 [*Greek Anth.* 16.310]). The third-century poet Nossis counts herself a second Sappho (*Greek Anth.* 7.718), and several writers wrote poems in imitation of hers (Theocritus 28; Catullus 51; Horace, *Carm.* 3.12); she was even considered a tenth muse (Catullus 35.16; Horace, *Carm.* 4.9.11; Plutarch, *Pyth. Or.* 6, *Erotikos* 762f–763a; *Greek Anth.* 7.17, 7.407, 9.66, 9.506, 9.571). And imperial women imitated her poetry and her dialect (LUCIAN, *Dial. meret.* 36; court ladies to HADRIAN's wife Sabina, Julia Balbilla, Caecilia Trebulla, and Damo, wrote imitative epigrams, Bernand 1960: nos. 28–31).

A few vases of the late sixth and fifth century BCE depict and name her (**44, 133**); there are other portraits, a mosaic from SPARTA and a bronze bust from the Villa dei Papyri, Herculaneum. Mytilene in Lesbos "honored Sappho, although she was a woman" (Aristotle, *Rhet.* 2.33) by minting coins with her portrait (**169, 206**). Other portraits are known from literature: Cicero, *Verr.* 2.4.126; *Greek Anth.* 2.11.

It is not clear when Sappho, her desire for women, and the name of her island home, Lesbos, become linked to female homoeroticism and the modern concept of LESBIANISM (cf. ANACREON 358). In the late fifth and fourth centuries BCE, Sappho became the subject of comedies, in which she expounds poetry and riddles (cf. Athenaeus 10.450e–f quoting Antiphanes) and men fall in love with her. OVID has her censured for her HOMOEROTIC feelings (Hallett 1989) and she renounces her love of girls (*Heroides* 15.199–201; Gordon 1997; cf. *Tristia* 2.365–6).

By the second century CE, Sappho was known as a homoerotic poet and lover of women (LUCIAN, *Dial. meret.* 5; Max. Tyr. 24.7). By the fifth century Sappho is condemned, her poems burnt by Gregory of Nazianzus in 381 CE and by Gregory VII in 1073. Georg Welcker (1816 [1845]) attempted to demonstrate that she could not have been lesbian not only because she had a daughter (and therefore was MARRIED), but also because lesbianism was vilified in antiquity, yet she and her poetry were much admired. He attributed her vicious reputation to the comic poets; his defense led to Sappho's rehabilitation as an acceptable author. In spite of William Mure's objections (1857) to Welcker's revisionism (Calder 1986: 131–56), literary critics continued to think Sappho innocent of any "scandal" (Edmonds 1922). Snyder's recent study (1997) accepts Sappho's desire for women but concentrates on how it operates in the poems. Sappho's major subjects (herself, EROS, and APHRODITE) imply a triangulation (PMG 31: Sappho, the groom, the bride), which may have been a "metamodel of lover, beloved, and memory" (Henry 1998).

Lefkowitz 1973; Stehle 1990.

Sappho 2, fictional character of Eresos (or Mytilene). This Sappho was at one time exiled to Sicily (*Marmor Parium*, 605–591 BC; cf. OVID, *Heroides* 15.51), loved Phaon of Mytilene, and eventually threw herself from the southern-most cliff of the island Leucas (*Suda, Sappho*; Aelian, *VH* 12.19; Strabo 10.8–9, quoting Menander; 334).

Phaon plied a ferry between Lesbos and the mainland; when he ferried APHRODITE for free, she gave him an unguent which made women DESIRE him (Servius 3.279); to Pliny (*HN* 19.8) this was *eryngô* (PLANTS). He was eventually caught in ADULTERY and murdered. Antiphanes and Plato Comicus wrote comedies entitled *Phaon*.

The Leucadian cliff became famous because of Sappho's death; SONGS were composed about it (Athenaeus 14.619d–e; Anacreon PMG 376); and many lovers threw themselves into the sea from there. An ancient catalogue of the leapers, however, does not include her (Athenaeus 14.618c; Photios s.v. *Leukátes, Phaon*); and some authors locate the cliff elsewhere (LUCIAN, *Dial. mort.* 9.2 on Chios; Statius, *Silvae* 5.3.155 near Calchis).

Edmonds 1928: 140–81.

Satires, a Roman literary genre that discusses hypocrisy and pretension humorously, bluntly, and bitingly (from *satur*, a mishmash). The Menippean satire originated with Menippus of Gadara (first half of the third century BCE) who wrote in a mix of prose and verse.

The earliest authors were Ennius and Lucilius; Varro wrote Menippean satires. Horace wrote two books (also called *sermones*, conversations) but of limited force that reflects the constraint of the times. Imperial satire became vicious but pointless: PETRONIUS satirizes everything; and Juvenal's satires are exaggerations on straw-men.

See also: NOVELS; THEATER

Satyrs and Silens, male followers of DIONYSUS. Silenus was the father of satyrs, and the two creatures become one by the early sixth century BCE. Satyrs have equine features (long, mule-like ears; a tail; and body hair), although Pliny (*HN* 5.46, 7.24, 8.216, 9.246) identifies them as a kind of ape (cf. Palestrina mosaic). They are usually depicted ithyphallic (**100, 207**), ready for sex (**6, 33, 46, 48,**

81, 109, 111, 203, 292, 296, 333, 335), and sneaking up on MAENADS or hermaphrodites (Osborne 1996: 78–80; cf. 83, 100).

Satyrs formed the stock chorus for the satyr plays (THEATER); ALCIBIADES in Plato's *Symposium* (215a ff.) likens Socrates to a silen; and men dressed as satyrs in the ANTHESTERIA (cf. 106). Terracotta satyr figurines were placed in children's and women's tombs as FERTILITY symbols (Parlama and Stampolides 2000: 329–30, no. 345).

See also: FAUNUS

Semen and Sperm Hippocratics believed that sperm arose from all parts of the body to travel to the brain where, like mucus, it was concocted, and thence dispensed through passages to the penis, generating pleasure; men who derive pleasure from anal penetration must have those passages rerouted to the anus (Aristotle, *Problems* 4.26).

A POMPEII graffito refers to *Severus sugusus* ("Severus, full of sap"; Warsher 1938–57: vol. VII.2 part 2); he may be the husband whose wife, in two graffiti from the same house, "wouldn't sell for any price" (*CIL* 4.3061; Varone 2001a: 162). Young men were thought to have abundent sperm (PLATO, *Laws* 839; Plutarch, *Erotikos* 751e).

See also: CONCEPTION; ORGASM

Semiramis (fl. 805 BCE), Sammu-ramat, wife of Shamshi-Adad V of Assyria and mother of Adad-Nirari III. According to Greek stories, she was the daughter of a goddess, born at Ashkalon and wife of Assyrian kings, especially Ninos who founded Nineveh (Diodorus Siculus 2.20.3 ff.; Reardon 1989); she herself founded Babylon, was the first to have EUNUCH SLAVES (Claudian, *in Eutrop.* 1.339; Ammianus 14.6), and had intercourse with a horse (Pliny, *HN* 8.64; cf. **217**).

Plutarch (*Erotikos* 753d–e) tells a moral:

> The Syrian Semiramis was the concubine of a house-born slave of the king, Ninos, who one day caught sight of her and fell in love. She grew to have such power that she asked to be allowed, for one day, to direct the affairs of state, and be crowned and seated on his throne. He granted this and issued orders for everyone to serve and obey her just as they would himself. At first her commands were moderate; then, when she saw that there was no opposition, she ordered Ninos to be seized, imprisoned, and finally put to death. Thereafter, she ruled gloriously over Asia for many years.

Sex in Art Sexual and erotic subjects were depicted in every Greek and Roman medium (wall paintings, TABELLAE, sculpture, mosaics, furniture [**207**], pottery, glass vessels, mirrors [**7, 230**], fingerrings, sealstones, cameos [**211**], LAMPS, and illustrated books [SORANUS's *Gynecology*; Parker 1992: 102]). WOMEN would have had access to all these objects.

Paintings

Vases depict erotic activity from at least the Geometric period (**29**). The PAIDERASTIC "hands up-and-down" position is first rendered on an Orientalizing jug (**30**) depicting a man and a woman. Under 200 vases depict sexually explicit scenes from the sixth through the early fifth century BCE (Sutton 1992: 7; SEXUAL ACTIVITIES), especially vases made for the SYMPOSIUM and Etruria. These diminish in the mid 5th c. when romantic eroticism, aimed at women, was just beginning (Sutton 1992). In the Hellenistic and Roman period MOULD-MADE BOWLS, other relief media, and wall paintings depict erotic activity.

Sexually explicit paintings always represented a small fraction of the total output, but they have been repeatedly illustrated (Grant and Mulas 1975; Jacobelli 1995; Guillaud and Guillaud 1990; Guzzo and Ussani 2000; Dover 1989; Kilmer 1993; Johns 1982; Marcadé 1962 and 1965; Clarke 2003), though not much studied (but see Clarke 1998). The paintings almost always depict a man and a woman having sex; rarely are two men involved (for two women: **61 [pl. 10], 291 VII**).

The PORNOGRAPHERS (Athenaeus 13.567b) painted portraits of hetairai (PROSTITUTES) from at least the late fifth century (Theodotê): Pausias (fourth century) painted Glykera and Leontion (pupil and friend of Epicurus and mistress of Metrodorus: Pliny, *HN* 35.99, 123–27, 137; cf. 21.4; Athenaeus 13.588b); Nikophanes (Pliny, *HN* 35.11, 137; Plutarch, *Mor.* 18b); Aristeides of Thebes (late fourth century BCE; Pliny, *HN* 35.98–100, 110); and Arellius (Augustan) who painted his mistresses as goddesses (cf. PHRYNE, fourth century). Easel paintings of women were in existence as early as the mid-fifth century (women portraits for the Heraia games; ATHLETICS), and Nossis's epigrams (third century) describe their realism (*Greek Anth.* 6.353, 354, and 604). At POMPEII many homes had small, circular portraits of women (see the house of Caecilius Jucundus); a Campanian painting shows a woman painting an actor's portrait (**335**; cf. Naples 9018 [Helbig 1868: 1443; Picard 1968: fig. 39] and Naples 9017 [Helbig 1868: 1444]); and Pliny discusses women portrait painters, who also invented modeling (*HN* 35.147–51; Athenagoras, *Presbeia* 17).

Sexually explicit wall paintings have survived from at least the Augustan period (**290**); they, and the Pompeii paintings, convey a suffused sexuality that must have been a signifier of Roman sophistication (cf. Kurke 1997: 118–19). Clement criticizes people who "place these monuments of shamelessness in your homes" (*Protr.* 4.53). Parrhasius of Ephesus (fl. 420–390 BCE; Xenophon, *Mem.* 3.10; Pliny, *HN* 35.65, 67–72; Quintilian, *In. Orat.* 12.10.5; Propertius 3.9.12; Athenaeus 12.543c–f, 15.687b; Aelian, *VH* 9.11) is the earliest easel painter known to have painted sexual pictures. His "ATALANTA FELLATING Meleager" was owned by TIBERIUS (Suetonius, *Tiberius* 44). Parrhasius also bought a SLAVE from Olynthus and had him tortured to death as a model for his representation of Prometheus (Seneca, *Controv.* 10.5.3). Another painting depicted HERA fellating ZEUS.

Sculptures

One three-dimensional sculpture depicts explicit sexual activity: Pan having intercourse with a she-goat (**245**); otherwise all sexual sculpture is small, portable, and in relief: appliqués (**281–286**), MOULD-MADE BOWLS (**182–193, 277–280**), LAMPS (**212–229**), tokens (**274, 275**), and vessels both metal (**287, 288 [pl. 43]**) and glass (**208, 209**). Erotic sculpture abounds: the "Knidia" (**18**; PRAXITELES), the sleeping HERMAPHRODITE (**175 [pls 35, 36]**), and a group of Pan, APHRODITE, and EROS (**173**).

The Knidia was a famous statue (copies begin in the second century BCE); a young man ejaculated onto her thigh and stained it (PRAXITELES). Other statues elicited DESIRE (LAÏS 1). Demetrios of Phaleron took the hetaira Lamia up to the Acropolis and had sex with her in the Parthenon, "not being able to 'marry' the statue of Athena" (Clement, *Protr.* 4.48). Pygmalion of Cyprus fell in love with an ivory statue of nude Aphrodite and had sex with it (*sunérkhetai*; Clement, *Protr.* 4.51; Philostephanus FGrH III:31); OVID (*Met.* 10.243–97) tells a different version: Pygmalion makes the statue and Aphrodite brings it to life; they MARRY and have a daughter Paphos.

Kleisophus the Selymbrian falls in love with the marble statue at Samos of Aphrodite (PROSTITUTES) and locks himself up in the temple, in the belief that he would be able to have intercourse with it. When he is unable, on account of the chilliness and inelasticity of the stone, he thenceforth desists from his desire. He sets out a small piece of meat and has intercourse with that.

(Athenaeus 13.605f)

Iphis of Cyprus is in love with Anaxaretê who spurns him; when he hangs himself at her door, she watches without feeling. Aphrodite turns her into a statue, Aphrodite Prospiciens ("looking on"; OVID 14.698 ff.; cf. VERTUMNUS AND POMONA).

See also: VIOLENCE

Sex Manuals Astyanassa, HELEN of TROY's maid (*therápaina*, a body servant) reportedly wrote the first sex manual, *On the Positions for Sexual Intercourse (perí tôn skhêmátôn tês Aphrodítês)*. The misogynistic lists of women by Hesiod and Semonides of Amorgos presume a similar catalogue. By the end of the fourth century BCE, however, catalogues of all sorts were being drawn up; some have survived (political constitutions; Theophrastus's *Characters*; medical treatises; and Apicius Caelius's cookbook *De Re Coquinari*). Sex manuals also belong to the taxonomy of knowledge (Parker 1992: 91) that is associated with Aristotelian philosophy. Just as Theophrastus compares human personalities to animal behavior, OVID (*Ars Am.* 3.769–88) assigns SEXUAL POSITIONS to female body types; and just as rhetoric's *figurae* constitute components of persuasive argument, so a sex manual's sexual positions (*figurae*) constitute components of sexual pleasure.

The earliest catalogue of sexual positions (Greek *skhêmata*, Latin *figurae*, *modi*) for heterosexual intercourse, seduc-

tion, and perhaps ORAL-GENITAL sex is mentioned by Timaios of Tauromenion (ca. 352–264 BCE; cf. LUCIAN, *Pseudologista* 24). The authors of these sex manuals (*anaiskhuntográphoi*, "writers of shameless things," Polybius 12.13.1) were said to be women (two men are known), and the manuals were meant to be the result of personal experience. Elephantis's sex manual, for instance, which TIBERIUS owned, described nine schemata.

The most cited author is Philainis of Samos (fl. ca. 370 BC). Fragments of a papyrus text (*POxy.* 39: 2891; Parker 1992: 94; second century CE) preserve bits of her sex manual:

frg 1 [col. i]: Philainis of Samos, daughter of Okymenes, wrote these things for those who plan to lead their life with knowledge and not carelessly ... having worked at it myself ... [col. ii] Concerning seductions: the seducer should go unadorned and uncombed so that he does not [appear] to the woman to be on the make ...

frg 3: ... with the thought ... we ... saying the [ ] woman is like a goddess ... the ugly one is charming, the older one is like a young girl. Concerning KISSES ...

The manual seems summary, rather like "Philainis's Notebook" (LUCIAN, *Amores* 28). The contents seem thin, but orderly, starting with advice on how men can seduce women, and continuing on to foreplay, and presumably sexual positions. Two texts have survived that incorporate aspects of the sex manual (SEXUAL POSITIONS). A catalogue-like depiction of sexual positions also occurs in art (59).

As "gourmet guides to sex," sex manuals were likened to cookbooks, both of which were criticized for over-elaborating the satisfaction of basic bodily needs (Diogenes Laertius 6.2.69; Plato, *Resp.* 389e, 580e; and Xenophon, *Symp.* 4.38); compare the modern sex manual *The Joy of Sex: A Cordon Bleu Guide to Love-making* by Alex Comfort, 1987, the title a parody of Irma Rombauer's *The Joy of Cooking*, 1931.

Philainis's sex manual is based on a popular, essentialist notion of how to perform sex (if one is to do it, it should be done "with knowledge"; SEXUAL ACTIVITIES); if sex manuals were thought to promote sexual immoderation, then theoretically they must have been considered "feminine" since the "feminine" was characterized by immoderation. Sex manuals were indeed considered *mollis* ("soft"; Martial 12.43.4), "suitable for men who acted like women and for moral weaklings and impotent emperors" – "naturally," therefore, sex manuals could only have been written by "women," and most probably by "women" who were outside "proper" society: SLAVES, PROSTITUTES, resident aliens. Sex manuals did not, however, discuss how to produce sexual pleasure for and in women: "The woman is the raw material" for men's pleasure (Myerowitz (1992: 136). Thus, it can be assumed that sex manuals were actually written for men, and probably therefore by men, "to create a normative intercourse and to reassure the male initiate that he will meet with nothing unexpected" (Parker 1992: 104). Taking his cue from Aiskhrion, M.L. West suggests that the fourth century BCE writer Polykrates wrote sex manuals under the name "Philainis" (1996: 20). Ancient sex manuals, therefore, may be modernly criticized for their masculinist nominalism (naming only what is pleasurable to men; what is not named is not important) and for creating the appearance of an acceptable set of sexual activities that, however, omit women as sexual subjects: ancient sex manuals are constituent of male-centered PORNOGRAPHY.

By the beginning of the Roman imperial period, sex manuals were also being illustrated (Parker 1992: 102); some POMPEII paintings (**291, 311**) probably reflect these illustrated manuals. Objects like

MOULD-MADE BOWLS (**182–193, 277–280**) carry so many depictions of people engaging in sexual activity, usually arranged in paratactic strings, that they can be thought of as visual sex manuals (cf. relief LAMPS **212–229**, appliqués **281–286**, and tokens **274, 275**). Several Greek vase paintings, some dating as early as the early sixth century BCE (**50**), carry such paratactic strings of couples having sexual intercourse, and these either reflect or stand for early text sex manuals.

Sexual Activities Here follows a schematic outline of some ancient practices discussed elsewhere in this book.

No penetration

MASTURBATION (hand-genital)

non-genital stimulation (BODY PARTS [breasts, feet], FROTTAGE; LESBIANISM)

pain (SEX IN ART; VIOLENCE): spanking (SANDALS), FLAGELLATION, singeing with oil lamps

VOYEURISM

Oral-genital sex

penis in mouth: FELLATIO, IRRUMATIO, auto-fellatio

mouth to vagina: CUNNILINGUS, RECIPROCAL POSITION FOR ORAL INTERCOURSE ("69")

mouth to anus: ANALINGUS

Penetration

(SEX MANUALS; SEXUAL POSITIONS; abbreviations in parentheses)

by DILDOES: penetration of the vagina, anus, or mouth

by penis: penetration of the vagina or anus

    Face to Face (**F**)

    "a tergo" (**AT**); *more canum* ("dog-style")

        penetrator standing or kneeling and penetratee leaning over (*kúbda*) or kneeling

    both reclining (**ATR**, "spooning")

Equestrian (**E**) (penetratee on top of reclining/sitting penetrator; *kélês*)

face-to-face (**EF**)

penetratee facing away (reversed; **ER**)

by penis: penetration of the thighs (intercrural; **I**; PAIDERASTIA)

See also: BESTIALITY; NECROPHILIA; ORGIES

Sexual Attitudes Although some writers have approved of sex for its pleasure (Diogenes commending MASTURBATION), most condemn it except for procreation (Boswell 1980: 130).

Hesiod (late eighth century BCE) comments that "the race of WOMEN" (*phúla gunaikôn*, *Theogony* 592) brings misery to MEN, but without them one cannot have CHILDREN who will care for their parents in their OLD AGE (cf. Euripides, *Oinomaos* fr. 571); Euripides adds that there should have been a better way to have children than through women (*Hippolytos* 616–25). Semonides of Amorgos (mid-seventh century) catalogues eight types of women: six hateful animals (sow, vixen, bitch, donkey, weasel, mare, monkey) and a mud-woman, plus one useful animal-woman, the bee (7).

Pleasure in sex was regarded with suspicion by philosophers (Cantarella 1992: 189–90); over-indulgence could lead to general profligacy (DESIRE). By the fifth century, sex had a good ("according to nature," *katá phúsin*) and bad purpose ("contrary to nature," *pará phúsin*). To determine what was "natural," philosophers looked to logic and to the SEXUAL ACTIVITY of ANIMALS, neither of which is appropriate (Boswell 1980, Foucault 1976 [1980]–1984 [1986], Winkler 1990).

PLATO'S early dialogues (ca. 400–388 BCE) regard sexual desire as a good thing. In his middle dialogues (ca. 388–61), he finds no disgrace in PAIDERASTIC LOVE, but he elaborates on the concept of two APHRODITES. His later dialogues (ca. 361–

47) stress that same-sex sex is unnatural and lacks self control (*akráteian*); desire for sexual intercourse was designed by the gods for begetting children "according to nature."

Musonius Rufus writes that "MARRIAGE is manifestly according to nature. For, to what other purpose did the creator of mankind first divide our human race into two sexes?" He condemns male-male sex as an "offense against nature" (*tólmêma pará phúsin*); and he argues against sex with PROSTITUTES and SLAVES as lacking self-control (fragments 14 and 12).

Seneca includes same-sex intercourse in a list of behaviors that are *contra naturam* (*Ep.* 122). St Paul has a similar list (1 Corinthians 6: 9–10; cf. 1 Timothy 1: 9–10); and he also condemns (without stating why) same-sex behavior, both male and female (Romans 1: 26–7). In another passage (1 Corinthians 7:8–9), Paul recommends celibacy, but if one has to have sex, it is better to MARRY than be damned. Philo, a Hellenized Jew, also denounces PAIDERASTIA, EFFEMINACY (*Decalogue* 168; *Hypothetica* 7.1; *Special Laws* 1.325, *Questions Genesis* 4.37), and non-procreative sex (*On Abraham* 134–7, 248; *Special Laws* 3.34–6, 113).

Later Christian writers all denounce same-sex activity and agree that sex is for procreation only. Clement: "to have sex for any other purpose than to produce children is to violate nature" (*Paid.* 2.10.95); this includes MASTURBATION (2.10.83, 91), masculine women and effeminate men (*Paid.* 3.3.18–21). Tertullian: sexual ABSTINENCE is best, since women lead men to fall from grace (*De cultu feminarum* 1), but sex is necessary for procreation and should be limited to marriage (*De Monog.* 3.1, 17.5); men should not dress effeminately (*De pallio*) and women should wear the veil (*De virginibus velandis*). Lactantius: "the passion for procreation should be used for pleasure" (2.12, 6.19). John Chrysostom: marriage tempers sexual desire and provides an alternative to prostitution and same-sex activity (*On Virginity* 1.1–2; 50.1.3–4), which confuses the "proper" gender and sex roles (*Homily* 4). And Augustine: sex should be only for procreation and take place only in marriage (*Good of Marriage* 13.15, 22.27, 23.31); nuns can love each other spiritually not carnally (*Epistle* 211); men should wear their HAIR short in imitation of Christ and women should go veiled in subordination to men and God (*Work of the Monks* 32.40); penetrated effeminate men are damned (*City of God* 7.26; *Lying* 9.15).

Sexual Differentiation Medically, MEN differed from WOMEN by being hotter and drier; in the womb, "insufficient accumulation of heat produced a female" (Corbeill 1997: 108). Men could become EFFEMINATE, becoming cooler and wetter (Brown 1988: 10–11). PLATO conjectured that the first humans were all males, but those who were effeminate by nature became, in the second incarnation, women and wives of true males (*Ti.* 90–91a). Aristotle characterizes a woman as a "male that does not produce seed" (*ágonon árrēn*; *Gen. An.* 728a18).

Men and women differed in gender, as well. Xenophon assigns women to "all work indoors" while men should "take charge of the outdoor activities" (*Oec.* 7.22); Aristotle (*Oec.* 1.1344.a.3–6; cf. *Pol.* 3.4.1277b.24f) and Hierokles agree (in Stobaeus, *Flor.* 3.696f).

Sexual Positions for Penetrative Intercourse (Grk *schêmata*, Lat. *figurae*), theoretically innumerable (OVID *Ars Am.* 2.678–80, *Rem. Am.* 407–8, 425, 525) but limited in practice (SEX IN ART). OVID's text (below) resembles a SEX MANUAL, listing five positions, two of which are repeated in Aristophanes (for abbreviations, see SEXUAL ACTIVITIES).

Ovid (*Ars Am.* 3.773–88)

F   The one who is remarkable for her

face, let her lie on her back;

AT   let them be viewed from behind, those whose backs are pleasing.

F   Milanion used to carry ATALANTA's legs on his shoulder: 775
if they are lovely, let them be seen in this way.

EF   Let the little one be carried on her horse; because she was so tall the Theban bride [Andromachê] never rode Hector like a horse.

ATR Let her press the covers with her knees and bend back her neck a little,
the woman who is worth looking at for her long flank.   780
For the one whose thighs are youthful and whose breasts are flawless,

F   let the man stand and let her spread out crosswise on the bed.
And don't think it sinful to let down your hair, like the Phylleian Mother [CYBELE],
with your locks spread out and your neck bent back.

ER   You also, whose belly Lucina [childbirth] has marked with wrinkles [stretchmarks],   785
like the swift Parthian use horses turned backward.
Venus has a thousand joys; the easiest and the one of least effort

ATR is when you lie down on your right side.

Aristophanes (*Peace* 894–901).

... when you have this lady.

AT   It will have ground-wrestling, getting down on all fours,   895
oiled up in the manner of a young athlete for pankration
to hit and to gouge, all at once with the punch (*púx*) and the prick (*péei*).

E   On the third day after these events, you will go in for horse-racing, one jockey out-jockeying another, chariots piled one on another   900 blowing and panting as the teams come to the finish.

It is possible that all figurae had mythological referents (cf. Martial 11.104.14; Johns 1982: 137): APHRODITE and Ares when caught by HEPHAESTUS (Homer, *Odyssey* 8.266–366); Briseis and ACHILLES (see below; OVID, *Ars Am.* 2.711–14; Martial 11.43.9); Jupiter and GANYMEDE (Plautus, *Menaechmi* 143–4); and Jupiter and Danaê (Terence, *Eunuchus* 583–5).

Depictions of intercourse "a tergo" are the most common (225; pl. 23), with equestrian intercourse a distant second (226, 227; pls 24, 25); depictions of other positions are rare, including the modern "missionary" position (woman supine, man on top), popular in American culture. The difference in cultural preferences may be meaningful: in American culture, couples prefer to face each other; in antiquity, men preferred to watch their partner without being looked at (Marks 1978).

Intercourse "a tergo" was called *kúbda* after the bent-over position of the woman (151; cf. Athenaeus 1.23d). "Erect" and "bent over" also described daily tasks assigned to men and to women (Scheidel 1995: 212); Aristotle (*Politics* 1.5.1254b.25–30) distinguishes between erect CITIZENS and bent-over SLAVES. In Greek art, the man usually stands, the woman standing and leaning forward; a variation has the woman's buttocks high, the "lioness pose" (*léaina*, 209). In Roman art, the couple usually reclines on a couch in a "spooning" position, perhaps to allow the viewer to see the act of penetration clearly (230). Intercourse "a tergo" between two males is rarely depicted (204). Some depictions have the woman leaning forward in such a way as to suggest anal intercourse (Sutton 1992: 11; 76) or "extra feeling" (Aristophanes, *Lys.* 230–40). Since the man is able to watch his partner, but not the partner him (without some difficulty), the position

may be "emphasizing male sexual dominance" (Zweig 1992: 83).

Anal intercourse could function as a type of CONTRACEPTION, and as a substitute for vaginal intercourse the first night of MARRIAGE, especially if the new bride were afraid of it (Martial 11.78.5–6; cf. PRIAPEA 3.6–7). As a regular activity it might have been censured (PEISISTRATOS). Briseis reportedly gave Achilles her anus to penetrate so he would forsake Patroklos (Martial 11.43.9).

"Equestrian" intercourse, *kélês*, was also referred to by several horseback riding terms (*hippeúô* and cognates; Aristophanes, *Lys.* 876–9; Plato Comicus 143 K-A; Heath 1986). A strap of cloth hanging from a support made equestrian sex easier for the penetratee to support himself (288 [pl. 43.5]) or herself (277.1.1), and for the male penetrator (282).

The "missionary" position, called in antiquity "Aphrodite's schema," was thought to be the most unnatural (Capitol. *Albin.* 11.7: "inter primos amatores aversae Veneris semper ignarus"; 205). OVID singles it out for the woman "who is remarkable for her face" (*Ars Am.* 3.773–5). In later antiquity the position becomes ideal: Artemidorus, writing in the second century CE asserts that it is the "natural" position for human beings, just as "a tergo" is the natural position for some animals (*Oneir.* 1.79, 91.12).

In Greek art, intercrural sex is occasionally depicted on Archaic and Classical vases 50, 58, 75): the older erastes and the younger eromenos stand to "face each other, embracing, as the older partner thrusts his penis between the thighs of the younger" (Keuls 1985: figs 249–50; Shapiro 1992: fig. 3.1). This is the only sexual position that regularly has the couple facing each other.

See also: ANALINGUS; BESTIALITY; CUNNILINGUS; DILDOES; FELLATIO; MASTURBATION; ORAL-GENITAL SEX; ORGIES; PORNOGRAPHY; RECIPROCAL

POSITION FOR ORAL-GENITAL
INTERCOURSE; VOYEURISM

Krenkel 1985, 1987.

Sexually Transmitted Diseases can be recognized in antiquity, such as herpes, gonorrhea, and chlamydia; others, like the ancient *campanus morbus*, are not known today. Syphilis is not known before 1495.

Diseases

Gonorrhea and chlamydia were common in antiquity. The symptoms of gonorrhea (gonococcus bacteria) are described in the Hippocratic corpus: abundant spermator-rhea (*profusio seminis*; Celsus 4.28) and an inflammation of the seminal vesicles. Chlamydia is also caused by a bacterial infection; it often goes undetected in women newly infected (75 percent) and in many men (50 percent). It can be natally transmitted to the fetus, leading to eye disease and pneumonia; in women it can lead to cancer of the cervix. In men, chlamydia can cause urethritis, proctitis, and epididymitis. In women, symptoms include vaginal discharge, bleeding after intercourse, bleeding between periods, abdominal or pelvic pain; in men, dis-charge from the penis, burning with urination, swollen and/or painful testicles. Similar symptoms were commonly re-ported in ancient Egypt.

Genital and oral ulcers and warts

Galen describes warts, ulcerations, canker sores, and calluses of the genitals ("Some-times, the penis is so eaten away under-neath the foreskin that the glans falls off; in which case the foreskin itself must be cut away"; "little tumors, which the Greeks call *phymata*, spring up around the glans," 8:437–52 Kühn). The Hippo-cratic corpus and Galen describe sores in the mouth as being related to sores on the genitals that appear during MENSTRUA-

TION and cause erosion on the labia (probably therefore a type of herpes: *Nat. mul.* 109, *Epid.* 3.7). The most common treatment for these diseases was cauteri-zation.

Anal warts and piles were called *ficus*, "figs," because of their resemblance to the seeds and fruit of the fig; besides cauter-ization, a poultice of fig was recom-mended (PLANTS). Martial and Juvenal allude to the creation of anal warts by anal intercourse.

Hemorrhoids, "a lesion, in which vein mouths rise up as from little heads, which at frequent intervals pour out blood. In women they may appear at the vulvar orifice" (Galen, *ibid.*).

A rash and set of lesions or warts on the face were called *campanus morbus* (Campanians reportedly liked oral sex; Vorberg 1965, s.v.), *mentagra* (especially when it appeared on the chin), and *impetigo* (Horace, *Sat.* 1.5.62; Knorr 2003).

See also: MEDICINE

Grmek 1989.

Slaves numbered a third of the population of Greece and Rome (Aristotle, *Politics* 1323a.5f). Slaves were born or sold into slavery, or captured. To Aristotle, slaves are "naturally, bent-over (*kúbda*), not erect like CITIZENS" (*Pol.* 1.5.1254b.25–30; WOMEN). New slaves, like new brides, are showered with *katakhúsmata* (figs, nuts, coins) when first brought into the house (Plutarch, *Erotikos* 753d). Slaves did not MARRY but merely cohabited (Latin *contubernium*).

Masters took sexual advantage of their slaves (VERGINIA; Haterius's maxim in LAWS). Epikrates falls in love with a slave boy who works in a perfume shop and offers to purchase not only his freedom but also that of his father and brother (Hypereides, *In Athenog.* 5–6). Greek vase painting shows men and women fondling their slaves (**95, 141**). A certain

Onesimos has children by his "worthy" (*khrestê*) slave Myrtis (Clairmont 1993: no. 2.406). Martial castigates women who lust after their litter bearers (2.49.2, 10.91). Vespasian orders that any woman who has an affair with a slave becomes his master's servant (Suetonius, *Vespasian* 11).

Pomeroy 1975; Evans-Grubbs 1993; Golden 1984; Scheidel 1995; Joshel and Murnaghan 1998.

Sodom, a city at the south end of the Dead Sea (Genesis 18:20–19:12). God sends two angels to discover ten righteous men in Sodom. A resident alien, Lot, offers the angels hospitality. All the men of Sodom demand that Lot bring out the strangers so they could "know" (*yada'*) them. Lot pleads with them not to do this wicked thing and offers his two virgin daughters; the angels strike the men blind. God then spares Lot and his family while He destroys Sodom and other cities.

A Levite resident alien in the city of Ephraim takes a concubine from Bethlehem (Judges 19:1–30); returning, they arrive late in Gibeah where they are given hospitality by an old man, also a resident alien. The men of the city surround the house and demand that the old man bring out his visitor so they might "know" (*yada'*) him. He asks the men not to do this wicked thing and offers his virgin daughter and the concubine. The men rape the concubine, who dies.

The verb to "know" (*yada'*) occurs 1,058 times in the Old Testament, only twelve times to refer to intercourse between a man and a woman (Bailey 1955); it is probable, therefore, that the resident alien status of the men in these two stories rendered their guests suspicious and the townspeople needed to be reassured who they were; it is probable, too, that the resident aliens misunderstood the townspeople's use of the Hebrew verb *yada'*. The townspeople's crime, therefore, is rape and violence towards people who should be offered hospitality (cf. Ezekiel

16:49–50, Matthew 10:15, and Luke 10:12).

By the late second century BCE, however, Sodom had become linked with sexual licentiousness (Jubilees 16:5–6 and 20:5–6) and this identification continued into the first century CE (Testament of the Twelve Patriarchs, Benjamin 9.1; Jude 7; 2 Peter 2:6–8), when the sexual sin is specified as same-sex male (Josephus, *Ant. Jud.* 1.200; Philo, *Questions Genesis* 4.37, *On Abraham* 135).

Solon, Athenian archon and lawgiver (594/3 BCE), and erastês to PEISISTRATOS (tyrant ca. 560–27; PAIDERASTIA). Solon's sexual legislation reportedly established public BROTHELS and a tax on PROSTITUTES (but see Philemon, fr. 3 K-A); forbade CITIZENS who had prostituted themselves from speaking in the assembly (Demosthenes 22.30–1); allowed citizens to beat ADULTRESSES seen out in public (AESCHINES, *In Tim.* 1.183); and advised men to have sex with their wives no fewer than three times a month (Plutarch, *Erotikos* 769a–b).

A series of Solon's LAWS attempted to protect boys in the GYMNASIUM from undesirables: "no one over the age of the boys is to enter" (a capital crime; Aeschines, *In Tim.* 1.10); SLAVES could not LOVE a freeborn boy, frequent the gymnasium, or anoint the boys' bodies with oil (fifty lashes with the whip; Plutarch, *Sol.* 1; Aeschines, *In Tim.* 1.138–9); except for the gymnasiarch, no adult man could attend the Hermaia games (ATHLETICS; Aeschines, *In Tim.* 9–12; Plato, *Lysis*); and, to prevent CRUISING, schools and gymnasia had daylight operating times (Aeschines, *In Tim.* 1.10).

Solon's poetry; Plutarch, *Sol.*

Songs Erotic laments were sung in honor of vegetation/fertility deities who died young: ADONIS and Linus, a youth or HERAKLES's MUSIC teacher (Apollodorus 2.63; Pliny, *HN* 7.204). The lament for

Linus was sung at harvest time and during the vintage (Homer, *Iliad* 18.570) and in many cultures (Herodotus 2.79).

Young women also DANCED while singing "Maiden Songs" (*parthénea*). Two long fragments of these by Alcman have survived, praising the grace and loveliness of the maidens, especially the leaders. The SPARTANS, while dancing, sang a song to APHRODITE and the EROTES (Edmonds 1967: 531, quoting LUCIAN, *Salt.* 11).

Scolia, drinking songs, were composed for and sung at SYMPOSIA. Athenaeus (15.693f–696a) cites twenty-five, of which several are erotic (BATH; BISEXUAL-ITY): for example, "the sow [*hús*, slang for cunt] has this acorn [*balanón*, literally "peg" = clitoris] but desires another [penis]. So I have one pretty girl and I desire another" (no. 20). And several songs form the ballad of ARISTOGEITON AND HARMODIUS (nos. 11–13).

LOVE songs included the conventional *paraklausíthyron*, sung ostensibly by the lover at his beloved's shut door (a metaphor for denied sexual access; OVID, *Ars Am.* 3.581). A popular love song at the time of POMPEII's destruction was inscribed in several places, including the House of Caecilius Iucundus and the VILLA OF THE MYSTERIES. The song is preserved in two elegaic lines: *quis amat valeat, pereat qui nexcit amare, bis tanto pereat quisquis amare vetat*, "whoever loves may they prosper; let them perish who cannot love; let them perish twice who deny love" (*CIL* 4.3200d, 4091, 5272, 6782, 9202; Varone 2001a: 62–3; cf. Helbig 1868: no. 1724).

Songs that were more bawdy (*moechicae*, "adulterous") were termed either "Locrian" songs or "Fescinnine" verses. Locrian songs were already known in the fourth century BCE and may date even earlier (Athenaeus 2.65a–b, 13.600a, 600f–601a, 14.639a quoting Klearchos of Soli). Fescinnine verses were Roman versions of Locrian songs, sung at weddings and as antiphonal harvest songs (Horace, *Epist.* 2.1.145–6). AUGUSTUS's verses

against Asinius Pollio were called Locrian (Macrobius, *Sat.* 2.4.21), perhaps too the song that NERO composed to ridicule Galba's revolt.

One Locrian song, sung by an ADULTERESS to her lover, is quoted by Athenaeus (15.697b–c; cf. OVID, *Ars Am.* 3.605–10):

> What are you doing? Do not betray us, please
> get up before he comes home and does to you
> some great harm, and to me even worse!
> It's daylight – see the sun through the door!

See also: MUSIC; THEATER

Soranus (fl. ca. 100–25 CE), a physician of Ephesus practicing at Rome. In his *Gynecology*, originally illustrated, book 1 explains it is written for intelligent MIDWIVES. A woman should remain a virgin until MENSTRUATION when the uterus is now ready for CONCEPTION and is large enough for the developing CHILD. Menstruation may cause some women to be pale, tired, and not hungry. The best age for conception is between fifteen and forty. Women should be healthy, have good digestion and loose bowels, be of a steady and cheerful mind, and should not be mannish. Permanent VIRGINITY, however, is healthful since intercourse itself is harmful. Conception will stop further menstruation. If the mother is strong during PREGNANCY, the child is a boy, if sluggish it is a girl. Passive exercises during pregnancy are good: reading aloud, massage, SINGING.

Book 2 discusses labor, the BIRTH process, and the care of the newborn. Midwives should prepare olive oil, warm water, soft sea sponges, wool, bandages, pillows, a birthing stool, and two beds. The midwife decides whether the newborn child is healthy by inspecting the genitals and making sure there are no obstructions in the cavities, all the joints are working properly, and the baby has a strong healthy cry. The infant should be washed in brine, wine, or urine; it should not be fed for two days because it already has nutrients from the mother. It should not drink the mother's breast milk because it is hard to digest. Care should be taken to select the right wetnurse. Watch out for overfeeding. Weaning should be tried around the fortieth day. The baby should be BATHED three times a day; after its bath it should be hung upsidedown to loosen the vertebrae. Teething should start in the seventh month.

Book 3 discusses medical problems of the uterus, among which is hemorrhaging after a difficult labor or miscarriage. The woman should lie down and sea sponges, soaked in cold water, should be placed on and around the genitals. Then a piece of wool soaked in the juice of opium, hypocist, and acacis should be placed up inside the uterus with a finger. This should stop the bleeding and the pain.

Book 4 discusses a difficult labor due to a hard and closed uterus, the large size of the fetus, or breech births. If the fetus does not come out naturally due to its size or death, the midwife must intervene with hooks to extract the child. After the extraction the region needs to be soothed.

See also: MEDICINE

Sotades (first half of the third century BCE), poet of Maroneia and inventor of "CINAEDIC" poetry. Sotades was famous for riddling verses that lampooned famous men (Athenaeus 14.620e–621a), among whom was Ptolemy Philadelphus, whose marriage with his sister (INCEST) he described as "poking his prick into an unholy hole." This last reportedly doomed him to being sealed in a lead jar and sunk at sea.

Burton (1885: "Terminal Essay," Section D) identifies a "Sotadic Zone" of tolerance for male-male sex around the earth: the Mediterranean, the Middle East, Afghanistan, much of Pakistan and India, Turkistan, China, Japan, the South Sea islands and the entire western hemisphere "where, at the time of its discovery, Sotadic LOVE was, with some exceptions, an established racial institution."

Sparta, a tent-city in southern Greece. Sparta had a rigorous system of AGE GRADES for both males and females, a military-sanctioned PAIDERASTIA for its youths and young men, and state-sponsored MARRIAGE and child rearing. Because girls also exercised NUDE they were renowned for their beauty (Homer, *Odyssey* 13.412; Aristophanes *Lys.* 79–83; Athenaeus 12.566a; Strabo 10.13); they also reportedly entered into paiderastic relationships with older adult women (LESBIANISM). Spartan warriors wore their HAIR long (Xenophon, *Lac.* 11.3) and donned red CLOAKS (Plutarch, *Mor.* 238f), both of which the Athenians thought EFFEMINATE.

Sterility, the inability to produce viable sperm or ova, probably not much considered in antiquity. The Hippocratic corpus advises that "women who are free from the extremes [of wet/cold, hot/dry] are those who conceive best – same with males" (*Aphorisms* 5.62–3; Hanson 1992: 46); presumably, therefore, WOMEN and MEN who suffered from these extremes could be sterile. Otherwise, men who could not engender CHILDREN were probably thought IMPOTENT, and women who did not conceive after intercourse were probably thought to have intervened (CONCEPTION; DIVORCE; FERTILITY).

Straton of Sardis (fl. 125 CE), Greek writer of some 100 PAIDERASTIC epigrams first arranged in one book, the *Paidikê Moúsa*, "the Boy Muse," eventually reworked into book 12 of the *Anthologia Palatina*. One of Straton's more famous poems is *Greek Anth.* 12.4:

I delight in the prime of a boy of
twelve, a thirteen year-old's better;
At fourteen he's Love's sweet flower,
and dearer yet's fifteen;
Sixteen belongs to the gods –
seventeen is for ZEUS, not me.
But if you want the older ones, play
no longer – it's for keeps.

Strophium, a broad breastband worn to
support the breasts. ATALANTA wears the
stophium when she wrestles Peleus (**123**).
A man can fall out of love with a woman
who has large breasts by requesting her
not to wear her strophium (OVID, *Rem.
Am.* 337–8) implying that its use makes
women more attractive (cf. *Ars Am.*
3.622). In Roman wall paintings most of
the women in sexually explicit scenes
wear the strophium (**291** I, **292, 299,
304, 314, 317, 320, 341**; cf. **279**).
Another use of the strophium was to
bind the orator's and actor's chest (**335**;
cf. **20**), perhaps to give him a stronger,
more projecting voice (cf. NERO); Pliny
wore a strophium around his head to cure
headache (Richlin 1997).

Sulpicia 1 (fl. 50 BCE), Roman woman
poet of the Republic. Six elegies have
survived among the works by Tibullus
(3.13–18). Apparently a freeborn Roman
woman, she speaks of her LOVE for a man
whom she calls "Cerinthus."

Sulpicia 2 (fl. 94/8 CE), Roman woman
poet under DOMITIAN, author of LOVE
poems to her husband Calenus of fifteen
years. Martial refers admiringly to her
twice (10.35, 10.38). One spurious fragment survives (*Sulpiciae conquestio, Epigrammata Bobiensia* 70).

Symposia, all-male drinking parties of the
Greek classical period. They were held in
the *ándron*, a large room in the Greek
house; guests reclined on 7–15 couches,
one or two men to a couch (BEDS). Special
vessel sets accommodated the wine. A
leader (symposiarch) decided how many
kraters of wine would be drunk ("three
for sensible men: one for health, one for
LOVE, and one for sleep"; Eubulus 94 K-
A), the ratio of water to wine (5:2 for
conversation), and the topic of conversation. Besides drinking, there could be
MUSIC and PROSTITUTES.
Both PLATO's and Xenophon's *Symposium* avoid sex directly. Plato hints at it
throughout since the topic is EROS, but the
men have dismissed the flutegirls; at the
end, ALCIBIADES talks of his love for
Socrates. In Xenophon's *Symposium*, the
host Kallias throws a symposium for his
eromenos to celebrate the boy's victory in
wrestling at the Greater Panathenaia. A
Syracusan troupe performs "DIONYSUS
leading Ariadnê to the bridal couch." The
guests are impressed: the MARRIED want
to leave to get back to their wives and the
bachelors want to marry.
Many sympotic vases of the classical
period depict symposia of several sorts.
Men with hetairai and/or flutegirls are the
most common (**68, 101 [pl. 11], 152, 156**;
cf. the Etruscan symposium **197**); some of
these show the beginnings of sexual activity (**94**).
Men-only symposia are commonly depicted (**155**). Other scenes have erotic
nuances: **49, 95, 127**. At the Haloa, a
mid-January festival in Eleusis honoring
DEMETER, hetairai held their own symposium from the fourth century BCE. A
number of fifth-century sympotic vases
show women-only symposia (**88, 128,
138**).

T

Tabellae, portable Roman paintings on wood panels with two hinged leaves. They exist by themselves (**290**) or are depicted in Roman art (wall paintings **329**, **321**; cameo **211**, mirror case **230**, and appliqué **284**). AUGUSTUS reportedly had one illustrating sexual positions (OVID, *Tristia* 2.521–4), and so did TIBERIUS (Suetonius, *Tiberius* 43–4). Clement (*Protr.* 4.53) denounces them for enflaming lust; Heliodorus claims magical power for them ("Ethiopian Tale" 4.8; NOVELS).

See also: PORNOGRAPHY

Brendel 1970: 30; Myerowitz 1992.

Thaïs (fl. 320–300 BCE), Athenian courtesan who accompanied ALEXANDER THE GREAT to Asia. She reportedly urged him during a SYMPOSIUM to set fire to Darius's palace. After Alexander's death she became courtesan to Ptolemy Soter and bore him two sons and a daughter Eirene who married the king of Soloi in Cyprus. Hipparchus and Menander wrote plays named for her (Athenaeus 11.484d–e, 13.567c).

Diodorus Siculus 17.72; Plutarch, *Alex.* 38; Curtius 5.7.3.

Theater While most plays had some sexual content (the pallaké Cassandra in Aeschylus's *Agamemnon*), Greek comedy (ARISTOPHANES) and SATYR plays had significant sexual content. Aristophanes's *Lysistrata*, for instance, is full of sexual jokes and its men characters all wore PHALLOI. Satyr plays, conventionally added to each trilogy of tragedies, were being produced by themselves by the middle of the fourth century, influencing the development of other sexually comedic forms, especially in Italy.

Mimes (short popular plays, employing dance and song; Richlin 1992b) were put on by traveling troupes in public and in private residences (cf. Xenophon's SYMPOSIUM). In the third century Theocritus and Herodas wrote mimes with sexual components. In the early empire, some mimes employed real rape and real ADULTERY (NERO). Pantomimes, a mime acted by a single actor, were brought to Rome in 22 BCE from the east. The pantomime DANCED the story, wearing a silk gown and mask with closed lips. The stories all had strong sexual content (LEDA or PROCNÊ; Juvenal 6.63, 7.92). Pantomimes were often EFFEMINATE (Richlin 1983: 92–3, 98; Pliny, *Pan.* 54.1) and DESIRED (Bathyllus by Maecenas, Tacitus, *Ann.* 1.54.3; Pliny *Ep.* 7.24; Edwards 1997: 67–8; Brown 1992: 180–3, 186–7).

The actor in *magodiae* parodied comedy in WOMEN's attire, tambourines, and cymbals, and made indecent gestures while acting the part of adulteresses and pimps (Athenaeus 14.621b–d; cf. Herodas, 36 and 40 Teubner). The south

Italian *phlyax* (Taplin 1986–7; Pontrandolfo 2000) turned myths and daily life into farces. Men's COSTUMES were padded with long phalloi either dangling or tied up in an exaggerated DOGKNOT. The Italian *palliata fabula* reworked Greek plays into Latin. The plots are stocked with lots of sexual jokes. The Italian *Atellana fabula* was a short piece depicting town-life using stock characters. Most date to the first century BCE but some are much later. During the festival, "Floralia," *fabulae Atellanae* used nude women (Lactantius 1.20.1).

AUGUSTUS had the actor Stephanio whipped and banished for being waited on by a woman dressed like a boy, and banished the actor Pylades because he used the "finger" to point at a man in the audience (Suetonius, *Augustus* 45.4). CALIGULA had sex with the pantomime Mnester and, dressed in a wig and long robe, acted and danced (Suetonius, *Caligula* 36). NERO often sang, danced, and played the lyre (Suetonius, *Nero* 12, 16, 23). DOMITIAN forbade actors on the public stage, and expelled a quaestor from the senate for acting and dancing (Suetonius, *Domitian* 3, 7, 8, 10).

Theogamia, Athenian festival celebrating the MARRIAGE (*gámos*) of ZEUS and HERA on 26 Gamelian (mid-February). Many mortal weddings also took place on and about the Theogamia.

See also: ANTHESTERIA; HIEROS GAMOS

Theognis (fl. late seventh or early sixth century BCE), elegiac poet of Megara. Many poems were written for the SYMPOSIUM; some 230 are addressed to his eromenos Kyrnis:

> Happy the lover who, having gone home
> to sleep with a beautiful boy, "works out" all day!
> (2.1335–6; cited in GYMNASIUM; PAIDERASTIA)

Thera, volcanic island in the south central Aegean. The Archaic capital exhibits seventh century BCE homoerotic graffiti (*IG* 12.3.536–601, esp. 536–49, and 12 Suppl. ad 537) hammered into the exposed rock west of the sanctuary and GYMNASIUM to Apollo Karneus. The inscriptions praise youths for their DANCING (no. 540: "Eumelas is the best dancer" and "Krimion is first in the KONISALOS"; cf. 536, 543). Other inscriptions include variations on the verb ôpheín, "to fuck": "Pheidipidas fucked here," and "Timagoras, Enferes, and I are fuckers"; cf. "Enpulos was a whore here" (*Énpulos entháde pórnos*), which Dover (1985: 125–6) reads as a "jocular obscenity." Other scholars interpret these inscriptions as implying ritual male-male intercourse during an AGE GRADE ceremony (Cantarella 1992: 7–8).

Theseus, legendary king of Athens, son of Aegeus (or POSEIDON). When he arrives in Athens, he wears a long chiton and long hair and is mistaken for a maiden (Pausanias 1.19.1; cf. 20). In the palace he foils MEDEA's attempts to POISON him. He then volunteers to lead the annual sacrifice of youths and maidens to king MINOS of Crete. With the help of Ariadnê he kills the Minotaur and takes her with him to the island of Dia (presumably Naxos; COUVADE), where he abandons her and sails to Athens (OSCHOPHORIA); Aegeus, thinking his son is dead, jumps to his death. Now king of Athens, Theseus leads an expedition against the AMAZONS, and, at the wedding of Pirithoös and Hippodameia, fights CENTAURS; Pirithoös and Theseus try to kidnap Persephonê from the Underworld but fail and Pirithoös must stay there. Theseus also kidnaps HELEN when she is twelve (he is fifty) and keeps her with his mother until her brothers CASTOR AND POLLUX invade Attica; Theseus then flees to Scyros where he is killed. At some point in his life he was said to have "favored" Tlepoleos, founder of Samos (Athenaeus 7.295a–b).

Thesmophoria, an all-WOMEN festival in honor of DEMETER in late October/early November. Most cities of Greece held this festival, which, when coupled with the immediately preceding festival Stenia, lasted five days. Stenia consisted of a night of dancing and ribaldry in honor of Iambê of Eleusis who, along with BAUBO, cheered Demeter; it may have been at the Stenia that women threw piglets and cakes into a cave to rot. The next day, the women gathered at the seashore.

The Thesmophoria begins with the day of *ánodos* (ascent), when all adult women (proper, metics, and PROSTITUTES) ascend to a sanctuary of Demeter (in Athens, on the Pnyx; in Corinth, on Acrocorinth). The second day, *nysteía*, "pure" women (not having had sex for three days) descend into the cave to retrieve the rotted remains of the piglets and cakes, and mix this material with seed for sowing. Since a slang term for a woman's vagina was *choíros*, "piglet," this part of the celebration directly links agricultural fertility with female fertility. On the last day, *kalligénia*, "beautiful offspring," the women feast.

Tiberius (42 BCE–37 CE), emperor Julius Caesar Augustus (14–37 CE), son of Tiberius Claudius Nero and Livia. He first marries Vipsania Agrippina, the daughter of Marcus Agrippa, and fathers two children by her, but, after Agrippa's death in 12, he is forced by Augustus to DIVORCE and marry JULIA MAIOR, Agrippa's widow and Augustus's daughter. After she gives BIRTH to a child that dies soon after, Tiberias stops having sex with her. He retires to Rhodes in 6, out of favor with Augustus. After Julia's banishment in 2, Augustus procures Tiberius a divorce. He returns to Rome in 2 CE.

Early in his reign, in 27, he retires to the island of Capri. There, Tiberius reportedly acquires infants to nurse on his penis, and boys and girls, whom he called *pisciculi*, "little fishes," to arouse him by nibbling at him when he goes BATHING, or

to play Pan and nymphs in special groves called *Caprinea*. He converts the latrines (*sellaria*; **pl. 37**) of Capri into male BROTHELS for which he procures "fancy boys," *sellarii* (CINAEDI), one of whom is the future emperor Vitellius (Suetonius, *Caligula* 16.1, *Vitellius* 3.2). He also acquires "men of gigantic proportions, whom he called *spintriae*, to copulate in threes to excite his failing DESIRES." He compiles an erotic library and art gallery, SEX MANUALS by Elephantis and paintings by Parrhasius, especially one that depicted ATALANTA FELLATING Meleager. And in his OLD AGE, he is accused of being a CUNNILICTOR; one woman kills herself afterwards, complaining of "the bad breath of the goat," *capri* in Latin, a phrase that became popular in Atellan farces (THEATER).

Once, at a sacrifice, he lusted after the incense bearer and had him brought to his chamber to rape both him and his flute-playing brother; when they complained, he had their legs broken. Since it was forbidden to execute virgins, he had the daughter of Sejanus raped first by the executioner. And he would trick men into drinking vast amounts of wine, and when they were tortured he would have their penises tied up so they were unable to urinate (DOGKNOT).

Suetonius, *Tiberius*.

Tiresias, mythological prophet of the Boeotians. He saw two copulating snakes on Mt Kyllene and was turned into a woman; later, he saw them again, and was turned back into a man (Hesiod, fr. 275 M-W; Apollodorus 3.6.7; TRANSSEXUALITY). He was therefore asked by the gods who enjoys sex more, MEN or WOMEN, and he answered "women, by a third." HERA was displeased and blinded him, but ZEUS granted him prophecy ([Hesiod], *Melampodia*). In another version, Tiresias was blinded because he saw ATHENA bathing (Callimachus 5). Both OEDIPUS and Odysseus consulted Tiresias (Sophocles,

Oedipus Turannos; Homer, *Odyssey* 10.490–5, 11.90–9).

Transsexuality, the change from one sex to the other. Ino-Leuothea raises the young DIONYSUS as a girl; also see CAENEUS; IPHIS; LEUKIPPOS 1; TIRESIAS. Lucius Mucianus claimed to have seen two transsexuals at Argos and Smyrna; and Pliny reports four in 171 BCE and himself inspected one from Thysdrus (*HN* 7.23; Aulus Gellius 9.4.12 ff.).

See also: HERMAPHRODITUS

Transvestism, wearing the COSTUME regarded as more appropriate for the other sex. Young men wore WOMEN's clothes at special occasions during adolescence (AGE GRADES; EKDYSIA; LEUKIPPOS 2; OSCHOPHORIA); ACHILLES is dressed as a girl on Skyros (Apollodorus 3.13.8); THESEUS is mistaken for a maiden (Pausanias 1.19.1); and HERAKLES, dressed as a woman, does women's work for Omphalê. SPARTAN youths spent a period in isolation that ended in a race, a beating, a procession in women's dress and grotesque masks (in the Sparta Museum), and a war DANCE. In Sparta and Cos (Plutarch, *Lyc.* 15, *Quaest. Graec.* 58), grooms donned women's clothes on their wedding night (perhaps MARRIAGE signaled CITIZENSHIP). In Argos the bride, however, wears a false beard on her wedding night (Plutarch, *Mor.* 245e–f; cf. Leitao 1995: 163).

To commemorate the woman poet Telesilla who, with an army of women, defended Argos against Kleomenes of Sparta (ruled 520–489), the Argives celebrated the Hyristic by switching clothes (Plutarch, *Mor.* 245c–f). At Erythrae, when the flatterers known as the Bowing Dogs (*próskunes*) killed king Knopos, they ruled for a time, wearing their hair long and women's clothing (Athenaeus 6.259c–d).

Men also dressed up as women in order to imitate women: the two youth companions of Theseus to kill the Minotaur (OSCHOPHORIA), LEUKIPPOS 2 to be with DAPHNE, Pentheus to infiltrate the Theban bacchants (Euripides, *Bacchae*), the beardless men as Thracian women to kill the Persian embassy (Herodotus 5.10), and the Theban soldiers to kill the Spartan garrison (Xenophon, *Hell.* 5.4.4).

Part of the characterization of EFFEMINACY (CINAEDI; PROSTITUTES) is the man's attention to his body, to wear makeup and to dress and act like a woman (Suetonius, *Caligula* 52). A set of late Archaic kylikes depict "male symposiasts reveling in extravagant eastern garb," interpreted as enacting *habrosúnê*, refined sensuality (Boardman and Kurtz 1986; Kurke 1997: 132), but they may also be mocking women. Surena, the victor of Carrhae, mocked Crassus by including in his triumphal procession a man labeled "Crassus" dressed as a woman (Plutarch, *Crass.* 32.4–6).

In THEATER, men played all roles until at least the late fourth century BCE, and they played several different roles in each play. Thus, HIPPOLYTOS could confront the sexuality of both father and stepmother if the same actor played Theseus and Phaidra in Euripides's *Hippolytos* (Rabinowitz 1995; cf Plautus, *Casina*). The long robes of concert musicians were feminine (Maas and Snyder 1989: 118–19) and Phaedrus (Plato, *Symp.* 179d) characterizes ORPHEUS, because he sang and played the kithara, as effeminate.

Trojan War, the events leading up to the Achaean attack on Troy, the ten years' siege there, and the returns of the various Greek heroes. The war can be dated ca. 1250 BCE (Thucydides), 1184 (Herodotus), or, according to archaeology, ca. 1190.

Preceding events
(*Cypria*, now lost)

Thetis, a nymph, is fated to have a son greater than his father, and so ZEUS has her MARRY the mortal Peleus. Their son is ACHILLES. All the gods attend the wedding, except Eris ("strife"), who throws a gold "apple" (*mêlon*) marked "To the fairest goddess." Three goddesses vie for the title, HERA, ATHENA, and APHRODITE; to settle the question, Paris, a son of king Priam and Hecuba of Troy, is chosen. Hera offers glory, Athena wisdom, and Aphrodite the hand of HELEN, wife of king Menelaus of SPARTA, and the most beautiful woman in the world.

Paris arrives in Sparta while Menelaus is away, and, with her consent, abducts her. When Menelaus discovers her ADULTERY, he persuades his brother Agamemnon, king of Mycenae (ATREUS), to honor the pledge all the suitors of Helen took, to maintain her honor. Agamemnon assembles the Achaeans at Aulis, where the fleet is delayed by an angry ARTEMIS until Agamemnon sacrifices his eldest daughter IPHIGENEIA to her.

The siege of Troy
(*Iliad*, and, now lost, *Aethiopis*, *Little Iliad*, and *Iliou Persis*)

Prior conditions must be met if the Achaeans are to take Troy, including: Philoctetes, left behind on Lemnos where he MASTURBATES, has to participate (he eventually kills Paris); and Achilles must kill the Trojan prince Troilos before he turns twenty, which he does by raping him to death.

When the *Iliad* begins its tale of ten days, nine years of fighting have gone by. Chryseis, daughter of a local priest of Apollo, has been taken by Agamemnon, which angers APOLLO. When Chryseis is returned to her father, Agamemnon demands Achilles's prize Briseis, which so angers Achilles that he refuses to participate in the fighting. His friend Patroklos (older than Achilles, and possibly his erastes) dons Achilles's armor and dies fighting Hector. Achilles, roused, kills

Hector. The *Iliad* ends with the funeral of Patroklus.

Soon after, Penthesileia, queen of the AMAZONS, arrives to help the Trojans. After fighting bravely she is eventually killed by Achilles, but only seconds after the two had fallen in LOVE at first sight (39, 124; NECROPHILIA). At her funeral, Achilles mourns; when Thersites mocks him for being in love, Achilles kills him too. Finally Achilles is killed by Paris, and Polyxena is sacrificed to him.

As a ruse, the Achaeans build the Trojan Horse and leave it before the gates of Troy. Helen tests the men inside, imitating the voices of their wives; when the men do not respond, the Trojans break down the walls and drag the horse in (Homer, *Odyssey* 4.271–89). That night, the Achaeans in the horse open the other gates of the city and let the rest of the Achaeans in to take it. During the final siege in the temple to Athena, Ajax the Lesser (the Locrian) rapes Cassandra (114), who then becomes Agamemnon's prize.

The return home
(*Odyssey*, and *Nostoi*, now lost)

Agamemnon goes directly back to Mycenae where his wife Clytemnestra and her lover Aegisthus kill both him and Cassandra. Menelaus, finding that Helen is a phantom, goes to Egypt to retrieve her.

Odysseus (*Odyssey*) is blown off course by POSEIDON and wanders the central Mediterranean for ten more years. He becomes the lover of CIRCE and Calypso, is almost the victim of the female Sirens who lure men to their death by SINGING sweetly, and of Scylla, a female monster that destroys ships. In his final adventure, washed ashore and NUDE, he meets Nausicaä daughter of Alkinoös of Phaiakia. She is content to MARRY him, and her father wants it, but Odysseus must get back to Ithaca.

While Odysseus is dallying in Phaiakia, his son Telemachos journeys to Sparta to get news of his father. At Pylos he teams up with his contemporary Peisistratos, son of Nestor; at Sparta, Helen gives him a wedding dress for his future bride. Meanwhile, his mother Penelopê is besieged by suitors pressing her to pick her next husband before Telemachos comes of age.

When Odysseus arrives, he challenges the suitors to a contest, wins it, and kills them all plus the WOMEN servants who had had sex with them. When Penelopê and Odysseus are finally alone they tell their stories and make LOVE.

V

Verginia In 450 BCE, a board of ten, the *decemviri*, usurp the leadership of Rome. Its head, Appius Claudius, DESIRES Verginia, the daughter of Lucius Verginius. Claudius's client Marcus Claudius takes her to Appius's court, where he claims she is his runaway SLAVE; Appius decrees her to be his property, but Verginia's fiancé Icilius forces Appius to rescind his order. Verginius leads his daughter back to court the next day; Appius again judges her to be a slave. Verginius, exclaiming "In the only way I can, my daughter, I claim your freedom," kills her. Shown her lifeless body and bloodstained clothes, the crowd overthrows the decemvirate and restores the republic. Verginius and Icilius are elected to office.

The story is repeated in the reign of TIBERIUS, when Claudius Regillianus, also a decemvir, tries to enslave a young freeborn woman to have sex with him (Suetonius, *Tiberius* 2.2).

See also: LUCRETIA

Livy 3.44–58; Joshel 1992.

Vertumnus and Pomona, an Etruscan god of the seasons and the Italian goddess of tree fruit. At Pomona's sanctuary Vertumnus, dressed as an OLD woman (TRANSVESTISM), tries to seduce her. "She" tells a story about a girl who rebuffs a young man's LOVE until he kills himself, and when she sees the funeral pass, she turns to stone. Pomona agrees to MARRY Vertumnus. A similar story concerns Parakyptousa (the Peeper) of Cyprus (Plutarch, *Erotikos* 766d); also Iphis and Anaxaretê (SEX IN ART [sculptures]), and the Biblical story of Lot's wife (Genesis 19).

Ovid, *Met* 14.622, 771.

Vestal Virgins, the six priestesses who maintained the sanctuary of Vesta, the Roman goddess of the hearth and family, in the Roman forum. In the temple, were the "sacred things that cannot be divulged": the Palladium (the statue of ATHENA taken from TROY), and the *fascinum*, an erect apotropaic PHALLUS (Pliny, *HN* 28.39; VILLA OF THE MYSTERIES at POMPEII).

Vestal Virgins were chosen at a young age from high-ranking families and had to commit to thirty years of chaste service, after which they were free to resume social life. They dressed like a Roman bride and matron, however. The last chief Vestal was Coelia Concordia in 380 CE and the cult was extinguished shortly after, in 394. Their sexual purity reflected Rome's (Seneca, *Controv.* 6.8; cf. 6.9). In 420 BCE, a Vestal named Postumia was indicted for sexual misconduct and acquitted, although she had "to abstain from jokes and to cultivate an appearance which was holy rather than smart" (Livy 4.44.11–12). The last Vestal to be punished for sexual misconduct was buried alive in the reign of DOMITIAN.

Worsfold 1932; Beard 1980 and 1995.

Villa of the Mysteries, an important villa to the northwest of POMPEII. The Great Frieze (ca. 50 BCE; Clarke 2003: figs 21–30) in room 5 depicts a woman readying herself for MARRIAGE (L–R): a standing woman (presumably the bride); a woman and NUDE boy reading from a scroll, and a PREGNANT woman with a tray of cakes; two WOMEN at a table; a woman pours water into a basin while Silenus plays the lyre; two fauns play the syrinx and attend goats; a woman swirls her mantle over her head as if startled, and looks diagonally across the room at the scene with the *fascinum* (veiled PHALLUS; see VESTAL VIRGINS); a seated SATYR holds up a bowl for a faun to look into while another faun holds up a speaking mask (both items of prophecy); DIONYSUS lounges in the lap of Ariadnê (opposite the major entrance to the room); a half-nude woman kneels to unveil the fascinum while a winged demon (Vanth) lifts a cane to strike her and another woman stands behind; the half-nude woman, now disheveled and weary, rests against the lap of a seated woman while a NUDE MAENAD (seen from behind) plays castanets and another holds a thyrsus; a seated woman (presumably the bride) arranges her HAIR with the help of another woman and PSYCHE who holds up a mirror to her (with her reflection painted in it, as if APHRODITE); and, finally, an older matron sits and surveys the entire frieze.

de Grummond 2002; Clarke 2003: 8–9, 47–57.

Violence, sexual violence, arose from men exercising great power. Men hitting WOMEN was thought natural, even if opprobrious (OVID, *Amores* 1.7). To yield (Peitho), to be passive, was women's duty: "rape is a compliment paid to an attractive woman" (Gordon 1997: 282; cf. Richlin 1992: 169).

Rape

The common Greek verb to have intercourse, *bineín*, implies violence, and the Latin *irrumo* denotes a rape of the mouth; the goddess of sex, APHRODITE/VENUS, is herself married to the god of war, ARES/MARS; and in Roman LAW, rape was only a crime against a freeborn CITIZEN. In war, the victors rape enemy women, kill their sons, and enslave all females. The early fifth century BCE LOVES OF THE GODS are actually rapes. Mars rapes the VESTAL VIRGIN Rhea Silvia (OVID, *Fasti* 3.11–48). CASTOR AND POLLUX rape the LEUKIPPIDAI (**107**). Jupiter gives Lara with her tongue ripped out to Mercury to rape. EROS rapes GANYMEDE (**80**). APHRODITE rapes Phaêthon (EOS; HERMAPHRODITUS). There is no instance of a female raping another female (but see KALLISTO). SATYRS characteristically accost MAENADS (**6, 33, 34, 83**; Osborne 1996: 78–80); CENTAURS rape women and youths. Boreas rapes the nymph Oreithyia; Hades rapes Persephonê; HEPHAESTUS unsuccessfully tries to rape ATHENA; so too the giant Tityos tries to rape LETO.

Peleus rapes Thetis (**85, 121 [pl. 13]**). THESEUS assaults the nereid Amphitritê.

Ajax rapes Cassandra at the altar of Athena at TROY, personalizing the rape of the city (**114**; Shapiro 1992: 65). Achilles rapes Troilos.

Men interpret the woman's fear of rape as attractive (**107**; Sutton 1992: 30–1): "fear itself became" Lekcothoê (OVID, *Met.* 4.230) and "chaste tears became" LUCRETIA (*Fasti* 2.757). CATULLUS 16 threatens anal and oral rape (FELLATIO). TIBERIUS had Sejanus's virgin daughter raped first, then strangled (Tacitus, *Ann.* 5.9). "The eldest daughter of king Ptolemaios Auletes could not endure the sexual demands of her husband Kybiosactes and had him strangled to death within a few days of her marriage" (Strabo 17.1.11; Krenkel 1981: 38); similarly, three young women of Miletos refused to MARRY barbarian Celts and killed themselves (Anyte, *Greek Anth.* 7.492).

Sadism
(SEXUAL ACTIVITIES [pain])

During sex men inflicted pain on both women and youths, and sometimes women on men, by slapping with SANDALS, occasionally by caning or whipping women (FLAGELLATION), and by burning women (**67**). Since the women who are beaten were PROSTITUTES, this violence also expresses differences in CLASS and status (cf. Sutton 1992: 32) and the differences that existed between citizen men and all women; thus, much sexual violence must have been against women in general. Women seemingly must die to prove men in power (VERGINIA, LUCRETIA) or to set men free (cf. Joshel 1992: 125).

EROS is bound in chains and amorini are depicted bound. The garden of the House of the Vettii at POMPEII held marble statues of infants with their hands bound behind them. Torture was applied to SLAVES and criminals to get information or confessions. The painter Parrhasius bought a slave to torture for his depiction of the pain of Prometheus (SEX IN ART [paintings]).

In Roman mosaics, CHILDREN are depicted as hunters and gladiators, attesting to the "Roman ability to see something cute or humorous in the killing of animals and men" (Brown 1992). Young and defenseless animals were represented as fearful. The emperor CLAUDIUS liked to watch *retiarii* die (gladiators who worked with nets), because he could see their uncovered faces (Suetonius, *Claudius* 34); after a bout in the arena, corpses were branded to make certain

they were really dead (Tertullian, *Apol.* 15.5).

Mutilation

Cotys, king of Thrace, in a fit of jealousy cuts up his wife alive, starting with her genitals (Athenaeus 12.532a).

See also: ATREUS; BODY MODIFICATION; PROCNÊ

Virginity, in antiquity, the state of a young woman not yet MARRIED (cf. Tertullian, *De virg. vel.*). In modern thought, the woman's intact hymen, a membrane across the mouth of the vagina, characterizes her virginity, her unpenetrated state. Ancient medical writers did not, however, claim an importance for the hymen (Aristotle and Galen) or even acknowledge its existence (Soranus 1.16–17; BODIES).

Sissa 1990; Hanson 1992: *passim*, n. 58.

Voyeurism, watching others have sex. "Always with doors wide open and unguarded, Lesbia, you receive your lovers; you do not hide your vices. The beholder gives you more pleasure than the lover" (Martial 1.34); Hostius Quadra set up a large mirror to watch himself be penetrated while performing CUNNILINGUS (Seneca, *Q nat.* 1.16). Voyeurs are inserted into Roman wall paintings of sexual scenes (often the *cubicularius*, chamber servant; **288, 290, 297**); and anonymous people stand in the upper zones of third and fourth style paintings as if watching the inhabitants of the room from half-open doors and windows. THEATER incorporates the notion of the voyeur when staging sexual activity (NERO), including PROSTITUTES MASTURBATING men in a play by Afranius (Ausonius 79).

See also: ORGIES; PORNOGRAPHY

W

Water eroticizes places. Water nymphs capture men (HERMAPHRODITUS; HERAKLES; IOLAOS). The CENTAUR Nessos attempts to rape HERAKLES's bride Deianeira at his river. Fetching water was eroticized since WOMEN were permitted to leave the house to do it; so too were the scenes on the water jars themselves: for example, two women in diaphanous chitons fetching water (98); ACHILLES ambushing Troilos at a fountain (201); at a fountain men accosting youths (37, 127) and women (130); and sexual intercourse (33, 48).

See also: BATHS

Women

Biography (AGE GRADES)

Greek

If the girl was accepted by her father (Athens) or by her tribe (SPARTA), she was allowed to live and given a name (in Athens, a compound abstraction). She is schooled at home in textile production, food preparation, household management, and child-rearing; some girls learn to play MUSIC and to read and write. By age twelve a girl begins the transition to adulthood and MARRIAGE (through rites like the ARKTEIA in Athens and footraces in Sparta; see ATHLETICS; LEUKIPPIDAI). In Sparta, she may become involved in a female form of PAIDERASTIA (see LESBIANISM). At age fifteen she is married to a man about fifteen years older; by age twenty she has given BIRTH at least once. After her husband's death, a woman is either under the guardianship of her son or her father's family, perhaps to marry again.

Roman

All first-born girls are raised by law; her name is the adjectival form of her father's surname. They remain at home and are schooled in the same subjects as their Greek counterparts. They marry at thirteen or fourteen and, depending on the type of marriage they choose, they remain under the guardianship of their father or pass to their husband's.

Greece and Rome

Girl infants can be exposed or killed at birth (cf. Hunt and Edgar 1970: 1, no. 105; Nixon 1995: 89). Females went through three main periods when chances of dying were great (Becker 2003): perinatal (stillborn and infants up to one month), weaning (2–4 years) and late adolescence (15–20 years), especially in first childbirth. After late adolescence, women's average age at death was midthirties (Varone 2001b: 166).

Women's bodies

Girls's BODIES were considered masculinate, needing to be "opened up," by intercourse and childbirth. Women were closer to nature than MEN (Aristotle, *Problems* 29; Ortner 1972). Their bodies are wet, spongey, and shaped like containers to hold the liquid necessary for MENSTRUATION: their uterus was an upturned jar, Pandora was shaped like a storage jar, women and/or their CHILDREN could be put out to the sea in chests (Augê, Danaê, the children of Rhea Silvia [Romulus and Remus]; Lissarrague 1995; Reeder 1995a). Their bodies were also like fleece (or fleecy like clouds; ARISTOPHANES, *Clouds* 341–3; CENTAURS); thus, when a girl is born, wool decorates her house doorway.

Female nature

Women formed a race apart (Hesiod, *Theogony* 592); their nature was unstable, prone to drunkenness (Athenaeus 10.440d, 10.429a–b, 441c–d) and gluttony (Athenaeus 3.97b–c, 4.161d–e, 5.179b–d), incapable of self-mastery, and dependent upon male guidance. Women were also prone to sexual voracity; they would even go after male SLAVES (Martial 2.49.2, 10.91; Juvenal 6.279, 331, 598).

Femininity and sexuality

Women's femininity becomes conventional by the late fifth century BCE. In vase paintings women cluster with their girl friends, play the lyre (also OVID, *Ars Am.* 3.319–20 [PROSTITUTES play auloi, however; see MUSIC]), assume graceful poses; EROS flutters nearby (cf. 85). Though women could take pleasure in sex (Aristophanes, *Lys.* 163–6; Ovid, *Ars Am.* 2.679–84, 717–32, and *Amores* 1.10.36 ff.; Parker 1992: 96), "decent women cannot, of course, bestow passionate love without impropriety" (Plutarch,

Erotikos 752c). Without frequent sexual intercourse, women could suffer from hysteria ("many have hanged themselves," Hippocrates, *Virg.* 1) or become masculine, with "a deepening voice and a beard," and die (Hippocrates, *Pop.* 6.8.32).

As consumers and comestibles

On Greek tombstones women select JEWELRY and admire their reflections in mirrors. They use COSMETICS, wigs, and false breasts to make themselves more attractive (Athenaeus 13.557e–558a, 568a; cf. Xenophon, *Oec.*; Horace, *Sat.* 1.2). Rome's Oppian LAW (215 BCE) curbed excesses: "no woman may carry more than half an ounce of gold, wear garments with purple trim, or ride in carriages." M. Porcius Cato argued against its repeal twenty years later: women are uncontrollable, their obsession with adorning their body signals the state's submission to luxury (Wyke 1994: 139).

Contrariwise, women were also seen as men's comestibles (Henry 1992: 260). In Sparta, young girls were stripped NUDE for guest-friends to admire (Athenaeus 13.566e). Prostitutes could be shared among men (Athenaeus 10.437e). And women were treated like food (Athenaeus 7.329c–d; cf. 4.238a–130d, 4.134d–137c).

Status

A proper woman was always a minor, dependent on her guardian; Roman wives, however, could remain under the guardianship of their father. The married woman's chief role was to bear legitimate children. If she was sterile or bore only daughters, she could be DIVORCED, returned to her former guardian, or given to one of her husband's friends (Wells 1979). When male guests visited, a woman was dismissed from the room; if found unchaste her father or brother could sell her to a BROTHEL. She married the man of her father's choice, her dowry maintained by her husband. Upper-class women stayed at home (Wells 1979): "the greatest glory of a woman is to be least talked about by men" (Thucydides 2.45.2; Plutarch, *Mor.* 242e). Priestesses were permitted to attend both the Athenian THEATER and the Olympics, but proper married women were not allowed at either (Pausanias 5.6.7; Podlecki 1990; Zweig 1992: 76). AUGUSTUS allowed women to see gladiatorial shows from the upper seats, but forbade them from Greek-style athletic contests (Suetonius, *Augustus* 44.3).

Women's work

This consisted primarily of indoor work, managing the household, producing textiles, rearing children, and preparing food (cf. Aristophanes, *Lys.* 710–30; Xenophon, *Oec.* 7.22; Aristotle, *Politics* 3.4.1277b.24f; Wyke 1994: 140). Women slaves were also MIDWIVES. In the rural areas, women had "the 'bent over' tasks (harvesting, weeding, gleaning, milking)." As day laborers and at various jobs in the cities, women could earn money (Scheidel 1995: 207, 211–13). For the "bent-over" tasks (*kúbda*), compare Aristotle's distinction between erect citizens and bent-over slaves (*Politics* 1254b.25–30).

Greek women worked on vases (**102**), wrote poetry (West 1996; Snyder 1989; cf. NMA 817, a tombstone of a woman author from Boeotia), and commissioned sculpture (McClees 1920: 16–28, 45); Roman women painted portraits (Helbig 1868: nos. 1443 [Naples 9017] and 1444; and Naples 9018 from POMPEII VI 1.10; cf. **335**). Women also won chariot races at the Olympic games and elsewhere (Pausa-

nias 3.8.1, 3.15.1, 3.17.6, 5.8.11, 5.12.5, 6.1.6, 6.5.10; Moretti 1953).

Women and religion (ANTHESTERIA; ATHLETICS; CLODIA; MAENADS; ORPHEUS; Turner 1983; Henderson 1987: 114–17; Whitehead 1986: 77–81; Simon 1991; Harris 1993)

Women frequented sanctuaries, dedicated objects, and conducted women-only festivals and rituals, such as (in Athens) the Stenia and THESMOPHORIA, the Haloa, the Hiketeria, the ADONIA, the Skira, and the ARKTEIA (Simon 1983; Keuls 1985: 352–7), and (in Rome) the Bona Dea (CLODIA). Women formed religious associations (*thíasoi*) that served various divinities (Pausanias 3.13.7, 3.16.1, 4.16.9); SAPPHO may have led a thiasos devoted to APHRODITE (Snyder 1989: 12; Cantarella 1992: 78–82).

Resentment

Women did not always tolerate their second-class status. Men could imagine women in revolt (Aristophanes, *Lysistrata*; Pherecrates, *Tyranny* [152 K-A]). In mythology, the women of Lemnos killed all the men (Apollodorus 1.9.17). At some all-women festivals, like the ADONIA, women jeer at men from rooftops; at the sanctuary of Mysian Demeter near Pellene, men and women insult each other (Pausanias 7.27.4); and on vases, women poke fun at the men's genitals (**86, 99, 105**).

See also: CONCEPTION; MEDICINE; PREGNANCY

Richlin 1997.

Z

Zeus/Jupiter/Jove, supreme divinity of classical antiquity, son of Kronos. Kronos castrates his father Ouranos (the sky; see APHRODITE; BODY MODIFICATION), and then mates with his sister Rhea (INCEST) to produce Hestia, DEMETER, HERA, Hades, POSEIDON, and ZEUS. Fearing his children would do the same to him, Kronos swallows them whole, except Zeus whom Rhea replaces with a stone (and Poseidon with a foal; Pausanias 8.8.2) and hides him in a cave in Crete.

Eventually Zeus forces his father to vomit forth his siblings and the stone (now the *ómphalos* at Delphi). He then rules the sky, Poseidon the sea, and Hades the underworld. Zeus's children are ARES, Hebe, and EILEITHYIA (from Hera); HERMES (Maia); ARTEMIS and APOLLO (LETO); DIONYSUS (Semelê, daughter of Cadmus of Thebes). He also has sexual liaisons with mortals (LOVES OF THE GODS).

Plate 26 Mould for a mould-made bowl from Pella (Hellenistic; Pella; **188**).

Plate 25 Discus lamp from Messene (1st c. CE; Messene; **227**).

Plate 27 Mosaic from Sousse (2nd–3rd c. CE; Sousse; **235**).

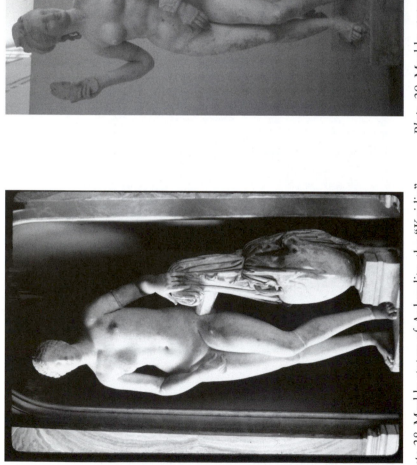

Plate 29 Marble statue group of Aphrodite, Pan, and Eros from Delos (3rd–2nd c. BCE; NMA; **172**).

Plate 28 Marble statue of Aphrodite, the "Knidia" by PRAXITELES (mid 4th c.; **18**).

Plate 30 Painting from the House of the Marine Venus, POMPEII (1st c. CE; **293**).

Plate 31 Mosaic from Maktar, Tunisia (2nd–3rd c. CE; Maktar; **236**).

Plate 32 Mosaic from El Jem, Tunisia (2nd–3rd c. CE; El Jem; **237**).

Plate 33 Painting from the House of the Vettii, POMPEII (1st c. BCE–1 c. CE; **305**).

Plate 34 Mosaic from El Jem, Tunisia (2nd–3rd c. CE; El Jem; **238**).

Plate 35 Marble hermaphrodite reclining on a (restored) couch, face (Rome, Altemps; **175**).

Plate 36 Marble hermaphrodite reclining on a (restored) couch, genitals (Rome, Altemps; **175**).

Plate 37 View of the latrine, Forum baths, Ostia (pp. 22, 27, 98).

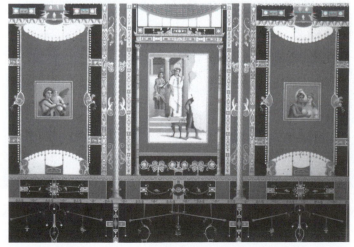

Plate 38 Reconstruction painting by G. Marsigli of the paintings on the tablinum north wall, House of Cæcilius Jucundus, POMPEII (p. 100).

Plate 39 General view of the peristyle garden, House of the Vettii, POMPEII
(p. 100).

Plate 40 General view of the southeast triclinium, House of the Vettii, POMPEII
(p. 101).

Plate 41 Red-figure kylix, Foundry Ptr.? (early 5th c. BCE; Tarquinia 5291; **93**).

Plate 42 Marble statue of Nero (Thessalonike; **243**).

Plate 43; 1–6 Silver "Warren" cup (1st c. CE; BM; **288**).

Bibliography

Abbreviations

ABV	Beazley 1956.
ARV^2	Beazley 1963.
BM	British Museum.
BMFA	Boston Museum of Fine Arts.
CVA	*Corpus Vasorum Antiquorum.*
EGF	Davies 1988.
FGrH	Jacoby 1954–1957.
K	Kock 1880–1888.
K-A	Kassel and Austin 1983-.
Liddell and Scott	Liddell and Scott 1996.
LIMC	Ackermann and Gisler 1981–1997.
NMA	National Museum, Athens.
NYMM	New York Metropolitan Museum.
OCD	Hornblower and Spawforth 1999
PMG	Page 1962.
RE	Gärtner and Wünsch 1980.

Cited studies

Ackermann, Hans Christoph, and Jean-Robert Gisler. (1981–97) *Lexicon Iconographicum Mythologiae Classicae*. Zurich/Munich: Artemis Verlag.

Adams, James N. (1982) *The Latin Sexual Vocabulary*. Baltimore: Johns Hopkins University Press.

Agence France-Presse. (1998) "Visit to an Ancient Brothel," *New York Times*, 17 February 1998: section F, p. 4, col. 6.

Ajootian, Aileen. (1997) "The Only Happy Couple: Hermaphrodites and Gender." In: *Naked Truths. Women, Sexuality, and Gender in Classical Art and Archaeology*, eds C. Lyons and A. Koloski-Ostrow, 220–42. London and New York: Routledge.

Akamates, I.M. (1993) *Pêlies mêtres aggeîôn apó tên Pélla. Sumbolê stê melétê tês ellênistikês keramikês*. Athens: Greek Ministry of Culture.

Albert, W.D. (1997) *Darstellungen des Eros in Unteritalien*. Amsterdam: Brill.

Aldeeb Abu-Sahlieh, Sami A. (2001) *Male and Female Circumcision among Jews, Christians and Muslims: Religious, Medical, Social and Legal Debate.* Warren Center PA: Shangri-La Publications.

Andronicos, Manolis, Manoles Chatzedakes, and Vassos Karageorghis. (1975) *The Greek Museums.* Athens: Ekdotike Athenon.

Bagnall, Robert S. (1991) "The Prostitute Tax in Roman Egypt," *Bulletin of the American Society of Papyrology* 28: 5–12.

Bailey, Derrick Sherwin. (1955) *Homosexuality and the Western Christian Tradition.* London: Longmans, Green and Co. (reprinted Hamden CT: Archon, 1975).

Bailey, Donald M. (1975) *A Catalogue of the Lamps in the British Museum,* 3: *Roman Provincial Lamps.* London: British Museum.

Bauman, Richard A. (1992) *Women and Politics in Ancient Rome.* New York: Routledge.

Beard, Mary. (1980) "The Sexual Status of Vestal Virgins," *Journal of Hellenic Studies* 70: 12–27.

——(1995) "Rereading (Vestal) Virginity." In: *Women in Antiquity: New Assessments,* eds R. Hawley and B. Levick, 166–77. London, Routledge.

Beare, W. (1955) *The Roman Stage,* 2nd edn. London: Methuen.

Beazley, John D. (1947) "Some Attic Vases in the Cyprus Museum," *Proceedings of the British Academy* 33: 195–244.

——(1956) *Attic Black-Figure Vase Painters.* Oxford: Oxford University Press. (ABV)

——(1963) *Attic Red-Figure Vase Painters,* 2nd edn. Oxford: Oxford University Press. (ARV, 2nd edn)

——(1971) *Paralipomena: Additions to Attic Black-Figure Vase-Painters and to Attic Red-Figure Vase-Painters,* 2nd edn Oxford: Clarendon Press. (*Paralipomena* 2nd edn)

Becker, Marshall Joseph. (2003) "Childhood among the Etruscans: Mortuary Programs as Indicators of the Age of Transition to Adult Status in Etruria," a paper read at *Coming of Age in Ancient Greece,* a symposium at Dartmouth College, 5–7 November 2003.

Benner, A.R., and F.H. Fobes. (1949) *Epistolaí erótikaí.* Cambridge MA: Harvard University Press.

Bérard, Claude, and Jean-Pierre Vernant. (1984) *Die Bilderwelt der Griechen. Schlüssel zu einer "fremden" Kultur.* Mainz: von Zabern.

Bernand, A., and E. Bernand, (1960) *Les inscriptions grecques et latines du Colosse de Memnon.* Paris: Institut Français d'Archéologie Orientale.

Betts, John H. (1981) "The Seal from Shaft Grave Gamma–A 'Mycenaean Chieftain?' " *Temple University Aegean Seminar* 6: 2–8.

Betz, Hans Dieter. (1986) *The Greek Magical Papyri in Translation, Including the Demotic Spells.* Chicago and London: University of Chicago Press.

Bianchi, Richard S. (1988) "Tattoo in Ancient Egypt." In: *Marks of Civilization,* ed. A. Rubin, 21–8. Los Angeles: University of California, Los Angeles, Museum of Cultural History.

Black, Jeremy, and Anthony Green. (1992) *Gods, Demons and Symbols of Ancient Mesopotamia.* Austin: University of Texas Press.

Bloedow, E. (1975) "Aspasia and the Mystery of the Menexenos," *Wiener Studien* 9: 32–48.

Boardman, John. (1974) *Athenian Black Figure Vases*. New York: Oxford University Press.

——(1975) *Athenian Red-Figure Vases. The Archaic Period*. London: Thames and Hudson.

——(1985) *Greek Sculpture: The Classical Period: A Handbook*. London: Thames and Hudson.

——(1989) *Athenian Red-Figure Vases. The Classical Period*. London: Thames and Hudson.

Boardman, John, and Max Hirmer. (1967) *Greek Art and Architecture*. New York: H.N. Abrams.

Boardman, John, and Donna Kurtz. (1986) "Booners," *Greek Vases in the J. Paul Getty Museum* 3: 35–70.

Boardman, John, and Eugenio LaRocca. (1975) *Eros in Greece*. New York: Erotic Art Book Society .

Bober, Phyllis. (1995) "Polykles and Polykleitos in the Renaissance: The 'Letto di Policreto'." In: *Polykleitos, the Doryphoros, and Tradition*, ed. Warren G. Moon, 317–26. Madison: University of Wisconsin Press.

Bodenstedt, Friedrich. (1981) *Die Elecktronmünzen von Phokaia und Mytilene*. Tübingen: Ernst Wasmuth.

Bonfante, Larisa. (1989) "Nudity as Costume in Classical Art," *American Journal of Archaeology* 93: 543–70.

——(1994) "Excursus: Etruscan Women." In: *Women in the Classical World. Image and Text*, eds Elaine Fantham, Helene Peet Foley, Natalie Boymel Kampen, Sarah B. Pomeroy, and H.A. Shapiro, 243–59. New York and Oxford: Oxford University Press.

Boswell, John. (1980) *Christianity, Social Tolerance, and Homosexuality: Gay People in Western Europe from the Beginning of the Christian Era to the Fourteenth Century*. Chicago: University of Chicago Press.

——(1994) *Same Sex Unions in Pre-modern Europe*. New York: Villard Books.

Boy Scouts of America. (1910) *Revised Handbook for Boys*. New York: Boy Scouts of America.

Brandt, Paul – see alias Licht, Hans.

Bragantini, I., and M. de Vos. (1982) *Le decorazioni della villa romana della Farnesina. Le Pitture*, 2.1. Rome: De Luca.

Branigan, Keith (ed.) (1998) *Cemetery and Society in the Aegean Bronze Age*. Sheffield: Sheffield Academic Press.

Bremmer, Jan. (1980) "A European Rite: Paederasty," *Arethusa* 13: 279–98.

——(1983) "The Importance of the Maternal Uncle and Grandfather in Archaic and Classical Greece and Early Byzantium," *Zeitschrift für Papyrologie und Epigraphik* 50: 173–86.

——(1990) "Adolescents, *Symposion*, and Pederasty." In: *Sympotica*, ed. Oswan Murray, 135–48. Oxford: Oxford University Press.

Brendel, Otto. (1970) "The Scope and Temperament of Erotic Art in the Graeco-Roman World." In: *Studies in Erotic Art*, eds Theodore Bowie and C.V. Christenson, 3–108. New York: Basic Books.

Brisson, Luc. (2002) *Sexual Ambivalence: Androgyny and Hermaphroditism in Graeco-Roman Antiquity* (trans. Janet Lloyd). Berkeley: University of California Press.

British Museum Department of Coins and Medals. (1963) *A Catalogue of the Greek Coins in the British Museum: The Tauric Chersonese, Sarmatia, Dacia, Moesia, Thrace, etc.* Bologna: Arnaldo Forni.

Brown, Peter. (1988) *The Body and Society: Men, Women, and Sexual Renunciation in Early Christianity.* New York: Columbia University Press.

Brown, Shelby. (1992) "Death as Decoration: Scenes from the Arena on Roman Domestic Mosaics." In: *Pornography and Representation in Greece and Rome*, ed. A. Richlin, 180–211. New York and Oxford: Oxford University Press.

Brunet, Gilbert. (1985) "L'hébreu kèlèb," *Vetus Testamentum* 35: 485–8.

Brunner, Helmut. (1991) Review of R. and J. Janssen, *Growing up in Ancient Egypt.* In: *Discussions in Egyptology* 21: 77–8.

Brunnsåker, Sture. (1971) *The Tyrant-Slayers of Kritios and Nesiotes: A Critical Study of the Sources and Restorations.* Stockholm: Swedish Institute in Athens.

Bullough, Vern L. (1975) *Sexual Variance in Society and History.* Chicago: Wiley.

Bürchner, L. (1882) "Griechische Münzen mit Bildnisse historischer Privatpersonen," *Zeitschrift für Numismatik* 9: 109–36.

Burton, Richard. (1885) *The Thousand Nights and a Night.* London: private.

Butler, Shane. (1998) "Notes on a Membrum Disiectum." In: *Women and Slaves in Greco-Roman Culture*, eds Sandra Joshel and Sheila Murnaghan, 236–55. London: Routledge.

Calder, William, III. (ed) (1986) *Friedrich Gottlieb Welcker. Werk und Wirkung.* (Hermes Suppl. 49.) Stuttgart: Steiner Verlag.

Cantarella, Eva. (1992) *Bisexuality in the Ancient World.* New Haven: Yale University Press.

Carpenter, Thomas H. (ed.) (1989) *Beazley Addenda: Additional References to ABV, ARV² and Paralipomena².* Oxford: Oxford University Press.

Carter, Tristan. (1988) "Reverberations of the International Spirit: Thoughts upon 'Cycladica' in the Mesara." In: *Cemetery and Society in the Aegean Bronze Age*, ed. Keith Branigan, 59–77. Sheffield: Sheffield Academic Press.

Cassio, Albio C. (1983) "Post-Classical *Lésbiai*," *Classical Quarterly* 33: 296–7.

Castriota, David. (1992) *Myth, Ethos, and Actuality. Official Art in Fifth-Century B.C. Athens.* Madison: University of Wisconsin Press.

Catalano, V. (1971) "La più antica epigrafe scherzosa ellenica grafita su pithos a Phaistos," *Giornale italiano di Filologia* 23: 308–24.

Charbonneaux, Jean, Roland Martin, and François Villard. (1971) *Archaic Greek Art (620–480 B.C.).* New York: G. Braziller.

Cimok, Fatih. (2000) *Antioch Mosaics.* Istanbul: A Turizm Yayinlari.

Clairmont, Christoph W. (1993) *Classical Attic Tombstones.* Kilchberg, Switzerland: Akanthus.

Clarke, John R. (1998) *Looking at Lovemaking: Constructions of Sexuality in Roman Art 100 B.C.–A.D. 250.* Berkeley: University of California Press.

——(2001) "Sex, Death, and Status: Nilotic Tomb Imagery, Apotropaic Magic, and Freedman Acculturation." In *La peinture funéraire antique, IVe siècle av. J.-C. – Ive siècle ap. J.-C. Actes du VIIe colloque de l'Association Internationale pour la Peinture Murale Antique (AIPMA), 6–10 Octobre 1998, Saint-Romaine-en-Gal – Vienne*, ed. Alix Barbet, 85–91. Paris: Editions Errance.

——(2003) *Roman Sex 100 BC–AD 250*. New York: H.N. Abrams.

Comfort, Alex. (1987) *The Joy of Sex: A Cordon Bleu Guide to Lovemaking*. New York: Crown Publishers.

Corbeill, Anthony. (1996) *Controlling Laughter: Political Humor in the Late Roman Republic*. Princeton: Princeton University Press.

——(1997) "Dining Deviants in Roman Political Invective." In: *Roman Sexualities*, eds Judith P. Hallet and Marilyn B. Skinner, 99–128. Princeton: Princeton University Press.

Crowther, N.B. (1977) "Weightlifting in Antiquity: Achievement and Training," *Greece and Rome* 24.2: 115–20.

——(1985) "Male Beauty Contests. The Euandria and Euaxia," *L'Antiquité Classique* 54: 285–91.

——(1980–1) "Nudity and Morality: Athletics in Italy," *Classical Journal* 76: 119–23.

Cruciani, Clauseia. (2000) "I suicido di Saffo nell' abride della Basilica Sotterranea di Porta Maggiore," *Ostraca* 9: 165–73.

d'Ambra, Eve. (1996) "The Calculus of Venus: Nude Portraits of Roman Matrons." In: *Sexuality in Ancient Art*, ed. Natalie B. Kampen, 219–32. Cambridge: Cambridge University Press.

d'Ambrosio, Antonio (ed.) (2001) *Women and Beauty in Pompeii* (trans. Graham Sells). Los Angeles: "L'ERMA" di Bretschneider and J. Paul Getty Museum.

Daremberg, Charles. (1877–1919) *Dictionnaire des antiquités grecques et romaines d'après les textes et les monuments*, in 5 volumes in 10. Paris: Hachette.

David, E. (1992) "Hair as Language," *Eranos* 90: 11–21.

Davies, M. (1988) *Epicorum graecorum fragmenta*. Göttingen: Vandenhoeck and Ruprecht. (EGF)

Davies, Mark I. (1987) "Merkins and Modes." In: *Images et société en Grèce ancienne: L'Iconographie comme méthode d'analyse. Actes du Colloque international, Lausanne 8–11 février 1984*, ed. Colin Martin, 243–8. (Cahiers d'Archéologie Romande 36.)

Davidson, James N. (1998) *Courtesans and Fishcakes*. New York: HarperCollins.

Dayagi-Mendels, M. (1989) *Perfumes and Cosmetics in the Ancient World*. Jerusalem: Israel Museum.

De Caro, Stefano. (2000) *The Secret Cabinet in the National Archaeological Museum of Naples*. Naples: Soprintendenza archeologica di Napoli e Caserta.

De Caro, Stefano, and Luciano Pedicini. (1996) *The National Archaeological Museum of Naples*. Naples: Electa Napoli.

de Grummond, Nancy T. (2002) "Mirrors, Marriage, and Mysteries," *Journal of Roman Archaeology* Suppl. 47: 62–85.

de Wit, C. (1972) "La circoncision chez les anciens Egyptiens," *Zeitschrift für ägyptische Sprache und Altertumskunde* 99: 41–8.

Dean-Jones, Lesley Ann (also see Jones, Lesley Ann). (1989) "Menstrual Bleeding According to the Hippocratics and Aristotle," *Transactions of the American Philological Association* 119: 177–92.

——(1991) "The Cultural Construct of the Female Body in Classical Greek Science." In: *Women's History and Ancient History*, ed. Sarah B. Pomeroy, 111–31. Chapel Hill: University of North Carolina Press.

——(1992) "The Politics of Pleasure: Female Sexual Appetite in the Hippocratic Corpus," *Helios* 19: 72–91.

——(1994) *Women's Bodies in Classical Greek Science*. Oxford: Clarendon Press.
De Felice, John. (2001) *Roman Hospitality. The Professional Women of Pompeii*. Warren Center PA: Shangri-La Publications.
Dessau, Herman (ed.) (1892–1916) *Inscriptiones latinae selectae*. Berlin: Weidman (ILS).
DeVries, Keith. (1997) "The 'Frigid Eromenoi' and Their Wooers Revisited: A Closer Look at Greek Homosexuality in Vase Painting." In: *Queer Representations. Reading Lives, Reading Cultures*, ed. Martin Duberman, 14–24. New York: New York University Press.
Dingwall, Eric John. (1925) *Male Infibulation*. London: John Bale, Sons and Danielsson.
Dittenberger, W. (1915–24) *Sylloge inscriptionum graecarum*, 3rd edn. Leipzig: S. Hirzelium.
Doumas, Khristos. (1992) *The Wall-Paintings of Thera*. Athens: The Thera Foundation.
Dover, Kenneth J. (1989) *Greek Homosexuality*, 2nd edn. Cambridge MA: Harvard University Press.
DuBois, Page. (1995) *Sappho is Burning*. Chicago: University of Chicago Press.
Dunbabin, Katherine M.D. (1999) *Mosaics of the Greek and Roman World*. Cambridge: Cambridge University Press.
Dunn, Laura Ann. (1998) "The Evolution of Imperial Roman Attitudes toward Same-sex Acts," unpublished Ph.D. dissertation, Miami University.
Edmonds, John M. (1922) "Sappho's Book as Depicted on an Attic Vase," *Classical Quarterly* 16: 1–14.
——(1928) *Lyra Graeca*. 4 vols, Cambridge MA: Harvard University Press.
——(1957–61) *The Fragments of Attic Comedy after Meineke, Bergk, and Kock*. Leiden: Brill.
——(1967) *Lyra Graeca, Being the Remains of All the Greek Lyric Poets from Eumelus to Timotheus Excepting Pindar*. 4 vols, Cambridge MA: Harvard University Press.
Edwards, Catherine. (1997) "Unspeakable Professions: Public Performance and Prostitution in Ancient Rome." In: *Roman Sexualities*, eds Judith P. Hallett and Marilyn B. Skinner, 66–95. Princeton: Princeton University Press.
Ehrenberg, V. (1951) *The People of Aristophanes*, 2nd edn. Oxford: Blackwell.
Ehrhardt, C. (1971) "Hair in Ancient Greece," *Echos du Monde Classique* 15: 14–9.
Ellis, Walter M. (1989) *Alcibiades*. London and New York: Routledge.
Elsom, Helen E. (1992) "Callirhoe: Displaying the Phallic Woman." In: *Pornography and Representation in Greece and Rome*, ed. A. Richlin, 212–30. New York and Oxford: Oxford University Press.
Ephraim, David. (1992) "Sparta's Social Hair," *Eranos* 90: 11–21.
Evans-Grubbs, Judith. (1993) " 'Marriage More Shameful than Adultery': Slave-Mistress Relationships, Mixed Marriages, and Late Roman Law," *Phoenix* 47: 125–54.
Faerman, Marina, Gita Kahila Bar-Gal, Dvora Filon, Charles L. Greenblatt, Lawrence Steger, Ariella Openheim, and Patricia Smith. (1998) "Determining the Sex of Infanticide Victims from the Late Roman Era through Ancient DNA Analysis," *Journal of Archaeological Science* 25: 861–5.
Fagan, Garrett G. (1999) *Bathing in Public in the Roman World*. Ann Arbor: University of Michigan Press.
Fantham, Elaine. (ed.) (1994) *Women in the Classical World. Image and Text*. New York and Oxford: Oxford University Press.

Faraone, Christopher A. (1999) *Ancient Greek Love Magic*. Cambridge MA: Harvard University Press.

Fellmann, B. (1978) "Zur Deutung frühgriechischer Körperornamente," *Jahrbuch des Deutschen Archaeologischen Instituts* 93: 1–29.

Flemming, R. (1999) "*Quae corpore quaestum facit*: The Sexual Economy of Female Prostitution in the Roman Empire," *Journal of Roman Studies* 89: 38–61.

Flory, Stewart. (1994) "Dressed to Kill: The Aesthetics of Archaic and Classical Greek Hoplite Warfare," *American Journal of Archaeology* 98: 333.

Foucault, Michel. (1976 [1980]–1984 [1986]) *The History of Sexuality*. Paris and New York: Vintage Press. Vol. 1: *An Introduction* (Paris 1976; New York 1980). Vol. 2: *The Use of Pleasure* (Paris 1984, New York 1985). Vol. 3: *The Care of the Self* (Paris 1984, New York 1986).

Fowler, Brenda. (2000) *Iceman: Uncovering the Life and Times of a Prehistoric Man Found in an Alpine Glacier*. New York: Random House.

Friedländer, P., and H.B. Hoffleit. (1948) *Epigrammata*. Berkeley and Los Angeles: University of California Press.

Garcia Romero, Fernando. (1995) "*Érós athlêtês*: les métaphores érotico-sportives dans les comédies d'Aristophanes," *Nikephoros* 8: 57–76.

Gardner, Jane F. (1989) "Aristophanes and Male Anxiety – the Defence of the Oikos," *Greece and Rome* 36: 51–61.

Garrett, Duane A. (1990) "Votive Prostitution Again," *Journal of Biblical Literature* 109: 681–2.

Goldschneider, Ludwig. (1941) *Etruscan Sculpture*. New York: Oxford University Press.

Golden, Mark. (1984) "Slavery and Homosexuality at Athens," *Phoenix* 38: 308–24.

Gordon, Pamela. (1997) "The Lover's Voice in *Heroides* 15: Or, Why Is Sappho a Man?" In: *Roman Sexualities*, eds Judith Hallett and Marilyn Skinner, 274–94. Princeton: Princeton University Press.

Gould, Thomas. (1963) *Platonic Love*. New York: Free Press of Glencoe.

Grandjouan, Clairé. (1961) *Athenian Agora, 6: Terracottas and Plastic Lamps of the Roman Period*. Princeton NJ: American School of Classical Studies at Athens.

Grant, Michael, and Antonia Mulas. (1975) *Eros in Pompeii: The Secret Rooms of the National Museum of Naples*. New York: William Morrow, and London: Octopus.

Graves, Robert. (1960) *The Greek Myths*. Harmondsworth: Penguin.

Green, Peter. (1979) "Ars gratia cultus: Ovid as Beautician," *American Journal of Philology* 100: 381–92.

Greenberg, David F. (1988) *The Construction of Homosexuality*. Chicago and London: University of Chicago Press.

Greifenhagen, Adolf. (1957) *Griechische Eroten*. Berlin: Walter de Gruyter.

——(1976) "Fragmente eines rotfigurigen Pinax." In: *In memoriam Otto J. Brendel: Essays in Archaeology and the Humanities*, eds Larissa Bonfante and Helga von Heintze, 43–8. Mainz: Philipp von Zabern.

Grémaux, René. (1989) "Mannish Women of the Balkan Mountains." In: *From Sappho to de Sade. Moments in the History of Sexuality*, ed. Jan Bremmer, 143–72. London: Routledge.

Griffin, Jaspar. (1976) "Augustan Poetry and the Life of Luxury," *Journal of Roman Studies* 66: 87–105.

Griffiths, Alan. (1990) "Arrows of Desire: Iole and Leto on Early Fifth-Century Vases," *Bulletin of the Institute of Classical Studies* 37: 131–3.

Grmek, Mirko D. (1989) *Diseases in the Ancient Greek World*. Baltimore: Johns Hopkins University Press.

Gruen, Erich. (1996) *Studies in Greek Culture and Roman Policy*. Berkeley: University of California Press.

Gudeman, A. (1890) "The Codex Matritensis of Plutarch and Plut. Cic. 29," *American Journal of Philology* 11: 312–18.

Guillaud, Jacqueline, and Maurice Guillaud. (1990) *Frescoes in the Time of Pompeii*. Paris and New York: Guillaud Editions.

Guzzo, Pietro Giovanni, and Vincenzo Scarano Ussani. (2000) *Veneris figurae: Immagine di prostituzione e sfruttamento a Pompei*. Naples: Ministero per i Beni e le Attività Culturali, Soprintendenza Archeologica di Napoli e Caserta.

Hägg, Thomas. (1983) *The Novel in Antiquity*. Berkeley: University of California Press.

Hall, Edith. (1989) *Inventing the Barbarian*. Oxford: Oxford University Press.

Hall, Robert G. (1992) "Epispasm: Circumcision in Reverse," *Bible Review* 8.4: 52–7.

Hallett, Judith. (1989) "Female Homoeroticism and the Denial of Roman Reality in Latin Literature," *Yale Journal of Criticism* 3: 209–27.

Hallett, Judith, and Marilyn Skinner (eds) (1997) *Roman Sexualities*. Princeton: Princeton University Press.

Halperin, David M. (1997) "Questions of Evidence: Commentary on Koehl, DeVries, and Williams." In: *Queer Representations: Reading Lives, Reading Cultures*, ed. Martin Duberman, 39–54. New York: New York University Press.

Hanson, Ann Ellis. (1992) "Conception, Gestation, and the Origin of Female Nature in the *Corpus Hippocraticum*," *Helios* 19: 31–71.

Harris, Diane. (1993) "Greek Sanctuaries, Forgotten Dedicants: Women, Children, and Foreigners in the Parthenon, Erechtheion, and Asklepieion," *American Journal of Archaeology* 97: 337 (abstract).

Harrison, Evelyn B. (1988) "Greek Sculptural Coiffures and Ritual Haircuts." In: *Early Greek Cult Practice*, eds Robin Hägg, Nanno Marinatos, and Gullug C. Nordquist, 247–54. Stockholm: Swedish Institute in Athens.

Heath, John R. (1986) "The Supine Hero in Catullus 32," *Classical Journal* 82: 28–36.

Helbig, Wolfgang. (1868) *Wandgemälde der vom Vesuv verschütteten Städte Campaniens*. Leipzig: Breitkopf und Härtel.

Henderson, Jeffrey. (1987) "Older Women in Attic Old Comedy," *Transactions of the American Philological Association* 117: 105–29.

——(1991) *The Maculate Muse: Obscene Language in Attic Comedy*, 2nd edn. Oxford: Oxford University Press.

Hendrix, Elizabeth. (2003). "Some Methods for Revealing Paint on Early Cycladic Figures." In: *Metron* (*Aegaeum* 24), eds Karen Foster and Robert Laffineur, 139–45. Liège: Université de Liège.

Henrichs, Albert. (1978) "Greek Maenadism from Olympias to Messalina," *Harvard Studies in Classical Philology* 82: 121–60.

Henry, Alan. (2002) "Hookers and Lookers: Prostitution and Soliciting in Late Archaic Thasos," *Annual of the British School at Athens* 97: 217–21.

Henry, Madeleine M. (1992) "The Edible Woman: Athenaeus's Concept of the

Pornographic." In: *Pornography and Representation in Greece and Rome*, ed. A. Richlin, 250–68. New York and Oxford: Oxford University Press.

——(1998) Review of Snyder 1997, *Bryn Mawr Classical Reviews* 98.8.11 (distributed through the internet, 16 August 1998).

Herdt, Gilbert. (1997) *Same Sex, Different Cultures: Exploring Gay and Lesbian Lives*. Boulder: Westview.

Holländer, Eugen. (1912) *Plastik und Medezin*. Stuttgart: F. Enke.

Hollein, Heinze-Günter. (1988) *Bürgerbild und Bildwelt der attischen Demokratie auf den rotfigurigen Vasen des 6.–4. Jahrhunderts v. Chr.* Frankfurt: Peter Lang.

Holmberg, Erik John. (1990) *The Red-Line Painter and the Workshop of the Acheloos Painter*. (*Studies in Mediterranean Archaeology* 87.) Jonsered: Paul Åström.

Hooks, Stephen M. (1985) "Sacred Prostitution in Israel and the Ancient Near East," unpublished Ph.D. dissertation, Hebrew Union College, Cincinnati.

Hooper, Richard W. (1999) *The Priapus Poems. Erotic Epigrams from Ancient Rome Translated from the Latin*. Urbana and Chicago: University of Illinois Press.

Hornblower, Simon, and Antony Spawforth (eds) (1999) *The Oxford Classical Dictionary*, 3rd edn. Oxford: Oxford University Press. (OCD)

Houdijk, Luc, and Paul Vanderbroeck. (1987) "Old Age and Sex in the Ancient Greek World," *Wissenschaftliche Zeitschrift der Wilhelm-Pieck-Universität* 36: 57–61.

Hubbard, Thomas K. (2003) *Homosexuality in Greece and Rome: A Sourcebook of Basic Documents*. Berkeley: University of California Press.

Hunt, A.S., and C.C. Edgar. (1970) *Select Papyri*. 4 vols, Cambridge MA: Harvard University Press.

Hurwitt, Jeffrey. (2002) "Reading the Chigi Vase," *Hesperia* 71: 1–22.

Instone, Stephen. (1990) "Love and Sex in Pindar: Some Practical Thrusts," *Bulletin of the Institute of Classical Studies* 37: 30–42.

Jacobelli, Luciana. (1995) *Le pitture erotiche delle terme suburbane di Pompei*. Rome: "L'ERMA" di Bretschneider.

Jacoby, Felix. (1954–1957) *Die Fragmente der griechischen Historiker*. Leiden: Brill. (FGrH)

Janan, Micaela. (forthcoming) *Individual and Group Identity in Ovid's Metamorphoses*.

Jocelyn, H.D. (1980) "A Greek Indecency and its Students: *laikázein*," *Proceedings of the Cambridge Philological Society* 206: 12–66.

Johns, Catherine. (1982) *Sex or Symbol: Erotic Images of Greece and Rome*. Austin: University of Texas Press.

Jones, Lesley Ann (also see Dean-Jones, Lesley Ann). (1987) "Morbidity and Vitality: The Interpretation of Menstrual Blood in Greek Science," unpublished Ph.D. dissertation, Stanford University.

Joshel, Sandra. (1992) "The Body Female and the Body Politic: Livy's Lucretia and Verginia." In *Pornography and Representation in Greece and Rome*, ed. Amy Richlin, 112–30. New York and Oxford: Oxford University Press.

——(1997) "Female Desire and the Discourse of Empire: Tacitus' Messalina." In: *Roman Sexualities*, eds Judith P. Hallett and Marilyn B. Skinner, 221–54. Princeton: Princeton University Press.

Joshel, Sandra, and Sheila Murnaghan (eds) (1998) *Women and Slaves in Greco-Roman Culture: Differential Equations*. London: Routledge.

Just, Roger. (1989/94) *Women in Athenian Law and Life*. London and New York: Routledge.

Kahil, Lily. (1977) "l'Artémis de Brauron. Rites et mystère," *Antike Kunst* 20: 86–98.

Kalogeropoulou, Athena. (1986) "Drei attische Grabreliefs." In: *Archaische und klassische griechische Plastik: Akten des internationalen Kolloquiums vom 22.–25. April 1985 in Athen, 2: Klassische griechische Plastik*, ed. Helmut Kyrieleis, 119–33, Mainz: Philipp von Zabern.

Kampen, Natalie B. (ed.) (1996) *Sexuality in Ancient Art*. Cambridge: Cambridge University Press.

Kapparis, Konstantinos. (2002) *Abortion in the Ancient World*. London: Duckworth.

Karouzou, S. (1968) *National Archaeological Museum. Collection of Sculpture: A Catalogue*. Athens: General Direction of Antiquities and Restoration.

Kassel, Rudolf, and Colin Austin (eds) (1983–) *Poetae Comici Graeci*. Berlin and New York: Walter de Gruyter. (K-A)

Keuls, Eva C. (1985) *The Reign of the Phallus: Sexual Politics in Ancient Athens*. Berkeley: University of California Press.

——(1990) "The Feminist View of the Past: A Comment on the 'Decentering' of the Poems of Ovid," *Helios* 17: 221–4.

Kilmer, Martin F. (1982) "Genital Phobia and Depilation," *Journal of Hellenic Studies* 102: 104–12.

——(1993) *Greek Erotica on Attic Red-Figure Vases*. London: Duckworth.

Kinsey, Alfred C. (1967) *Sexual Behavior in the Human Female*. New York: Pocket Books.

Kleiner, Diana E.E. (1992) *Roman Sculpture*. New Haven: Yale University Press.

Knigge, Ursula. (1988) *Der Kerameikos von Athen. Führung durch Ausgrabungen und Geschichte*. Athens: Deutsches Archäologisches Institut Athen.

Knorr, Ortwin. (2003, forthcoming) "*Campanus morbus*," *Classical Quarterly* 53.

Koch-Harnack, Gundel. (1983) *Knaben Liebe und Tiergeschenke: Ihre Bedeutung im päderastischen Erziehungssystem Athens*. Berlin: Gebrüder Mann Verlag.

——(1989) *Erotische Symbole*. Berlin: Gebrüder Mann Verlag.

Kock, T. (ed.) (1880–8) *Comicorum atticorum fragmenta*. Leipzig: Teubner.

Koehl, Robert B. (1986) "The Chieftain Cup and a Minoan Rite of Passage," *Journal of Hellenic Studies* 106: 99–110.

Korshak, Yvonne. (1987) *Frontal Faces in Attic Vase Painting of the Archaic Period*. Chicago: Ares Publishers.

Krenkel, Wilhelm A. (1970) "Zur Prosopographie der antike Pornographie," *Wissenschaftliche Zeitschrift der Wilhelm-Pieck-Universität Rostock* 19: 615–19.

——(1979a) "Masturbation in der Antike," *Wissenschaftliche Zeitschrift der Wilhelm-Pieck-Universität Rostock* 28: 159–78.

——(1979b) "Pueri meritorii," *Wissenschaftliche Zeitschrift der Wilhelm-Pieck-Universität Rostock* 28: 179–89.

——(1980) "Fellatio et Irrumatio," *Wissenschaftliche Zeitschrift der Wilhelm-Pieck-Universität Rostock* 29: 77–88.

——(1981) "Tonguing," *Wissenschaftliche Zeitschrift der Wilhelm-Pieck-Universität Rostock* 30: 37–54.

——(1985) "Figurae Veneris, I," *Wissenschaftliche Zeitschrift der Wilhelm-Pieck-Universität Rostock* 34.4: 50–7.

——(1987) "Figurae Veneris, II," *Wissenschaftliche Zeitschrift der Wilhelm-Pieck-Universität Rostock* 36: 49–56.

——(1989) "Tribaden," *Wissenschaftliche Zeitschrift der Wilhelm-Pieck-Universität Rostock* 38: 49–58.

Kühn, Karl Gottlob (ed.) (1821–33 [1964–5]) *Klaudiou Galenou Apanta. Claudii Galeni Opera omnia*. Hildesheim: Olms.

Kurke, Leslie. (1997) "Inventing the *Hetaira*: Sex, Politics, and Discursive Conflict in Archaic Greece," *Classical Antiquity* 16: 106–50.

Kurtz, Donna C., and John Boardman. (1971) *Greek Burial Customs*. London: Thames and Hudson.

Lacey, W.K. (1980) "2 B.C. and Julia's Adultery," *Antichthon* 14: 127–42.

Lapatin, Kenneth D.S. (1997) Review of *Polykleitos, the Doryphoros, and Tradition*, ed. Warren G. Moon (Madison: University of Wisconsin Press, 1995), *Sculptors and Physicians in Fifth-century Greece: A Preliminary Study*, by Guy P.R. Métraux (Montreal: McGill-Queen's University Press, 1995), and *The Aphrodite of Knidos and Her Successors: A Historical Review of the Female Nude in Greek Art*, by Christine M. Havelock (Ann Arbor: University of Michigan Press, 1995), for *Art Bulletin* 79: 148–56.

Lavelle, Brian. (1986) "The Nature of Hipparchos' Insult of Harmodios," *American Journal of Philology* 107: 318–31.

Lee, Hugh M. (1988) "SIG³ 802: Did Women Compete against Men in Greek Athletic Festivals?" *Nikephoros* 1: 103–10.

——(1994) "Athletics and the Bikini Girls from Piazza Armerina," *Stadion* 10: 45–76.

Lefkowitz, Mary R. (1973) "Critical Stereotypes and the Poetry of Sappho," *Greek, Roman and Byzantine Studies* 14: 113–23.

Lefkowitz, Mary R., and Maureen B. Fant. (1992) *Women's Life in Greece and Rome: A Source Book in Translation*. Baltimore: Johns Hopkins University Press.

Leick, Gwendolyn. (1994) *Sex and Eroticism in Mesopotamian Literature*. London: Routledge.

Leitao, David D. (1995) "The Perils of Leukippos: Initiatory Transvestism and Male Gender Ideology in the Ekdusia at Phaistos," *Classical Antiquity* 14: 130–63.

——(1998) "A Male Pregnancy Ritual from Amathous, Cyprus, and the Strategies of Replacement," *Abstracts of the American Philological Association, 130th Annual Meeting*, 143. New York: American Philological Association.

Lempesi, Angelike. (2000–) *The Sanctuary of Hermes and Aphrodite at Syme Viannou*. Athens: Athens Archaeological Society.

Levine, Daniel. (2002) "The Bare Feet Speak: Nonverbal Messages of Barefootedness," *American Journal of Archaeology* 106: 284.

Levine, Molly Myerowitz (also see Myerowitz 1992). (1995) "The Gendered Grammar of Ancient Mediterranean Hair." In *Off With Her Head! The Denial of Women's Identity in Myth, Religion, and Culture*, eds Howard Eilberg-Schwartz and Wendy Doniger, 76–130. Berkeley: University of California Press.

Lewis, Naphtali, and Meyer Reinhold. (1959) *Roman Civilization*. New York: Columbia University Press.

Licht, Hans (alias Paul Brandt). (1925–8) *Sittengeschichte Griechenlands*. Dresden and Zurich: Paul Aretz.

——(1932; [reprint 1963]). *Sexual Life in Ancient Greece*. London: George Routledge and Sons.

Lilja, Saara. (1983) *Homosexuality in Republican and Augustan Rome. Commentationes Humanarum Litterarum* 74. Helsinki: Societas Scientiarum Fennica.

Lind, Hermann. (1988) "Ein Hetärenhaus am Heiligen Tor?," *Museum Helveticum* 45: 158–69.

Lissarrague, François. (1995) "Women, Boxes, Containers: Some Signs and Metaphors." In: *Pandora. Women in Classical Greece*, ed. Ellen D. Reeder, 91–101. Princeton: Princeton University Press.

Lloyd, G.E.R. (ed.) (1978) *Hippocratic Writings* (trans. J. Chadwick and W.N. Mann). London: Penguin.

Love, Iris. (1972) "A Preliminary Report of the Excavations at Knidos, 1970," *American Journal of Archaeology* 76: 61–76.

Lullies, Reinhard, and Max Hirmer. (1960) *Greek Sculpture*. New York: H.N. Abrams.

Lutz, Cora E. (1947) *Musonius Rufus: The Roman Socrates*. New Haven: Yale University Press.

Lyne, R.O.A.M. (1980) *The Latin Love Poets: From Catullus to Horace*. Oxford: Oxford University Press.

Maas, Margaret, and Jane Snyder. (1989) *Stringed Instruments in Ancient Greece*. New Haven: Yale University Press.

MacLachlan, Bonnie. (1992) "Sacred Prostitution and Aphrodite," *Studies in Religion* 21: 145–62.

Makowski, John F. (1996) "Bisexual Orpheus: Pederasty and Parody in Ovid," *Classical Journal* 92: 25–38.

Mantas, K. (1995) "Women and Athletics in the Roman East," *Nikephoros* 8: 125–44.

Marcadé, Jean. (1962) *Eros Kalos: Essay on Erotic Elements in Greek Art*. Geneva: Nagel.

——(1965) *Roma Amor: Essay on Erotic Elements in Etruscan and Roman Art*. Geneva: Nagel.

Marinatos, Spyridon, and Max Hirmer. (1960) *Crete and Mycenae*. New York: H.N. Abrams.

Marks, Margaret. (1978) "Heterosexual Coital Position as a Reflection of Ancient and Modern Cultural Attitudes," unpublished Ph.D. dissertation, State University of New York-Buffalo.

Markussen, Erik Poulsgaard. (1979) *Painted Tombs in Etruria*. Rome: "L'ERMA" di Bretschneider.

McClees, Helen. (1920) *Study of Women in Attic Inscriptions* (Columbia University Studies in Classical Philology 14). New York: Columbia University Press.

McClure, Laura. (2002) "Prostitution in the Ancient World," a conference, 12–14 April 2002, at the University of Wisconsin Madison (http://classics.lss.wisc.edu/prostitution/home.html).

McCudy, G.H. (1932) "A Note on the Jewelry of Demetrius the Besieger," *American Journal of Archaeology* 36: 27–8.

McGarry, Jane. (1989) "The Athenian Prostitute," *Pegasus* (University of Exeter Classical Society) 32: 21–7

McGinn, Thomas A.J. (1989) "The Taxation of Roman Prostitutes," *Helios* 16: 79–110.

——(1998a) *Prostitution, Sexuality, and the Law in Ancient Rome*. New York: Oxford University Press.

——(1998b) "Caligula's Brothel on the Palatine," *Echos du Monde Classique* n.s. 17: 95–107.

——(2002) "Pompeian Brothels and Social History," *Journal of Roman Archaeology* Suppl. 47: 62–85.

McManus, Barbara F. (1990) "Multicentering: The Case of the Athenian Bride," *Helios* 7: 225–35.

Meinardus, Otto. (1967) "Mythological, Historical, and Sociological Aspects of the Practice of Female Circumcision among the Egyptians," *Acta Ethnographica Academiae Scientarum Hungaricae* ser. 9, 16: 387–97.

Miller, Margaret C. (1997) *Athens and Persia in the Fifth Century BC: A Study in Cultural Receptivity*. Cambridge: Cambridge University Press.

Miller, Stephen. (1991) *Arete. Greek Sports from Ancient Sources*. Berkeley: University of California Press.

Montserrat, Dominic. (1996) *Sex and Society in Graeco-Roman Egypt*. London and New York: Kegan Paul International.

Montague, Holly. (1992) "Sweet and Pleasant Passion: Female and Male Fantasy in Ancient Romance Novels." In: *Pornography and Representation in Greece and Rome*, ed. A. Richlin, 231–49. New York and Oxford: Oxford University Press.

Moon, Warren G. (1979) *Greek Vase-Painting in Midwest Collections*. Chicago: Art Institute of Chicago.

Moretti, Luigi. (1953) *Iscrizioni agonistiche greche*. Rome: Bardi.

Mulas, Antonia. (1978) *Eros in Antiquity*. New York: Erotic Art Book Society.

Mure, William. (1857) "Sappho and the Ideal Love of the Greeks," *Rheinisches Museum* 12: 564–93.

Myerowitz, Molly (also see Levine 1995). (1992) "The Domestication of Desire: Ovid's *Parva Tabella* and the Theater of Love." In: *Pornography and Representation in Greece and Rome*, ed. A. Richlin, 131–57. New York and Oxford: Oxford University Press.

Neumann, Günter. (1965) *Gesten und Gebärden*. Berlin: Walter de Gruyter.

Nixon, Lucia (1995) "The Cults of Demeter and Kore." In: *Women in Antiquity. New Assessments*, eds Richard Hawley and Barbara Levick, 75–96. London: Routledge.

Nussbaum, Martha C. (1994) "Platonic Love and Colorado Law: The Relevance of Ancient Greek Norms to Modern Sexual Controversies," *Virginia Law Review* 80.7: 1515–651.

Oakley, John H. (1995) "Nuptial Nuances." In: *Pandora. Women in Classical Greece*, ed. Ellen D. Reeder, 63–73. Princeton: Princeton University Press.

Oakley, John H., and Rebecca Sinos. (1993) *The Wedding in Ancient Athens*. Madison: University of Wisconsin Press.

Obermayer, Hans Peter. (1998) *Martial und der Diskurs über männliche "Homosexualität" in der Literatur der frühen Kaiserzeit*. Tübingen: Gunter Narr Verlag.

O'Brien, Joan V. (1993) *The Transformation of Hera: A Study of Ritual, Hero, and the Goddess in the Iliad*. Boston MA: Rowman and Littlefield.

Oden, Robert A. (2000) *The Bible without Theology: The Theological Tradition and Alternatives to It*. Urbana: University of Illinois Press.

Ogden, Daniel. (1996) *Greek Bastardy in the Classical and Hellenistic Periods*. Oxford: Oxford University Press.

——(1999) *Polygamy, Prostitutes and Death: The Hellenistic Dynasties*. London: Duckworth with the Classical Press of Wales.

Olender, Maurice. (1983) "L'enfant Priape et son phallus." In: *Souffrance, Plaisir, et Pensée*, ed. Jacques Caïn, 141–64. Paris: Société d'édition "les Belles Lettres."

Ortner, Sherry B. (1972) "Is Female to Male as Nature is to Culture?" *Feminist Studies* 1: 5–21.

Osborne, Robin. (1996) "Desiring Women on Athenian Pottery." In: *Sexuality in Ancient Art*, ed. Natalie B. Kampen, 65–80. Cambridge: Cambridge University Press.

Padgug, Robert. (1989) "Sexual Matters: Rethinking Sexuality in History." In: *Hidden from History: Reclaiming the Gay and Lesbian Past*, eds Martin B. Duberman, Martha Vicinus, and George Chauncey Jr, 54–64. New York: NAL Books.

Page, Denys L. (ed.) (1962) *Poetae melici graeci*. Oxford University Press, Oxford. (PMG).

——(1974) *Supplementum lyricis graecis*. Oxford: Oxford University Press.

Palagia, Olga. (1998) *The Pediments of the Parthenon*. Leiden: Brill.

Papaefthimiou-Papanthimou, A. (1979) *Skênê kaí súnerga tou kallopismoú ston krêtomukênaïkó khôro*. Salonika: Aristotle University of Thessalonike.

Papalas, Anthony J. (1991) "Boy Athletes in Ancient Greece," *Stadion* 17: 165–92.

Parke, Herbert W. (1977) *Festival of the Athenians*. Ithaca NY: Cornell University Press.

Parker, Holt N. (1992) "Love's Body Anatomized: The Ancient Erotic Handbooks and the Rhetoric of Sexuality." In *Pornography and Representation in Greece and Rome*, ed. Amy Richlin, 90–111. New York and Oxford: Oxford University Press.

Parlama, Liana, and Nicholas Stampolides. (2000) *The City beneath the City: Antiquities from the Metropolitan Railway Excavations*. Athens: N.P. Goulandris Foundation, Museum of Cycladic Art.

Paszthory, E. (1990) "Salben, Schminken und Parfüme im Altertum. Herstellungsmethoden und Anwendungsbereiche im östlichen Mediterraneum," *Antike Welt*, Sondernummer.

Paul, A.J. (1993) "Eros and a Depilation Scene by the Dinos Painter," *American Journal of Archaeology* 97: 330.

Pavese, Carlo Odo. (1996) *L'auriga di Mozia*. Rome: "L'ERMA" di Bretschneider.

Peck, Harry Thurston. (1898) *Harpers Dictionary of Classical Antiquities*. New York: Harper, cited online on "Perseus": http://perseus.tufts.edu.

Percy, W. Armstrong. (1996) *Pederasty and Pedagogy in Archaic Greece*. Urbana: University of Illinois Press.

Pfrommer, M. (1980) "Ein Eros des Praxiteles," *Archäologische Anzeiger*, 532–44.

Pinney, Gloria Ferrari. (1986) "Money Bags?" *American Journal of Archaeology* 90: 218.

——(1995) "Fugitive Nudes: The Woman Athlete," *American Journal of Archaeology* 99: 303–4.

Podlecki, Anthony J. (1990) "Could Women Attend the Theatre in Ancient Athens?" *Ancient World* 21: 22–43.

Pollini, John. (1999) "The Warren Cup: Homoerotic Love and Symposial Rhetoric in Silver," *Art Bulletin* 81: 21–52.

Pomeroy, Sarah B. (1975) *Goddesses, Whores, Wives and Slaves: Women in Classical Antiquity*. New York: Schocken Books.

Pontrandolfo, Angela. (2000) "Dionisio e personaggi fliaciei nelle immagine pertane," *Ostraca* 9: 117–34.

Preziosi, Patricia G., and Saul S. Weinberg. (1970) "Evidence for Painted Details in Early Cycladic Sculpture," *Antike Kunst* 13: 4–12.

Pugliese Carratelli, Giovanni. (1990–2003) *Pompei: Pitture e mosaici*. Rome: Istituto della enciclopedia italiana.

Rabinowitz, Nancy S. (1992) "Tragedy and the Politics of Containment." In: *Pornography and Representation in Greece and Rome*, ed. A. Richlin, 36–52. New York and Oxford: Oxford University Press.

——(1995) "The Erotics of Greek Drama: The Contribution of the Cross-Dressed Actor," *Abstracts of One Hundred Twenty-Seventh Meeting, American Philological Association*, 132. Worcester MA: American Philological Association.

——(2002) "Excavating Women's Homoeroticism in Ancient Greece: The Evidence from Attic Vase Painting." In: *Among Women: From the Homosocial to the Homoerotic in the Ancient World*, eds Nancy S. Rabinowitz and Lisa Auanger, 106–66. Austin: University of Texas Press.

Rabinowitz, Nancy S., and Lisa Auanges. (eds) (2002) *Among Women: From the Homosocial to the Homoerotic in the Ancient World*. Austin: University of Texas Press.

Rawson, Beryl. (ed.) (1991) *Marriage, Divorce and Children in Ancient Rome*. Oxford: Oxford University Press.

Reardon, B.P. (ed.) (1989) *Collected Ancient Greek Novels*. Berkeley: University of California Press.

Reed, Joseph D. (1995) "The Sexuality of Adonis," *Classical Antiquity* 14: 317–47.

Reed, Nancy B. (1987) "The *Euandria* Competition at the Panathaia Reconsidered," *Ancient World* 15: 59–64.

Reeder, Ellen D. (1995a) "Women as Containers." In: *Pandora. Women in Classical Greece*, ed. Ellen D. Reeder, 195–9. Princeton: Princeton University Press.

Reeder, Ellen D. (ed.) (1995b) *Pandora. Women in Classical Greece*. Princeton: Princeton University Press.

Rehak, Paul. (1999) "The Aegean Landscape and the Body: A New Interpretation of the Thera Frescoes." In *From the Ground Up: Beyond Gender Theory in Archaeology. Proceedings of the Fifth Gender and Archaeology Conference, University of Wisconsin-Milwaukee, October 1998*, eds N.L. Wicker and B. Arnold, 11–22. Oxford: Archaeopress.

Reinhold, M. (1980) "Roman Attitudes toward Egyptians," *Ancient World* 3: 97–103.

Reinsberg, Carola. (1989) *Ehe, Hetärentum und Knabenliebe im antiken Griechenland*. Munich: C.H. Beck.

Richardson, Lawrence R. Jr. (1963) "Furi et Aureli, comites Catulli," *Classical Philology* 58: 93–106.

—(1988) *Pompeii: An Architectural History*. Baltimore: Johns Hopkins University Press.

Richlin, Amy. (1983) *The Garden of Priapus: Sexuality and Aggression in Roman Humor*. New Haven: Yale University Press.

Richlin, Amy. (ed.) (1992a) *Pornography and Representation in Greece and Rome*. New York and Oxford: Oxford University Press.

—(1992b) "Reading Ovid's Rapes." In: *Pornography and Representation in Greece and Rome*, ed. Amy Richlin, 158–79. New York and Oxford: Oxford University Press.

—(1993) "Not Before Homosexuality: The Materiality of the Cinaedus and the Roman Law Against Love Between Men," *Journal of the History of Sexuality* 3: 523–73.

—(1997) "Pliny's Brassiere." In: *Roman Sexualities*, eds Judith Hallet and Marilyn Skinner, 197–220. Princeton: Princeton University Press.

Richter, Gisela M.A. (1934) "The Menon Painter = Psiax," *American Journal of Archaeology* 38: 548–54.

—(1960) *Kouroi. Archaic Greek Youths. A Study of the Development of the Kouros Type in Greek Sculpture*. London: Phaidon Press.

—(1966) *The Furniture of the Greeks, Etruscans and Romans*. London: Phaidon.

—(1988) *Korai. Archaic Greek Maidens. A Study of the Development of the Kore Type in Greek Sculpture*. New York: Hacker Art Books.

Riccobono, S. (1940–3; 1992, trans. Cantarella) *Fontes juris romani antejustiniani*. Florence: G. Barbera.

Riddle, John M. (1992) *Contraception and Abortion from the Ancient World to the Renaissance*. Cambridge MA: Harvard University Press.

—(1997) *Eve's Herbs: A History of Contraception and Abortion in the West*. Cambridge MA: Harvard University Press.

Riddle, John M., J.W. Estes, and J.C. Russell. (1994) "Ever Since Eve – Birth Control in the Ancient World," *Archaeology* 47.2: 29–35, with letters to the editor in *Archaeology* 47.4: 8–10.

Ridgway, Brunilde Sismondo. (1974) "A Story of Five Amazons," *American Journal of Archaeology* 78: 1–18.

—(1990) *Hellenistic Sculpture*, 1: *The Styles of ca. 331–200 B.C.*. Madison: University of Wisconsin Press.

Robertson, Martin. (1992) *Art of Vase Painting in Classical Athens*. Cambridge: Cambridge University Press.

Robinson, David M., and Edward J. Fluck (1937) *A Study of the Greek Love Names, Including a Discussion of Pederasty and a Prosopographia*. Baltimore: Johns Hopkins University Press.

Rombauer, Irma. (1931) *The Joy of Cooking*. Indianapolis and New York: Bobbs Merrill.

Romm, James S. (1994) *The Edges of the Earth in Ancient Thought*. Princeton: Princeton University Press.

Sanson, David. (1988) *Greek Athletics and the Genesis of Sport*. Berkeley: University of California Press.

Sargent, Barnard. (1986) *L'homosexualité initiatique dans l'Europe ancienne*. Paris: Payot.

Scanlon, Thomas F. (2002) *Eros and Greek Athletics*. Oxford: Oxford University Press.

Schäfer, Jörg. (1968) *Hellenistische Keramik aus Pergamon*. Berlin: de Gruyter.

Schauenburg, K. (1981) "Eros im Tempel," *Archäologische Anzeiger*, 344–8.

Scheidel, W. (1995) "The Most Silent Women of Greece and Rome: Rural Labour and Women's Life in the Ancient World," *Greece and Rome* 42: 202–18.

Schmidt, Evanmaire. (1962) *The Great Altar of Pergamum*. Leipzig: VEB Edition.

Seeberg, A. (1971) *Corinthian Komos Vases (Bulletin of the Institute of Classical Studies of the University of London* suppl. 27). London: Institute of Classical Studies of the University of London.

Serwint, Nancy. (1987) "Greek Athletic Sculpture from the Fifth and Fourth Centuries B.C.: An Iconographic Study," unpublished Ph.D. dissertation, Princeton University.

——(1993) "Female Athletic Costume at the Heraia," *American Journal of Archaeology* 97: 403–22.

Sestieri, Pellegrino C. (1955) *Il nuovo museo di Paestum*. Rome: Ministero della Pubblica Istruzione.

Shapiro, Harvey Allen. (1981a) "Courtship Scenes in Attic Vase-painting," *American Journal of Archaeology* 85: 133–43.

——(1981b) *Art, Myth, and Culture: Greek Vases from Southern Collections*. New Orleans: New Orleans Museum of Art, Tulane University.

——(1987) "Kalos-Inscriptions with Patronymic," *Zeitschrift für Papyrologie und Epigraphik* 68: 107–18.

——(1992) "Eros in Love: Pederasty and Pornography in Greece." In *Pornography and Representation in Greece and Rome*, ed. A. Richlin, 53–72. New York and Oxford: Oxford University Press.

Siebert, Gérard. (1984) "Un bol à reliefs inscrit à représentations érotiques," *Antike Kunst* 27: 14–20.

Simms, Ronda R. (1997) "A Date with Adonis," *Antichthon* 31: 45–53.

——(1998) "Mourning and Community at the Athenian Adonis," *Classical Journal* 93: 121–41.

Simon, Erika. (1983) *Festivals of Attica: an Archaeological Commentary*. Madison: University of Wisconsin Press.

Simon, Stephen J. (1991) "The Functions of Priestesses in Greek Society," *Classical Bulletin* 67: 9–13.

Sinn, Ulrich. (1979) *Die homerische Becher. Hellenistische Keramik aus Makedonien*. Berlin: Gebrüder Mann.

Sissa, Giulia. (1990) "Maidenhood without Maidenhead." In: *Before Sexuality*, eds D.M. Halperin, J.J. Winkler, and F. Zeitlin, 339–64. Princeton: Princeton University Press.

Skinner, Marilyn B. (1996) "The Sexuality Wars in Contemporary Classical Scholarship," *Thamyris* 3.1: 103–23 (reproduced at: http://www.uky.edu/ArtSciences/Classics/gender.html).

Small, Jocelyn Penny. (1986) "The Tragliatella Oinochoe," *Römische Mitteilungen* 93: 63–96.

Smallwood, E. Mary. (1959) "The Legislation of Hadrian and Antoninus Pius against Circumcision," *Latomus* 18: 334–47.

Snyder, Jane McIntosh. (1989) *The Woman and the Lyre. Women Writers in Classical Greece and Rome*. Carbondale: Southern Illinois University Press.

——(1997) *Lesbian Desire in the Lyrics of Sappho*. New York: Columbia University Press.

Sourvinou-Inwood, Christiane. (1987) "A Series of Erotic Pursuits: Images and Meanings," *Journal of Hellenic Studies* 107: 131–53.

——(1988) *Studies in Girls' Transitions: Aspects of the Arkteia and Age Representation in Attic Iconography*. Athens: Kardamitsa.

——(1990) "Ancient Rites and Modern Constructions: On the Brauronian Bears Again," *Bulletin of the Institute of Classical Studies, London* 37: 1–14.

Spiro, Friedrich. (1900) "Ein Leser des Pausanias." In: *Festschrift Johannes Vahlen zum 70. Geburtstag*, ed. Johannes Vahlen, 135–8. Berlin: G. Reimer.

Stampolides, Nikolaos K. (1992) *Ta sphragísmata tês Dêlou, 2: o erôtikós kúklos*. Paris: École française d'Athènes.

Stehle, Eva. (1990) "Sappho's Gaze: Fantasies of a Goddess and a Young Man," *differences* 2: 88–125.

Steingräber, Stephen. (ed.) (1985) *Etruscan Painting. Catalogue Raisonné of Etruscan Wall Paintings*. New York: Johnson Reprint Corporation: Harcourt Brace Jovanovich.

Stewart, Andrew, F. (1995) "Reflections." In: *Sexuality in Ancient Art*, ed. Natalie Kampen, 136–54. Cambridge: Cambridge University Press.

——(1997) *Art, Desire, and the Body in Ancient Greece*. Cambridge: Cambridge University Press.

——(1990) *Greek Sculpture: An Exploration*. New Haven: Yale University Press.

Stillwell, Richard, William L. MacDonald, and Marian Holland McAllister. (eds) (1976) *Princeton Encyclopedia of Classical Sites*. Princeton: Princeton University Press.

Strong, Rebecca Anne. (1997) "The Most Shameful Practice: Temple Prostitution in the Ancient Greek World," unpublished Ph.D. dissertation, University of California at Los Angeles.

Sutton, Robert F. Jr. (1981) "The Interaction between Men and Women Portrayed on Attic Red-figure Pottery," unpublished Ph.D. dissertation, University of North Carolina, Chapel Hill.

——(1992) "Pornography and Persuasion on Attic Pottery." In: *Pornography and Representation in Greece and Rome*, ed. Amy Richlin, 3–35. New York and Oxford: Oxford University Press.

Sweet, Waldo. (1985) "Protection of the Genitals in Greek Athletics," *Ancient World* 11: 43–52.

Symonds, John Addington. (1883) *A Problem in Greek Ethics*. Edinburgh: Ballantyne and Hanson.

——(1891) *A Problem in Modern Ethics*. Privately printed.

Talalay, Lauren E. (1991) "Body Imagery of the Ancient Aegean," *Archaeology* 44: 46–9.

Taplin, Oliver. (1986–7) "Phallology, *Phlyakes*, Iconography and Aristophanes," *Bulletin of the Institute of Classical Studies* 32–3: 92–104.

Tara, S.L. (1985) "*Eisí tríkhes*. An Erotic Motif in the Greek Anthology," *Journal of Hellenic Studies* 105: 108–28.

Tatton-Brown, V. (1982) "The Archaic Period, the Classical Period, and the Hellenistic Period." In *Footprints in Cyprus*, ed. D. Hunt, 98–109. London: Trigraph.

Taylor, Rabun (1997) "Two Pathic Subcultures in Ancient Rome," *Journal of the History of Sexuality* 7: 319–71.

Thatcher, Oliver J. (ed.) (1901) *The Library of Original Sources*, 3: *The Roman World*. Milwaukee: University Research Extension Co.

Thompson, D.J. (1988) *Memphis under the Ptolemies*. Princeton: Princeton University Press.

Thoas, Y. (1980) "Marriages endogamiques à Rome. Patrimoine, pouvoir et parenté depuis l'époque archaïque," *Revue historique de droit français et étranger* 58: 345–82.

Travlos, John. (1971) *Pictorial Dictionary of Ancient Athens*. New York: Praeger.

Treggiari, Susan. (1981) "Contubernales, in CIL VI," *Phoenix* 35: 42–69.

——(1991) *Roman Marriage: "Iusti Coniuges" from the Time of Cicero to the Time of Ulpian*. Oxford: Oxford University Press.

Turner, Judy Ann. (1983) "Hiereiai: Acquisition of Feminine Priesthoods in Ancient Greece," unpublished Ph.D. dissertation, University of California, Santa Barbara.

Van Der Eijk, Philip J. (1999) "Antiquarianism and Criticism: Forms and Functions of Medical Doxography in Methodism." In: *Ancient Histories of Medicine*, ed. Philip Van Der Eijk, 397–452. Leiden: Brill.

Van Straten, F.T. (1981) "Gifts for the Gods." In: *Faith, Hope and Worship: Aspects of Religious Mentality in the Ancient World*, ed. H.S. Versnel, 65–151. Leiden: Brill.

Varone, Antonio. (2001a) *Erotica Pompeiana. Love Inscriptions on the Walls of Pompeii* (trans. Ria P. Berg). Rome: "L'ERMA" di Bretschneider.

——(2001b) *Eroticism in Pompeii* (trans. Maureen Fant). Los Angeles: "L'ERMA" di Bretschneider and J. Paul Getty Museum.

Venit, Marjorie S. (1988) "The Caputi Hydria and Working Women in Classical Athens," *Classical World* 81: 265–72.

Vermeule, Cornelius C. III. (1963) *Greek, Etruscan and Roman Art. The Classical Collections of the Museum of Fine Arts, Boston*. Boston MA: Museum of Fine Arts, Boston.

Vicinus, Martha. (1994) "Lesbian History: All Theory and No Facts or All Facts and No Theory?," *Radical History Review* 60: 57–75.

Vollmer, Friedrich (ed.) (1910) *Poetae latini minores*. Leipzig: Teubner.

von Bothmer, Dietrich. (1957) *Amazons in Greek Art*. Oxford: Oxford University Press.

von Gennep, Arnold. (1909/1960) *Les Rites de Passage: étude systématique des rites de la porte et du seuil, de l'hospitalité, de l'adoption, de la grossesse et de l'accouchement, de la naissance, de l'enfance, de la puberté, de l'initiation, de l'ordination, du couronnement des fiançailles et du mariage, des funérailles, des saisons, etc.* Paris: É. Nourry (translated 1960: London, Routledge).

Vorberg, Gaston. (1932 [reprint 1965]) *Glossarium eroticum*. Stuttgart: Püttmann [Hanau: Müller und Kiepenheuer].

Warmington, E.H. (ed.) (1967) *Remains of Old Latin*. Cambridge MA: Harvard University Press.

Warsher, Tatiana. (1938–57) *Codex Topographicus Pompeianus*. Unpublished typescript in 23 vols (or more), consulted at Duke University, Department of Classical Studies library, but also available in the Blegen Library, The University of Cincinnati, the American Academy in Rome, and elsewhere.

Webster, Thomas B.L. (1972) *Potter and Patron in Classical Athens*. London: Methuen.

Welcker, Friedrich Gottlieb. (1816 [1845]) "Sappho von einem herrschenden Vorurtheil befreyt." In *Kleine Schriften*, 2: *Zur griechischen Literaturgeschichte*, by F.G. Welcker, 80–144. Bonn: E. Weber (reprint, Osnabrück: O. Zeller, 1973).

Wells, Wendy. (1979) "Mercenary Prostitution in Ancient Greece," *Quest* 5: 76–80.

West, Martin L. (1992) *Ancient Greek Music*. Oxford: Oxford University Press.

——(1996) *Die griechische Dichterin: Bild und Rolle*. Stuttgart: B.G. Teubner.

Whitehead, D. (1986) *The Demes of Attica*. Princeton: Princeton University Press.

Wilcken, Ulrich. (1978) *Urkunden der Ptolemäerzeit*. Berlin: Walter de Gruyter.

Williams, Caroline Ransom. (1905) *Couches and Beds of the Greeks, Etruscans and Romans*. Chicago: Chicago University Press.

Williams, Craig. (1999) *Roman Homosexuality: Ideologies of Masculinity in Classical Antiquity*. Oxford: Oxford Uuniversity Press.

Winkler, John J. (1990) *The Constraints of Desire: The Anthropology of Sex and Gender in Ancient Greece*. New York: Routledge.

Worsfold, Thomas Cato. (1932) *The History of the Vestal Virgins of Rome*. London: Rider.

Wroth, Warwick. (1894) *Catalogue of the Greek Coins in the British Museum*, 17: *Troas, Aeolis, and Lesbos*. London: British Museum.

Wycherley, Richard Ernest. (1957) *Athenian Agora*, 3: *Literary and Epigraphical Testimonia*. Princeton NJ: American School of Classical Studies at Athens.

Wyke, Maria. (1994) "Woman in the Mirror: The Rhetoric of Adornment in the Roman World." In: *Women in Ancient Societies: An Illusion of the Night*, eds Léonie J. Archer, Susan Fischler, and Maria Wyke, 134–51. New York: Routledge.

Younger, John G. (1992) "Bronze Age Representations of Aegean Jewelry." In *Eikon* (*Aegaeum* 8), eds J. Crowley and R. Laffineur, 257–93. Liège: Université de Liège.

——(1995) "Bronze Age Representations of Aegean Bull-Games, III." In *Politeia* (*Aegaeum* 12), eds R. Laffineur and P.B. Betancourt, 507–45. Liège: Université de Liège.

——(1997) "Gender and Sexuality in the Parthenon Frieze." In: *Naked Truths. Women, Sexuality, and Gender in Classical Art and Archaeology*, eds C. Lyons and A. Koloski-Ostrow, 120–53. London and New York: Routledge.

——(1998) *Music in the Aegean Bronze Age*. Jonsered: Paul Åström (*Studies in Mediterranean Archaeology*, pocket book 96).

——(1998–2000) "Waist Compression in the Aegean Late Bronze Age," *Archaeological News* 23: 1–9.

Zahn, Wilhelm. (1828–59). *Die schönsten Ornamente und merkwürdigsten Gemälde aus Pompiji, Herkulanum und Stabiae, nebst einigen Grundrissen und Ansichten nach den an Ort und Stelle gemachten original Zeichnungen*. Berlin: G. Reimer.

Zilliacus, Henrik. (1941) *Vierzehn Berliner griechische Papyri: Urkunden und Briefe*. Berlin: Helsingfors.

Zimmermann, K. (1980) "Tätowierte Thrakerinnen auf griechischen Vasenbildern," *Jahrbuch des deutschen archäologischen Instituts* 95: 163–96.

Zweig, Bella. (1992) "The Mute Nude Female Characters in Aristophanes' Plays." In: *Pornography and Representation in Greece and Rome*, ed. A. Richlin, 73–89. New York and Oxford: Oxford University Press.

Ancient sources cited

For abbreviations, see Hornblower and Spawforth 1999: xxi–xliv.

Manuscripts

Achilles Tatius (late 2nd c. CE) – 84–5

1.18 – 15
2.35 – 8, 5.27 – 84–5
3.7 – 90

Aelian (second half 2nd c. CE)

de Natura Animalium
6.1 – 2
3.9 – 8, 21

Varia Historia
9.11 – 119
10.2 – 65
10.18 – 85
12.19 – 117
13.33 – 114

Aelius Lampridius (3rd c. CE)

Alexander Severus
24 – 113

Elagabalus – 114–15

Aeschines (ca. 397–22 BCE)

Epistles
10.3–8 – 75

In Timarchum – 3, 32
1.10 – 126
1.10 – 53
1.41 – 82
1.74 – 111
1.9–12 – 126
1.19–32 – 66
1.56.7 – 15
1.85 – 58
1.138–9 – 126
1.183 – 66, 126

Aeschylus (?525/4–456/5 BCE)

Eumenides
658–66 – 34

Libation Bearers
896–8 – 25

Myrmidons
fr. 228 Mette – 2

Prometheus Bound
135 – 115

Alcaeus (b. ca. 625/20 BCE)

fr. 130.32 Lobel-Page – 18

Alcman (b. 625/20–ca. 605 BCE)

36 Diehl – 45
Parthénea – 68

Alexis (ca. 375–275 BCE)

206 K-A – 27

Ammianus (ca. 330–65 CE)

14.6 – 47, 117
22.9.15 – 2

Anacreon (fl. 536/5 BCE)

PMG
346 – 107, 109
347 – 7
358 – 7, 68, 116
376 – 117
fr. 45 – 45–6
fr. 369 Diehl – 45–6

Anaxilas (4th c. BCE)

K-A
fr. 21 – 107–8

Andocides (ca. 440–390 BCE)

in Alc.
4.42 – 18

Anecdota Par. (Anecdota Graeca ed. J.A. Cramer)

2.154.20–25 – 2

Antiphanes (fl. 385 BCE)

"On Hetaeras" – 111, 117
101 K-A – 26

Antoninus Liberalis (mid-2nd c. CE)

17 – 45–69
21 – 8

Apollodorus (ca. 180–post 120 BCE)

1.2.6 – 44
1.3.2 – 3
1.9.9, 11, and 12 – 3
1.9.17 – 141
2.1.4 – 81
2.5.4 – 30
2.63 – 126
3.1.2–4 – 81

3.4.3 – 41
3.6.7 – 132
3.13.8 – 133
3.12.2 – 52
3.14.3 and 4 – 3
3.14.6 – 15
3.101 – 64
3.116 – 58
5.1.6 and 9 – 81

Apollonius (3rd c. CE) – 78

1.57 scholiast – 29
2.188 ff. – 22

Apuleius (b. ca. 123 CE)

Apology
10 – 106

Metamorphoses – 85
2.11.2 – 50
4.28 – 12
10.22 – 19

Archilochus (d. 652 BCE)

196A West = S478 Page = Campbell 1976: 463:
15–16 – 36

Aretaeus Cappadocius (1st c. CE)

De causis et signis acutorum morborum
2.5.4 – 2

Aristides (ca. 100 BCE)

Milesian Tales – 84

Aristides Quintilianus (3rd c. CE)

1.13 – 32

Aristophanes (ca. 455–386 BCE)

Acharnians
527–30 – 14
790–2 – 9
1199–1200 – 25

Clouds
8–10 – 22
341 ff. – 140
358–63 – 115
373 – 23

Athenagoras (late 2nd c. CE)

Presbeia

Augustine (354–430 CE)

City of God

Epistle

Good of Marriage

Lying

Trinity

Work of the Monks
32.40 – 122

Aurelius Victor (fl. 360–89 CE)

Liber de Caesaribus
28.6 – 67

Ausonius (4th c. CE)

Epigrams
70.5 – 8, 92
79 – 138
79.7 – 43
82.1–6 – 26, 37
83 – 87
86.1–2, 87.7 – 37
92 – 67

Barnabas

Epistle
10.6 – 9

Acts – 110

Bible (canonical and lost books)

Acts 10–11, 15 – 24
1 Corinthians 6: 9–10, 7:8–9 – 122
1 Corinthians 7:18 – 24
Deuteronomy 23:18–19 – 109
Ezekiel 16:49–50 – 126
Galatians 2.3 – 24
Genesis 17 – 23–5
Genesis 18:20–19:12 – 126, 136
Genesis 19 – 136
Genesis 38.10 – 36
Jubilees 16:5–6 and 20:5 – 126
Jude 7 – 126
Luke 10:12 – 126
1 Maccabees 1:15 – 24
Matthew 10:15 – 126
2 Peter 2:6–8 – 126
Romans 1:26–27 – 122
1 Timothy 1:9–10 – 122
Testament of the Twelve Patriarchs, Benjamin
  9.1 – 126

Callias (fl. 446–430 BCE)

1 K-A – 3

Callimachus (first half 2nd c. BCE)

5 – 132
6.146 – 20

Callisthenes (d. 327 BCE)

FGrH 124 F34 – 5

Cassios Dio (ca. 164–post 229 CE)

43.20.2 ff. – 62
45.1 – 9
58.2.4 – 70
59 – 29
62.13.1–2 – 84
65.16 – 115
67.2.3 and 68.2.4 – 23, 67
69.8.2 – 17
77.16.1 – 34, 87
80 – 45

Catullus (ca. 84–54 BCE) – 20, 30

15 – 3
16 – 31, 137
25 – 43
35.16, 51 – 116
61 – 59
63 – 16
74 – 3
79.4, 80, 88.8 – 49
99 – 27

Celsus, Iuventius (fl. 106–31 CE)

de medicina
4.25.3 – 24
4.28 – 125
7.25.1–2 – 24

Chariton (early 2nd c. CE)

"The Story of Khaireas and Kallirhoê" –
  84–5

Cicero (106–43 BCE)

Att.
1.13.3, 16.2.5 – 34, 63

Cael.
3.6 – 34, 63
61–7 – 17

de Or.
70.232 – 47

Dom.
10.25 – 61
 92 – 34

Fam.
1.9.15 – 34
8.12 and 14 – 67
8.13.3, 14.4 – 31

Har. Resp.
27.38 – 34
27.59 – 49, 61

Inv.
31.51 – 14

Phil.
2.2.5 – 49
2.44–5 – 108
3.6 – 67

Q Fr.
2.3.2 – 34

Sest.
16.19 – 34

Tusc.
4.70 – 53, 86

Verr.
2.3.9, 23 – 39, 45
2.4.126 – 116
2.4.135 – 29, 45–6, 104

Claudian (370–ca. 404 CE)

in Eutrop.
1.339 – 47, 117

Clement of Alexandria (ca. 150–215 CE)

Protrepicus
4.47 – 95
4.48, 51 – 104, 119
4.53 – 95, 119, 130

Paidogogos
2.10.95, 2.10.83, 91; 3.3.18–21 – 122
2.11 – 115

3, 3.18–21 – 122

Stromata
3.6.50, 4.51.1 – 65

Columella (1st c. CE)

11.3.29, 10.109.372 – 10

Cratinus (late 5th c. BCE)

F354 K-A 294 – dildoes

Cheiron fr. 9 Koch – citizenship

Curtius (late 1st–early 2nd c. CE)

6.53 – eunuchs   000
5.7.3 – Thais   000
10.1.25 – eunuchs   000

Deinarchus (ca. 360-post 292/1 BCE)

2.17 – 32

Demosthenes (384–22 BCE)

22.30–1 – 108, 126
23.53 – 66
27.4, 29.43 – 74
30.61, 73 – 108
36 – 75
59 – 83
59.66 – 66
59.85–6, 113–14 – 14

Digest (529 CE) – 58
3.1.1.5 – 66
3.1.1.6 – 31
47.10.15.15–23 – 66
48.6.3.4 and 5.2 – 67
48.8.3.5, 8.11.1 – 26, 67
48.19.38.5 – 1
Novel 77, 141 – 67

Dio Chrysostom (ca. 40/50–post 110 CE) – 108

1.1–2 – 82
66.25, 26 – 115

Diodorus Athenaeus (4th c. BCE)

FGrH 372 F40 – 14

Diodorus Siculus (fl. 60–30 BCE)

2.20.3 ff. – 117
3.53–54 – 6
4.16, 4.28 – 7
4.24.4, 4.29.4 – 61
4.83 – 110
17.72 – 130
17.77.1–3 – 7

Diogenes Laertius (first half 3rd c. CE)

2.105 – 108
6.2.69 – 120
6.16 – 14

Dionysius of Halicarnassus (Augustan)

Antiquitates romanae
2.25 – 3, 77
7.9.3–4 – 93
16.9 – 66

Ennius (239–169 BCE)

Euhemerus 134–8 – 116

Epigrammata Bobiensia

70 – 129

Epicrates

Antilais – 65

Eratosthenes (285–194 BCE)

Catasterismi
1.1.1–11 – 63

Etymologicum Magnum

s.v. thallophoros – 18

Eubulus (ca. 405–335 BCE)

94 K-A – 129

Euphorion (mid-5th c. BCE)

107 Powell, p. 49 – 75

Eupolis (late 5th c. BCE)

1 Edmonds 1957 – 37

Euripides (ca. 480–8 BCE)

Hipp. – 133

Bacchae – 133
1062 – 87

Chrysippus – 65

Cycl.
323–9 – 22

Hecuba
558–70 – 25

Helen
140 – 30
1459–61 – 58

Hipp.
31–3 – 58
616–25 – 122
1425–7 – 54

Ion – 50

Iph. Aul.
548–9 – 45
732 – 75

Iph. Taur.
1439 ff. – 5
1462 – 105

Phaetho
233–5 – 59

Eustathius (12th c. CE)

Commentary on the Iliad
24.29 – 75

Eutropius (fl. 363 CE)

I 90 ff.; p. 77B – 65

Festus (late 2nd c. CE)

Gloss. Lat.

31 – 46
39 – 105

Firmicus Maternus (fl. 334–43 CE)

Mathesis
5.2.4, 5.3.11 and 17, 5.6.8., 6.30.15 – 14

Gaius (fl. 160–78 CE)

Institutes
3.220–4 – 66
4.18.4 – 67

Galen (129–99 or 216 CE)

Kühn 1821–33 [1964–65]
5:29–30 – 87
8:437–52 – 125
8:451–2 – 1, 40
9.12 – 2, 24
12:232 – 2, 84
12:249 – 37, 47, 78, 80
12:283 – 64
12:416 – 78

Gellius, Aulus (b. 125–8–post 180 CE)

Noctes atticae
1.5.2–3 – 44
1.8 – 65
6.1.2–5 – 9
6.12.3–4 – 43
9.4.12 ff. – 133
10.10 – 76
10.15 – 4

Gorgias (ca. 485–38 BCE)

Isocrates
10 – 55

Greek Anthology

2.11 – 116
5.19.1– 92
5.38 [37], 104.3–4, 105 – 49
5.170 – 68
5.202, 203 – 116
5.208.1 – 92
6.1, 18–20 – 65
6.275 – 2
6.350 – 62

6.353, 354 – 15, 119
7.14, 17 – 116
7.492 – 138
7.718 – 68, 116
9.66 – 116
9.332 – 69, 111
9.338 – 85
9.506, 571 – 116
9.604 – 5, 119
9.605 – 15
11.328.9 – 49
11.329 – 9, 47
12.4 – 128–9
12.34 – 92
12.187 – 19, 20, 37
12.192 – 53
12.222 – 92
16.310 – 116

Harpocration (2nd c. CE)

pornikón télos – 109

Heliodorus (early 3rd c. CE)

"Ethiopian Tale of Theagenes and
  Kharikleia" – 85
4.8 – 130

Hephaestion (fl. 130 CE)

15.59 – 106

Herodian (fl. 130 CE)

5 – 45

Herodotus (ante 480–post 443 BCE)

1.34–45 – 16
1.59–65, 6.131 – 93
1.80 – 38
1.93 – 46
1.105 – 56
1.199 – 110
1.216 – 47
2.79 – 127
2.112–20 – 55
2.134–5 – 113, 116
3.92 – 47
4.67 – 56
4.110–117, 4.159 ff. – 7
4.172, 4.176, 4.180 – 46
5.10 – 133
5.55, 6.109, 6.123 – 12
6.126–131 – 4

9.129 – 18
14.294 – 52
14.295 – 45–6
18.490 ff. – 74
18.570 – 127
22.230–5 – 52
23.101 – 112

Odyssey – 134–5
4.120–305 – 55
4.271–89 – 134
6.292 scholiasts A and D – 18
8.266 – 11, 124
10 – 32
10.275 ff. – 72
10.490–5 – 133
11.90–9 – 133
11.248–50 – 105
11.300 ff. – 30
13.412 – 86, 128
18.212 – 45
21.152 – 87
23.191–206 – 19
24.6 – 112
24.78–9 – 2

Homeric Hymns

Apollo – 69

Demeter
412 – 11, 40, 96

Horace (65–8 BCE)

Ars P.
414 – 1

Carm.
3.10 – 70
3.12 – 116
3.14.5 – 70
3.24.52–4 – 40
4.9.11 – 116

Epist.
2.1.145–6 – 127

Ep.
5.11–82 – 72
5.58 – 8
8 – 50
17 – 72

Sat.
1.2 – 27, 140

1.5.54 – 47
1.5.62 – 47, 125
1.8 – 106
2.8.51 – 11

Hyginus (mid-1st c. BCE)

Fabulae
14.4 – 29
40.1 – 81
185 – 9
254.3 – 25

Hypereides (389–22 BCE)

Eux.
3 – 109

In Athenog.
5–6 – 125

Isaeus (BCE 420–330 BCE)

6.19 – 27
6.21 – 107
6.49–50 – 14

Isocrates (436–338 BCE)

4.42, 4.68, 4.70, 7.75, 12.193 – 7

Jerome (ca. 347–420 CE)

Regulae Sancti Pachomii
94, rule 104 – 58

John Chrysostom (347–407 CE)

On Virginity
1.1–2; 50.1.3–4 – 122–3

Homily
4 – 122–3

Josephus (b. 37/8 CE)

Bell. Jud.
4.8.4 – 81

Ant. Jud.
12.241 – 24
1.200 – 126

In Ap.
2.141 – 24

Julian (2nd c. CE)

Epistles
89(301b) – 84

Justin (3rd or 4th c. CE)

Epit. Hist.
18.5 – 110

Justin Martyr (ca. 100–65 CE)

1 *Apology* 27 – 29, 109

Juvenal (fl. 120–40 CE) – 63

2 – 34, 43
2, 3, 5, 9, 11 – 63
2.41 – 79
2.43–8 – 66
2.44–50 – 31
2.63 scholiast – 9
2.117–142 – 73
2.143–8 – 79
3.66 – 110
6.63–6 – 39, 130
6.73 – 1
6.114 ff. – 80
6.127 – 98, 111
6.185 ff. – 79
6.279 – 140
6.300–1 – 50
6.311 ff. – 23, 68
6.331 – 140
6.333 ff. – 19
6.365 – 110
6.379 schol. – 24
6.419 – 17
6.598 – 140
7.82–92 – 39, 130
9.130–3 – 31
14 – 24

Lactantius (ca. 240–320 CE)

Divine Institutes
1.20.1 – theater 139
1.22.9 ff. – faunus 49
2.12, 6.19 – 122

Libanius (314–ca. 393 CE)

Progymn. narr 2 – 58

Little Iliad – 134

fr. 19 *EGF* – 55

Livy (59 BCE–17 CE)

1.57–60 – 71
3.13.2 – 108
3.44–58 – 136
4.44.11–12 – 137
8.22 – 97
8.28 – 66
23.21 – 67
27.11.4 – 56
30.12–15 – 7
39.6.7–9 – 109
39.8–18 – 17

Longinus (1st c. CE)

De subliminibus
44.5 – 42

Longus (late 2nd or early 3rd c. CE)

"The Pastoral Story of Daphnis and Khloê"
– 85

Lucan (39–65 CE)

Pharsalia
5.735–815 – 19

Lucian (ca. CE) 120–180

Alexander
p. 665 – 9

Amores
13, 15, 16 – 104
28 – 68, 120

Anacharsis
36–7 – 86

Apophras
28 – 47

Conviv.
16.35.46 – 39

Dial. deor.
7.3 – 45
16.14.2 – 58

Dial. meret.
5 – 58, 62, 71, 117
36 – 116

Dial. mort.
9.2 – 117

Eikones
4, 6 – 104
18 schol. – 116

Lucani vita – 39

Pseudologista
24 – 120

Salt.
11 – 27

Lucilius (180–2/1 BCE), Loeb edn (Warmington)

56 – 21
61 – 26, 55, 107
63 – 27
251 – 3
254–8 – 31
306–7 – 23

Lucretius (early 1st c. BCE)

4.1269–76 – 36

Lysias (?459–ca. 380 BCE)

Eratosthenes – 3, 66
1.6–14 – 74
3 – 92
3.21–6 – 110
16, 25, 26, 31 – 32

Lysippus (late 5th c. BCE)

5 K-A – 26

Machon (mid-3rd c. BCE)

376–86 – 95

Macrobius (early 5th c. CE)

In Somn
1.2.6–12 – 84

Sat.
1.12.24 – 49
2.4.21 – 127

Manetho (fl. 280 BCE)

4.312 – 14, 51
4.358 – 68

Martial (ca. 40–104 CE) – 77

1.24 – 73
1.34 – 138
1.34.8 – 110
1.77 – 26
1.83.1–2 – 8
1.90 – 68
1.96 – 18, 31
2.17.1 – 108
2.28 – 19, 25, 49, 113
2.47.4 – 3
2.49.2 – 126, 140
2.50 – 49
2.62 – 27, 55, 77
2.82, 2.83 – 49
2.84 – 28
3.51, 3.68.1–4 – 17
3.72 – 72, 26
3.74 – 24, 55, 77
3.75.3 – 11
3.77 – 37, 49
3.81 – 26, 37, 47
3.95 – 27
3.96 – 26
4.17 – 49
4.43 – 26
4.50 – 49
4.7 – 27, 77
4.71.5–6, 4.84.1 – 49
5.46 – 27
6.2 – 67
6.26 – 37, 60, 87
6.55.5 – 49
6.56 – 27, 55, 77
6.66.1–9 – 49, 108
6.70 – 25
7.32.9 – 2
7.35 – 17, 30
7.55 – 49
7.62 – 27
7.67, 7.70 – 68, 77

Maximus of Tyre (2nd c. CE)

Menander (342/1–291/0 BCE)

Musonius Rufus (30–102? CE; fl. 60–101 CE)

Mythographi Vaticani

Oribasius (ca. 320–400 CE)

Origen (184/5–254/5 CE)

Orosius (early 5th c. CE)

Ovid (43 BCE–17 CE) – 89–90

3.639–40 – 18
3.769–88 – 120
3.773–88 – 127
3.775–6 – 14

Fasti
2.155–92 – 64
2.318–24 – 56
2.757, 3.11–48 – 137
3.167–258 – 63
3.827 – 15
4.221–44. – 16
5.433 – 26
6.651ff – 14

Heroides
4 – 57
7 – 41
9.53–118 – 56
15 – 89, 116–17
15.199–201 – 68, 177
16.149–52 – 15
18–19 – 57

Medic. – 36

Met
1.452 ff. – 39
1.462–567 – 69
2.409–40 – 64
2.433 – 71
2.844–75 – 48
3.342–407 – 83
3.605–91 – 41
4.217–33 – 12, 64, 71, 137
4.285–399 – 56
6.524–585 – 106
7.688a–865 – 45
8.45–150 – 57
9.666–797 – 61
9.731–5, 762–3 – 69
10.1–11, 84 – 89
10.150–61 – 52
10.215 – 58
10.238–46 – 110
10.243–97 – 119
10.298ff – 60
10.519–36 – 2–3
11.301–17 – 56, 64, 71
12.189–209 – 29
13.396 –58
13.750–897 – 97
13.900–14.74, 14.320–96 – 32
14.622 – 136
14.654–771 – 64, 136
14.698ff – 120
14.771 – 136

Pont.
3.3.57–8 – 89

Rem. Am.
327 – 47
337–8 – 129
354 – 36
407–8, 425 – 123
437–40 – 81
525 – 123
549–54 – 11
797–8 – 10

Tristia
1.3 – 89
2.308–14 – 70, 86
2.345–6, 361–470 – 89
2.365–6 – 117
2.443–4 – 84
2.497–546 – 89
2.519–20 – 39
2.521–8 – 16, 130

Palaephatus (late 4th BCE)

14 – 9

Parthenius (1st c. BCE)

Amat. Narr.
5 – 69

Pausanias (fl. 150 CE)

1.2.1 – 7
1.8.5 – 12
1.15.2, 17.2 – 7
1.18.5 – 44
1.19.1 – 131, 133
1.20.1–2 – 95
1.20.3, 22.5 – 82
1.23.5–6 – 47
1.24.3 – 57
1.25.2 – 7
1.29.15 – 12
1.30.1 – 9
1.37.3 – 54
1.41.7 – 7
1.44.1 – 85
2.4.7 – 110
2.5.1 – 12
2.10.3 – 19
2.20.6 – 3
2.20.8–10 – 7
2.23.8 – 82

4.37 – 122, 126

Special Laws
1.325, 3.34–6, 113 – 58, 122

Philonides (late 5th c. BCE)

fr. 5 – 109

Philostephanus (3rd c. BCE)

FGrH3:31 – 119

Philostratus (3rd c. CE?)

Gym.
31–40 – 2, 21

Imag.
1.24 – 58

Phlegon of Tralles (early 2nd c. CE)

Mirabilia – 56

Photius (810–93 CE)

kunodésmê – 42
lámbda – 37
Leukátes – 117
Phaon – 117
siphniázein – 47

Pindar (?518–post 446 BCE)

fr. 128c. 7–8 Snell-Maehler – 58
fr. 150 Bowra – 29

Isthm.
7.22–22b – 18

Nem.
3.19 – 18

Ol.
1 – 15
1.40–5 – 93
7.154c schol. – 45
8.19–20 – 18
10.95–105 – 15, 78

Pyth.
2.42 – 56
4.123 – 18
4.214 – 72
9 – 15

Plato (ca. 429–327 BCE) – 96-7

Alc.
103a – 5
141d – 91–3

Chrm.
155d – 92, 96

Euthydemus
282b – 96

Gorgias
481d–482d – 96
493–494e – 31

Hipp.
228d – 57

Laws
636b–c – 58, 93, 97
636e – 68
737c–8a – 31
783ab – 40
833c–834d – 4, 15
836c – 8, 97
838e – 58, 97
839a – 57, 97, 118
839e–840c – 2
841d – 57

Lysis – Solon
204b–206a, 207a – 92, 96

Menex.
236b schol., 235e – 14

Phaedo
64d, 81b, 82c, 83b and d, 114e – 40

Phaedrus
231a–256d – 96
235b – 116
250e–251a – 58, 97
255b–e – 9

Prt.
309a–d – 96
315e – 72–3

Resp.
389e, 580e – 120
425c–457b, 458d – 86
459d – 87
468c – 74
620b – 14

Sull.
2.2–4, 8–13, 147–17, 326–9 – 19

Thes.
20 – 37
26–28 – 7

Pollux (2nd c. CE)

Onomasticon
2.171 – 42
2.174 – 26
6.188 – 68
7.96 – 41
7.203 – 106
15.102 – 39

Polybius (ca 200–118 BCE)

12.13.1 – 120
12.15.104 – 37
14.11.3–4 – 111
31.25.2–6 – 27

Praeparatio Sophistica
199 p. 85B de Borries – 42

Priapea (Hooper 1999) – 105–6

3.6–7 – 36, 114
12.10–15 – 26
19, 27, 34 – 106
40 – 106, 108
53 – 53, 106
62 – 49
63.17 – 78
64.1 – 43
78.5 – 26

Priscian Caesariensis (5th–6th c. CE)

Institutio de arte grammatica
3 [I:574–8] 1992 – 105

Priscianus, Theodorus

2.11 Rose 133 – 59, 84
Add. p. 340.16 – 26

Procopius (6th c. CE)

Anecdota
11.34–36 – 67

Propertius (ca. 54/47–2 BCE)

1.6.29 – 106
3.9.12 – 119
3.14.1–4 – 15
4.7 – 106
4.7.15 – 108
4.8 – 27, 106

Ptolemy Mathematicus (fl. 146–170 CE)

Tetnabiblos
III 18f. 44r 33 – 68

Quintilian (35–post 90 CE)

Institutes
4.2.69 – 67
5.9.14 – 17

In. Orat.
12.10.5 – 119

Rufus

Onomastikon
112 – 26

Sappho (fl. 600 BCE) – 116–17

Edmonds 1928
12 – 107
82 – 116

PMG
16, 31 – 116–17
39 – 115
47, 48 – 68
49 – 116
54 – 34
82, 91 – 116
94 – 67–9
95, 98, 102, 121 – 116
126 – 68
130 – 45
132, 132, 144 – 116

Semonides (mid-7th c. BCE) – 120, 122

Seneca the Elder (50 BCE–40 CE)

Controv.
1.2.22 – 106

De monog.
3.1, 17.5 – 122

De cultu feminarum
1 – 122

De pallio – 122

De virginibus velandis – 122, 138

Theocritus (early 3rd c. BCE)

1.64–142 – 85
1.81 – 106
3 – 85
6 – 97
7 – 91
7.106–8 – 50
12.27–38 – 95
18 – 15
28 – 116–17
scholia (C. Wendel, *Scholia in Theocritum Vetera* [Leipzig: Teubner 1914]) – 75

Theodosian Code (429–38 CE) – 67

Theognis (mid-6th c. BCE)

1335–6 – 15
1345–8 – 52

Theophilus (late 2nd c. CE)

Ad Autolycum
3.3 and 8 – 49

Theophrastos (372/69–288/5 BCE)

Characters – 120
21.3 – 54–5

De signis
1.4 – 72–3

Thucydides (b. 460/55–ca. 400 BCE)

1.6.4–5 – 85
2.45.2 – 141
5.54.3 – 12

Tibullus (54/48–19 BCE)

1.4 – 106
2.4.32 – 8

3.13–18 – 129
8, 9 – 27

Timaeus (ca. 350–260 BCE)

FGrH 566 F83 – 85

Timocles (late 4th c. BCE) K-A

2.13 – 26
32.3 – 66

Tyrtaeus (mid-7th c. BCE)

10.26–7 – 86

Tzetzes (12th c. CE)

Historiarum variarum Chiliades
8.375 – 105

Ulpian (d. 223 CE)

Edicts
paragr. 192 – 66

Valerius Maximus (1st c. CE)

2.1.4 – 42
5.4.1 – 25
6.1.7, 9 – 58, 60
6.1.10–12 – 56
6.7.1–3 – 80
8.11.4 – 105
9.1.8 – 28

Varro (116–27 BCE)

Sat. Men.
48 B, 70 Cèbe – 37

Ling.
7.97 – 95

Velleius Paterculus (20/19 BCE–30/31? CE)

2.45.1 – 34

Vergil (70–19 BCE)

Aen.
1 – 40

1.317 – 7
2 – 75
4 – 40
7.19–20 – 32
7.765–82 – 57
11.532 ff. – 7

Ecl.
2.56 – 46

G.
3.258–63 – 57
4.453–525 – 89

Vettius Valens (fl. 152–62 CE)

1.1, 2.16, 2.36 and 38 – 14

Xenophon (b. ca. 430)

Anab.
4.3 and 19 – 109

[*Ath. pol.*]
1.10–12 – 32, 86
50.2 – 108

Cyr. – 84

Hell.
5.4.4 – 133
6.4.16 – 86

Lac.
11.3 – 128

Mem.
1.3.11–12 – 90
1.3.13 – 40
2.2.13 – 32
3.3.12–13 – 18
3.10 – 119
3.11 – 107

Oec. – 140
3.15 – 14
7.5 – 74
7.22 – 123, 141
12–13 – 74

Symp. – 129–30
1.9–10 – 15
4.17 – 18
4.38 – 120
8.32 – 72–3

Xenophon of Ephesus (early 2nd c. CE)

1.2 – 15

Inscriptions

Corpus Inscriptionum Latinarum (CIL)

1.196 – 17
1.236 – 108
4.760+p. 196 – 88, 99
4.1383 – 102
4.1512–47 – 46, 69
4.1516 – 103
4.1645+p. 463 – 103
4.1649 – 103
4.1665 – 101
4.1751+pp. 211, p. 464 – 98
4.1781 + p. 464 – 103
4.1825+p. 212, 464 – 102
4.1830 – 55, 107
4.2048+p. 215 – 102
4.2060 – 100
4.2066 – 78
4.2145 – 102
4.2193 – 98, 111
4.2210 – 95
4.2260+p. 216 – 57
4.2273 + p. 216 – 49, 98
4.2319b+p.216 – 101
4.2321 – 102
4.3042 – 102
4.3061 – 102, 118
4.3062 – 102
4.3200d – 127
4.3938 – 101
4.4082 – 100
4.4087 – 100
4.4091 – 127
4.4345 – 102
4.4353 – 102
4.4397 – 102
4.4547 – 101
4.4592 – 101
4.4699 – 101
4.4818 – 102
4.4917 – 101
4.4954 – 8, 101
4.4977 – 102
4.5007 [=3299+3300] – 102
4.5037=3310 – 102
4.5178 – 101
4.5203 – 98

4.5204 – 98
4.5206 – 98
4.5272 – 127
4.5296+p. 705 – 103
4.5358 – 101
4.5373 – 102
4.6782 – 127
4.7080 – 102
4.7339 – 111
4.8149 – 102
4.8259 – 102
4.8260a – 111
4.8321a – 102
4.8384 – 102
4.8454 – 98
4.8512 – 101
4.8767 – 102
4.8805 – 101–3
4.8820 – 102
4.8843 – 8
4.8898 – 8
4.9027 – 49, 101
4.9202 – 127
4.9848 – 102
4.10004 – 26
4.10085b – 102
4.10151 – 101
4.10153f – 101
4.10156 – 101
6.579 – 17
11.6721[5] – 26

Inscriptiones Graecae (IG)

2^2.956 [= $Syll$.3 667], 957, 958 – 18

2^2.1237.123–5 – 69
2^2.4671 – 16
5^1.170 – 60
5^1.1390.26 – 66
7.52 – 85
12.3.536–601, esp. 536–49, and 12 Suppl. ad 537 – 131
12.5.173 – 54
12.5.199 – 81

Inscriptiones Latinae Selectae (Dessau ed. 1892–1915) (ILS)

18 – 17

Supplementum Epigraphicum Graecum (SEG)

27.261 – 53, 108

Oxyrinchus Papyri (POxy.)

vol. 39: 2891 – 120

Sylloge Inscriptionum Graecarum (W. Dittenberger ed. 1915–1924) (SIG)

1219.17 – 66
1266 – 3

The Twelve Tables (Warmington ed. 1967)

4.6.6 – 76

Works of art cited

Minoan-Myceaean

1   "Taureador" frescoes, Knossos (HM; Marinatos and Hirmer 1960: pl. XVII) (p. 25).
2   boxing boys, Akrotiri, Thera (NMA; Doumas 1992: pls 79–81) (p. 85).
3   "Snake Goddesses," Knossos (HM; Younger 1998–2000: figs 3–4) (p. 25).
4   "Harvester Vase," Ayia Triada (HM; Younger 1998–2000: pls 1 top, 2) (p. 25).
5   "Chieftain Cup," Haghia Triada (HM; Koehl 1986) (p. 92; **pl. 4**).

Greek

Coins

6   silver staters Thasos, (5th c.; British Museum Department of Coins and Medals. 1963: 216 nos. 1–17; Vorberg 1965: 385): ithyphallic satyr rapes maenad (pp. 117, 137)

Mirrors

7   cover, Corinth (BMFA 08.32c; Reinsberg 1989: fig. 76; Brendel 1970: fig. 27; Mulas 1978: 60, 61; Johns 1982: figs 95, 112; Stewart 1995: fig. 58, 1997: figs 114, 115; Clarke 2003: figs 16 and 17): exterior (relief): man and woman have "a tergo" intercourse reclining (cf. **230**; interior (etched): man about to have "a tergo" intercourse with woman who leans over and reaches to insert his penis into her vagina (pp. 45, 88, 104, 118).

Sculpture

Limestone/marble

Relief
8   metopes, temple of Apollo, Gortyn (HM; 7th c.; Stewart 1990: fig. 33, 1997: fig. 26): nude Leto? and Artemis? flank Apollo (pp. 14, 69, 86).
9   Bassae frieze (BM 524; Stewart 1990: pl. 451): nude woman about to be raped by centaur (p. 86).
10 tombstone of "Dermys and Kittylos" (NMA; 7th c.; Stewart 1990: pl. 61): two youths embrace (p. 93).
11 tombstone, Phalanna (Larisa; Boardman 1985: fig. 55): two young women face each other, pulling (left) or touching (right) her veil; left woman holds out an "apple" to right woman who touches it (p. 68).

12 tombstone, Pharsalos (Louvre; Boardman 1985: fig. 54): two young women hold flowers; left woman offers a purse (p. 68; **pl. 9**).
13 tombstone, Piraeus (Piraeus; Lullies and Hirmer 1960: pl. 182; Clairmont 1993: no. 2.156): nude youth "Chairedemos" and adult "Lykeas" in chiton, both soldiers (p. 73; **pl. 12**).
14 tombstone (Pushkin; Clairmont 1993: no. 2.354): adult and youth, both soldiers, face each other (p. 73).

In the round
15 korê, "Lady of Auxerre" (7th c.; Louvre; Richter 1988: no. 18). (p. 25).
16 korê, "Nikandre" (7th c.; Delos; Richter 1988: no. 1) (p. 25).
17 kouros (Delos; Richter 1960: no. 17; 7th c.) (p. 25).
18 "Knidia," Praxiteles (mid-4th c.; Stewart 1990: pls 502–7): nude Aphrodite arises from a bath (Lapatin 1997) (pp. 11, 86, 104; **pl. 28**).
19 Crouching Aphrodite with Eros, Doidalses of Bithynia (late 4th c.; Ridgway 1990: pls 112–13) (pp. 11, 45).
20 "Charioteer," Motya, Sicily (Motya; 5th or 4th c.; Pavese 1996): youth in a chiton and strophium stands in a pronounced contrapposto (actor? cf. 335; Theron of Acragas?) (pp. 86, 129, 131).

Bronzes
21 bronze cuirass, Olympia (Olympia; 5th c.; Andronicos *et al.* 1975: 213 fig. 30) (p. 23).

Terracottas
22 statue group, Olympia (Olympia; Dover 1989: first ill.): adult god carries boy holding a cock (p. 52).
23 votive relief (NYMM 24.97.92; ca. 425–400; Van Straten 1981: 100, fig. 43): Asklepios?, Hygieia, woman gives birth (p. 20).
24 votive relief (private collection; 4th c.?; Keuls 1985: fig. 124): woman gives birth (p. 20).
25 votive relief, Heraion of Sele (Paestum; Sestieri 1955: pl. 34): Eileithyia (p. 44).
26 phallus, Chios (BM 1888.6–1.496C; 7th c.; Johns 1982: b/w fig. 49) (p. 95).

Wood
27 statuette group (Samos; Reinsberg 1989: fig. 4; Neumann 1965: fig. 30): Zeus squeezes breast of Hera (p. 25).

Tomb painting
28 "The Diver," Paestum (Paestum; late 6th c.; Dover 1989: second ill.): men and youths on couches (p. 19).

Vase paintings

Geometric
29 column krater (BM; Reinsberg 1989: fig. 3): man grabs woman by the wrist to take her aboard ship (p. 118).

Orientalizing
30 jug, Afrati (HM; Reinsberg 1989: fig. 108; Neumann 1965: fig. 32): man and woman face each other, "hands-up-and-down" position (p. 118).
31 aryballos, Corinthian (BM terracotta 1676; Johns 1982: b/w fig. 74): male genitalia (p. 95).
32 "Chigi" oinochoe, Corinthian (Villa Giulia; late 7th c.; Hurwitt 2002): (bottom) boys hunt hares; (middle) youths on horses, charioteer, lion hunters, judgment of Paris; (top) hoplites (p. 4).

Black-figure

Caeretan
33   hydria (Vienna 218; Koch-Harnack 1989: fig. 74): satyrs have frontal intercourse with women (pp. 117, 137, 139).

Attic
34   amphora, Acheloos Ptr. (BM 1856.12–26.1086; Johns 1982: b/w fig. 13): satyr with an erection carries off a maenad (p. 137).
35   amphora, Amasis Ptr. (Paris Cabinet des Medailles 222; Boardman 1985: fig. 85): 2 maenads, arms about their shoulders, trip up to Dionysos (p. 72).
36   kylix, Amasis Ptr. (BMFA 01.651; ABV 157.86; Keuls 1985: fig. 256; Johns 1982: b/w fig. 73; Mulas 1978: 42): two men masturbate; a dog defecates under each handle (pp. 8, 22, 78).
37   hydria, Antimenes Ptr. (Leyden XVe28; ABV 266.1; Charbonneaux *et al.* 1971: fig. 348) man ogles youth bathing in a fountain house (pp. 18, 139).
38   lekythos, Diosphos Ptr. workshop, Athens (Parlama and Stampolides 2000: no. 289): (A) orgy, man has frontal intercourse with awoman, woman has frontal equestrian intercourse with man; man and woman kiss; (B) "three couples are engaged in sodomy" (men having anal intercourse?); below the handle, two couples "entwined under the same blanket" (p. 64).
39   amphora, Exekias (BM B 210; ABV 144.7;Boardman 1974: fig. 98): (tondo) Achilles kills Penthesileia (p. 134).
40   amphora, Exekias (*ABV* 145.14): (A) death of beardless Achilles; (B) death of bearded Antilochos (p. 2).
41   lekythos, Ptr of Athens 9690 (NMA 9690; ABV 505; Keuls 1985: fig. 300): two satyrs flank phallus (p. 95).
42   pinax fragments, Paseas, Athens Acropolis? (AM 1984.131, 132 or private collection; Greifenhagen 1976: color pl.; Robertson 1992: fig. 38; Reinsberg 1989: fig. 87): (fragment 1) man has "a tergo" intercourse with woman reclining on a couch; (fragment 2) woman stands on a couch, her body arched, presumably having "a tergo" intercourse; at right, the legs of a man to right on a third couch [possibly this man is having intercourse with the third woman at extreme left in 43]
43   pinax fragment, Paseas? (Athens Acropolis; Vorberg 1965: 708): two couples, each consisting of a youth having "a tergo" intercourse with awoman; a third woman's head at left (belonging to the couple on 42.2?) (p. 88).
44   hydria, Sappho Ptr. (Warsaw Goluchow 32; Beazley 1971: 246; Boardman 1985: fig. 311): Sappho plays a barbitos (p. 116).
45   amphora (Munich 1541; Stewart 1997: fig. 70; Scanlon 2002: fig. 7–5): Atalanta wrestles Peleus (p. 14).
46   cup, one-handled (BM 1865.11–18.43; Johns 1982: color pl. 26): satyr has "a tergo" intercourse with male donkey (pp. 117, 119).
47   dinos (NMA 19363): two women share cloak (p. 33; **pl. 8**).
48   hydria (Florence 3809; Korshak 1987: fig.3): (shoulder) satyr has "a tergo" intercourse with a mule (pp. 19, 117, 139).
49   kylix (AM 1974.344; Koch-Harnack 1989; fig. 78; Johns 1982: b/w fig. 76): (interior) male symposium; male genitals as kylix foot (pp. 50, 95, 129).
50   kylix (Berlin 1798; Dover B634, illustrated; Reinsberg 1989: fig. 57): men have intercourse with youths and women (pp. 121, 124).
51   kylix (Florence 3897; Keuls 1985: fig. 71): men carry a phallus-float (p. phallus).
52   kylix (Florence; Vorberg 1965: 582–5): (A) (upper zone) battle; (lower zone) orgy, standing man with erection faces standing woman; woman stands on her head, her legs spread while a man mounts her from above; man and woman stand having oral sex ("69"); woman lies supine on elevated platform while man crouches below to have intercourse; woman stands supporting the other end of the elevated platform while man faces her; man about to have intercourse with woman "a tergo"; woman has facing 'equestrian' intercourse with a seated man; man and woman have "a tergo" intercourse; (B) (upper zone) family scene (man, woman, two children); orgy, two men have anal intercourse; man defecates into oinochoe; man urinates?, two men stand having anal "a tergo" intercourse while a third figure kneels to fellate the penetrated man;

man with an erection; two figures stand facing each other; more figures; (lower zone) centaurs (pp. 88, 113).

53 kylix (Villa Giulia 20776): two women share cloak (p. 33).

54 kylix sherds, Athens Acropolis (probably 1623a, 1648a, 1685a, 1669ab; Vorberg 1965: 4): orgy, (a) man and woman on a couch, three couples having "a tergo" intercourse; (b) man having frontal anal intercourse with supine man while woman lies supine below; (c) man and woman have facing equestrian intercourse (p. 88).

55 kylix, eye (Berlin; Furtwängler 2052; Vorberg 1965: 486–8): men and women having intercourse; male genitals as kylix foot (pp. 50, 95).

56 lekythos (Munich; ABV 469.71; Keuls 1985: fig. 161): man has "a tergo" intercourse with a doe (p. 19).

57 lekythos (Vatican 35605): two men share cloak (p. 33).

58 pyxis, tripod (Oxford MS; Shapiro 1981b: no. 62; Reinsberg 1989: fig. 96a–c): (B) two women share cloak; (C) intercrural intercourse (pp. 33, 124).

Cypriote archaic

59 bowl, Achna (E. Cyprus): line of dancing women, couples copulating (Tatton-Brown 1982: 76) (p. 120).

Attic red-figure

60 kylix, Akestorides Ptr. (once Basel market; Keuls 1985: fig. 64): (interior) Hyakinthos rides Apollo as swan, its neck inserted between his thighs (p. 58).

61 kylix, Apollodorus (Tarquinia; Beazley 1971: 333.9bis; Kilmer 1993: R207 color plate backwards; Keuls 1985: fig. 151; Mulas 1978: 53): (interior) nude woman seated on floor facing and touching standing nude woman's pubic area (with hair) as she holds a plemochoe (pp. 68, 119; **pl. 10**).

62 bell krater, Berlin Ptr. (Tarquinia RC 7456; ARV^2 206.126; Keuls 1985: fig. 33): Europa, Zeus as bull (p. 48).

63 kylix, Briseis Ptr. (AM 1967.305; Reinsberg 1989: fig. 64; Johns 1982: b/w fig. 109; Keuls 1985: fig. 158): (interior) man has "a tergo" intercourse with woman (pp. 88, 115).

64 kylix, Briseis Ptr. (Tarquinia 703; ARV^2 408.32): (AB) youth holds out leather bag to woman; (interior) cloaked youth stands in front of seated youth, leather bag hangs on wall above (p. 107).

65 kylix, Brygos Ptr (AM 1967.304; ARV^2 378.137; Reinsberg 1989: fig. 89; Keuls 1985: fig. 254; Johns 1982: b/w fig. 81): (interior) man with erection feels boy's genitalia (pp. 22, 115).

66 kylix, Brygos Ptr. (Berlin F2309; Reinsberg 1989: fig. 45): (interior) boy helps adult man vomiting (pp. 54–5).

67 kylix, Brygos Ptr. (Florence 3921; ARV^2 372.31; Vorberg 1965: 187–8; Reinsberg 1989: fig. 51; Keuls 1985: figs 167–170; Johns 1982: b/w figs 93, 108; Mulas 1978: 47–9): (A) orgy, man-woman-man group, man canes a kneeling woman, man carries woman while he has frontal intercourse with her while another man holds a lit oil lamp below her buttocks; (B) orgy, man carries woman while he has frontal intercourse with her, man spanks a kneeling woman with a sandal, man dances, man has "a tergo" intercourse with woman; (interior) flutegirl and nude man (pp. 82, 87–8, 111, 138).

68 hydria, CA Ptr. (Naples RC 144; Johns 1982: color pl. 32): symposium, male and female (pp. 82, 107, 129).

69 bell krater, Dinos Ptr. (BM F65; ARV^2 1154.55; Reinsberg 1989: fig. 119; Keuls 1985: fig. 263; Johns 1982: b/w fig. 9): (A) crowned youth about to have facing equestrian intercourse with seated youth; man and woman look on (pp. 28, 108).

70 bell krater, Dinos Ptr. (Harvard 9.1988; Paul 1993): Eros singes a standing bride's pubic hair (p. 55).

71 calyx krater, Dinos Ptr. (Bologna 300; ARV^2 1152.7; Scanlon 2002: 185, fig. 7–3): at a wash basin nude Atalanta prepares for the footrace; Aphrodite and Eros attend a nude Meilanion at the turning post (p. 86).

72 aryballos, Douris (NMA 15375; ARV^2 447.274; Robertson 1992: fig. 85): "Eros" and "Anteros" flank a running youth (pp. 9, 45).

73 kylix, Douris (Berlin 2289; ARV^2 435.95; Keuls 1985, figs 153, 232): (AB) komos of men, their

penises tied back on itself (p. 42); (interior) woman sits, bares leg (wool basket in front) to woman standing, holding aside the shoulder of her chiton (pp. 42, 68).

74   kylix, Douris (BMFA 1970.223; ARV^2 444.241; Kilmer 1993: R577; Johns 1982: b/w fig. 111): (interior) man has "a tergo" intercourse with woman; inscription "Hold still!" (p. 104).

75   kylix, Douris (BMFA 01.8029; Mulas 1978: 34 top): Eros and Ganymede (or Zephyros and Kyakinthos) have intercrural intercourse (p. 124).

76   kylix, Douris (BMFA 1970.233): (interior) man has "a tergo" intercourse with woman (p. 124).

77   kylix, Douris (NYMM 52.11.4; ARV^2 437.114; Reinsberg 1989: fig. 83, 102; Keuls 1985: fig. 266): (AB): men and youths; (interior) man offers seated youth a leather bag (p. 108).

78   kylix, Douris (Vatican 16545; ARV^2 437.116; Dover R637 illustrated): (A) man talks to cloaked youth, men and youths; (B) youths, boy, man (p. 40).

79   psykter, Douris (BM E768; ARV^2 446.262; Robertson 1992: fig. 86; Bérard *et al.* 1984: fig. 171 color; Johns 1982: b/w fig.on p. 12+13, fig. 2, color pl. 3): two satyrs with their penises tied back on itself; satyr pours wine into a kantharos balanced on a crouching satyr's erection; Hermes (pp. 20, 42, 88).

80   kylix, Douris, style (BMFA 13.94; ARV^2 1570.30; Koch-Harnack 1989: fig. 58; Kilmer 1993: R603; Richlin 1992a: fig. 3.6): (interior) Eros (erect) and Ganymede have intercrural intercourse (pp. 70, 137).

81   kylix, Epiktetos (BM E35; ARV^2 74.38; Kilmer 1993: R126): satyr has intercourse with an amphora (p. 118).

82   kylix, Epiktetos (Leningrad 14611; ARV^2 75.60; Kilmer 1993: R132; Keuls 1985: fig. 73; Reinsberg 1989: fig. 43): (interior) nude woman with two dildoes (pp. 26, 41).

83   kylix, Epiktetos (Naples RP 27669; Johns 1982: figs 67, 92; Keuls 1985: fig. 139): (A) satyr creeps up on nude woman; (B) nude woman and donkey with an erection (pp. 19, 118, 137).

84   kylix, Epiktetos (Orvieto Faine; ARV^{2}1705.79bis; Kilmer 1993: R134; Vorberg 1965: 109 top): (AB) preparation for heterosexual orgy (woman about to kneel on pillow; youth in front about to be fellated; youth with an erection); (interior) man has "a tergo" intercourse with woman (p. 88).

85   epinetron, Eretria Ptr. (NMA 1629; ARV^2 1250.34; Keuls 1985: fig. 234; Reinsberg 1989: fig. 24): (front, around plastic woman's head) Peleus abducts Thetis; A: marriage of Alkestis; B: marriage of Harmonia (pp. 19, 45, 137, 140).

86   lekythos, squat, Eretria Ptr (BMFA 95.48; ARV^2 1248.1688; Keuls 1985: fig. 1): Amazono-machy: Amazon aims spear at warrior's genitals (p. 141).

87   calyx krater, Euphronios (Berlin 2180; ARV^2 13.1; Boardman 1989: fig. 24.1; Keuls 1985: fig. 50; Neumann 1965: fig. 12): athlete tying up penis, youth points to discobolus's penis (p. 42).

88   psykter, Euphronios (Leningrad 644; ARV^2 16.15; Korshak 1987: fig. 19): symposium, three nude women (p. 129).

89   kylix, Euthymides (Berlin 2278 (ARV^2 21.1; Robertson 1992: fig. 46; Keuls 1985: fig. 54): (interior) Achilles and Patroklos (p. 2).

90   kylix, Euthymides (NYMM 56.171.61 (ARV^2 50.192; Kilmer 1993: R88): nude woman holds kylix with male genitals for kylix foot (pp. 50, 95).

91   amphora, Flying Angel Ptr. (Paris Petit Palais 307; ARV^2 279.2; Keuls 1985: fig. 77; Johns 1982: fig. 50; Kampen 1996: fig. 77): (A) nude woman carrying a bird with phallus head to a basket of dildoes; (B) nude woman points a dildo at her anus (p. 41).

92   kylix, Foundry Ptr. (Berlin 3757; Keuls 1985: fig. 149; Reinsberg 1989: fig. 46): (interior) nude woman urinating (p. 23).

93   kylix, Foundry Ptr.? (Tarquinia 5291; ARV^2 405.1): man (husband) takes woman (wife) by the wrist (p. 95 [**pl. 41**]).

94   kylix, Gales Ptr. (Yale University 163; ARV^2 36; Kilmer 1993: R82 illustrated; Reinsberg 1989: fig. 38): (interior) youth with erection fondles flutegirl (pp. 82, 129).

95   kylix, Hegesiboulos Ptr (NYMM 07.286.47; Reinsberg 1989: fig. 113): (AB) symposium, man feels the genitals of serving boy (pp. 125, 129).

96   pelike, Hephaistos Ptr (Rhodes 12887; ARV^2 1116.40; Keuls 1985: fig. 241): man with leather bag and woman with lyre (p. 28).

97   pelike, Hasselmann Ptr. (BM E819; ARV^2 1137.25; Kilmer 1993: R940 illustrated; Parke 1977: 100): woman and phallus-cakes (p. 40).

98 hydria, Hypsis (Rome, Torlonia 73; Boardman 1989: fig. 44): (shoulder) two women in diaphanous chitons fetch water at a fountain (p. 139).

99 amphora, Kleophrades Ptr. (Munich 2344; ARV^2 182.6, 1632; Beazley 1971: 340; Keuls 1985: fig. 333; Boardman, 1989: fig. 132.1): maenads dance, maenad aims thyrsos at satyr's testicles (p. 141).

100 hydria, Kleophrades Ptr. (Rouen 538.3; ARV^2 188.61; Keuls 1985: fig. 308; Osborne in Kampen 1996: fig. 32; Kilmer 1993: R318): (shoulder) satyr with an erection, satyr with an erection bending over a sleeping maenad (pp. 72, 117–18).

101 bell krater, Louvre G521 Ptr (Vatican 9098; ARV^2 1441.3): symposium, youths and flutegirl (pp. 82, 119 [pl. 11]).

102 hydria, Leningrad Ptr (Milan private coll.; ARV^2 571.73; Venit 1988): Nikai crown youths potting; at extreme right, woman painting/chasing pot (p. 141).

103 hydria, Leningrad Ptr (Warsaw 142290; Reinsberg 1989: fig. 9): women bathe the nude groom (p. 18).

104 kylix, Makron (Toledo): youth and man offer leather bags to women (p. 107 [pl. 5]).

105 kylix, Makron (Munich 2654; ARV^2 462.47; Brendel 1970: fig. 9; Mulas 1978: 22–3; Johns 1982: color pl. 20; Keuls 1985: fig. 310): maenad aims thyrsos at satyr's testicles (p. 141).

106 kylix, Makron (Munich 2657; Johns 1982: b/w fig. 69): (interior) bearded man with extra beard and a fall of hair, wears a broad belt that supports a satyr tail and phallus (p. 118).

107 hydria, Meidias Ptr. (BM E224; Sutton 1992: 30–31 fig. 1.12): (upper zone) Rape of the Leukippidae; (lower zone) Judgment of Paris (pp. 69, 137).

108 kantharos, Nikosthenes Ptr. (BMFA 95.61; ARV^2 132; Boardman 1974: fig. 99.1; Mulas 1978: 45; Reinsberg 1989: fig. 49): (A) youth prepares to have reverse equestrian intercourse with another youth; youth prepares to insert double-ended dildo into woman's anus as she fellates youth, a second double-ended dildo hangs on the wall above; (B) youth pushes woman, woman flees, youth pushes woman (pp. 41, 88).

109 kylix, Nikosthenes Ptr., circle (Berlin 1964.4; ARV^2 1700; Brendel 1970: fig. 20; Reinsberg 1989: fig. 79; Keuls 1985: fig. 262; Stewart 1997: 188 fig. 122; Johns 1982: fig. 71): (A) orgy, satyr fellates satyr, satyr has anal intercourse with satyr, satyr masturbates; (B) Herakles and Apollo struggle for the tripod; (interior) Ares sits (pp. 73, 88, 117–18).

110 kylix, Nikosthenes Ptr. (Turin 4117; Dover R243, illustrated; Reinsberg 1989: fig. 116): (AB) two nude youths bend over and touch bottoms, while a third youth stands in back and puts his erect penis between them (p. 88).

111 kylix, Nikosthenes Ptr., circle (BMFA 08.30a; Keuls 1985: fig. 74): (interior) woman about to have frontal equestrian intercourse with satyr, also holding a double-ended dildo (pp. 41, 118).

112 kylix, Oltos (once Berlin; ARV^2 66.121; Kilmer 1993: R114; Keuls 1985: fig. 75; Reinsberg 1989: fig. 44; Stewart 1997: fig. 99): (AB) on a single couch, man has "a tergo" intercourse with woman, woman has facing equestrian intercourse with man; (interior) nude woman with auloi stradles an amphora (pp. 82, 86, 88).

113 kylix, Onesimos (BMFA 65.873; Beazley 1971 360; Kilmer 1993: R463): (interior) man accosts youth; inscriptions "let me," "won't you stop?" (p. 104).

114 kylix, Onesimos (J. Paul Getty 86.AE.161; Robertson 1992: fig. 33): (AB) Ajax accosts nude Cassandra (pp. 86, 134, 137).

115 kylix, Onesimos, manner (Harvard; ARV^2 331.20; Beazley 1971: 361): woman holds lighted oil lamp to vagina, to singe herself (p. 55).

116 aryballos, Onesimos imitator (BMFA 98.879; ARV^2 1646): youth and cloaked boy, youths, hunting dog (p. 40).

117 lekythos, Ptr. of London E342 (Univ. of Arkansas; Shapiro 1981b: no. 62): youth offers leather bag to woman (p. 107).

118 bell krater, Pan Ptr. (BMFA 10.185; ARV^2 550.1; Robertson 1992: fig. 148; Keuls 1985: fig. 331): Pan attacks Daphnis (pp. 19, 85).

119 column krater, Pan Ptr. (Berlin, Staatliche Museen 3206; Keuls 1985: frontispiece; Johns 1982: b/w fig. 120): nude woman carries colossal phallus (p. 95).

120 pelike, Pan Ptr. (NMA 9683; ARV^2 554.82; Keuls 1985: fig. 49): Herakles attacks circumcised Egyptians (p. 46).

121 kylix, Peithinos (Berlin, Charlottenburg 2279; ARV² 115.2; Reinsberg 1989: fig. 117; Keuls 1985: figs 37, 196, 197; Johns 1982: fig. 82; Mulas 1978: 40; Licht 1925–8: 3, fig. on p. 148): (A) three youths barter with women; (B) youth stands dejected; three youths embrace boys; man embraces youth; (interior) Thetis as a lion attacks Peleus (pp. 28, 115, 137; pl. 13).

122 kylix, Pedieus Ptr. (Louvre G13; ARV² 86.a; Reinsberg 1989: fig. 50; Keuls 1985: fig. 166; Brendel 1970: fig. 17; Johns 1982: b/w fig. 107; Vorberg 1965: 189–90, and 640; Clarke 2003: fig. 15): (A) orgy, youth has "a tergo" intercourse with woman on table while she fellates another youth, woman fellates youth, youth confronts dog; (B) orgy, youth has "a tergo" intercourse with woman, youth grabs woman, woman fellates youth; (interior) youth embraces female lyrist (pp. 8, 88, 107).

123 volute krater fragment, Peleus Ptr. (ARV² 1039.9; Scanlon 2002: 190, fig. 7–7): Atalanta wrestles "Hippomenes" (pp. 14, 129).

124 kylix, Penthesileia Ptr. (Munich 2688; ARV² 879.1; Robertson 1992: fig. 167; Keuls 1985: figs 28, 29): (interior) Achilles kills Penthesileia (pp. 62, 134).

125 kylix, Penthesileia Ptr. (Philadelphia L637–1; ARV² 880.3; Keuls 1985: fig. 56): (interior) youth, his penis tied back on itself, exposes himself to a maiden (p. 42).

126 kylikes, Penthesileia Workshop (once Munich [ARV² 904.71], Bologna 420 [ARV² 904.72]): (AB) Eros pursues youth; (interior) athlete tying up penis (p. 42).

127 hydria, Phintias (BM E159; ARV² 24.9; Robertson 1992: fig. 21): (body) man ogles youths at fountain; (shoulder) symposium, man and youth (pp. 129, 139).

128 hydria, Phintias (Munich 2421; ARV² 23.7; Keuls 1985: figs 133, 134; Boardman 1975: fig. 38; Reinsberg 1989: fig. 61; Robertson 1992: fig. 20): (body) youth at music lesson; (shoulder) symposium, two women (p. 129).

129 kylix, Phintias (J. Paul Getty 82.AE.31; ARV² 1620.12bis; Kilmer 1993: R47.1): (A) nude woman masturbates youth; (B) youth masturbates in presence of older nude woman (p. 78).

130 hydria, Pig Ptr. (Detroit 63.13; Beazley 1971: 389.40; Moon 1979: no. 95; Keuls 1985: fig. 213;): (shoulder) men and women at fountain (p. 139).

131 kylix, Pistoxenos Ptr (Zimmerman 1980; Robertson 1992: 157): Thracian women kill Orpheus (p. 89).

132 stamnos, Polygnotos Workshop (Louvre C9682; Koch-Harnack 1989: fig. 99; Johns 1982: b/w fig. 110; Reinsberg 1989: fig. 78): (A) man and youth hold woman aloft; man has frontal intercourse with her while the youth masturbates; (B) two men with erections (one with a sandal) accost flutegirl (pp. 78, 82, 88, 111).

133 hydria, Polygnotos Group (NMA 1260; ARV² 1060.145; Beazley 1971: 445; Edmonds 1922): Nike crowns Sappho reading a scroll: "Gods! Winged words, I begin, airy words but pleasant" (p. 116).

134 alabastron, Psiax (Odessa; Richter 1934) nude Greek warrior giving "the finger" to Persian (looking down his arrow at the Greek) (p. 113).

135 kantharos, Q Ptr. (BMFA 95.36; ARV² 381.182; Keuls 1985: figs 31, 32, 314; Richlin 1992a: fig. 3.3; Robertson 1992: fig. 271): (A) Zeus and woman; (B) Zeus and Ganymede; (interior) nude maenad wears satyr's loin-cloth with an erection (p. 36).

136 stamnos, Siren Ptr. (New York, Shelby White and Leon Levy Coll.; Beazley Archives 5343; Scanlon 2002: figs 7–9): partially draped man fondles the breast of nude woman bathing (pp. 18, 25).

137 plastic vase (Amazon on horse), Sotades, Meroë (BMFA 21.2286; Vermeule 1963: 113, pl. 94; Beazley Archives 209548): Amazonomachy (p. 6).

138 krater, Telos Ptr. (Budapest, private coll.; ARV² 1426.27; Keuls 1985: fig. 138): symposium, pairs of women (p. 129).

139 kylix, Thalia Ptr. (Berlin 3251+Florence I B 49; Krenkel 1981: pls 1 and 2; Brendel 1970: fig. 13; I: Reinsberg 1989: fig. 52; Johns 1982: b/w fig. 117; Kilmer 1993: R192 illustrated; Vorberg 1965: 538): (AB) man lifts woman up for "a tergo" anal intercourse, youth performs cunnilingus on standing woman, youth and woman dance, woman leads man, man and woman dance, woman; (interior) below a couch, woman lies masturbating; on the couch, man has frontal intercourse with woman, while a second woman spanks him with a sandal; at left, youth masturbates (pp. 38, 78, 88, 107, 111).

140 kylix, Triptolemos Ptr. (Tarquinia; ARV² 367.94; Keuls 1985: fig. 145; Johns 1982: b/w fig. 106; Mulas 1978: 57): (interior) balding man has frontal intercourse with woman (p. 54).

141 pelike, Truro Ptr. (Taranto; Keuls 1985: fig. 81): seated woman touches the breast of standing woman (slave?) (pp. 25, 125).

142 pyxis, Washing Ptr. (Würzburg 541; ARV² 1133.196; Robertson 1992: figs 235 and 236): preparing the bride; two Erotes wrestle (p. 9).

143 loutrophoros (BMFA 03.802; Sutton 1992: fig. 1.10) groom takes the bride by the wrist (p. 74).

144 oinochoe fragment (BMFA 98.936; Beazley Archives 1337; ca. 425–375 BCE): "Tyrannicides" (p. 12).

145 A group of vases, "Anacreontic" or "Booners" (Boardman and Kurtz 1986): symposium, effeminate men (p. 8).

146 amphora (Leningrad B1555; Reinsberg 1989: fig. 71): youth hands cloaked woman a leather bag, her hand out to receive it (pp. 40, 107).

147 disk (NMA: Vorberg 1965: 131): phallus bird with testicles surrounded by three vulvae (p. 26).

148 hydria (Villa Giulia 50635): man offers youth a hare (p. 70; pl. 3).

149 hydria (Würzburg 530; Keuls 1985: fig. 163): (shoulder) boy with sandal markings, kneeling nude woman, youth reclining (p. 86).

150 hydria (Madrid 11130; Scanlon 2002: fig. 7–2): Aphrodite?, Meilanion, "apples," Atalanta, her father Schoineus (p. 14).

151 jug (private collection; Reinsberg 1989: fig. 98; Keuls 1985: fig. 261): nude Greek holds erect penis and approaches Persian bending over; inscription below spout, "I am Eurymedon; I stand bent over" ("Eurumédôn eimí kúbade ésteka") (p. 124).

152 kylix (Basel Kä 415; Keuls 1985: figs 143, 144; Reinsberg 1989: fig. 34): (A) symposium, men and nude women; (B) youth with nude woman and man with nude woman (pp. 107, 129).

153 kylix (once Basel market; Keuls 1985: fig. 148): (interior) middle age hetaira looking at herself in a mirror (pp. 65, 107).

154 kylix (Louvre; Vorberg 1965: 447): (interior) boy holds spoon up to the penis of a youth whose arms are flung out (to catch his semen?) (p. 88).

155 kylix (Munich 2410 (Reinsberg 1989: fig. 34): symposium, two men on a couch (p. 129).

156 kylix (NYMM; Reinsberg 1989: fig. 32): symposium, men and women on couches (pp. 107, 129).

157 kylix (Toledo 64.126; Moon 1979: no. 101; Keuls 1985: fig. 51): (AB) boys and men; (interior) lyre-player youth, his penis tied back on itself, and dancing man (p. 42).

158 kylix (Villa Giulia 50404; ARV² 1565; Keuls 1985: fig. 78; Johns 1982: b/w fig. 27): (AB) komos; (interior) two women erect phallus (p. 95; pl. 22).

159 pelike (Mykonos; Reinsberg 1989: fig. 96; Dover R502): intercrural intercourse, man and youth holding a hare and leashed dog (p. 8; pl. 7).

160 pyxis (NYMM 1972.118.148; Sutton 1992: fig. 1.9): Eros pours water over nude bride (pp. 11, 18).

Attic white-ground

161 "bobbin" (votive inyx), Penthesileia Ptr. (NYMM 28.167; ARV² 890.175; Robertson 1992: fig. 172; Shapiro 1985, 1992: fig. 3.10): (A) Eros (or Zephyros) grabs youth (or Hyakinthos); (B) Eros crowns boy victor (pp. 45, 58, 72).

162 cup, stemless (Palermo 2132b), Selinus: three youths stand, two hold leather bags (p. 108 [fig. 6]).

163 kylix fragment, Brauron (Keuls 1985: fig. 282): woman at fountain, wearing a diaphanous chiton through which her pubic hair is visible (p. 55).

164 kylix (Gotha 48; ARV² 20; Reinsberg 1989: fig. 107): (interior) youth embraces boy, dog jumps at caged hare (p. 8).

165 lekythos, Douris (Cleveland 66.114; Moon 1979: no. 104; Scanlon 2002: fig. 7–1): Atalanta runs with Eros, Pothos, and Himeros? (p. 14).

166 lekythos, Eretria Ptr. (NYMM 31.11.13; ARV² 1248.9; slide; Robertson 1992: figs 239, 240): Amazonomachy; Achilles and Patroklos (p. 2).

South Italian red-figure

167 oinochoe (J. Paul Getty 72.AE.128; Keuls 1985: fig. 275): Kallisto changing into a bear (p. 64).

168 fragment (private collection; Keuls 1985: fig. 276): Kallisto changing into a bear (p. 64).

Hellenistic

Coins

169 Lesbos (Mytilene, Old Samos Museum; 250–200 BCE): obverse: head of Sappho to right; reverse: lyre with MYT(ILENE) (p. 116).

Gem

170 agate ringstone (Leiden Coin Cabinet 1648; Clarke 2003: fig. 62): two men look at each other while having reclining anal intercourse (the penetrated man with erection); inscription: "Panther [cf. 188], drink, live in luxury, embrace. One must die for time is short. Live well, Greek!" (p. 108)

Sculpture

Marble statues
171 "Laocoön" (Vatican; early 2nd c.; Lullies and Hirmer 1960: pls 262–3): snakes entwine around Laocoön, priest of Poseidon at Troy, and his two sons (pp. 21, 23).
172 Aphrodite, Pan, and Eros, Delos (NMA): Pan (no erection) tugs at Aphrodite; she threatens him with a sandal; Eros tugs at Pan's horn (p. 21; **pl. 29**).
173 "Old Fisherman" (2nd c.?; Stewart 1990: pl. 755) (pp. 21, 119).
174 "Old Woman" with jug (2nd c.?; Stewart 1990: pls 753–4) (pp. 21, 107).
175 hermaphrodite reclining on a (restored) couch (Rome, Altemps [Brendel 1970: fig. 32]; other copies in the Louvre MA 231 [Johns 1982: b/w fig. 85; Clarke 2003: figs 73 and 74] and NMA [Licht 1925–8: 3, 179]) (pp. 56, 119; **pls 35, 36**).
176 Pan, Athens, Olympieion (NMA; 4th c./Hellenistic; Karouzou 1968: 93, no. 683): seated, his penis tied back on itself (p. 42; **pl. 15**).
177 phalloi, Delos, sanctuary of Dionysos (Brendel 1970: fig. 6; Mulas 1978: 24–5; Johns 1982: b/w fig. 1) (p. 95).

Marble relief
178 altar to Zeus, Pergamum (Berlin, Pergamum; mid-2nd c.; Schmidt 1962): gigantomachy (p. 23).
179 "Visit to the Poet," in several copies (Johns 1982: color pl. 22: Naples RP 6713): (L) man and woman recline on couch, as if she had been fellating him; (R) drunken Dionysus supported by a satyr leads a procession of satyrs (and perhaps one or two maenads) (p. 104).

Terracotta
180 man and woman recline on a couch, kissing (St Germaine-en-Laye 72474; 2nd c. CE; Johns 1982: fig. 100) (pp. 8, 64).

Vessels

181 phallus-shaped drinking vessel (Pella) (pp. 34, 50; **pl. 21**).

Mould-made bowls (pp. 82, 119, 121)
182 Arezzo Museo Civico (Licht 1925–8: 3, 170): man and woman have frontal intercourse ($\approx$ 186).
183 Bregenze 13.1439 (Clarke 2003: fig. 93): man and woman have frontal intercourse; man has "a tergo" anal intercourse with another man.
184 Berlin and Dresden (Licht 1925–8: 3, 194): man and woman have "a tergo" intercourse reclining.

185 Mytilene, New Mytilene Museum: 6 (originally?) woman has facing equestrian intercourse with man, man and woman have facing intercourse; perhaps the same mould as 186.

186 Mytilene, Old Mytilene Museum 24219: woman has facing equestrian intercourse with man; man and woman have facing intercourse reclining; perhaps the same mould as 185.

187 Pegamum fragments (Schäfer 1968): 1. facing intercourse: E22–23, E28; 2. facing intercourse: E25–27, E 30, E 31 (mould); 3. "a tergo" intercourse: E19+E20, E21; 4. "a tergo" intercourse reclining: E48+49, E50, E51, E52; 5. facing equestrian intercourse: E32+E33, E34, E35+36, E38 (appliqué); 6. facing equestrian intercourse: E38, E39, E42; 7. reverse equestrian intercourse: E44, E45+46; 8. woman (nude) approaches: E53, E55 ≈ 192.i and 193.3.

188 Pella (Akamates 1993: no. 322): 1. "a tergo" intercourse reclining: "be direct!"; 2. man points spear at woman; "pantheress" (sexual characterization? cf. 170); 3. facing equestrian intercourse: "I'm close" ≈ 189.3; 4. man and woman nude, he with erection, embrace on the floor: "come on, bitch"; 5. man on stool, she climbs up: "come on up" ≈ 192.g (Fig. 17; pl. 26).

189 Pella (Akamates 1993: no. 323): 1. man and woman have facing intercourse: "come on"; 2. man and woman have "a tergo" intercourse: "find the hole!"; 3. woman has facing equestrian intercourse with man (his arm across his head): "I'm close" ≈ 188.3; 4. man striding left to previous couple: "I've got you"; 5. man on stool, woman about to climb up for facing equestrian intercourse: "allow me"; 6. man sits on couch, woman reclines: "slowly"; 7. "a tergo" intercourse kneeling: "come on."

190 Macedonia (Sinn 1979: MB 64 and 65): "cinaedi" in a grist-mill: L-R: man ("mill owner"), man pressing a press, man with club, man pulling another (with erection?) away ("cinaedi"), man tied to a pole ("punished"), nude man squatting and reaching out to touch a mule's erection, man with club, man at a basin, man pressing a press ("mill pressers") (p. 31).

191 Macedonia (Sinn 1979: MB 66): man tied to pole, another is being beaten ("cinaedus, adulterer"), woman has facing equestrian intercourse with seated man = 192.g (p. 31).

192 Macedonia (Sinn 1979: MB 67): a. man runs right (cf. 189.4); b. facing equestrian intercourse = MB 69; c. man strides right; d. "a tergo" intercourse kneeling 193.6; e. flutegirl; f. facing intercourse on altar = 193.7; g. man on stool = 191 ≈ 188.5 68; h. man to left; i. woman approaches, man reclines = 187.8, 193.3.

193 Peyrefitte Coll. (Siebert 1984); 1. Eros and Pysche embrace: "bravo, Psyche" (p. 112); 2. man and woman have facing intercourse: "hold me close"?; 3. woman approaches, man reclines: "I'm beautiful" = 187.8 and 192.i; 4. man and woman dance, woman plays the sambuke: "what noise the sambuke makes"; 5. man with erection approaches woman on stool: "just what I want"; 6. man and woman have "a tergo" intercourse (192.d): "come on!"; 7. man and woman have facing intercourse: "you're expert" = 192.f; 8. man and woman have "a tergo" intercourse: "push it in when you want."

Etruscan

Sculpture

194 Terracotta sarcophagus (Villa Giulia; 6th c. BCE; Goldschneider 1941: 27 left figure, pls 10–13): couch on which a husband and wife recline together (**pl. 1**).

195 Marble sarcophagus lid (BMFA 81.145; 4th c.; Vermeule 1963: 201 no. 184): man and woman recline on bed (p. 57; **pl. 2**).

Tomb paintings

Chiusi

196 della Scimmia (ca. 480/470 BC; Steingräber 1985: no. 25): (rear wall) bearded boxers, each with a thong around the hips to which, or with which, the penis is tied (p. 42).

Tarquinia

197 4260 (early 5th c. BCE; Steingräber 1985: cat. 156; Markussen 1979: no. 159): (rear wall), a symposium of a man and woman in the pediment, banquet scene in the main panel. Right and left walls: "remains of erotic scenes with groups of two and three figures" (pp. 112, 129).

198 delle Bighe (also Stackelberg; early 5th c.; Steingräber 1985: cat. 47; Markussen 1979: no. 50): athletes; (at the rear corners) stands of spectators, below which recline nude and clothed youths and men, among whom two pairs of youths have "a tergo" anal intercourse and kiss (pp. 46, 73, 107).

199 della Fustigazione (Tomba 1701; Caning; early 5th c.; Steingräber 1985: cat. 67): (right wall) nude bearded man canes woman while he has "a tergo" intercourse with her while she fellates a nude youth; at right, nude youth holds a whip, woman cowers, a nude man with whip (pp. 50, 88, 11).

200 delle Leonesse, (ca. 520 BCE; Steingräber 1985: cat. 77; Marcadé 1965: pl. on p. 27): (rear wall), at right, woman in a transparent chiton plays castanets, makes the sign of the "horns," and dances with blond nude youth (p. 113).

201 dei Tori (ca. 530 BCE; Steingräber 1985: cat. 120; Markussen 1979: no. 168; Marcadé 1965: pl. on p. 19; Brendel 1970: fig. 5): (back wall frieze) man stands to have facing vaginal intercourse with woman supine on the back of a second man kneeling; man stands to have "a tergo" intercourse with a person (painted a light brown but no breasts are visible); (below) Achilles ambushes Polyxena and Troilos at the fountain (pp. 88, 139).

Vase paintings

202 amphora (Berlin 1684; Licht 1925–8, 3: fig. on p. 73): male aulete with erection and having an orgasm (pp. 82, 88).

203 amphora (Corneto; Vorberg 1965: 328): satyr masturbates (pp. 78, 118).

204 amphora (Naples 27670; Marcadé 1962: pl. on p. 39C; Vorberg 1965: 462–3): two youths have "a tergo" anal intercourse, each with his right arm outstretched (pp. 46, 88, 107, 124).

205 oinochoe, "Tragliatella" (Small 1986; Mulas 1978: 35–7): man and woman atop a bench (?) have facing vaginal intercourse; below the bench, man and woman (?) have facing anal (?) intercourse; maze labeled "truia"; two men with shields on horseback; nude man with staff; seven warriors; man, daughter, wife; woman at cippi. The vase is probably funerary: man and daughter bid farewell to the deceased woman, in whose honor warriors are depicted as dancing and men on horseback are depicted as having completed the *Troiae lusus* (a maze-like set of movements) (pp. 88, 124).

Roman

Coins

206 Lesbos (1st–3rd c. CE; (Wroth 1894: no. 169; Bodenstedt 1981): (p. 116).

Furniture

207 Bronze tripod censor, Pompeii, the Praedia of Julia Felix (II.4.2; Naples 27874; De Caro 2000: fig. on p. 33; Marcadé 1965: pl. on p. 115): three ithyphallic satyrs, each with a single leg, support the bowl, each with hand extended palm out (pp. 117–18).

Glass vessels

208 cameo unguentarium, Ostippo, Spain (Clarke 2003: figs 57–9): man about to have anal intercourse with reclining woman; man and youth have "a tergo" anal intercourse reclining (repeated on a color glass fragment, BM) (pp. 108, 119).

209 cameo fragment (NYMM 81.10.349; Clarke 2003: fig. 89): man and woman have "a tergo" intercourse (pp. 119, 124).

Jewelry

Amulets
210 phalloi, *mano fica* (Johns 1982: b/w figs 45, 53, 55–7, color pl. 10; Marcadé 1965: pl. on p. 101A; De Caro 2000: fig. on p. 39) (pp. 19, 72, 95).

Cameo
211 sardonyx (Naples 25847; De Caro 2000: fig. on p. 11): (tabella) woman prepares for reverse equestrian intercourse with man (pp. 118, 130).

Lamps (in general: pp. 66, 104, 119, 121)

Erotic
212 plastic, dwarf riding phallus, Arles (FAN.91.00.2067; Clarke 2003: fig. 105) (p. 42).
213 plastic, handle = vagina (BM Q1025; Johns 1982: b/w fig. 58) (p. 26).

Bestiality
214 discus (BM Q871; Johns 1982: fig. on p. 97, fig. 88): Leda and swan (pp. 47, 67).
215 discus (BM Q900; Johns 1982: b/w fig. 91): pygmy negro woman sits on dildo on top of crocodile (pp. 19, 41, 47).
216 discus (Vorberg 1965: 95 lower left, and 601): crocodile mounts pygmy (p. 19).
217 discus, Athens (BM Q3271; Bailey 1975): horse having frontal intercourse with woman (pp. 19, 118).
218 discus, Cyprus (BM Q2578; Bailey 1975): man has frontal intercourse with woman on a horse; below, woman has frontal intercourse with the horse (p. 19).

Oral-genital
219 handle, Ephesos (Berlin 7597.96; Vorberg 1965: 129): man performs cunnilingus (p. 38).
220 discus (Munich [Vorberg 1965: 185; Brendel 1970: fig. 44] and Nicosia [Johns 1982: b/w fig. 116 = Marcadé 1962: 59, "Herakleion"; Clarke 2003: fig. 86]): man performs cunnilingus while woman fellates him (pp. 38, 113).
221 discus, Pompeii (Naples RP 27864; Reinsberg 1989: fig. 83; Johns 1982: b/w fig. 115; Marcadé 1965: pl. on p. 102, top; Clarke 2003: fig. 85): woman fellates man (p. 50).
222 discus (Vorberg 1965: 184): woman fellates man (p. 88).
223 discus (Vorberg 1965: 186): orgy, man-woman-man group (p. 88).

Intercourse
224 discus (Vorberg 1965: 410): man with dildo kneels before woman for facing intercourse (p. 41).
225 discus, Athens, Cave of Pan (NMA): man has "a tergo" intercourse with woman (p. 124; **pl. 23**).
226 discus, Sparta (Sparta): woman has facing equestrian intercourse with man (p. 124; **pl. 24**).
227 discus, Messene (Messene): woman has reverse equestrian intercourse with man (p. 124; **pl. 25**).

Masturbation
228 discus (Rome and Brussels; Vorberg 1965: 230 top): old philosopher masturbates (pp. 78, 87–8).

Orgy
229 late discus, Kavousi (HM; Clarke 2003: fig. 99): man holds woman up for frontal intercourse while another man stands in back for "a tergo" anal intercourse (p. 88).

Mirror

230 Rome (Capitoline; 1st c. CE; Mulas 1978: 72/3; Johns 1982: fig. on p. 116, color pl. 35; Richlin 1992a: fig. 7.10 [exterior]; Boardman and LaRocca 1975: 162–63; Clarke 2003: fig. 18): (cover) man and woman have "a tergo" intercourse, reclining (cf. 7). Above, an open tabella (man and woman having "a tergo" intercourse) (pp. 8, 104, 118, 124, 130).

Mosaics

Pompeii

231 House of Menander (I.10.4; Bragantini *et al.* 1981–92): negro with erection carries two phallic water pitchers; below, abstract vagina (pp. 26, 46).

232 (Naples; Marcadé 1965: pl. on p. 40): Nilotic scene with three boats, each with a man having intercourse with woman (two frontal, one "a tergo") (p. 88).

Elsewhere

233 Antioch, Syria (Antioch; Cimok 2000: pl. xxx): man offers amorini for sale (p. 45).

234 El Jem A16, Tunisia (El Jem): Nilotic scenes, pygmies and cranes (p. 46; **pl. 14**).

235 Sousse, Tunisia (Sousse): Zeus as eagle abducts Ganymede (p. 52; **pl. 27**).

236 Maktar, Tunisia (Maktar): Venus adjusts her sandal (p. 11; **pl. 31**).

237 El Jem, House of Venus, Tunisia (Sousse): Venus arranges her hair (p. 11; **pl. 32**).

238 El Jem, Tunisia (El Jem): amorini at the vintage (pp. 45, 99; **pl. 34**).

239 Antioch, House of the Evil Eye, Syria (ca. 150 CE; Clarke 2003: 76): dwarf with large phallus plays an aulos; eye stabbed by a knife and trident and attacked by animals; inscription, "same to you" (pp. 82, 95).

240 Ostia, House of Jupiter the Thunderer (Clarke 2003: fig. 75; Johns 1982: b/w fig. 46), entrance: phallus (p. 95; **pl. 19**).

241 Sousse, Tunisia: phallus flanked by two vaginas; inscription: "O favor!" (Sousse Mus.; Marcadé 1965: pl. on p. 105A) (p. 26; **pl. 20**).

Sculpture

Limestone/marble

In the round

242 Augustus, Primaporta (Vatican; Kleiner 1992: fig. 42) (p. 23).

243 Nero with Polykleitan body (Thessaloniki) (pp. 21, 36, 83, 86; **pl. 42**).

244 women with Aphrodite body (d'Ambra 1996: figs 92–5) (p. 21).

245 Pan has frontal intercourse with she-goat, Herculaneum, Villa of the Papyri (Naples RP 27709; 2nd c. BCE; De Caro 2000: fig. on p. 25; Brendel 1970: fig. 8; Johns 1982: color pl. 1; Marcadé 1965: pl. on p. 114; Clarke 2003: fig. 8) (pp. 19, 119).

246 Antinoös as Herakles (Chalkis) (pp. 10, 53; **pl. 16**).

247 Priapus, House of Vettii, room x (Clarke 2003: figs 2 and 72) (pp. 95, 101, 105).

248 Venus adjusts her sandal, Pompeii, II.4.6, tablinum (Naples 152798; De Caro 2000: fig. on p. 34; Varone 2001a: pl. 6) (p. 99).

Reliefs

249 altar, Aquilea (Aquilea; Trajanic; Olender 1983: pl. 1 after p. 164): Aphrodite recoils, looking at infant Priapus (pp. 45, 95).

250 sarcophagus (Naples RP 27710; 2nd c. CE; Johns 1982: b/w figs 31, 65; color pl. 23): ithyphallic herm; female Pan reaches back to insert the herm's phallus; Ariadnê sleeps; two fauns support drunk Dionysus; male ithyphallic Pan approaches female Pan, a curtain behind draped on trees (p. 104).

251 relief (Naples 27713; De Caro 2000: fig. on p. 37): goose has intercourse with hen (p. 8).

252 relief (Naples 6688; De Caro 2000: fig. on p. 27): "Alcibiades" and courtesans (p. 5).

Bronzes

Statuettes
253 Ethiopian lyre-player with long, infibulated penis (Rome, Museo Kircheriano: Holländer 1912: fig. 248) (p. 24).
254 hermaphrodite (Terme) (p. 56).
255 Priapus (Naples 27717 [Johns 1982: b/w fig. 33], 27729 [De Caro 2000: fig. on p. 32], BM 1824.4–71.4 [Johns 1982: b/w fig. 22]) (p. 105).

Tintinabula
256 hermaphrodite rides a phallus-bat (Vorberg 1965: 222) (pp. 56, 95).
257 gladiators (BN 1856.12–26.1086 [Johns 1982: color pl. 13, right], Naples 27853 [De Caro 2000: fig. on p. 35]) (p. 95).
258 Mercuries (Naples RP 27854 and 27855; Johns 1982: b/w figs 39 and 54; Marcadé 1965: pl. on p. 56) (pp. 56, 95).
259 phallus with lion/dog hindlegs (BM 1856.12–26.1086; Johns 1982: color pl. 13, left; Clarke 2003: figs 7, 63) (p. 95).
260 phalloi, winged, with lion/dog hindlegs (Naples [Marcadé 1965: pl. on p. 93 left and right], Trier G92 [Brendel 1970: fig. 1; Johns 1982: b/w fig. 52]) (p. 95).
261 bird-phallus-quadruped (Naples 27839 and 27840; De Caro 2000: fig. on p. 36) (p. 95).

Terracottas
262 woman bust (Vorberg 1965: 485): phallus between the breasts (pp. 14, 41, 51).
263 women displaying their genitals, Egypt (Johns 1982: 75) (p. 26).
264 Baubo (Grandjouan 1961: 24) (p. 18).
265 Pan-like figure with exaggerated phallus, Pompeii (Naples RP 27732; Johns 1982: b/w fig. 34) (p. 95).
266 pregnant woman (Palestrina) (p. 105).
267 uterus (Wilcox Collection, University of Kansas) (p. 27; **pl. 17**).
268 vulva (Città Castellana) (26; **pl. 18**).

Signs (shop, street)

Pompeii
269 painted shop, IX.12.6, Chaste Lovers, bakery (De Caro 2000: fig. on p. 36; Varone 2001a: pl. 19; Clarke 2003: fig. 71): bearded Mercury with large phallus holds a leather bag (pp. 56, 95).
270 stone relief phalloi (p. 95)
    street signs: I.20.5 (Johns 1982: color pl. 12), IX.5
    shop signs: VI.14.33 (taberna), VII.1.36 (bakery), VII.2.32/33 (caupona), VII.3.22/23, VII.4.27, VII.4.27, IX.1.14, IX.7.2 (fullery: Clarke 2003: fig. 66)
    bakeries, over ovens: VI.9.17–21 (Clarke 2003: figs 68 and 69), VII.1.36, IX.1.3/33,
    street pavers: VII.13 (Clarke 2003: fig. on p. 7, and fig. 64).

Leptis Magna
271 street sign (Johns 1982: b/w fig. 3): phallus (p. 95).
272 street sign (Johns 1982: b/w fig. 77): centaur with exaggerated phallus, phallus-nose, and apotropaic motifs (snake, bird, eye, scorpion); inscription "MAL E R" (p. 95).
273 street sign (Johns 1982: b/w fig. 123): winged phallus with lion/dog hindlegs, phallus-tail; individual apotropaic motifs (clenched hand and eye) (pp. 95, 113).

Tokens and gaming pieces (pp. 88, 119, 121)

274 (Vorberg 1965: 386–7)
    two figures have facing intercourse
        386 top left, rev. XIII and 386 middle left, rev. III; 387 first row left, rev. XIIII
    two figures having facing intercourse reclining

387 second row right, rev. VIII
two figures having "a tergo" intercourse
386 middle right, rev. II; 386 bottom left, rev. VII?; 386 bottom right, rev. VII?;
387 first row right, rev. VII?; 387 first row left, rev. I
two figures having facing equestrian intercourse
387 third row right): (rev. II)
two figures having reverse equestrian intercourse
387 second row left, rev. XIII
387 fourth row left, rev. XIII
man-woman-man group
387 third row left, rev. VIIII
275 AM (Johns 1982: b/w fig. 122, left): woman (?) fellates man (pp. 50, 119, 221).

Vessels

Terracotta

Vessels
276 Knidian jugs (late 1st–2nd c. CE; Princeton 56.104: Johns 1982: b/w fig. 104; Berlin: Brendel 1970: figs 34–36): male negro head for spout: in relief, three couples have frontal intercourse; woman has reverse equestrian intercourse with man (p. 46).

Mould-made bowls (pp. 82, 119, 121)
277 Arretine vase moulds (AM 1966.252, NYMM [Brendel 1970: fig. 39; Johns 1982: figs 16, 101, 102]; and BMFA RES 13.109 [Clarke 2003: figs 54, 55]): men and women have facing equestrian and facing vaginal intercourse (Johns 1982: figs 101, 102) (p. 124).
278 Arretine vases (AM [Johns 1982: color pl. 30], Berlin [Brendel 1970: fig. 37, 38, 40, 41]; Richlin 1992a: fig. 7.5.; Boardman and LaRocca 1975: 166 bottom): men and women have frontal and facing and reverse equestrian intercourse; and man and youth recline.
279 Samian bowl (Museum of London A.21474 and others [Johns 1982: b/w figs 17, 23, 29, 102, 103; Clarke 2003: fig. 92], Naples [Marcadé 1965: pl. on p. 39A, B]): ithyphallic Pan; man and woman having "a tergo" intercourse; two men having "a tergo" anal intercourse; man with an erection and playing auloi walks toward woman who bends over and reaches behind her as if to guide the man's penis (pp. 82, 119).
280 Roman-British beaker (Cambridge 81–320; 3rd c. CE; Johns 1982: fig. 78): man, his exaggerated penis ejaculating, strides right to woman bending forward and holding a phallus or dildo; nude charioteer drives a team of four phalloi toward man having "a tergo" anal intercourse with another man(?), surrounded by phalloi (pp. 41, 88).

Appliqués (pp. 119, 121)
281 Arles: reverse equestrian (Marcadé 1965: pl. on p. 82A), "a tergo" (82B); man reclines, flaccid while woman sits as if for facing equestrian intercourse wearing a shield and wielding a sword (inscription: "arise! it's a shield" [= vagina], 84A).
282 BM 1912.11–25, 12–256 (Johns 1982: b/w figs 15, 114): reverse equestrian intercourse; inscription: "you have plowed me!" (p. 124).
283 Châlon-sur-Saône (Marcadé 1965: pl. on pp. 86, 87): facing intercourse; reverse equestrian.
284 Lyons 2000.0.2679 (Marcadé 1965: pl. on p. 85 top; Clarke 2003: fig. 94): facing intercourse, inscription: "I fuck well; turn to me"; 2000.0.2567 (Clark fig. 95): reverse equestrian, inscription: "you woman alone conquer"; CEL 7645 (Clark fig. 96): man in boat has anal "a tergo" intercourse with woman, inscription: "navigating Venus," sea animals below (p. 11); E 032 (Clarke fig. 97): man has "a tergo" intercourse with man having "a tergo" intercourse with woman; E 001 (Clark fig. 98): two men recline on a couch facing each other, the woman has equestrian intercourse perhaps with both men; inv. no. unknown (Marcadé 1965: pl. on p. 84C, 85 middle L and R, bottom): facing intercourse, woman fellates seated man, "a tergo" intercourse (pp. 88, 130), facing intercourse.

285 Nîmes 90851.1106 (Clarke 2003: fig. 100): man and woman have facing intercourse; inv. no. unknown (Clarke fig. 106): facing equestrian, inscription: "do you see how well you open me."
286 Vienne CIM 67.00.180 and inv. no. unknown (Marcadé 1965: pl. on p. 88 middle L and R): reverse equestrian, inscription: "I like it that way"; inv. no. unknown (Marcadé 88 bottom): facing intercourse.

Bronze
287 bowl, Pompeii (Naples PR; Johns 1982: color pl. 4; Marcadé 1965: pl. on p. 37): maenad (youth?) has reverse equestrian intercourse with satyr (p. 119).

Silver
288 Warren cup, "Palestine" (BM; Johns 1982: fig. 84, color pl. 25; Pollini 1999; Clarke 2003: figs 52, 53, 60, 61): (A) man and youth in reverse equestrian intercourse; (B) youth and boy have "a tergo" intercourse, reclining (pp. 27, 104, 108, 119, 124 [**pl. 43**]).

Wall paintings

Boscotrecasa
289 Villa of Agrippa Postumus, room 19 (NYMM 20.192.16 and 17; Guillaud and Guillaud 1990: figs 234 and 233, respectively): (E wall) Perseus frees Andromeda; (W wall) Polyphemus and Galatea (pp. 90, 97).

Rome, Farnesina Villa, decorated for the wedding of Julia and Agrippa, 19 BCE?
290 (Palazzo Massimo; Bragantini and de Vos 1982: pls 40, 86; Clarke 2003: figs 9, 11; Guillaud and Guillaud 1990: figs 182–5; Richlin 1992a: figs 7.3, 4): half-nude woman kisses nude? man; tabella: nude man and dressed woman sit facing each other; outline painting of seated Venus contemplating a flower (pp. 62, 104, 119, 130, 138).

Pompeii
291 Suburban Baths near the Porta Marina (Jacobelli 1995: 107–17; Guzzo and Ussani 2000: 21–6; Varone 2001a: pls 13, 14, 26, 27; Clarke 2003: figs 79–83, 85, 87, 88, 90, 91), "apodyterium," S wall, top frieze depicts seven bins (*capsae*), each numbered in Roman numerals, above which are (left to right):
   VIII man with large testicles
   VII   man has "a tergo" anal intercourse with man being fellated by woman, on whose vagina another woman performs cunnilingus
   VI   man has "a tergo" anal intercourse with man having "a tergo" intercourse with woman
   V   man having "a tergo" intercourse with woman
   IIII   man performs cunnilingus on woman
   III   woman performs fellatio on man
   II   man and woman have "a tergo" intercourse reclining
   I   man and woman have facing equestrian intercourse (pp. 19, 38, 50, 68, 78, 98, 119, 121, 129).
292 I.9.1, Bell'Impluvio (I.9.1, cubiculum 11; Guzzo and Ussani 2000: p. 27 no. A, fig. on p. 43; Marcadé 1965: pl. on p. 76): nude man reclines on a couch and welcomes the woman on to it (pp. 116, 118, 129).
293 II.3.3, Marine Venus (rear wall of garden; Guillaud and Guillaud 1990, fig. 309 and 310; Varone 2001a, pl. 5): Venus reclines on shell (p. 99; **pl. 30**).
294 II.4.4, Pinarius Cerealis (room a; Guillaud and Guillaud 1990: figs 294, 296): self-mutilation of Attis (p. 56).
295 V.1.18, Epigrammatist (Naples 27705, peristyle; Guillaud and Guillaud 1990; fig. 386): satyr attacks nude maenad (p. 19).
296 V.1.26, Caecilius Jucundus (Naples 110590; Guillaud and Guillaud 1990: fig. 70; Varone 2001a: pl. 7): satyr fondles the breast of maenad (pp. 25, 100, 118).

297 V.1.26, Caecilius Jucundus (peristyle l; Naples RP 110569; Marcadé 1965:, pl. on p. 15; Richlin 1992a: fig. 7.2; Grant and Mulas 1975: 156–7; Guzzo and Ussani 2000: fig. on p. 44; De Caro 2000: fig. on p. 28; Guillaud and Guillaud 1990: fig. 385; Clarke 2003: figs 12–14 [plan]): (in preparation) man reclines and reaches for the woman who sits in front of him, facing away (pp. 100, 138).

298 VI.1.6, Vestals (Guillaud and Guillaud 1990: fig. 300): Narcissus unveiling himself (p. 83).

299 VI.10.1, caupona on the Via di Mercurio (Guzzo and Ussani 2000: fig. on p. 19; Clarke 2003: figs 41–5): man with erection holds glass of red wine; woman leans forward with glass of red wine (pp. 25, 98, 129).

300 VI.10.1, caupona on the Via di Mercurio (room b; Clarke 2003: figs 41–5): woman stands, breasts exposed; man is nude with erection and leans forward to touch her genitals (p. 98).

301 VI.15.1, Vettii (fauces, W. wall; Johns 1982: color pl. 6; Varone 2001a: pl. 22; Clarke 2003: fig. 3): Priapus weighs his phallus against a leather bag (of money?) (pp. 100, 105, 107).

302 VI.15.1, Vettii (triclinium n, E. wall; Johns 1982: color pl. 19; Varone 2001a: pl. 24): maenads kill Pentheus (p. 101).

303 VI 15.1, Vettii (cubiculum x, E wall; Marcadé 1965: pl. on p. 129; Guzzo and Ussani 2000: fig. on p. 33 top; Varone 2001a: pl. 16): man has facing intercourse with woman (p. 101).

304 VI.15.1, Vettii, cubiculum x (Guzzo and Ussani 2000: p. 26 no. 1, fig. on p. 33 bottom; Guillaud and Guillaud 1990: fig. 390; Varone 2001a: pl. 167; Clarke 2003: fig. 1): man and woman have facing equestrian intercourse (pp. 25, 64, 129).

305 VI.15.1, Vettii (triclinium q; Guillaud and Guillaud 1990: figs 24, 25): amorini as manufacturers (pp. 45, 101; **pl. 33**).

306 VI.15.1, Vettii (triclinium p; Varone 2001a: pl. 1): Daedalus delivers the cow to Pasiphaê (pp. 81, 101).

307 VI.16.33, thermopolium bar (Bragantini 1981–1992: I, 371–3; Pugliese Caratelli 1990–2003: 5, 963): ejaculating phallus; two men masturbating (p. 88).

308 VII.2.6, Paquius Proculus (Naples 9195; tablinum g; Guillaud and Guillaud 1990: fig. 394): Cupid and Psyche kiss passionately (pp. 46, 112).

309 VII.2.23, Punished Cupid (Naples 9257; Guillaud and Guillaud 1990: fig. 248): Venus and Anteros look at Peitho restraining Eros in chains (pp. 9, 45).

310 VII.2.23, Punished Cupid (Naples 9249; tablinum; Guillaud and Guillaud 1990: figs 244–5; Varone 2001a: pl. 2): Mars reaches for Venus's breast (pp. 25, 52).

311 VII 2.25, Chariot (Quadriga, peristyle f; Naples 27698; Marcadé 1965: pl. on p. 31 top; Varone 2001a: pl. 19): (dado) Nilotic scene, crocodiles; in a boat, man-woman-man group; on a raft, man and woman have "a tergo" intercourse (pp. 50, 88, 121).

312 VII.4.48, Hunt (excedra 15; Naples 27687; De Caro 2000: fig. on p. 20; Varone 2001a: pl. 9): Polyphemus kisses Galatea (p. 97).

313 VII.4.31.51, Painted Capitals (excedra 22; Naples ADS 625; Bragantini et al. 1981–1992: water color by G. Marsigli, 24 Feb. 1833): Cupid Seller (p. 45).

314 VII.9.33, King of Prussia (cubiculum 3; Naples 27690; De Caro 2000: fig. on p. 47; Marcadé 1965: pl. on p. 30 bottom; Vorberg 1932: 234; Grant and Mulas 1975: 161; Guzzo and Ussani 2000: fig. on p. 17; Guillaud and Guillaud 1990: fig. 392; Varone 2001a: pl. 12; Clarke 2003: fig. 107): man has "a tergo" intercourse with woman; inscription "push it in slowly" (pp. 104, 129).

315 VII.12.18–20, brothel (entrance; Clarke 2003: fig. 34): Priapus with a double phallus (p. 106).

316 VII.12.18–20, brothel (atrium, N wall; Marcadé 1965: pl. on p. 119; Guzzo and Ussani 2000: fig. on p. 9): man has "a tergo" intercourse with woman (pp. 88, 98).

317 VII.12.18–20, brothel (atrium, S wall; Marcadé 1965: pl. on p. 123; Richlin 1992a: fig. 7.6; Grant and Mulas 1975: 33 top; Guzzo and Ussani 2000: fig. on p. 11, top; Clarke 2003: fig. 36): woman has facing equestrian intercourse with man (pp. 98, 104, 129).

318 VII.12.18–20, brothel (atrium, S wall; Marcadé 1965: pl. on p. 120; Guzzo and Ussani 2000: fig. on p. 11 bottom; Clarke 2003: fig.37): man has "a tergo" intercourse with woman (pp. 98, 104).

319 VII.12.18–20, brothel (atrium, W wall; Marcadé 1965: pl. on p. 117 bottom; Guzzo and Ussani 2000: fig. on p. 15 bottom; Clarke 2003: fig. 39): woman has reverse equestrian intercourse with man (p. 98).

320 VII.12.18–20, brothel (atrium, W wall; Marcadé 1965: pl. on p. 107; Guzzo and Ussani 2000: fig. on p. 14; Clarke 2003: figs 33, 38, 40); man has "a tergo" intercourse with woman (pp. 98, 104, 129).

321 VII.12.18–20, brothel (atrium, W wall; Marcadé 1965: pl. on p. 117 top; Guzzo and Ussani 2000: fig. on p. 15 top): man and woman recline on couch, possibly having "a tergo" intercourse (p. 130).

322 VIII.2.23, "Little" Palaestra (Pugliese Carratelli 1990–2003: pl. 220): victorious boxer and defeated boxer posed as if having "a tergo" intercourse (p. 15).

323 IX.2.10, house (cubiculum): Polyphemus kisses Galatea (pp. 64, 97).

324 IX.3.5, Marcus Lucretius Fronto (Naples 8992; De Caro and Pedicini 1996: fig. 180): Hercules in the court of Omphalê (pp. 82, 98, 105).

325 IX.5.14–16, House of the Restaurant, brothel? (cubiculum, N wall; Marcadé 1965: pl. on p. 127; Guzzo and Ussani 2000: fig. on p. 36; Clarke 2003: fig. 48): man has facing intercourse with woman (p. 98).

326 IX.5.14–16, Restaurant, brothel? (cubiculum f; Marcadé 1965: pl. on p. 50; Guzzo and Ussani 2000: fig. on p. 35 bottom; Clarke 2003: fig. 49): man and woman have "a tergo" intercourse (pp. 19, 98, 104).

327 IX.5.14–16, Restaurant brothel? (cubiculum, S wall; Marcadé 1965: pl. on p. 31 bottom; Guzzo and Ussani 2000: fig. on p. 37; Clarke 2003: fig. 51): woman has facing equestrian intercourse with man (p. 98).

328 IX.5.14–16, Restaurant brothel? (cubiculum f; Marcadé 1965: pl. on p. 71; Richlin 1992a: fig. 7.8; Guzzo and Ussani 2000: fig. on p. 35 top; Clarke 2003: fig. 50; Brendel 1970: fig. 43): woman has facing equestrian sex with man (pp. 88, 98).

329 IX.8.6, Centenary (cubiculum 43, N wall; Marcadé 1965: pl. on p. 126; Guzzo and Ussani 2000: fig. on p. 40; Guillaud and Guillaud 1990: fig. 384; Clarke 2003: fig. 6): woman has reverse equestrian sex with man (pp. 98, 130).

330 IX.8.6, Centenary (cubiculum 43, S wall; Marcadé 1965: pl. on p. 79; Johns 1982: color pl. 2; Richlin 1992a: fig. 7.7; Guzzo and Ussani 2000: fig. on p. 39; Clarke 2003: figs 4 and 5); woman has facing equestrian sex with man (p. 98).

331 IX.12.6, Chaste Lovers (triclinium; Varone 2001a: pl. 10): two pairs of man and woman on a couch; the pair at left seem to be kissing (she has slipped off one sandal) (p. 116).

332 Doctor, a banqueting couch (Naples 113196; De Caro 2000; fig. on pp. 24–5; Marcadé 1965: pl. on p. 36; Brendel 1970: fig. 31): pygmies performing an erotic show under an awning: two boys have reverse equestrian intercourse (p. 104).

333 Via degli Augustali (Naples 110878; Guillaud and Guillaud 1990: fig. 387; De Caro 2000: fig. on p. 21): (not the C. degli Epigrammi): kneeling maenad (dropped thyrsos at right) pushes against the face of a reclining satyr; we see the maenad from the back – the painting copies a sculpture which was in the *natatio* of the villa at Oplontis, and there is a mosaic as well; in these copies, the maenad is a hermaphrodite (pp. 56, 118).

Rome

334 Basilica Sotteranea, Porta Maggiore (Augustan; Cruciani 2000): Sappho leaps off short cliff into the arms of a triton in the sea (p. 117).

Provenance unknown, Naples Museum

335 9019, Herculaneum or Stabiae (Guillaud and Guillaud 1990: fig. 242): actor wearing a strophium sits in a chair; woman kneels to write something below a painting of a tragic mask (pp. 118–19, 129, 141).

336 9256 (De Caro 2000: fig. p. 19): Mars undresses Venus and touches her breast (pp. 11, 25, 52).

337 27683 (Marcadé 1965: pl. on p. 35): Nike crowns mule having "a tergo" intercourse with lion (p. 9).

338 27696 (Marcadé 1965: pl. on p. 90; Guzzo and Ussani 2000: fig. on p. 49 right; De Caro 2000: fig. on p. 42; Guillaud and Guillaud 1990: fig. 389; Varone 2001a: pl. 11; Brendel 1970: fig. 46): man has "a tergo" intercourse with woman (p. 104).

339 27697 (Marcadé 1965: pl. on p. 59; Johns 1982: color pl. 37; Guzzo and Ussani 2000: fig. on p. 52; De Caro 2000: fig. on p. 45): man has facing intercourse with woman (pp. 88, 104).

340 27700 (De Caro 2000: fig. on p. 22; Johns 1982: color pl. 29): Pan recoils from a hermaphrodite (pp. 19, 56).
341 inv. no. unknown (Marcadé 1965: pl. on p. 76): nude man reclines on a couch and welcomes the woman to it (pp. 25, 116, 129).
342 inv. no. unknown, Stabiae (Helbig 1868: 164–5 no. 824): woman sells amorini to woman (p. 45).

Index